Get the eBook FREE!
(PDF, ePub, Kindle, and liveBook all included)

We believe that once you buy a book from us, you should be able to read it in any format we have available. To get electronic versions of this book at no additional cost to you, purchase and then register this book at the Manning website.

Go to https://www.manning.com/freebook and follow the instructions to complete your pBook registration.

That's it!
Thanks from Manning!

Data-Driven Cybersecurity

Data-Driven Cybersecurity
Reducing risk with proven metrics

Mariano A. Mattei

Foreword by Joseph Steinberg

MANNING
SHELTER ISLAND

For online information and ordering of this and other Manning books, please visit www.manning.com. The publisher offers discounts on this book when ordered in quantity.

For more information, please contact

    Special Sales Department
    Manning Publications Co.
    20 Baldwin Road
    PO Box 761
    Shelter Island, NY 11964
    Email: orders@manning.com

© 2025 Manning Publications Co. All rights reserved.

No part of this publication may be reproduced, stored in a retrieval system, or transmitted, in any form or by means electronic, mechanical, photocopying, or otherwise, without prior written permission of the publisher.

Many of the designations used by manufacturers and sellers to distinguish their products are claimed as trademarks. Where those designations appear in the book, and Manning Publications was aware of a trademark claim, the designations have been printed in initial caps or all caps.

∞ Recognizing the importance of preserving what has been written, it is Manning's policy to have the books we publish printed on acid-free paper, and we exert our best efforts to that end. Recognizing also our responsibility to conserve the resources of our planet, Manning books are printed on paper that is at least 15 percent recycled and processed without the use of elemental chlorine.

The author and publisher have made every effort to ensure that the information in this book was correct at press time. The author and publisher do not assume and hereby disclaim any liability to any party for any loss, damage, or disruption caused by errors or omissions, whether such errors or omissions result from negligence, accident, or any other cause, or from any usage of the information herein.

Manning Publications Co. 20 Baldwin Road PO Box 761 Shelter Island, NY 11964	Development editor: Rebecca Johnson Technical editor: Laura D. Bell Review editor: Dunja Nikitović Production editor: Keri Hales Copy editor: Lana Todorovic-Arndt Proofreader: Olga Milanko Typesetter: Tamara Švelić Sabljić Cover designer: Marija Tudor

ISBN 9781633436107
Printed in the United States of America

To my parents, Angelo and Rachael (Tocco) Mattei, who bought me my first Zenith 3000 computer back in high school and always supported all my endeavors

brief contents

PART 1 BUILDING THE FOUNDATION 1

- 1 ■ Introducing cybersecurity metrics 3
- 2 ■ Cybersecurity analytics toolkit 21
- 3 ■ Implementing a security metrics program 44
- 4 ■ Integrating metrics into business strategy 68

PART 2 THE METRICS THAT MATTER... 89

- 5 ■ Establishing the foundation 91
- 6 ■ Foundations of cyber risk 126
- 7 ■ Protecting your assets 145
- 8 ■ Continuous threat detection 174
- 9 ■ Incident management and recovery 192

PART 3 BEYOND THE BASICS: ADVANCED ANALYTICS, MACHINE LEARNING, AND AI 219

- 10 ■ Advanced cybersecurity metrics 221
- 11 ■ Advanced statistical analysis 248
- 12 ■ Advanced machine learning analysis 265
- 13 ■ Generative AI in cybersecurity metrics 289

contents

foreword xv
preface xviii
acknowledgments xx
about this book xxii
about the author xxv
about the cover illustration xxvi

PART 1 BUILDING THE FOUNDATION 1

1 ■ Introducing cybersecurity metrics 3

1.1 Understanding metrics 5

1.2 Significance of metrics in cybersecurity 6

1.3 Traditional vs. innovative metrics 7

1.4 The changing landscape of cybersecurity 8

1.5 The importance of frameworks in cybersecurity 11

HITRUST framework 12 ■ Center for Internet Security CIS Top 18 framework 14 ■ NIST Cybersecurity Framework v2.0 16

1.6 AI and predictive cybersecurity metrics 17

1.7 Defending against AI 19

2 Cybersecurity analytics toolkit 21

- 2.1 Tool selection 22
  - *Key tool selection factors 23*
- 2.2 Dashboard development 25
  - *Choosing the right metrics 25* • *Knowledge points 26*
  - *Dashboard example 27*
- 2.3 Statistical analysis 31
  - *Trend analysis 32* • *Correlation analysis 34* • *Probability distribution 36*
- 2.4 Integrated security analytics environment 38
  - *Integrated security analytics environment exercise 39*
- 2.5 Continuous improvement and iteration 39
  - *Iteration techniques 41* • *Continuous improvement cycle 41*

3 Implementing a security metrics program 44

- 3.1 Introducing metrics program design 45
  - *Key components of a security metrics program 45*
- 3.2 METRICS methodology 46
  - *Measure 47* • *Evaluate 48* • *Threshold 48* • *Report 49*
  - *Improve 49* • *Communicate 50* • *Sustain 51*
- 3.3 Using the METRICS methodology example 52
  - *Step 1: Measure 52* • *Step 2: Evaluate 53* • *Step 3: Threshold setup 53* • *Step 4: Report 54* • *Step 5: Improve 55*
  - *Step 6: Communicate 56* • *Step 7: Sustain 56* • *Exercise summary 56*
- 3.4 Building a metrics dashboard 57
  - *Different dashboards for different stakeholders 57* • *Security dashboard example 57*
- 3.5 Tools and technologies for metrics collection 60
  - *Open source tools for metrics collection 60* • *Commercial tools for metrics collection 60* • *Automation and integration 61*
  - *Scripting for metrics collection 61*
- 3.6 Common pitfalls in metrics programs 65
  - *Pitfall 1: Overreliance on quantitative metrics 66* • *Pitfall 2: Misalignment with business goals 66* • *Pitfall 3: Stagnation and complacency 66*

4   *Integrating metrics into business strategy*   68

4.1   Business alignment   69

Business-aligned security metrics example   69   ▪   Mapping metrics to business performance   70   ▪   Supporting innovation with metrics   70

4.2   Security metrics alignment with business strategy exercise   72

*Step 1: Understanding MediHealth's business objectives   72
Step 2: Selecting key metrics   72   ▪   Step 3: Mapping metrics to business goals   73   ▪   Step 4: Measuring metrics   73
Step 5: Communicating the Metrics   74*

4.3   Security metric reporting   75

*Presenting metrics in executive reports   76   ▪   Demonstrating return on investment   78   ▪   Communication strategies   79
Metrics communication exercise   83*

PART 2   THE METRICS THAT MATTER 89

5   *Establishing the foundation*   91

5.1   Governance   92

5.2   Organizational context   93

Understanding the differences between mission, vision, and values   96   ▪   Strategic objectives   97   ▪   Organizational metrics   97   ▪   Organizational metrics exercise   98

5.3   Risk management strategy   100

*Risk mitigation   101   ▪   Risk management metrics   102
Risk management metrics exercise   103*

5.4   Roles, responsibilities, and authorities   105

*Roles, responsibilities, and authorities metrics   106
Roles and responsibilities metrics exercise   107*

5.5   Policy, processes, and procedures   108

*Policy, processes, and procedures metrics   110
Policy, processes, and procedures metrics exercise   111*

5.6   Oversight   113

Governance structure   114   ▪   Simulated governance structure   114   ▪   Governance exercise   116   ▪   Oversight metrics   117   ▪   Oversight metrics exercise   118

- 5.7 Cybersecurity supply chain risk management 119
  - *Supply chain risk management practices 120*
  - *Cybersecurity supply chain risk management metrics 121*
  - *Supply chain risk management metrics exercise 123*
- 5.8 Governance metrics 124
- 5.9 Answer to exercise 5.6.3 124

6 Foundations of cyber risk 126

- 6.1 Identify 127
- 6.2 Asset management 128
  - *Asset management metrics 129 ▪ Asset management metrics exercise 130*
- 6.3 Risk assessments 131
  - *NIST 800-30: Guide for conducting risk assessments 132*
  - *Risk assessment metrics 134 ▪ Risk assessment metrics exercise 138*
- 6.4 Continuous improvement 140
  - *Continuous improvement metrics 140*
- 6.5 Identity metrics exercise 142

7 Protecting your assets 145

- 7.1 Identity management, authentication, and access control 146
  - *Authentication 147 ▪ Access control 148 ▪ Identity and credential management 149 ▪ Context-based identity proofing and credential binding 149 ▪ User, service, and hardware authentication 150 ▪ Identity assertion, protection, conveyance, and verification 150 ▪ Access permissions management 152 Physical access controls 152 ▪ Types of security controls 153 Identity management, authentication, and access control metrics 153 ▪ Identity and access management dashboard exercise 154*
- 7.2 Awareness and training 156
  - *Awareness and training metrics 156 ▪ Awareness and training metrics exercise 157*
- 7.3 Data security 158
  - *Data at rest 159 ▪ Data in transit 160 ▪ Data in use 160 Data backup and recovery 161 ▪ Data security metrics 161 Data security metrics exercise 162*

7.4 Configuration management 164
   *Software maintenance 164 ▪ Hardware maintenance 164
   Log maintenance 164 ▪ Unauthorized software prevention 165
   Secure software development 165 ▪ Platform metrics 167
   Platform security metrics exercise 167*

7.5 SDLC testing exercise 169

7.6 Technology infrastructure resilience 170
   *Networks 170 ▪ Environmental threats 170 ▪ Resilience
   mechanisms 171 ▪ Resource capacity 171*

7.7 Protection metrics 171

7.8 Answer to exercise from section 7.5 172

8 Continuous threat detection 174

8.1 Implementing continuous threat monitoring systems 175
   *Defining strategy 176 ▪ Establishing architecture, implementing
   data collection, and analysis 177 ▪ Responding to findings 177*

8.2 Open source alternative to continuous threat detection 178

8.3 Continuous monitoring metrics 179
   Continuous monitoring metrics exercise 180

8.4 Understanding ATLAS 182
   *ATLAS methodology 182 ▪ Review and update 184
   ATLAS benefits 184*

8.5 Determining valid threat detections 185
   *False rejection rate 185 ▪ False acceptance rate 185
   Equal error rate 185 ▪ FRR, FAR, and EER metrics 186
   FRR, FAR, and ERR exercise 186*

8.6 Adverse event analysis 188
   *Adverse event analysis metrics 188 ▪ Adverse event analysis
   metrics exercise 189*

8.7 Alternatives to ATLAS and Wazuh 190

9 Incident management and recovery 192

9.1 Incident management 193

9.2 Planning and preparation 195

9.3 Testing an IRP 196
   *Tabletop exercise example 197 ▪ Tabletop exercise metrics 199
   Table for tabletop exercise evaluation sample 200*

- 9.4 Detection and documentation 200

  Three-tier severity model 202 • *Five-tier severity model 202* • *Changing severity over time 203* • *Practical example of incident documentation 203* • *Chain of custody 204* • *Incident management metrics 204* • *Incident management metrics exercise 205*

- 9.5 Incident triage and analysis 206

  Case study: Financial institution data breach 208 • *Incident metrics 208* • *Incident metrics exercise 209* • *Incident metrics table 210*

- 9.6 Notification and communication 210
- 9.7 Containing validated incidents 212
- 9.8 Evidence gathering and forensic analysis 213
- 9.9 Eradication of incidents 214

  Incident response metrics 215

- 9.10 Recovering to operational status 216
- 9.11 Post-incident and lessons learned 216

  Incident reporting and communication metrics 216 • *Incident reporting and communication metrics exercise 217*

PART 3 BEYOND THE BASICS: ADVANCED ANALYTICS, MACHINE LEARNING, AND AI 219

10 Advanced cybersecurity metrics 221

- 10.1 Risk exposure and predictive analysis 222
- 10.2 Risk exposure and predictive metrics 223

  Risk exposure index 224 • *Predictive threat index 225* • *Risk exposure and predictive metrics exercise 226* • *Using open source tools to calculate REI and PTI 228* • *How cybersecurity teams work together with open source solutions 228*

- 10.3 Advanced threat detection 229

  Anomaly detection 230 • *Time to predict 230* • *Dynamic risk scoring 232* • *Advanced threat detection metric exercise 233*

- 10.4 Effectiveness of AI in cybersecurity 235

  False-positive suppression rate 235 • *AI-based decision accuracy rate 236* • *Effectiveness of AI in cybersecurity exercise 237*

CONTENTS

10.5   Cloud and network threat management   238

Cloud threat detection 238 ▪ Cloud threat detection accuracy 239 ▪ Attack surface index 239 ▪ Cloud and network threat management metric exercise 240

10.6   Incident management   241

Threat hunting 241 ▪ Incident impact estimation 242 Incident management metric exercise 243

10.7   Continuous improvement   243

Risk mitigation 244 ▪ Time to predict 244 Continuous improvement metric exercise 245

11   Advanced statistical analysis   248

11.1   Continuous improvement with statistical metrics   249

Key concepts for continuous improvement 250 ▪ Free resources for statistical analysis 250

11.2   Using statistical metrics for continuous improvement   251

11.3   Implementing a feedback loop   251

11.4   Finding hidden relationships in data   251

11.5   Using moving averages to track trends   254

Moving averages example 254 ▪ Detailed description of the plots 255

11.6   Grouping similar events for better insights   256

11.7   Forecasting cybersecurity trends   258

ARIMA in action 259

11.8   Bayesian inference   261

Interpreting the results 262

11.9   Statistical models for vulnerability management   262

Interpreting the results 264

12   Advanced machine learning analysis   265

12.1   Code requirements   266

What is AI 266

12.2   DBSCAN for threat detection   267

DBSCAN example 268

- 12.3 Random forest and SVM for threat detection 270

  Random forest and SVM exercise 270 ▪ Isolation forest and autoencoders exercise 274

- 12.4 Natural language processing 277

  NLP exercise 278

- 12.5 Deep learning 281

  Deep learning exercise 282

- 12.6 Reinforcement learning 285

  Reinforcement learning example in Python code 285

13 Generative AI in cybersecurity metrics 289

- 13.1 Understanding generative AI 290
- 13.2 Open source generative AI alternatives 290

  LM Studio 290 ▪ Ollama 291 ▪ LM Studio vs. Ollama 291 Why we chose LM Studio for this chapter 292

- 13.3 A note on LLMs 292
- 13.4 Prompt engineering 293

  Why prompt engineering matters 293

- 13.5 Prompt engineering in cybersecurity 293

  Basics of prompt engineering 293 ▪ Open source vs. cloud API integration 294

- 13.6 Generating and analyzing cybersecurity data 296

  Generating synthetic cybersecurity data 297 ▪ Analyzing the output 301

- 13.7 Enhancing reporting and visualization 302

  Failed login reasons reporting 305

- 13.8 Automating incident response and trend analysis 306

  Setting the context 306

- 13.9 Exploring generative AI 310

  Learning resources 310 ▪ Inspiration to experiment 311 Your next steps 311

- 13.10 Limitations and ethical considerations 311

index 315

foreword

Throughout the three decades of my involvement in the world of cybersecurity, one area in which I have seen consistent underperformance, even by otherwise mature and extremely competent organizations, has been in the realm of establishing, utilizing, and interpreting key performance indicators (KPIs) for the management of cyber risk.

Unlike the many areas of business that sport obvious sets of metrics offering easy-to-understand, actionable intelligence—and where modern professionals can learn from numerous decades of others' experience generating and acting on highly meaningful measurements—the world of cybersecurity is not only relatively young and quickly changing, but also one in which the most significant events that demand the greatest attention and should factor most heavily into KPI measurements are often invisible to those responsible for measuring them.

Cybersecurity professionals cannot simply measure the number of breaches, or the financial or operational outcomes thereof; cybersecurity KPIs must capture unseen risks, evolving threats, and preventative actions—many of which have results that are not only intangible in the short term, but also impossible to correlate to their original investments of time, money, and effort. How does one capture the fact, for example, that a particular investment within a cybersecurity program motivated an attacker to pursue a different target than originally conceived?

Furthermore, many metrics adopted over the years may at first glance seem meaningful but ultimately prove to be dangerously misleading. For example, when metrics show that an organization is consistently experiencing a reduced number of breaches with diminishing financial effects on a quarter-over-quarter basis, does that translate to a notable and commendable improvement? Or does it indicate that the organization's cybersecurity management has deteriorated relative to emerging threats and that the organization is increasingly failing to both recognize when it has been breached and properly account for the business effects accumulating beneath the surface, eventually rearing its ugly head in catastrophic fashion?

Operators are not the only ones facing the difficulty in establishing and utilizing proper KPIs. I have seen boards obsess over detailed figures that should be irrelevant at the cyber-risk-management oversight level, and other boards effectively shirk responsibility by paying no more than lip service to overseeing the CISO. Failures to measure occur in both directions.

Likewise, even today, differences in experience, approach, and attitude often create communication and understanding gaps between business stakeholders and security teams—a problem that often yields KPIs that are either too broad, vague, and/or abstract to be meaningful, or far too detailed and technical to provide meaningfully actionable information for those overseeing risk management at a board level.

Moreover, it is important to keep in mind that both budget and time limitations ensure that most cyberwarriors do not have access to every possible tool they would like to have in their arsenals. Even if they did have everything they wanted, unlike those measuring financial performance, cybersecurity teams always work with data that is never fully accurate, complete, or totally reliable.

What complicates matter even further is the reality that one of the important goals of an effective cybersecurity program is to mitigate against as-yet-unknown risks. As such, KPIs must account not only for measuring what we know, but also for how well we can predict the future and measure things about which we do not yet know or even fully comprehend—and that is no easy task.

As the author discusses in this book, despite the inherent challenges involved, the effort to create meaningful KPIs is far from being a lost cause. *Data-Driven Cybersecurity* provides readers with valuable, practical, and actionable advice about selecting, implementing, and utilizing meaningful metrics—not just in a general sense, but also as relevant to readers' own specific environments.

Through the use of case studies, this book delivers to readers wisdom learned from both the successes and failures of others, thereby potentially saving people and organizations both time and money, while also minimizing the risk of the serious cybersecurity-related aggravations that often emerge when parties responsible for cybersecurity utilize inadequate, improper, and/or misleading metrics.

As will become clear to readers of this book, establishing cybersecurity-related KPIs is not a simple, one-size-fits-all endeavor—the skills necessary for achieving success in such an effort simply cannot be learned overnight. And, yes, we must admit that the dynamic nature of cybersecurity and the constantly evolving threat landscape associated with it complicates KPI development and implementation. We know that some things that may be highly relevant as you read these words today may become obsolete tomorrow (or even by the time you read the next sentence).

That said, as described throughout this book, we can create effective KPIs and utilize them to meaningfully reduce our exposure to cyber risks. In fact, not only *can* we do so, but we *must*.

—Joseph Steinberg, Cybersecurity Expert Witness and Board Member,
Lecturer, Columbia University

preface

When I first stepped into the world of cybersecurity from software engineering over 20 years ago, it was a rapidly evolving field, brimming with potential and vulnerabilities. Over time, I noticed an unsettling pattern: despite technological advances, many organizations still neglect to measure the effectiveness of their security programs. A chief financial officer would never attend a meeting without clear data, charts, and metrics in hand. Why, then, should a CISO or security leader do any differently?

This realization pushed me to explore how data-driven insights could elevate an organization's security posture from reactive to proactive. In my roles, spanning AI innovation and cybersecurity, I saw firsthand how metrics, when used properly, could tell compelling stories that influence stakeholders, justify investments, and save companies from potentially devastating breaches.

In *Data-Driven Cybersecurity: Reducing risk with proven metrics*, I share the lessons I've learned across fintech, biotechnology, pharmaceuticals, and beyond. The book begins with foundational topics: what constitutes a good security metric, how to align cybersecurity goals with broader business objectives, and the dos and don'ts of a robust security management program. As you move forward, you'll discover hands-on examples of Python and Jupyter Notebooks that make collecting and visualizing metrics straightforward—no advanced coding knowledge is required. For those looking to push the envelope, I also discuss advanced statistical methods, machine learning approaches, and even generative AI techniques that can forecast potential threats and anomalies in real time.

I hope that this book will encourage CISOs, security practitioners, and even curious newcomers to embrace a data-centric mindset. By combining deep cybersecurity expertise with measurable analytics, we can make our organizations and the world safer.

Thank you for picking up this book. I trust it will provide you with both the inspiration and the practical tools to measure and elevate your cybersecurity program. Let's start telling better security stories—with data.

acknowledgments

Writing a book, especially on such a rapidly evolving topic, requires time, focus, energy, and inspiration. My family has given me all three in abundance, and I can't express enough gratitude for their patience and understanding. Their willingness to let me disappear into my office for hours, dive into research and revisions, and still greet me warmly at the dinner table is a deeply cherished gift. My children, Cienna, Elia, Emmy (Mariano), Luca, and my better half, Michelle DiBruno, and my two stepdaughters Santina and Alessia, thank you for supporting me.

I also want to thank the incredible team at Manning Publications. From the earliest stages of this project, they believed in my vision and provided unwavering guidance. Their editorial insights, thorough reviews, and tireless efforts behind the scenes transformed raw ideas into a cohesive book. Their professionalism and passion made this journey both rewarding and enjoyable.

I owe a special debt of gratitude to Dr. Mary Grace Giraldo, who guided me during my master's degree program in data integrity and information assurance at Temple University. Her mentorship expanded my perspective on cybersecurity, taught me the importance of data-driven risk management, and encouraged me to bring these insights to a wider professional audience.

A heartfelt thank-you also goes out to Derek Fischer. Derek is a talented author at Manning and a professor at Temple University who introduced me to the Manning team. His encouragement and belief in my work were instrumental in getting this project off the ground. I'm grateful for that personal introduction and his continued support throughout the writing process.

Thanks to all the reviewers: Aditya Visweswaran, AJ Bhandal, Andrew Oswald, Anil Kumar Moka, Anupam Mehta, Brandon Darlington-Goddard, Charan Akiri, Deepak

Bhaskaran, Dipen N. Kumar, Gianluigi Spagnuolo, Krutik Poojara, Mark Furman, Mayuresh Dani, Michael Langdon, Mike Biocchi, Mukund Sarma, Paul Love, Peter Sellars, Pierluigi Riti, Richard Vaughan, Saidaiah Yechuri, Samarth Shah, Sankalp Kumar, Sarthak Munshi, Shirin Bhambhani, Sudin Baraokar, Sumanth Gangashanaiah, Suraiya Khan, Tyler Chewning, and Venkata Reddy Thummala. Your suggestions helped make this a better book.

Finally, to everyone who read early drafts, tested code snippets, or offered constructive feedback, your contributions matter more than you know. This project is as much yours as it is mine, and I'm honored to share these pages with you.

about this book

Who should read this book

This book is for any cybersecurity practitioner who wants to measure the effectiveness of their information security program and turn raw data into meaningful narratives for leadership. Whether you're a newly appointed security analyst, a seasoned CISO, or a manager juggling both IT and security responsibilities, these chapters will equip you with practical metrics strategies.

If you've ever struggled to convey security's value to upper management, justify budget requests, or figure out which alerts matter most, the techniques and examples here will help you build a compelling data-driven case. You don't need to be a coding expert—basic familiarity with cybersecurity concepts and a willingness to explore simple Python scripts will get you up and running quickly.

How this book is organized: A road map

Data-Driven Cybersecurity: Reducing risk with proven metrics is divided into 13 chapters. The following list provides a quick overview:

- *Chapter 1: Introducing cybersecurity metrics*—Lays out the rationale for measuring security and demonstrates how metrics can drive strategic decisions.
- *Chapter 2: Cybersecurity analytics toolkit*—Shows you how to set up basic analytic tools, such as Python and Jupyter Notebooks, to begin collecting and visualizing data.
- *Chapter 3: Implementing a security metrics program*—Discusses core frameworks and processes for a robust security program, ready to be measured and monitored.

- *Chapter 4: Integrating metrics into business strategy*—Explores how to align security goals with broader corporate objectives, ensuring executive buy-in.
- *Chapter 5: Establishing the foundation*—Examines governance, risk, and compliance fundamentals so you can understand the big picture before diving into technical details.
- *Chapter 6: Foundations of cyber risk*—Explains metrics related to IAM processes, from provisioning and deprovisioning to least-privilege enforcement.
- *Chapter 7: Protecting your assets*—Focuses on asset inventory, classification, and vulnerability management metrics.
- *Chapter 8: Continuous threat detection*—Covers how to measure performance in real-time threat detection scenarios (SIEM, IDS/IPS) to ensure ongoing protection.
- *Chapter 9: Incident management and recovery*—Demonstrates how to measure the effectiveness of incident response processes and post-incident reviews.
- *Chapter 10: Advanced cybersecurity metrics*—Dives deeper into specialized metrics, dashboards, and scenario-driven KPIs.
- *Chapter 11: Advanced statistical analysis*—Introduces concepts like regression and anomaly detection that can identify security trends and outliers.
- *Chapter 12: Advanced machine learning analysis*—Explores ML algorithms you can use for threat hunting, predictive modeling, and beyond.
- *Chapter 13: Generative AI in cybersecurity metrics*—Looks at using LLMs and other AI models to enhance everything, from automated reporting to advanced threat detection.

About the code

This book contains practical code snippets in Python, displayed in numbered listings and inline examples. We've formatted them in a `fixed-width font like this` for clarity. Sometimes code is also **`in bold`** to highlight code that has changed from previous steps in the chapter, such as when a new feature adds to an existing line of code.

In many cases, the original source code has been reformatted; we've added line breaks and reworked indentation to accommodate the available page space in the book. In rare cases, even this was not enough, and listings include line-continuation markers (➥). Additionally, comments in the source code have often been removed from the listings when the code is described in the text. Code annotations accompany many of the listings, highlighting important concepts.

The primary development environment is a simple Jupyter Notebook, chosen for its ease of use, interactive nature, and immediate data visualization capabilities. Once the book is published, readers can download all code examples from the Manning Publications website. I've also included instructions for installing necessary dependencies and libraries in the code repository. The software requirements are

- Python 3.10+
- Jupyter Notebook/Lab
- Basic libraries such as `pandas`, `matplotlib`, `scikit-learn`, and any additional libraries explicitly mentioned in each chapter

Feel free to adapt these examples to your own environment. No advanced Python knowledge is needed; the scripts are intentionally approachable, focusing on data analysis and dashboard generation over complex architecture or design patterns.

You can get executable snippets of code from the liveBook (online) version of this book at https://livebook.manning.com/book/data-driven-cybersecurity. The complete code for the examples in the book is available for download from the Manning website at https://www.manning.com/books/data-driven-cybersecurity, and from GitHub at https://github.com/Mariano215/Security_Metrics.

liveBook discussion forum

Purchase of *Data-Driven Cybersecurity* includes free access to liveBook, Manning's online reading platform. Using liveBook's exclusive discussion features, you can attach comments to the book globally or to specific sections or paragraphs. It's a snap to make notes for yourself, ask and answer technical questions, and receive help from the author and other users. To access the forum, go to https://livebook.manning.com/book/data-driven-cybersecurity/discussion.

Manning's commitment to our readers is to provide a venue where a meaningful dialogue among individual readers and between readers and the author can take place. It is not a commitment to any specific amount of participation on the part of the author, whose contribution to the forum remains voluntary (and unpaid). We suggest you try asking the author some challenging questions lest his interest stray! The forum and the archives of previous discussions will be accessible from the publisher's website as long as the book is in print.

Other online resources

- Personal blog/website: https://www.linkedin.com/in/mariano-a-mattei
- Business website: https://www.matteiinfosec.com
- For broader community discussions, consider checking out subreddits like r/cybersecurity and r/datascience, or Q&A sites such as Stack Overflow for any Python-related queries.

about the author

MARIANO MATTEI is an author, an adjunct professor in the Computer and Information Sciences Department at Temple University, and a certified chief information security officer with over 30 years of experience in cybersecurity and AI innovation. He has overseen security transformations across the biotechnology, pharmaceutical, and medical device sectors, integrating robust cyber defenses with AI-driven capabilities in clinical trials, manufacturing automation, quality systems, and regulatory compliance frameworks.

Throughout his career, Mariano's work has spanned predictive analytics for risk management, AI-powered threat detection, process optimization, and regulatory AI governance. By uniting cutting-edge artificial intelligence with proven cybersecurity methodologies, he helps organizations stay ahead of evolving threats, while maintaining strict compliance standards.

Mariano earned his master's degree in cyber defense and information assurance from Temple University, where his deep commitment to data-driven decision-making crystallized. This passion led him to write *Data-Driven Cybersecurity: Reducing risk with proven metrics*, a practical guide offering real-world metrics and insights for elevating any security program to enterprise-level excellence.

about the cover illustration

The figure on the cover of *Data-Driven Cybersecurity*, titled "L'Acquavitaio," or "The Buyer," is taken from a book by Francesco de Bourcard published in 1853. Each illustration is finely drawn and colored by hand.

In those days, it was easy to identify where people lived and what their trade or station in life was just by their dress. Manning celebrates the inventiveness and initiative of the computer business with book covers based on the rich diversity of regional culture centuries ago, brought back to life by pictures from collections such as this one.

Part 1

Building the foundation

Chapters 1–4 lay the groundwork for a data-driven approach to cybersecurity. In these early chapters, you'll explore the basics of measuring security, discover how to launch a metrics program that aligns with business goals, and learn how to tell a compelling story using data. Whether you're a seasoned security veteran or new to this field, establishing the right mindset and methodology is essential before you dive deeper into everyday metrics. By the end of part 1, you'll have a solid framework for why metrics matter, how they fit into your organization's strategy, and what tools you'll need to begin collecting them effectively.

Introducing cybersecurity metrics

This chapter covers
- Metric types and their practical applications
- Common frameworks for cybersecurity programs
- The significance of metrics in modern cybersecurity
- The changing landscape of cyber threats

In 2006, British mathematician Clive Humby famously said, "Data is the new oil." While this sentiment captures the transformative power of data, it is important to recognize a key distinction: oil is finite, while data is seemingly boundless, especially as AI begins to generate its own data. In today's digital landscape, data has become an ever-growing resource that powers business strategies, product development, and organizational success. However, like crude oil, raw data requires refinement—analysis, context, and interpretation—to become valuable.

This is particularly true in cybersecurity, where metrics act as the refining process that transforms raw data into actionable insights. Metrics help organizations interpret and monitor risks, enable them to measure performance, and ensure their security posture is aligned with overarching business goals. Critical vulnerabilities can remain hidden without proper metrics, leaving organizations exposed to risks.

For example, the infamous 2017 Equifax breach exposed inadequate metrics in patch management processes. A vulnerability in their Apache Struts framework went unpatched, ultimately resulting in the theft of sensitive information for over 147 million people. The breach might have been mitigated had metrics been in place to monitor patch compliance or prioritize high-risk vulnerabilities. This case underscores the importance of metrics: they bridge the gap between raw data and informed decision-making, turning potential threats into opportunities for resilience and growth.

Cybersecurity metrics include quantifiable measures that turn raw data into actionable intelligence, thus enabling organizations to track, assess, and improve their security efforts. These metrics achieve three core benefits: benchmarking and measurement, prioritizing actions, and communicating insights effectively. For instance, tracking the time to provision or de-provision user access benchmarks the efficiency of access control processes, helping identify delays and set targets for improvement. Measuring the frequency and severity of failed login attempts prioritizes actions by highlighting where to focus additional training, strengthen authentication measures, or implement multifactor authentication. Finally, visualizing trends such as patching compliance over time or incident response times provides a clear and effective way to communicate progress to stakeholders, which makes it easier to secure buy-in for additional resources or policy changes.

Metrics bridge the gap between operational performance and strategic goals, ensuring cybersecurity efforts are effective and aligned with business objectives. By focusing on benchmarking, prioritizing, and communication, organizations can use metrics to drive continuous improvement and build resilience against evolving threats. In the same way that businesses use financial data to navigate opportunities and challenges, cybersecurity metrics enable organizations to assess their security posture and address vulnerabilities proactively. Without these metrics, organizations are left blind to potential threats and unable to respond effectively. Metrics help in several key ways: they allow organizations to measure their cybersecurity maturity over time, prioritize the most critical actions, and communicate the status of security efforts to internal and external stakeholders in clear, quantifiable terms.

This book explores how to employ cybersecurity metrics to strengthen defenses and align security efforts with the organization's strategic goals. By transforming raw data into actionable intelligence, readers will learn how to safeguard critical digital assets and remain resilient in an evolving threat landscape.

Metrics help us

- *Benchmark and measure*—Metrics taken over time assist us in strengthening our cyber maturity. Cyber maturity refers to an organization's ability to manage its cybersecurity posture effectively.
- *Prioritize actions*—We can help prioritize remediations by analyzing our metrics.

- *Communicate*—Metrics can help internal and external stakeholders stay informed in a clear and quantifiable manner.
- *Visualize*—Tracking metrics across different time periods provides valuable insights, which enables informed decision-making.

1.1 Understanding metrics

Metrics are quantifiable measures used to assess the status and performance of specific processes, programs, and activities. In cybersecurity, metrics provide insights to help organizations make informed decisions, track progress, and improve their security posture. By translating complex cybersecurity data into actionable insights, metrics bridge the gap between technical aspects of cybersecurity and strategic business objectives. Furthermore, metrics will vary depending on the organization.

Effective cybersecurity metrics are actionable, relevant, and reliable. *Actionable metrics* provide insights that can influence decision-making. *Relevant metrics* align with organizational objectives and risk management strategies. For example, monitoring the number of unpatched systems can help prioritize vulnerability management efforts. *Reliable metrics* are consistent and accurate, ensuring decision-makers can rely on both the information and the analysis resulting from it.

Setting clear and measurable goals is essential for utilizing metrics effectively. These goals provide a target for what the organization aims to achieve within its cybersecurity program, maintaining alignment with overall company strategies and supporting proactive cybersecurity measures. Metrics are a powerful tool for measuring progress toward these goals, offering insights that drive improvement and inform decision-making.

However, it's important to recognize that overemphasizing metrics can lead to unintended consequences, such as metrics-driven behaviors. In these cases, teams may focus more on improving specific numbers to meet targets rather than addressing the root causes of security problems. This tendency can result in gaming metrics, where efforts are directed at manipulating measurements rather than at achieving genuine progress. Organizations must use metrics thoughtfully to avoid this pitfall, treating them as indicators of underlying trends rather than as ultimate objectives. By focusing on the bigger picture, metrics can remain a means to an end, enhancing security posture and resilience, rather than becoming an end in themselves.

Cybersecurity metrics can be categorized into different types, each serving a specific purpose in assessing and improving an organization's security posture:

- *Quantitative metrics*—They provide numerical data on specific aspects of cybersecurity, such as the number of detected incidents or the average response time to threats. These metrics offer clear, measurable insights that can be tracked over time.
- *Qualitative metrics*—They focus on aspects that are not easily quantified, such as the effectiveness of a training program or its effects on organizational culture. These metrics add valuable context and depth to complement numerical data.

- *Leading indicators*—These constitute forward-looking metrics that predict trends and potential risks, such as tracking the number of phishing attempts to identify early warnings of future attacks.
- *Lagging indicators*—These are backward-looking metrics that measure the outcomes of past actions, such as the number of resolved incidents or the average downtime caused by a breach, and provide insight into the effectiveness of security measures.

Organizations can better understand and use their data to anticipate risks and evaluate past performance by categorizing cybersecurity metrics into these types. To further refine our understanding of metrics, we categorize them into possible, direct, derived, and indirect:

- *Possible metrics*—These metrics can be tracked and maintained but are not necessarily industry standards. Organizations must evaluate the value derived from collecting and preserving these metrics.
- *Direct metrics*—These metrics can be collected and measured directly. They are straightforward and easily identifiable, such as the number of identity and credential management-related incidents per year.
- *Derived metrics*—They are calculated using a combination of other metrics or data over time, providing added value and meaning. An example is the ratio of successful to failed authentication attempts.
- *Indirect metrics*—This type involves metrics from other business measurements that offer further insights when used alongside direct or derived metrics. For instance, cybersecurity incident reduction following training can be an indirect metric indicating the effectiveness of training programs.

By understanding and implementing these metrics, organizations can continuously assess their cybersecurity resilience, identify incident trends, and evaluate the return on investment of their cybersecurity programs. Such a proactive approach enables companies to allocate resources better, manage risks better, and enhance their overall security posture.

1.2 Significance of metrics in cybersecurity

Cybersecurity metrics enable companies to customize their specific strategies based on unique data. Rather than taking a blanket, customary approach, companies can fine-tune their decisions based on actual data about their company. Furthermore, they can identify trends and patterns that better inform their decisions by analyzing data from past and current intelligence. This targeted, proactive approach anticipates potential problems before they materialize.

Resource management is another key consideration that plays a vital role in decision-making. Most companies have limited cybersecurity resources and most often have roles that share cybersecurity responsibilities. By using metrics to provide information highlighting areas of need, companies can better allocate scarce resources requiring immediate attention. This could mean effectively deploying additional controls, investing in new technologies, or enhancing programs.

Data quantification in cybersecurity also aids in risk management by providing a measurable way to assess risks. By quantifying risks, organizations can better evaluate the exposure, likelihood, and potential effects of incidents. This quantification allows companies to prioritize risk mitigation strategies effectively. Metrics provide tangible data that can be used to manage risk more efficiently, ensuring that resources are allocated to the areas of highest concern and that the most significant risks are addressed promptly.

Many companies face the dual challenge of protecting their assets, while adhering to strict regulatory requirements. Demonstrating compliance with these regulations and effectively communicating with stakeholders are critical responsibilities. As the threat landscape evolves, regulations are becoming increasingly stringent, demanding more from organizations in terms of accountability and transparency. Cybersecurity metrics provide a verifiable way to showcase adherence to industry standards, best practices, and legal obligations. By maintaining detailed records of compliance-related metrics, organizations can streamline audits, simplify regulatory reviews, and minimize the risk of penalties and fines.

Transparency and communication are essential; metrics are invaluable in this information exchange. Cybersecurity is increasingly becoming a mandated reporting topic. There is no better way to demonstrate the company's cybersecurity posture and effectiveness than with clear and quantitative security metrics. This helps build trust with key stakeholders, customers, investors, and partners.

Effective internal communication is essential for aligning cybersecurity efforts with the company's strategic goals. By sharing cybersecurity metrics across all divisions, organizations can nurture a culture of security awareness and collaboration, which ensures that each division, department, manager, and employee understands their role in protecting the company's critical assets, data, and systems.

Metrics are crucial in providing evidence-based insights that support informed decision-making, enhance accountability, and ensure compliance with regulatory requirements. In addition, metrics improve communication across teams and stakeholders by offering a clear picture of cybersecurity performance. As cybersecurity programs evolve, metrics have become indispensable for maintaining resilience, driving strategic decisions, and strengthening overall security posture.

1.3 Traditional vs. innovative metrics

Traditional metrics focus on quantifying the effectiveness of controls within a cybersecurity program, including the number of detected security incidents, the time to detect, the time to respond, and similar. The benefits lie in their simplicity. Traditional metrics offer clear, tangible data that can be tracked over time. For example, a decrease in the time to detect an incident would indicate an improvement in security capabilities. These metrics play a crucial role in measuring cybersecurity programs.

As we have learned from past experiences, traditional metrics have limitations. As cyber threats evolve, so must our methods for measurement. Typically, traditional metrics are reactive in nature, as they are measured after the fact. Therefore, they do not capture the complexity of modern cybersecurity attack vectors such as insider threats or multistage attacks. Relying only on traditional metrics may skew the view of the company's cybersecurity posture and fail to implement continuous improvement plans effectively.

Innovative metrics are designed to provide dynamic, proactive measurements that assess an organization's ability to anticipate, adapt, and mitigate cyber threats before they escalate into breaches. These metrics incorporate advanced techniques such as predictive analytics, threat intelligence, and behavioral analysis to offer forward-looking insights. For instance, metrics that track anomalous user behavior can signal potential insider threats or compromised accounts, thus enabling early intervention.

However, it's important to clarify that such metrics must be paired with proactive controls and policies. Without mechanisms to enforce preventive measures, these metrics may still be reactive, tracking incidents after they occur rather than preventing them. For example, a well-defined policy might require using secure libraries for password hashing across all applications. Metrics that monitor compliance with this requirement can identify gaps early, allowing action to be taken before insecure configurations lead to vulnerabilities. The key is in tracking and creating an environment where such problems are addressed before they manifest as exploits.

When implemented alongside robust policies and preventive controls, innovative metrics go beyond traditional measurements, providing actionable insights into organizational resilience and security effectiveness. Their ultimate goal is to enable early detection, track compliance, and enhance an organization's ability to achieve successful security outcomes.

The cybersecurity ecosystem is not static. It requires flexible, adaptive metrics to fend off attacks proactively rather than reactively. By combining traditional and innovative metrics, companies can have a more holistic and well-rounded measurement platform. This approach would best prepare companies to handle the sophistication of today's modern cybersecurity threat landscape.

Innovative metrics present a challenge because they also introduce the need for advanced analytics, machine learning, and artificial intelligence (AI). Throughout the book, we explore these new technologies and traditional statistical analysis in depth.

1.4 The changing landscape of cybersecurity

From the first moment digital data was generated, cybersecurity has evolved alongside every technological advancement. It involves a constant battle between attackers and defenders, where adversaries continuously refine their techniques, while security teams work to stay ahead. While it's often said that defenders need to be right all the time and attackers only need to succeed once, this oversimplifies the reality of modern defense strategies. Today, organizations implement layered security controls, resilience planning, and continuous monitoring to account for potential failures. The goal is not just to prevent every attack but to detect, respond, and recover swiftly, minimizing effects and ensuring that a single failure does not lead to catastrophic consequences.

With recent breakthroughs in AI, both attackers and defenders have a new set of highly valuable tools at their disposal. These advancements significantly increase the complexity and severity of attacks, affecting all industries worldwide.

One of the predominant trends in cybersecurity is the evolution of phishing attacks beyond deceptive emails into highly targeted, multichannel social engineering campaigns. Attackers now use *vishing* (voice-based phishing) and *smishing* (SMS-based phishing), alongside more sophisticated forms such as *spear phishing* (targeting specific individuals) and *whaling* (targeting executives). Business email compromise (BEC) attacks have become more refined, often incorporating deepfake tactics such as voice cloning to increase credibility. Imagine receiving an email about resetting your password, followed by a phone call from someone who sounds exactly like a trusted IT staff member. The cloned voice walks you through the process while the attacker simultaneously captures your credentials on a cloned system. This convergence of social engineering and emerging technology makes these attacks increasingly difficult to detect, which reinforces the need for robust training and multifactor verification protocols.

Beyond phishing, another growing threat is the rise of supply-chain attacks. Organizations are no longer just direct targets; they are often exploited as a stepping-stone to breach a larger entity. The infamous Target breach serves as a stark reminder—attackers first compromised an HVAC vendor with access to Target's network, using it as an entry point to infiltrate the retailer's systems. This case highlights the importance of securing internal systems and third-party vendors, ensuring that supply chain security is a core component of an organization's defense strategy.

Ransomware is one of the leading cybersecurity attack vectors. Hackers encrypt data for ransom and conduct crypto viral extortion, threatening to release compromised data on the dark web if a ransom is not paid. These tactics force companies to reconsider their data protection and recovery strategies.

Each type of hacker has a specific set of motivators, as referenced in table 1.1. Things are not always black and white, but it is essential to understand the types of hackers and their motivations to better defend against them. This table will provide you with an insight into why your critical data and systems may, or may not, be targeted.

Table 1.1 Types of hackers and their primary motivating factors

Hacker type	Motivating factors
Cybercriminals	Profit
Nation-state	Geopolitical
Terrorist groups	Ideological violence
Thrill seekers	Satisfaction
Insider threats	Discontent
Hackers	Variable

State-sponsored hacking has become a significant concern, with attacks often aimed at espionage, sabotage, or influencing geopolitical landscapes. These sophisticated campaigns frequently target intellectual property, sensitive government data, or critical infrastructure. For example, the Stuxnet worm, widely attributed to a joint effort by state actors, targeted Iran's nuclear facilities, causing physical damage to centrifuges and delaying the country's nuclear program. Another example is the SolarWinds attack, believed to be conducted by a state-sponsored group, which infiltrated numerous U.S. government agencies and private companies, stealing sensitive data and creating long-term vulnerabilities. These examples highlight how well-funded and organized state-sponsored groups operate on a scale that challenges traditional defenses and legal frameworks.

Geopolitical factors must also be integrated into a proper cybersecurity strategy, as they typically move lockstep with increases in state-sponsored attacks. Understanding the capabilities of potential adversaries and developing proper contingency plans are critical for a more holistic solution to cybersecurity defenses.

Because of the changing cybersecurity ecosystem, companies must adapt and shift their focus to more proactive approaches to cyber defense. In that, metrics must evolve to reflect this paradigm shift. You can see this shift taking place as more companies move from traditional *security information and event management* (SIEM) systems to *security orchestration, automation, and response* (SOAR) systems.

SIEMs focus on collecting, correlating, and analyzing security events to provide insights into potential problems. Alerts are generated but must be manually triaged and responded to. Typically, the response times are longer than in a SOAR system.

SOARs also collect, correlate, and analyze security events but focus more on orchestration and automation, taking instant action without manual intervention. Alerts are automated and can be reviewed to determine whether an event occurred or the system generated a false positive. SOARs integrate multiple systems for more effective and responsive incident handling by enriching alerts with additional data that helps further clarify the nature of the events.

Figure 1.1 summarizes the difference in functions between SIEM and SOAR systems. While they both support the aggregation of log data and can generate alerts, a SOAR system is typically preferred for companies who have the budget and means to implement it. SIEMs still serve an important role in many companies, with many utilizing both SIEM and SOAR systems in some way.

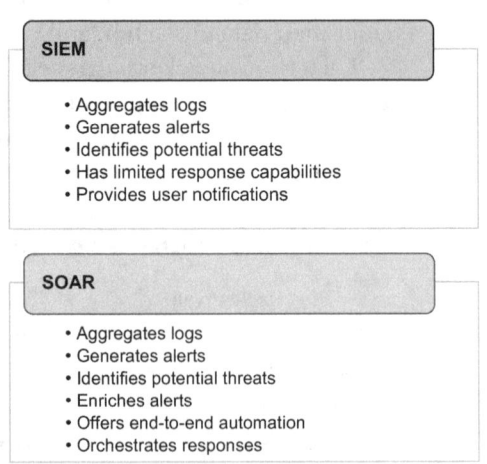

Figure 1.1 A comparison of the main functionality of SIEM vs. SOAR

Today, and for the foreseeable future, the cybersecurity threat landscape demands a dynamic approach to the implementation of cyber defenses, measurement of their efficacy, and informed decision-making based on analysis of cybersecurity metrics.

1.5 The importance of frameworks in cybersecurity

Cybersecurity frameworks provide structured guidelines representing the industry's best practices, helping organizations manage and mitigate risk. They serve as a scaffold for evaluating, planning, implementing, and maintaining cybersecurity programs. The NIST Cybersecurity Framework (NIST CSF) is widely adopted in the United States, while ISO/IEC 27001 remains a leading standard for information security management internationally.

Beyond improving security, these frameworks also add significant business value. Compliance with recognized frameworks is often a prerequisite for market access, particularly when working with government agencies or regulated industries. For example, in the United States, FedRAMP compliance is mandatory for cloud service providers working with federal agencies, while in Japan, ISMAP serves a similar role for government procurement. Organizations that adhere to these standards strengthen their security posture and enhance their credibility in the marketplace. Businesses with recognized certifications often have an advantage in competitive situations, as customers may prioritize vendors with well-established security credentials.

Moreover, some companies use cybersecurity frameworks to comply with regulatory requirements, protect against threats, or align their cybersecurity program with business objectives. These frameworks allow diverse companies to express their cybersecurity implementation universally.

For our purposes, we reference various cybersecurity frameworks to illustrate key points, without focusing exclusively on any single one. Frameworks such as NIST CSF V2.0, ISO/IEC 27001, and HITRUST provide structured approaches to managing and reducing cybersecurity risks. These frameworks are widely adopted across industries, offering organizations a consistent way to establish, assess, and improve their security postures. The availability of crosswalks that map these frameworks to one another makes them versatile and adaptable tools. This tactic ensures that the principles discussed in this book, particularly regarding cybersecurity metrics, are universally applicable and valuable, regardless of an organization's specific framework.

While this book uses NIST CSF V2.0 as a foundation for its discussions, the focus is not on NIST itself but on the broader application of cybersecurity metrics across frameworks. This approach allows readers to benefit from the insights provided here, no matter which framework they rely on.

Understanding the variety of cybersecurity frameworks available is essential for tailoring an organization's risk management and compliance approach. Frameworks such as HITRUST, CIS Controls, and NIST CSF offer unique perspectives and methodologies for addressing cybersecurity challenges. While each framework has its distinct focus and application, they share common goals: enhancing security posture, ensuring regulatory compliance, and reducing risk. The following sections explore several popular frameworks, examining how they contribute to cybersecurity strategies and where metrics play a critical role in their implementation and evaluation.

1.5.1 HITRUST framework

HITRUST started with the 1996 Healthcare and Health Information Portability and Accountability Act (HIPAA) but has since grown into one of the leading frameworks as a comprehensive set of baseline security controls. It is one of the gold standards in cybersecurity certifications in the United States—a proprietary yet highly recognized certifiable, prescriptive framework.

When we refer to HITRUST as "prescriptive," we mean that the framework provides detailed, specific instructions on achieving and maintaining a high level of cybersecurity. Unlike more flexible or high-level guidelines, *prescriptive frameworks* outline exact steps, controls, and measures organizations should follow. This approach reduces ambiguity and helps ensure consistent implementation across different organizations.

In the context of HITRUST, the necessary controls are established, with their implementation, measurement, and management specified. In addition, detailed procedures, policies, and practices that organizations must adhere to are included to achieve compliance. This level of detail helps organizations clearly understand the requirements and implement them effectively to enhance their cybersecurity posture.

To be certified under HITRUST, organizations must achieve a set score on a validated assessment. This certification process evaluates how well an organization has implemented the prescribed controls and practices. The assessment scores the organization's adherence to these detailed requirements, ensuring that they meet the high standards set by the HITRUST framework.

The HITRUST framework is divided into 19 domains, each containing controls crafted based on selected factors relevant to the organization's environment and risk profile. To achieve HITRUST certification, organizations are evaluated based on their adherence to specific illustrative procedures within these controls. Each control is rated according to their adherence to the following principles:

- *Policy*—High-level strategic direction and principles that define purpose and scope (this is the *why*)
- *Procedure*—Detailed, step-by-step instructions on how to implement the policies (this is the *how*)
- *Implemented*—Actual application or execution of the policies and procedures (this is the *what*)
- *Measured*—The importance of continuously measuring the effectiveness of cybersecurity controls and practices
- *Managed*—Ongoing management of cybersecurity practices (i.e., actively updating policy, procedures, and implementation of controls based on measurements)

Each principle carries a specific weight contributing to the overall score of the control statement, thereby reflecting the maturity and comprehensiveness of the organization's cybersecurity posture.

As shown in figure 1.2, HITRUST implementation includes weights for each requirement. The core areas assessed during certification are policy, procedure, implemented, measured, and managed. These principles are not just theoretical; they represent specific, actionable requirements that organizations must meet to achieve certification. *Policy* and *procedure* provide strategic and operational guidelines, while *implemented* focuses on actual execution. *Measured* and *managed*, although not mandatory for initial certification, are crucial for a mature cybersecurity program. *Measured* involves the regular assessment of the effectiveness of the controls, accomplished through metrics, as discussed in this book. *Managed* ensures continued improvement through analysis of these metrics. Including these principles in a mature cybersecurity program supports ongoing cybersecurity practices and aligns with the core idea of this book.

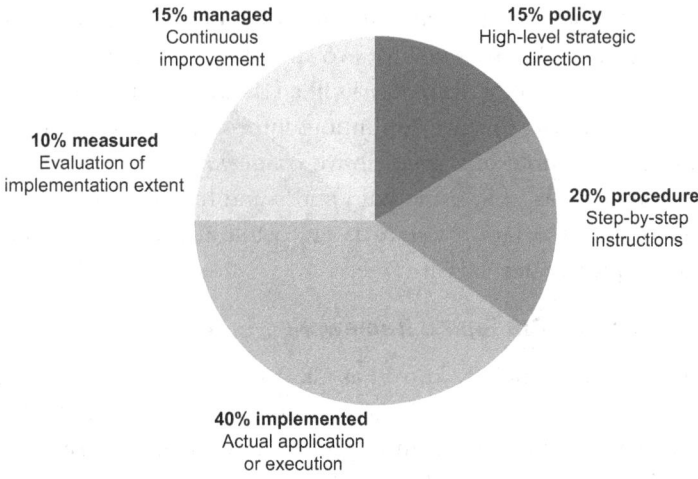

Figure 1.2 HITRUST scoring criterion by percentage. The percentages indicate the weights placed on each category for scoring purposes.

Achieving HITRUST certification through a validated assessment requires organizations to score at least 75% on key control measures, primarily focusing on policy, procedure, and implementation. Many companies choose to limit their assessment scope to these areas, often excluding more advanced maturity levels such as measured and managed. While this approach ensures compliance with HITRUST's requirements, it does not necessarily equate to strong security.

As the industry saying goes, compliance does not equal security. How an organization approaches compliance determines whether it becomes a meaningful security investment or merely a checked box. Organizations that treat compliance as a strategic initiative—deeply integrating its principles into decision-making—benefit from stronger security postures and reduced risk exposure. In contrast, those who view compliance as a regulatory hurdle may pass audits, while remaining vulnerable to real-world cyber threats.

For example, a healthcare provider may achieve HITRUST certification by demonstrating its policies and procedures for multifactor authentication (MFA). However, if it fails to enforce MFA across all critical systems, attackers can still exploit unprotected access points. Similarly, an organization may implement a documented patch management process but leave high-risk vulnerabilities unpatched for months due to operational constraints, creating exploitation opportunities. Therefore, true security requires going beyond the minimum requirements and adopting a mindset where compliance is not just about meeting standards but continuously strengthening and adapting security controls to address evolving risks.

This chapter emphasizes the importance of going beyond compliance to build a robust cybersecurity posture. Organizations have access to valuable data, tools, and methods to analyze and report on their security metrics. Using these resources ensures compliance and strengthens defenses against evolving threats. The following sections explore how organizations can align frameworks like HITRUST with a proactive cybersecurity approach, using metrics to drive continuous improvement and resilience.

HITRUST is a prime example of a prescriptive framework. There are many other frameworks to choose from as well, some paid and some free (commercial vs. open source). HITRUST is a proprietary framework, and while it is quickly becoming the gold standard in the United States, it is not free.

1.5.2 Center for Internet Security CIS Top 18 framework

The CIS Top 18 framework, officially known as CIS Controls Version 8, was released in May 2021, and it is a set of prioritized and actionable cybersecurity best practices designed to mitigate the most pervasive and significant cyber threats. By categorizing the top 18 security threat vectors, the CIS Top 18 aims to provide controls specifically crafted for immediate and practical implementation to improve an organization's security posture. Table 1.2 shows the CIS Top 18 and the description of the categories and controls in each organizational category.

These controls are divided into basic, foundational, and organizational categories, each targeting different cybersecurity aspects:

- *Basic controls (1–6)*—Focus on cyber hygiene to protect against the most common attacks. This category covers asset management, continuous vulnerability management, secure configurations, controlled administrative privileges, email and browser protections, and maintenance and monitoring of audit logs.
- *Foundational controls (7–16)*—Address the best technical practices and strategies. This includes email and browser protections, malware defense, data recovery,

Table 1.2 CIS TOP 18 Controls Version 8

#	CIS Critical Security Control (v8)	Purpose
1	Inventory and control of enterprise assets	Know every device that touches the network and manage it continuously to eliminate blind spots.
2	Inventory and control of software assets	Track and authorize all software so only approved, secure applications can run.
3	Data protection	Safeguard sensitive data in motion and at rest, preventing unauthorized disclosure or alteration.
4	Secure configuration of enterprise assets and software	Harden systems and applications with proven baseline configurations to reduce the attack surface.
5	Account management	Establish and maintain the full lifecycle of user and service accounts to prevent abuse.
6	Access control management	Enforce leastprivilege and role-based access so users can reach only what they truly need.
7	Continuous vulnerability management	Identify, prioritize, and repair vulnerabilities relentlessly to stay ahead of exploits.
8	Audit log management	Collect, protect, and analyze logs to detect anomalies and support investigations.
9	Email and web browser protections	Harden email and browsing pathways (i.e., common entry points) to block phishing and driveby attacks.
10	Malware defenses	Deploy antimalware at multiple layers to prevent, detect, and respond to malicious code.
11	Data recovery	Ensure reliable, protected backups and tested recovery procedures to restore data after incidents.
12	Network infrastructure management	Secure, maintain, and segment network devices to limit lateral movement and exposure.
13	Network monitoring and defense	Continuously inspect network traffic for suspicious activity and respond in near real time.
14	Security awareness and skills training	Educate workforce regularly so human behavior reinforces—rather than undermines—security controls.
15	Service provider management	Govern and monitor third-party providers to ensure they meet your security expectations.
16	Application software security	Build and maintain software securely through coding standards, testing, and remediation.
17	Incident response management	Prepare, detect, contain, and recover from security incidents swiftly and methodically.
18	Penetration testing	Validate the effectiveness of all controls by emulating real-world attacker techniques.

secure network configurations, access control, wireless technologies, and awareness and training.

- *Organizational controls (17 and 18)*—Focus on people, processes, and technologies to manage and improve organizational security posture. This includes incident response, penetration testing, and red team exercises.

CIS Top 18, free with registration, provides a pragmatic approach to cybersecurity by emphasizing prioritization, scalability, and actionable steps. It can be used in isolation or in combination with other frameworks to better defend against cyberattacks.

1.5.3 *NIST Cybersecurity Framework v2.0*

The NIST Cybersecurity Framework (CSF), released in February 2024, offers a structured approach to achieving cyber maturity, guiding organizations to prioritize and implement flexible controls tailored to their needs. Widely adopted across industries in the United States, this voluntary framework emphasizes the importance of evolving cybersecurity practices to counter ever-changing threats. Although it lacks official certification, the NIST CSF provides a comprehensive, cost-effective strategy that complements existing cybersecurity programs by focusing on foundational aspects and promoting a logical, risk-based approach to enhance security measures.

NIST recently released version 2.0 of the NIST CSF v2.0. The latest version comprises six primary functions: govern, identify, protect, detect, respond, and recover. These functions serve as the high-level strategic view of the cybersecurity lifecycle and risk management. As shown in table 1.3, the six functions encompass their own elements of the cybersecurity lifecycle.

Table 1.3   NIST CSF v2.0 with six main functions and categories

Category	Function
Govern	Organizational context
	Risk management
	Supply-chain risk
	Roles and responsibilities
	Policies and procedures
	Oversight
Identify	Asset management
	Risk management
	Improvement
Protect	Access control
	Awareness and training
	Data security
	Platform security
	Infrastructure resilience
Detect	Continuous monitoring
	Adverse event analysis
Respond	Incident response
	Incident analysis
	Incident reporting
	Incident mitigation
Recover	Incident recovery
	Incident communication

These functions serve as the high-level strategic view of the cybersecurity lifecycle and risk management:

- *Govern*—Involves defining the organization's cybersecurity risk management strategy, expectations, policies, and procedures, as well as how they are communicated and monitored
- *Identify*—Involves developing organizational understanding to manage cybersecurity risk to critical systems, assets, data, and capabilities
- *Protect*—Involves defining safeguards to deliver critical services
- *Detect*—Includes all activities used to identify the occurrence of an event
- *Respond*—Includes all actions taken in response to cybersecurity incidents
- *Recover*—Involves restoring capabilities or services impaired by a cybersecurity event

NOTE In cybersecurity, events, incidents, and breaches represent a progression of severity. An *event* is any activity that warrants further analysis to determine its significance. If an event is found to violate the company's security policies, it is classified as an *incident*. A *breach* occurs when an incident results in compromise, unauthorized access, or theft of data, systems, or networks. This hierarchy helps organizations prioritize their responses and allocate resources effectively.

The six functions are divided into 23 categories, which are further divided into 108 subcategories. These subcategories represent the specific controls that organizations can implement in their cybersecurity programs.

In this book, we use the NIST CSF version 2.0 to guide the conversation around metrics. I've selected NIST CSF v2.0 due to its widespread popularity, both in the United States and globally. Nearly all cybersecurity frameworks, regardless of industry, can map directly to NIST CSF, making it a versatile tool for discussing metrics across a wide range of security programs.

That said, it's important to note that it is not necessary to implement NIST CSF v2.0 to benefit from the metrics covered in this book. While we will reference the framework for structure, the metrics are relevant and applicable to any cybersecurity framework, whether we use ISO 27001, COBIT, CIS Controls, HITRUST, or another standard. Our focus is on using metrics to measure, evaluate, and strengthen our cybersecurity efforts practically and meaningfully. This approach will allow you to align metrics with your organization's specific needs and objectives, regardless of the framework you implement.

1.6 AI and predictive cybersecurity metrics

AI is a broad term that encompasses various technologies, including machine learning (ML), natural language processing (NLP), and generative AI with large language models (LLMs). In cybersecurity, AI is used to identify complex patterns and correlations that human analysts might overlook. When trained on high-quality historical and real-time data, machine learning models can recognize subtle indicators of compromise, enabling predictive security measures.

However, AI models are only as effective as the data they are trained on and the algorithms that power them. Poor quality, biased, or incomplete data can lead to false positives, missed threats, or misleading insights. Likewise, AI decision-making algorithms must be carefully designed, tested, and validated to avoid errors that could undermine security efforts.

Despite these challenges, AI's predictive capabilities allow organizations to shift from reactive to proactive security strategies. When properly trained and deployed, AI can enhance threat detection, improve response times, and strengthen defenses against emerging cyber threats by identifying trends and anomalies that traditional security monitoring systems might miss. The key to success lies in continuously refining AI models, ensuring high-quality data inputs, and integrating AI-driven insights with human expertise for a balanced and effective cybersecurity posture.

Anomaly detection and automation can help improve decision-making processes by providing actionable insights at speeds and accuracy that were previously impossible. For example, AI can sift through global threat intelligence feeds, identify emerging threats, and advise on preventive measures or automate responses instantaneously. These new technologies are transformative.

All these features mean that companies can implement more effective cybersecurity strategies that go beyond simply responding to threats—they can anticipate, predict, and proactively mitigate risks before they escalate. The key to employing AI effectively in cybersecurity lies in data quality, model validation, and continuous refinement. The metrics used for AI-driven security analysis typically focus on predictive accuracy, speed, and efficacy, ensuring that the system is fast and reliable in detecting threats.

However, AI's effectiveness is directly tied to the quality and structure of the data it processes. Data cleansing is critical before feeding them into an AI model, which includes removing duplicates, handling missing values, and filtering out noise or irrelevant data. If the data is inaccurate or biased, AI-generated insights will be flawed, potentially leading to false positives or overlooked threats.

Another essential step is validating what AI is inferring versus what it can actually figure out based on its knowledge base. Just because AI detects a pattern does not mean it fully understands a cyber threat's underlying context. Security teams must evaluate AI-generated predictions against real-world security incidents and fine-tune models to reduce errors and improve accuracy.

The good news is that you don't need to build AI algorithms from scratch. Many open source libraries and frameworks, such as scikit-learn, TensorFlow, and PyTorch, already provide prebuilt models for cybersecurity applications. The key tasks are to collect high-quality, representative data, ensure AI systems are learning the right patterns, and continuously monitor and refine outputs to maintain effectiveness in an evolving threat landscape.

This book provides practical examples of how AI can be used to enhance cybersecurity metrics. You will learn to utilize AI-driven tools to predict and identify threats before they become significant problems. We will explore how AI enhances the accuracy and efficiency of cybersecurity metrics, offering actionable insights that lead to faster detection and response to threats. However, while AI offers significant advantages, it is not without its risks. Problems such as AI hallucinations, where systems generate false or misleading outputs, can undermine decision-making. Additionally, improperly handling sensitive information when interacting with AI systems poses a serious security risk. By the end of this book, readers will understand how to integrate AI into their cybersecurity metrics strategy and mitigate these potential dangers to maximize its effectiveness.

The following chapters follow NIST CSF v2.0 through a logical progression, collecting important metrics along the way. We will not attempt to boil the ocean. Instead, we will establish and develop metrics, continuously refining and expanding them, offering analysis along the way, and identifying use cases.

1.7 Defending against AI

Artificial intelligence will become more integrated into cybersecurity strategies as advancements in AI continue to grow rapidly. It is important to mention that adversaries also employ AI to formulate more sophisticated attack methods. AI-driven cybersecurity threats—such as automated phishing, adaptive malware to avoid detection, an increase in zero-day (never-before-seen) malware, and more sophisticated social engineering attacks using deepfakes—pose new challenges for defenders.

AI brings significant advantages to cybersecurity but also introduces several challenges, including bias, false positives, and limitations due to inadequate training data. One of the biggest concerns is bias in AI models, which can lead to disproportionate risk assessments. For instance, an AI-based fraud detection system trained predominantly on historical data from one industry may misclassify transactions from another industry, leading to unnecessary account lockouts or missed fraud attempts.

Another problem is false positives, where AI flags legitimate behavior as a security threat. Consider an intrusion detection system (IDS) that incorrectly identifies a surge in network traffic as a DDoS attack, triggering unnecessary incident response measures. False positives erode trust in AI-driven security tools and lead to alert fatigue, where security teams start ignoring real threats due to an overwhelming number of false alarms.

Cybersecurity frameworks combine AI-driven tools with traditional security measures to mitigate these risks in a layered defense strategy. AI is not a standalone solution. Instead, it works alongside signature-based detection, rule-based systems, behavioral analysis, and human oversight to create a more comprehensive security posture.

A real-world example of AI-assisted cybersecurity is PyRIT (Python Risk Identification Toolkit), an open source tool designed to simulate, test, and analyze security risks in automated environments. PyRIT uses AI to identify potential vulnerabilities in an enterprise environment, simulate attack scenarios, and assess the effectiveness of security controls. By integrating AI with traditional security methodologies, organizations can enhance threat detection, while reducing the risks associated with AI biases and false positives.

Ultimately, AI should be viewed as an enhancement rather than a replacement for human security expertise. The key to success lies in continually refining AI models, improving data quality, and layering AI-driven analytics with established security protocols to ensure robust, reliable threat detection and response.

This book provides strategies to overcome these challenges, such as improving data quality for AI algorithms and successfully integrating AI into existing security infrastructures. Readers will learn to implement AI-driven metrics effectively through practical examples and exercises. We will discuss practical solutions for managing false positives, enhancing model accuracy, and easing the learning curve for IT teams, ensuring that AI-driven metrics are reliable and practical for everyday cybersecurity operations.

Summary

- Cybersecurity metrics quantify the effectiveness of cybersecurity programs and guide informed decisions by highlighting strengths and weaknesses.
- Frameworks such as NIST CSF emphasize the importance of metrics in aligning security practices with industry standards and best practices.
- Traditional metrics measure the effectiveness of controls, providing insight into the current security posture and improving it.
- Innovative metrics provide proactive measurements to anticipate and mitigate potential threats, thus enhancing security management efficiency.
- The dynamic cybersecurity threat landscape necessitates continuous monitoring and proactive measurement strategies to stay ahead of adversaries.
- AI enhances the predictive capabilities of cybersecurity metrics, leading to more efficient resource allocation and faster response times.

Cybersecurity analytics toolkit

This chapter covers
- Key components of a cybersecurity toolkit
- How to choose the right tools
- Designing insightful dashboards
- Statistical analysis for threat detection
- How to integrate AI in security analytics

A cybersecurity analytics toolkit consists of multiple integrated tools that work together to support various stages of security analytics. The main components for any specific scope include data collection, processing, visualization, and automation. Each of these tools enhances the efficiency and effectiveness of security teams. Figure 2.1 demonstrates the composition of each toolkit, highlighting how various parts operate within the defined scope.

Data collection involves gathering data from various sources—logs, network traffic, endpoint activity, and similar. Tools such as security information and event management systems (SIEMs) and intrusion detection systems (IDSs) are typically used for this purpose. Once collected, the data must be processed and normalized for analysis. This process involves parsing, enriching, and correlating data to make it suitable for deeper investigation and interpretation. Furthermore, large datasets require effective visualization tools to help display complex information in an easy-to-understand format. Dashboards and graphs are commonly used to highlight trends, anomalies, and security events.

Automation empowers teams to respond to threats faster, and integration enables seamless coordinated work of various tools. Furthermore, automation also includes automating alerts, reporting, and incident management. The value of a cybersecurity analytics toolkit lies in its ability to deliver timely and accurate insights that support an organization's overall security posture.

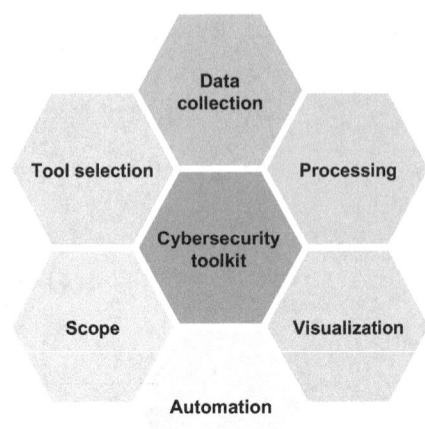

Figure 2.1 Cybersecurity toolkit consisting of the proper scope, tool selection, data collection, processing, visualization, and automation

2.1 Tool selection

This section focuses on selecting cybersecurity analytics tools that support data collection, analysis, and visualization for security operations. These tools may include SIEM platforms (e.g., Splunk or IBM QRadar), threat intelligence platforms (e.g., ThreatConnect), log management systems (e.g., Elastic Stack), and data visualization software (e.g., Tableau or Power BI), tailored to cybersecurity needs.

The selection process should consider factors such as functionality, ease of integration, and long-term support, ensuring the tools meet the organization's specific security objectives. For example, some tools may be ideal for threat detection, while others are designed to support compliance or incident response. When choosing tools, the decision-making process should be guided by a clear understanding of the organization's specific needs, existing infrastructure, current resources, and budgetary requirements. Furthermore, when selecting open source or commercial tools, several key factors should be considered, such as functionality, ease of integration, and long-term support.

When evaluating potential tools, it is necessary to identify your organization's primary security objectives and ask yourself whether you need a tool that excels in data collection, analysis, or visualization. You also need to determine whether you focus on compliance, threat detection, or incident response. Prioritizing your organizational needs will help narrow the options available.

As your organization grows, so will your data and security needs. You should choose tools with scalability in mind to adapt to these changes in growth, new operations, requirement changes, or security challenges. The tools you select should easily integrate with your existing systems and infrastructure. This is important for data collection and processing tools as it helps prevent data silos and allow smooth information flow.

How easily your enterprise can use the tool will significantly affect its success. Complex learning curves may not be suitable for all organizations. Take the time to consider your team's expertise and look for solutions that align with them and provide an easy-to-use interface.

2.1.1 Key tool selection factors

There are several key tool categories based on functionality. For data collection and monitoring, tools such as Wireshark, Sysmon, and OSQuery are designed to collect data from various sources, including network traffic, endpoints, and servers.

Threat intelligence tools such as MISP (https://www.misp-project.org/) and Anomali ThreatStream (https://www.anomali.com/products/threatstream) collect valuable information on emerging threats and vulnerabilities. These tools help organizations stay informed about adversaries' latest attack vectors and tactics. There are many open source and commercial options available to choose from. Both have their intrinsic benefits and drawbacks, as shown in table 2.1.

Table 2.1 The pros and cons of open source vs. commercial software

Tool	Pros	Cons
Open source	Cost-effective, highly customizable, and backed by active community support. Open source tools are ideal for organizations with skilled technical staff who want to avoid licensing fees.	May require more time and expertise to set up and maintain. Support is community driven, which may not be ideal for organizations needing immediate help.
Commercial	Offer more out-of-the-box functionality, user-friendly interfaces, and professional support. These tools often include advanced features and capabilities that might not be available in open source alternatives.	Licensing costs can be high and flexibility may be limited due to vendor lock-in or lack of customization options.

SIEM solutions, such as Splunk, ELK Stack, and QRadar, are critical in real-time threat detection, anomaly detection, and event correlation. These tools collect logs from multiple sources, normalize the data, and apply predefined rules to detect potential security incidents. However, SIEMs are only as effective as their configurations—if rules are too broad, they may generate overwhelming false positives, leading to alert fatigue for security teams. Conversely, overly restrictive rules may miss emerging threats, reducing the SIEM's effectiveness. Fine-tuning correlation rules, refining detection thresholds, and using machine-learning-driven analytics are essential to making SIEMs more efficient and reducing noise.

In addition to SIEMs, vulnerability management tools such as OpenVAS, Tenable Nessus, and Qualys help organizations identify and prioritize vulnerabilities. These tools automate security scanning, evaluate system weaknesses, and assign risk scores to discovered vulnerabilities, allowing security teams to focus on the most high-impact threats. By integrating SIEM data with vulnerability scanning results, security teams can correlate detected exploits with known system weaknesses, strengthening incident response and risk management strategies.

Ultimately, SIEMs and vulnerability scanners work best with proactive tuning, regular rule updates, and contextual threat intelligence. Without proper optimization, organizations risk becoming overwhelmed by false alarms or blindsided by undetected threats, making continuous refinement an essential practice for effective security operations.

Understanding the advantages and limitations of open source and commercial tools facilitates making better, more informed decisions. It is necessary to take the time to evaluate tool compatibility with existing infrastructure and systems. You also need to develop the ability to categorize tools based on their core functions. Table 2.2 lists the features of some of the software we have previously mentioned.

Table 2.2 Specific features, with pros and cons of various popular open source and commercial software

Category	Name	Features	Pros	Cons
Data collection	Wireshark	Network traffic analysis	Open source, comprehensive packet analysis	Requires technical expertise to interpret data
	Sysmon	Windows system monitoring	Lightweight, detailed logging capabilities	Limited to Windows environment
Threat intelligence	MISP	Threat data sharing and management	Community-driven, integrates with other tools	Complex setup and configuration
	Anomali	Threat intelligence aggregation and analysis	Professional support, extensive threat database	Expensive licensing
SIEM	ELK Stack	Real-time log collection, search, and visualization	Open source, highly customizable	Requires manual configuration
	Splunk	Comprehensive SIEM with advanced analytics	Intuitive UI, robust support	High licensing costs
Vulnerability management	OpenVAS	Vulnerability scanning and assessment	Open source, good coverage of known vulnerabilities	Limited support options
	Tenable Nessus	Vulnerability scanning and complex auditing	Professional support, extensive plugin library	Costly licensing for enterprise use

Depending on your specific environment, team expertise, and security requirements, choosing the right tool requires investigation and evaluation. The best fit must take these factors into consideration.

2.2 Dashboard development

A well-designed dashboard is invaluable for communicating the organization's security posture, identifying trends, and making informed decisions. By visualizing security metrics, dashboards make complex data accessible and actionable for various stakeholders—from security analysts to executives.

The purpose of a dashboard is to transform raw data into meaningful visualizations that can be quickly interpreted and acted upon. A good dashboard should meet the principles of clarity, relevance, accessibility, and consistency.

The information should be easy to understand immediately. It is necessary to avoid clutter and keep visualizations simple. In addition, clear labels, concise text, and a logical layout should be used to guide the viewer through the information. In addition, only the most relevant metrics should be displayed for the intended audience. For instance, a dashboard for security analysts might focus on operational data such as vulnerability status and incident response times, while an executive dashboard would highlight high-level metrics such as risk exposure and compliance status.

The dashboard should be accessible to its audience in terms of both physical access (web, desktop, or mobile) and cognitive load (avoiding overwhelming complexity). It should be designed to consider accessibility best practices to ensure it's usable by individuals possessing varying levels of technical expertise. A consistent design should be maintained throughout the dashboard, including colors, fonts, and iconography. Consistency helps create a sense of familiarity and reduces the viewer's cognitive load.

Dashboards should be designed to prompt action. Metrics should be connected to potential actions or decision points. For example, if a dashboard shows an increase in failed login attempts, the user should be able to easily drill down into the data and investigate further.

2.2.1 Choosing the right metrics

Selecting the right metrics is crucial for building a meaningful dashboard. The metrics displayed should align with business goals, support decision-making, and show trends over time. Metrics should reflect the organization's business objectives and risk management strategies. For example, if the organization is focused on achieving SOC2 compliance, access control violations or encryption key management metrics should be prioritized.

Furthermore, it is necessary to choose metrics that support decision-making and provide actionable insights rather than just raw numbers. For instance, tracking the average time to patch critical vulnerabilities can directly inform resource allocation and risk prioritization, ensuring security teams focus on the most pressing threats. While real-time data is essential for immediate incident response, trend data is equally important as it allows stakeholders to see how security posture evolves, identifying whether efforts lead to tangible improvements or whether new gaps are emerging.

However, metrics should not remain static. As organizational goals, technologies, and threat landscapes evolve, the relevance of specific metrics may shift. Regularly reviewing and refining cybersecurity metrics ensure they continue providing meaningful insights and remain aligned with business priorities and emerging risks. However, metrics that used to be valuable might become obsolete, and new threats may require the introduction of fresh measurement criteria. Organizations can establish a continuous feedback loop to ensure that security metrics remain dynamic, actionable, and aligned with evolving cybersecurity challenges.

Different stakeholders have different data needs. A one-size-fits-all approach rarely works, so dashboards should be tailored for specific roles.

SECURITY ANALYST DASHBOARD

This dashboard is designed for operational use and includes metrics such as

- Real-time incident alerts
- Detailed views of security events
- Vulnerability status and remediation efforts
- Threat intelligence feeds and indicators of compromise (IoCs)

A security dashboard provides analysts with data to detect, investigate, and respond to security incidents.

EXECUTIVE DASHBOARD

This dashboard provides a high-level overview for senior leadership. It typically contains

- Overall risk exposure and trend analysis
- Compliance status and gaps
- Metrics related to the return on investment (ROI) of security investments
- Security incident trends and their effects on business operations

An executive dashboard communicates the organization's security posture in a business context, helping executives make strategic decisions.

COMPLIANCE DASHBOARD

This dashboard focuses on regulatory and compliance metrics, such as

- Compliance status for frameworks like SOC2, HIPAA, or GDPR
- Number of controls in place versus required controls
- Audit findings and remediation status

A compliance dashboard provides compliance officers and auditors with data needed to ensure adherence to regulatory standards.

2.2.2 Knowledge points

Learning to use charts, graphs, and tables effectively is crucial as well. You need to select the right visualization type for each metric—bar charts for comparative analysis, line graphs for trends, and pie charts for proportional data. It is also important to understand how to create dashboards that convey complex security metrics in a format that is easy to interpret for both technical and nontechnical audiences.

Dashboards are used to visualize risk data, allowing stakeholders to grasp potential threats and make proactive decisions. For example, an operational dashboard would highlight metrics such as incident response times, vulnerability status, and network traffic anomalies. In contrast, an executive dashboard would feature high-level metrics such as risk exposure, compliance status, and key incident trends.

2.2.3 Dashboard example

Let's build a sample dashboard for a fictional company, TechGuard Solutions, a mid-sized company specializing in software development. It has recently seen a spike in phishing attacks targeting its employees. The security team wants to monitor these incidents closely and provide executives with an overview of the organization's security posture. The objective is to create two dashboards:

- *Executive dashboard*—This dashboard will focus on high-level metrics to provide a strategic overview of the security landscape.
- *Security analyst dashboard*—This dashboard will provide real-time operational data to enable swift detection and response to security incidents.

To build our sample dashboards, we take the following steps.

DEFINE METRICS

Choose five key metrics for the executive dashboard and five for the security team dashboard:

- Executive dashboard metrics
  - *Risk exposure score*—Measures the overall risk level of the organization based on factors like vulnerability severity and recent incidents
  - *Compliance status*—Shows the compliance status with regulatory frameworks like SOC2 and HIPAA
  - *Number of critical security incidents*—Tracks the number of incidents classified as critical over the past quarter
  - *Mean time to resolve (MTTR)*—The average time to resolve security incidents
  - *Financial consequences of security incidents*—Provides an estimate of the financial losses resulting from incidents
- Security analyst dashboard metrics
  - *Real-time security alerts*—Number of alerts triggered within the past 24 hours, segmented by severity
  - *Top attack vectors*—Lists the most common attack vectors, such as phishing, malware, or brute-force attacks
  - *Phishing detection rate*—Tracks the detection rate for phishing attempts, showing how effective the defenses are

- *Vulnerability status*—Displays the number of open vulnerabilities categorized by severity
- *Incident response time*—Tracks the time to respond to each incident, helping measure team efficiency

CREATE VISUALIZATIONS

Select appropriate visualizations (e.g., line charts, bar charts, pie charts):

- Executive dashboard
  - *Risk exposure score*—A gauge chart visually representing the risk level, ranging from low (green) to high (red)
  - *Compliance status*—A simple bar chart showing the percentage of controls met for each compliance framework
  - *Number of critical security incidents*—A line chart showing trends over the past quarter
  - *Mean time to resolve*—A bar chart comparing MTTR across different incident categories (e.g., phishing, malware)
  - *Financial consequences of security incidents*—A pie chart breaking down the financial impact into categories such as data loss, legal fees, and lost productivity.
- Security analyst dashboard
  - *Real-time security alerts*—Real-time updating ticker or heatmap used to show the count of alerts by severity
  - *Top attack vectors*—A bar chart displaying the frequency of different attack vectors over the past 30 days
  - *Phishing detection rate*—A gauge chart showing the percentage of detected phishing attempts
  - *Vulnerability status*—A stacked bar chart showing open vulnerabilities categorized by low, medium, high, and critical severity
  - *Incident response time*—A scatter plot showing the distribution of response times for incidents, helping identify outliers

DESIGN DASHBOARDS

Create wireframe designs for both dashboards, showing the placement of each metric and visualization:

- Executive dashboard design
  - *Title*—"TechGuard Solutions: Executive Security Overview."
  - *Section 1: Risk exposure*—Use a gauge chart to display the overall risk exposure score. The gauge should have three sections: low (green), moderate (yellow), and high (red).

- *Section 2: Compliance status*—A bar chart showing the percentage of compliance achieved for each framework. SOC2, HIPAA, and ISO27001 should be displayed as separate bars with compliance percentages.
- *Section 3: Security incident overview*—Use a line chart to show the number of critical security incidents over the past quarter. Include a trend line to visualize changes over time.
- *Section 4: Mean time to resolve*—A bar chart is used to compare MTTR for different categories of incidents (e.g., phishing, malware).
- *Section 5: Financial consequences*—A pie chart is used to break down the estimated financial impact of security incidents into categories such as data loss, legal fees, and lost productivity.

- Security Analyst Dashboard Design
    - *Title*—"TechGuard Solutions: Security Operations Overview."
    - *Section 1: Real-time alerts*—A real-time heatmap showing the number of alerts by severity (low, medium, high).
    - *Section 2—Top attack vectors*: A bar chart displaying the top five attack vectors and their frequency over the past month.
    - *Section 3—Phishing detection rate*: A gauge chart showing the detection rate for phishing attempts, with a target range (e.g., above 80%)
    - *Section 4—Vulnerability status*: A stacked bar chart showing the number of open vulnerabilities categorized by severity (low, medium, high, critical)
    - *Section 5—Incident response time*: A scatter plot showing incident response times for the past 30 days, highlighting outliers with significantly high response times

Table 2.3 lists the metrics and example values for the executive dashboard.

Table 2.3 Executive dashboard example values

Metric	Value
Risk exposure score	7.5
SOC 2 compliance %	85%
HIPAA compliance %	90%
Critical security incidents (Q3)	5
MTTR (phishing incidents)	2 days
Financial consequences (Q3)	$150k

Figure 2.2 is an example of TechGuard executive dashboard, showing what it could look like.

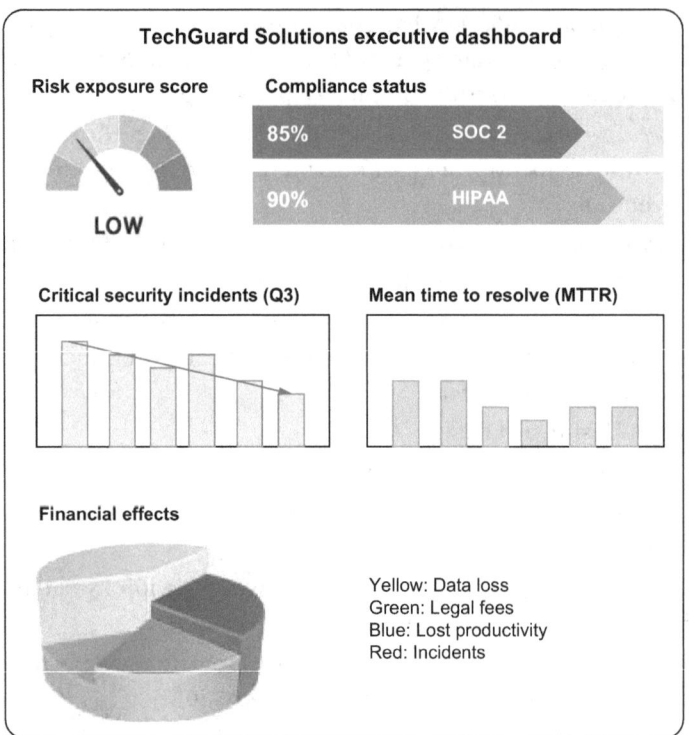

Figure 2.2 Example TechGuard executive dashboard

Table 2.4 lists the metrics and example values for the security analyst dashboard.

Table 2.4 Security analyst dashboard example values

Metric	Value
High severity alerts	15
Medium severity alerts	30
Low severity alerts	50
Top attack vector (phishing)	25 incidents
Phishing detection rate	92%
Critical vulnerabilities	10
High vulnerabilities	25
Medium vulnerabilities	40
Low vulnerabilities	70
Average incident response time	3 hours

Figure 2.3 is an example of TechGuard security analyst dashboard, showing what it could look like.

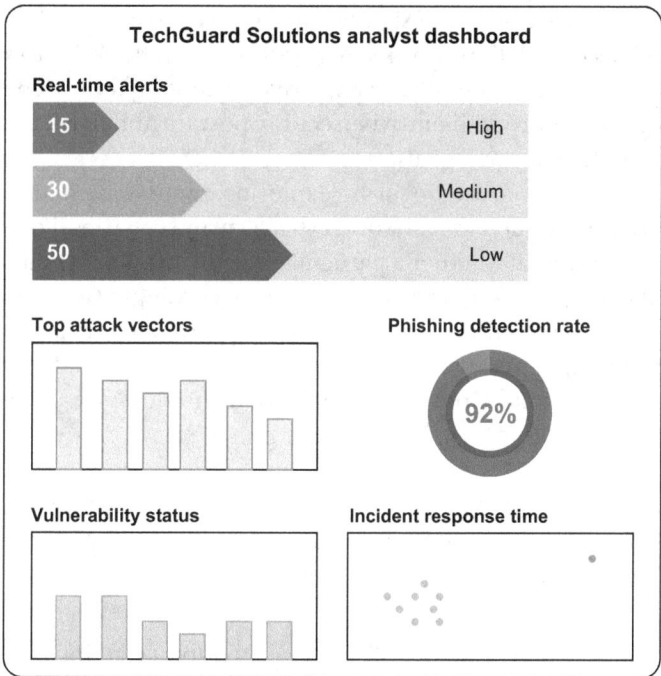

Figure 2.3 Example TechGuard security analyst dashboard

INTERPRET RESULTS

The final step is interpreting results:

- *Executive dashboard*—The executive dashboard indicates a moderate risk level and good compliance posture, but noticeable financial consequences due to recent security incidents. This finding suggests a need for enhanced preventive measures to reduce the number of incidents.
- *Security analyst dashboard*—The real-time dashboard highlights phishing as the top attack vector. In addition, the high number of critical vulnerabilities suggests that the vulnerability management program needs strengthening.

2.3 Statistical analysis

Statistics enhance cybersecurity strategies by helping analysts understand patterns, spot anomalies, and predict potential security incidents. While some may see statistics as purely academic or mathematical, the reality is that these techniques offer practical value for identifying trends, determining the relationships between different variables, and assessing overall risk.

In a cybersecurity toolkit, statistical techniques can uncover unusual behaviors, such as spikes in login attempts or irregular data transfers, which may indicate a security threat. Analysts can detect early warning signs and proactively address vulnerabilities by using methods such as correlation analysis, regression, and time series forecasting. Statistical analysis is invaluable in identifying immediate and long-term trends, allowing organizations to build a more resilient cybersecurity posture and make data-driven decisions that align with their security goals.

To provide a solid foundation, we begin by exploring some core statistical techniques and how they can be applied to real-world cybersecurity scenarios. For example, a simple trend analysis can reveal whether a particular type of attack is becoming more frequent over time, allowing teams to prioritize defenses accordingly. Correlation analysis, however, can identify connections between seemingly unrelated data points, such as login times and failed login attempts, thus uncovering potential insider threats or compromised accounts. Let's take a look at both of these techniques.

2.3.1 Trend analysis

Trend analysis helps identify whether a particular metric increases, decreases, or stays constant over time. Cybersecurity is often used to monitor incidents such as malware detections, failed login attempts, or data exfiltration alerts.

TREND ANALYSIS EXERCISE

Suppose a security team tracks the number of phishing attempts targeting their organization over the last 12 months. By applying trend analysis, they can determine whether phishing is becoming a more frequent problem.

The code presented in the following listing creates a simple line plot to visualize the monthly trend of phishing attempts over a year. Using a dataset that records phishing attempts for each month, the code loads this data into a DataFrame, then plots the number of phishing attempts on the y-axis against each month on the x-axis. The result is a line chart that makes it easy to see how phishing attempts increase over time, helping analysts spot trends and possibly anticipate future spikes.

Listing 2.1 Using trend analysis to create a simple line plot

```
import pandas as pd
import matplotlib.pyplot as plt

# Example dataset: Phishing attempts recorded over 12 months
data = {'Month': ['Jan', 'Feb', 'Mar', 'Apr', 'May', 'Jun',
                  'Jul', 'Aug', 'Sep', 'Oct', 'Nov', 'Dec'],
        'Phishing_Attempts': [23, 25, 30, 35, 40, 45, 50, 60, 7
                              5, 80, 85, 90]}
```

- Imports pandas, a data manipulation library, to handle and structure the dataset
- Imports matplotlib.pyplot for creating visualizations, specifically a line plot in this example
- Defines a dictionary with data on phishing attempts, recording the number of attempts each month. The dictionary includes two keys: Month (for month names) and Phishing_Attempts (for the count of phishing incidents).

Statistical analysis

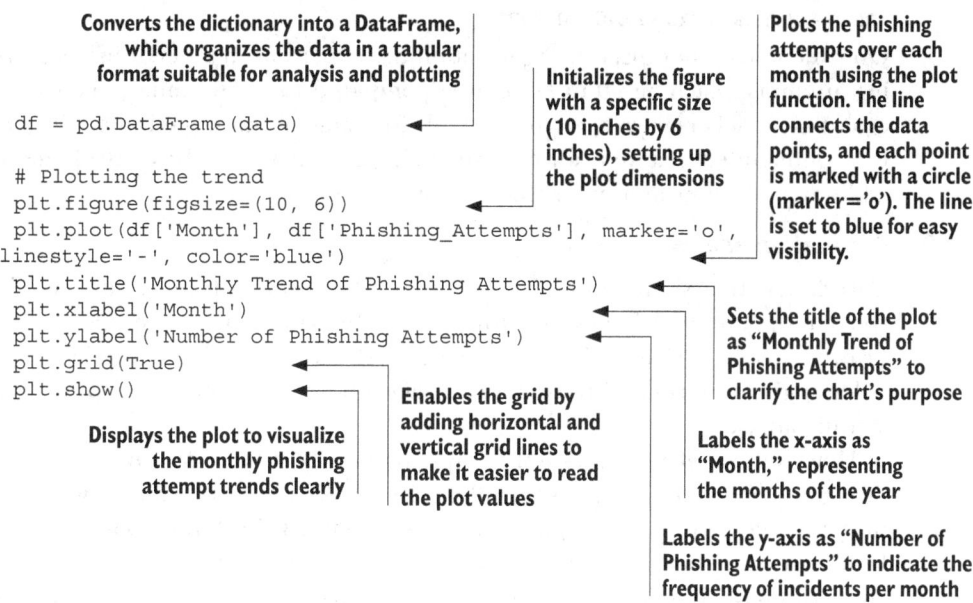

```
df = pd.DataFrame(data)

# Plotting the trend
plt.figure(figsize=(10, 6))
plt.plot(df['Month'], df['Phishing_Attempts'], marker='o',
linestyle='-', color='blue')
plt.title('Monthly Trend of Phishing Attempts')
plt.xlabel('Month')
plt.ylabel('Number of Phishing Attempts')
plt.grid(True)
plt.show()
```

- Converts the dictionary into a DataFrame, which organizes the data in a tabular format suitable for analysis and plotting
- Initializes the figure with a specific size (10 inches by 6 inches), setting up the plot dimensions
- Plots the phishing attempts over each month using the plot function. The line connects the data points, and each point is marked with a circle (marker='o'). The line is set to blue for easy visibility.
- Sets the title of the plot as "Monthly Trend of Phishing Attempts" to clarify the chart's purpose
- Labels the x-axis as "Month," representing the months of the year
- Labels the y-axis as "Number of Phishing Attempts" to indicate the frequency of incidents per month
- Enables the grid by adding horizontal and vertical grid lines to make it easier to read the plot values
- Displays the plot to visualize the monthly phishing attempt trends clearly

Figure 2.4 illustrates the output produced by the analysis Python code. The graph shows an upward trend in phishing attempts over the last 12 months, suggesting that the organization needs to bolster its defenses against phishing attacks by providing additional training to employees or investing in more robust email filtering technologies.

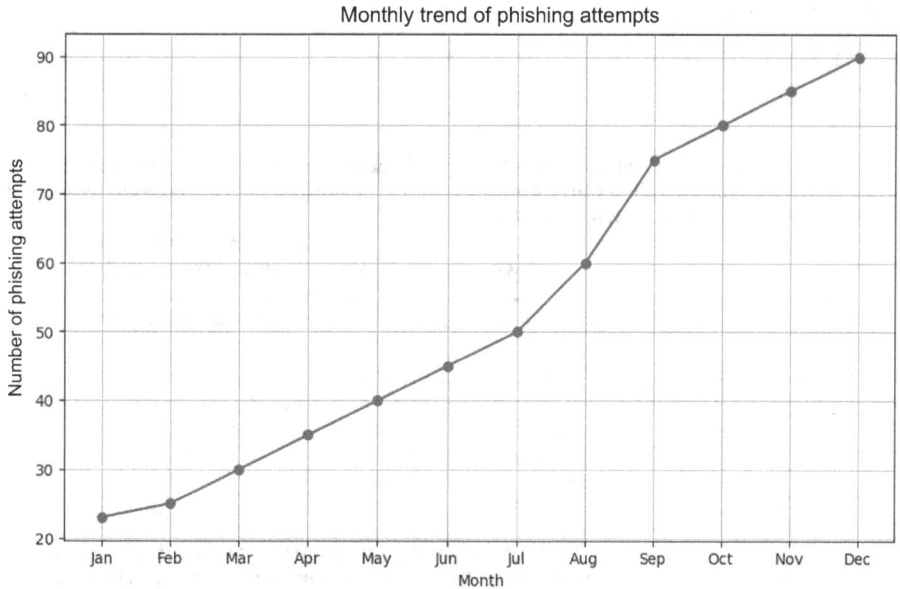

Figure 2.4 Monthly trend analysis of phishing attempts for the trend analysis exercise Python code

TREND ANALYSIS EXERCISE CISO REPORT

Over the last 12 months, our organization has experienced a steady increase in phishing attempts, reaching 90 in December compared to 23 in January. This trend indicates that attackers have been increasingly focusing on our organization. As a result, it is recommended that we prioritize enhancing our email security controls and provide additional phishing awareness training for employees.

2.3.2 Correlation analysis

Correlation analysis measures the strength and direction of the relationship between two or more variables. In cybersecurity, this can help identify whether specific behaviors or events are associated with an increased risk. For example, a correlation between failed login attempts and phishing campaigns might indicate an ongoing credential-stuffing attack.

However, correlation does not imply causation. Just because two factors are linked does not mean that one causes the other directly. A high correlation between login failures and late-night hours might suggest malicious activity, but it could also be due to legitimate employees working across different time zones. Misinterpreting correlation as causation can lead to false alarms, wasted resources, and ineffective security responses.

To avoid misinterpretation, correlation analysis should be paired with contextual understanding, additional data validation, and security expertise to distinguish true threats from normal user behavior patterns.

CORRELATION ANALYSIS EXERCISE

Let's analyze the relationship between employee login times and the frequency of failed login attempts to identify whether abnormal login times are correlated with potential unauthorized access attempts. The following listing shows the correlation analysis Python code.

Listing 2.2 Analyzing login attempts with correlation analysis

```python
import seaborn as sns
import pandas as pd
import matplotlib.pyplot as plt

# Sample dataset: Login times and failed login attempts
data = {'Login_Hour': [8, 9, 10, 11, 12, 13, 14, 15, 16, 17,
                      18, 19, 20, 21, 22, 23, 0, 1, 2, 3],
        'Failed_Login_Attempts': [2, 3, 4, 5, 3, 6, 7, 5, 8,
                                  9, 12, 13, 10, 8, 7, 5, 2,
                                  3, 4, 5]}
```

- Imports seaborn as sns, a data visualization library that provides statistical graphics, including heatmaps
- Imports pandas as pd, a library for data manipulation and analysis, in this case used to create a DataFrame
- Imports matplotlib.pyplot as plt, which provides plotting capabilities, such as setting up figure dimensions and displaying plots
- Defines a dictionary data containing two lists: Login_Hour, which represents the hour of the day (in 24-hour format) during which logins occurred, and Failed_Login_Attempts, which represents the number of failed login attempts for each hour

Statistical analysis

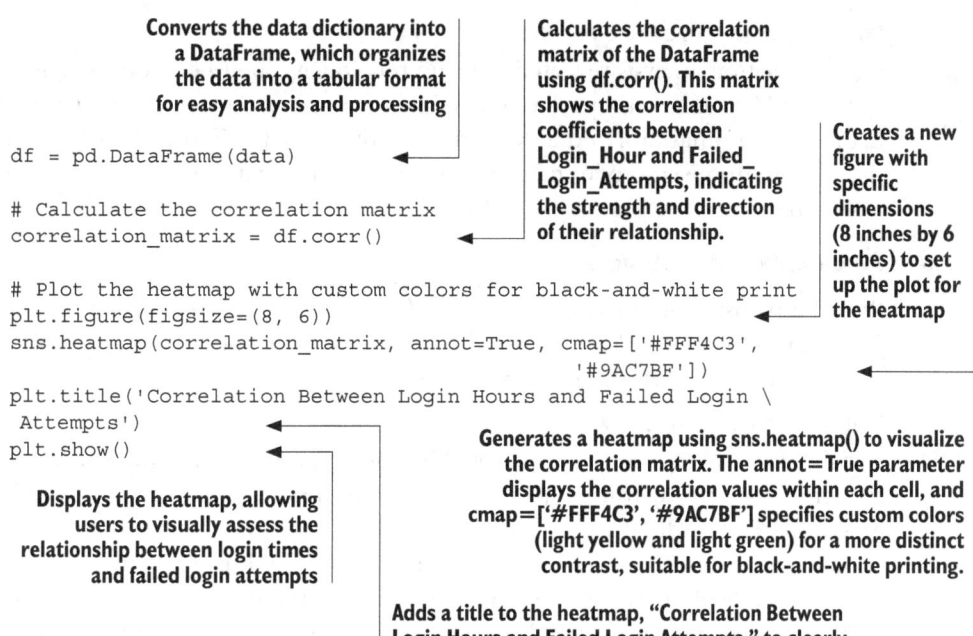

Figure 2.5 illustrates the code output. The heatmap shows a high positive correlation between login hours during late nights (post 11 PM) and failed login attempts, suggesting that an increase in failed attempts often accompanies unusual login times. This insight could be used for adjusting monitoring policies so they pay closer attention to login attempts during these times.

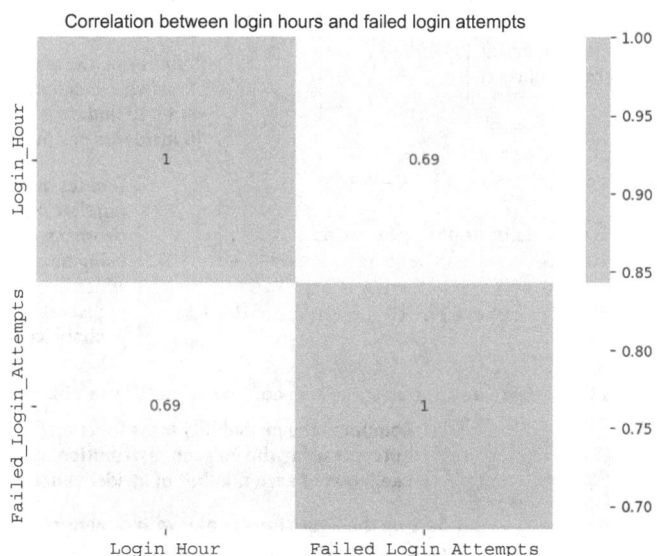

Figure 2.5 Correlation analysis Python code output

CORRELATION ANALYSIS CISO REPORT

Our correlation analysis revealed a strong relationship between abnormal login hours (post 11 PM) and the frequency of failed login attempts. This finding suggests a potential pattern of unauthorized access attempts during late-night hours. To mitigate the risk of compromised credentials, it is recommended that stricter authentication controls and monitoring policies be enforced during these hours.

2.3.3 Probability distribution

Probability distributions show how the values of a variable are spread or distributed. This can help model the likelihood of different outcomes, such as predicting how many security incidents might occur within a certain period.

PROBABILITY DISTRIBUTION EXERCISE

Imagine we want to estimate the probability of experiencing several malware incidents in a given month. By using a probability distribution, we can forecast these incidents and prepare accordingly.

The code presented in the following listing uses the Poisson distribution to model the probability of different numbers of malware incidents occurring in a given month, based on an average rate. The Poisson distribution is well-suited for events that occur randomly over a fixed interval, such as monthly malware incidents. Here, we assume an average of 10 incidents per month. The code calculates the probability of observing 0 to 20 incidents and visualizes this distribution using a bar chart, helping analysts understand the likelihood of various outcomes for malware incidents.

Listing 2.3 Measuring probability of malware incidents with probability distribution

```python
import numpy as np
import matplotlib.pyplot as plt
from scipy.stats import poisson

# Average number of malware incidents per month
mu = 10  # Average incidents

# Create a range of possible outcomes (0 to 20 incidents)
x = np.arange(0, 21)

# Calculate the probability for each outcome using Poisson distribution
pmf = poisson.pmf(x, mu)

# Plot the distribution
plt.figure(figsize=(10, 6))
```

- Imports NumPy to handle numerical operations, including array manipulation
- Imports Matplotlib for visualization of statistical distributions
- Imports the Poisson distribution function from scipy.stats for modeling discrete probability distributions
- Defines mu, the average number of malware incidents per month, set to 10, indicating an expected 10 incidents per month
- Creates an array of possible outcomes (from 0 to 20 incidents) using np.arange(), which provides a range of discrete values for probability calculations
- Computes the probability mass function (PMF) for each outcome using the Poisson distribution, calculating the likelihood of each number of incidents occurring
- Sets up the figure for the plot with dimensions of 10 inches by 6 inches for better visualization

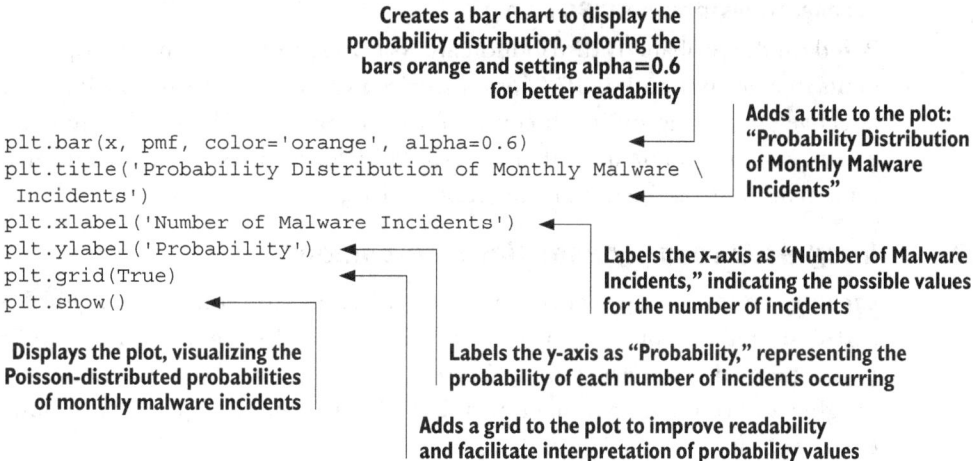

Figure 2.6 illustrates the output of the probability distribution Python code The graph shows that the most likely number of malware incidents in a month is around 10, with decreasing probabilities for values higher or lower than this. This insight can help teams allocate resources, ensuring there are enough personnel available to handle the expected volume of incidents.

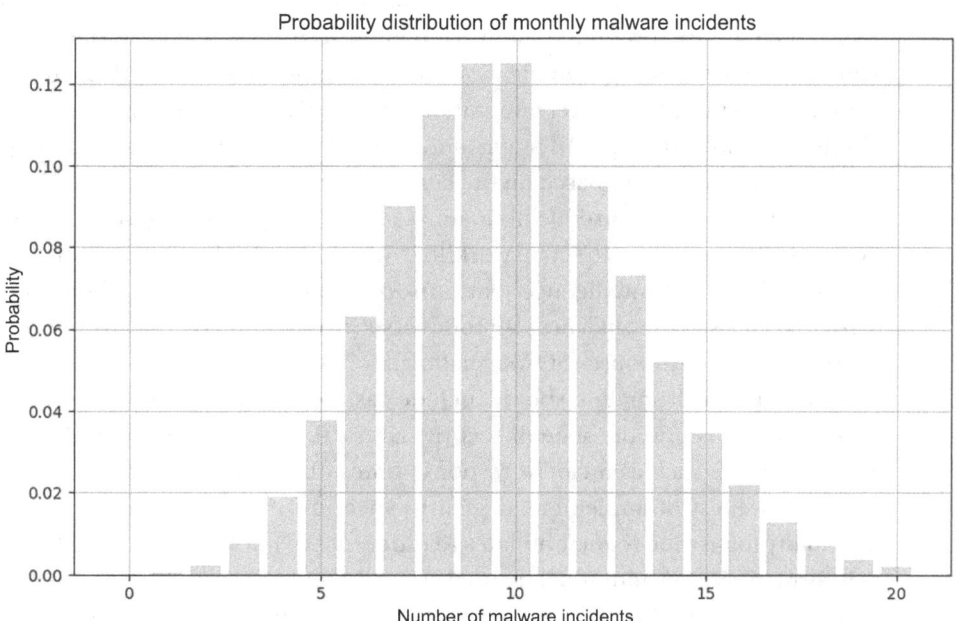

Figure 2.6   Probability distribution Python code output

PROBABILITY DISTRIBUTION CISO REPORT

Based on the probability distribution analysis, the most likely number of malware incidents in a given month is 10. This data-driven estimate allows us to allocate resources effectively, ensuring sufficient coverage to address the anticipated volume of security events. It is recommended that we regularly review these estimates to ensure they remain accurate as the threat landscape evolves.

2.4 Integrated security analytics environment

Creating an integrated security analytics environment requires thoughtful planning and a strategic approach to tool selection, data flow management, and automation. The goal is to ensure that different tools work together, exchanging data and insights and reducing manual effort. Let's break down the key steps in building this environment.

The first step is selecting the right tools for your organization's needs. This involves choosing tools that complement each other and can integrate smoothly. SIEM solution tools such as Splunk, IBM QRadar, or ArcSight collect logs and events from across the network, providing a centralized view of security activities. Solutions such as Threat-Connect or Anomali can enrich alerts with context, indicating whether an IP address or URL is associated with known malicious activity.

Analytical tools such as the ELK Stack (Elasticsearch, Logstash, Kibana) or commercial solutions such as Microsoft Sentinel enable deeper analysis and visualization of collected data. It's important to establish data flow so that the tools can share data, which can be achieved through application programming interfaces (APIs), data export/import mechanisms, or direct integrations provided by the vendors. Maintaining a consistent data flow to keep all systems updated in real-time is crucial, enabling them to make accurate decisions based on the latest information.

Automation is key to reducing manual efforts and facilitating faster detection and response. It is necessary to set up workflows where the SIEM system automatically sends alerts to the threat intelligence platform for context enrichment, then forwards the enriched alerts to the analytics tool for deeper investigation or a security orchestration, automation, and response (SOAR) platform for automated response.

Integrated environments should include dashboards and reporting mechanisms that provide insights into the state of security across the organization. Dashboards should display metrics such as incident response times, the number of detected threats, and the effectiveness of implemented security measures. Automated reporting facilitates the ability to provide regular updates to different stakeholders, ensuring that everyone is informed without additional manual effort.

Insights gathered from the integrated environment are used to fine-tune detection rules, update threat models, and improve the security program's overall effectiveness. This continuous feedback loop helps the organization adapt to new threats and remain resilient.

2.4.1 Integrated security analytics environment exercise

Imagine a healthcare organization, SecureHealth, that needs to build an integrated security analytics environment to protect sensitive patient data and ensure compliance with regulations such as HIPAA. They use Splunk as their SIEM system, ThreatConnect as their threat intelligence platform, and the ELK stack for analytics and visualization.

Here is the outline of the integrated security analytics exercise:

- *Tool integration*—SecureHealth integrates Splunk with ThreatConnect using APIs, enabling automatic enrichment of alerts with threat intelligence data. They then connect Splunk with the ELK stack, ensuring that all enriched alerts are forwarded to Elasticsearch for advanced analytics and visualization in Kibana.
- *Data flow and automation*—SecureHealth configures workflows so that any alert generated in Splunk is automatically enriched with contextual data from ThreatConnect (e.g., is the source IP involved in known attacks?). If the enrichment confirms a high-risk activity, the alert is sent to their SOAR platform for further automated investigation or response actions, such as blocking the IP or alerting the on-call analyst.
- *Automated reporting*—SecureHealth sets up a reporting schedule where weekly compliance reports are automatically generated and sent to the compliance team, while a real-time dashboard provides executives with a high-level overview of the security posture and the number of incidents detected and resolved in the past month.
- *Continuous improvement*—SecureHealth reviews the automated reports and conducts post-incident analyses using the ELK stack. They use these insights to update their Splunk detection rules and fine-tune their threat intelligence feeds to prioritize the latest emerging threats in the healthcare sector.

The architecture diagram in figure 2.7 illustrates the data flow between the SIEM, threat intelligence platform, and analytics tools. We include elements such as automated workflows, APIs for data exchange, and real-time dashboards for monitoring and reporting.

This diagram depicts a unified security environment where all tools contribute to a common goal of enhanced threat detection, response, and reporting. With an integrated security analytics environment, organizations can achieve comprehensive visibility, faster response times, and improved overall security posture.

2.5 Continuous improvement and iteration

Building a cybersecurity analytics toolkit is not a one-time effort. As threats evolve and the organization's security landscape changes, the tools, techniques, and processes used to defend against them must also adapt accordingly. Continuous improvement is the key to maintaining an effective security posture. Organizations should adopt a continuous improvement approach to refine their security analytics toolkit based on changing needs, feedback, and new developments in the industry.

40 CHAPTER 2 *Cybersecurity analytics toolkit*

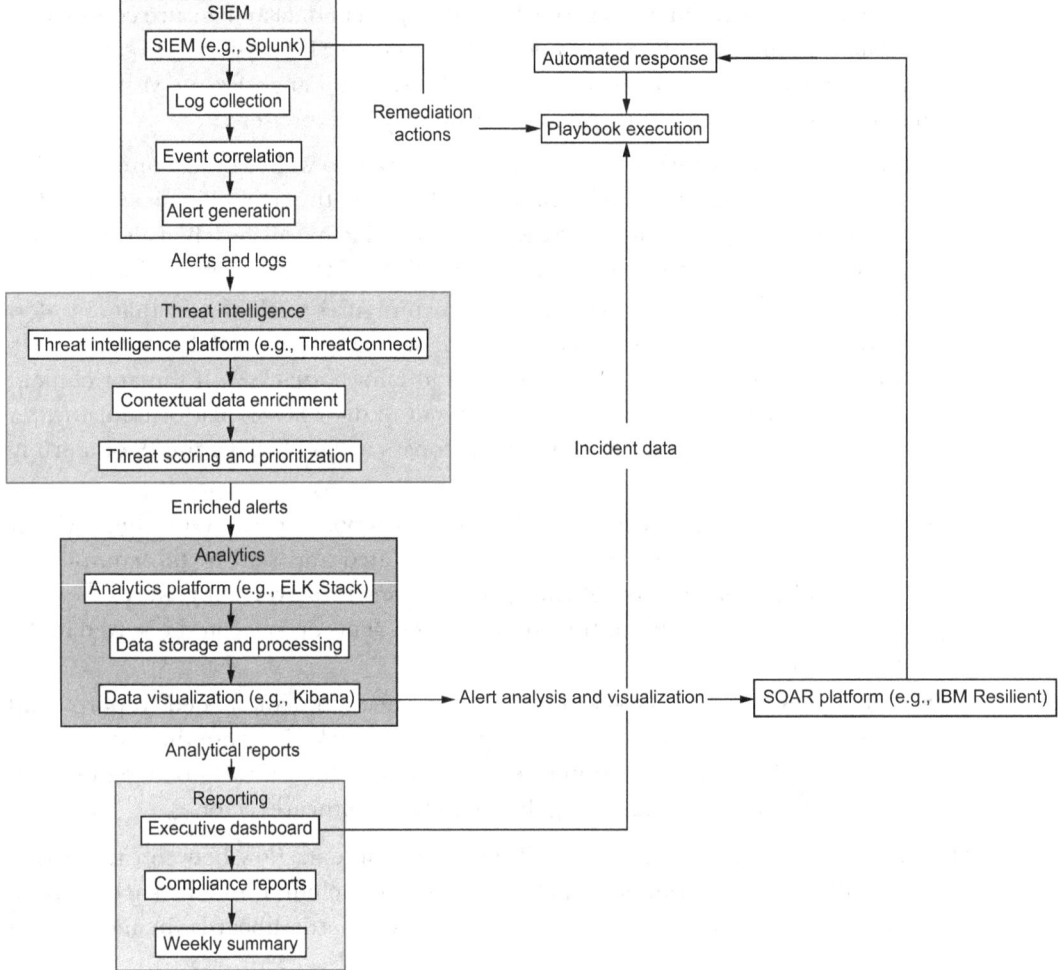

Figure 2.7   Example of an integrated security analytics environment.

In cybersecurity, stagnation can be just as dangerous as complacency. A security analytics toolkit that remains static is at risk of becoming outdated and ineffective. New threat vectors, technological advancements, and business shifts can all contribute to gaps in coverage if the tools and processes are not regularly updated. A proactive approach to continuous improvement ensures that the organization remains resilient and capable of addressing emerging risks.

2.5.1 Iteration techniques

Iteration based on feedback loops is one of the most effective ways to maintain the relevance of a cybersecurity analytics toolkit. Regular reviews and assessments help identify inefficiencies, coverage gaps, or areas for enhancement, which can involve

- *Feedback loops*—Gather feedback from all stakeholders, including security analysts, engineers, and executives. Determine which areas of the analytics toolkit provide the most value and which need improvement.
- *Regular tool evaluation*—Regularly evaluate the current tools to see if they meet the organization's requirements. For instance, a tool that was effective for detecting traditional malware may not be sufficient for identifying sophisticated multistage attacks.
- *Adapting to new threats*—As new threats and technologies emerge, the organization must assess how well these changes can be handled using current tools. If a new type of attack becomes prevalent, consider adding or upgrading tools that specialize in detecting or mitigating such attacks.
- *Integration of new technologies*—Taking into account that AI and machine learning capabilities improve consistently, consider incorporating these into the toolkit to enhance detection, analysis, and response.

2.5.2 Continuous improvement cycle

Implementing a continuous improvement cycle involves more than just adopting new tools—it also means revisiting and refining existing processes. This iterative cycle can be broken down into the following steps:

1. *Review and assess*—Regularly review the effectiveness of tools and processes. Identify new requirements based on recent incidents, business changes, or technological developments.
2. *Plan and develop*—Based on the assessment, create a plan for improving or adding to the toolkit. This can include adopting new tools, refining existing configurations, or enhancing processes.
3. *Implement and test*—Roll out the planned changes, ensuring they are thoroughly tested in a controlled environment before full deployment. Testing should include assessing the effect of changes on overall system performance and security posture.
4. *Evaluate and refine*—After implementation, measure the effect of changes using key metrics such as detection rate, false-positive reduction, or incident response time. Use these insights to refine the toolkit further.

CONTINUOUS IMPROVEMENT EXERCISE

Imagine a mid-sized healthcare organization that relies on automated alerts and dashboards to monitor compliance with HIPAA regulations. Over time, they notice an increase in phishing attempts targeting employees. The organization could iterate by adding an anti-phishing tool to the existing suite, training employees to spot phishing emails, and updating alert thresholds to detect suspicious email activity better. Once these changes are implemented, the organization will monitor the results and continue refining its approach based on feedback and new attack trends.

To illustrate this process, figure 2.8 depicts the continuous improvement cycle within a cybersecurity analytics environment.

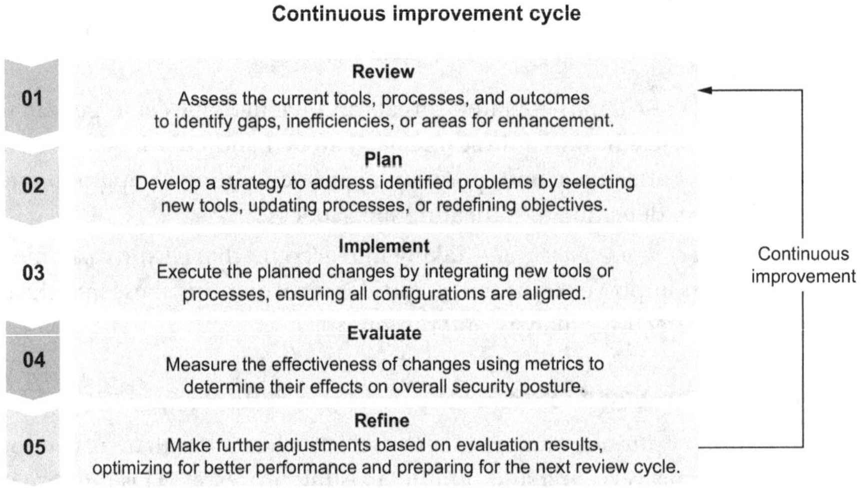

Continuous improvement cycle

01 Review
Assess the current tools, processes, and outcomes to identify gaps, inefficiencies, or areas for enhancement.

02 Plan
Develop a strategy to address identified problems by selecting new tools, updating processes, or redefining objectives.

03 Implement
Execute the planned changes by integrating new tools or processes, ensuring all configurations are aligned.

04 Evaluate
Measure the effectiveness of changes using metrics to determine their effects on overall security posture.

05 Refine
Make further adjustments based on evaluation results, optimizing for better performance and preparing for the next review cycle.

Continuous improvement

Figure 2.8 Continuous improvement cycle diagram as an example of how an organization can implement their toolkit

Continuous improvement should not be viewed as an optional process but as an integral part of a cybersecurity strategy. Organizations that commit to iterative enhancements of their analytics toolkit will be better equipped when facing new challenges and stay ahead of adversaries. The ability to adapt quickly and effectively separates mature security programs from those that are merely reactive.

Embracing a culture of continuous improvement enables organizations to shift from a reactive to a proactive security posture, providing stronger defenses and more resilient security operations.

Summary

- A cybersecurity analytics toolkit includes tools for data collection, analysis, and visualization, enabling organizations to monitor, detect, and respond more effectively to security threats.

- When selecting tools, organizations should consider functionality, integration ease, and scalability, ensuring that each tool aligns with security objectives and can adapt to future needs.
- Effective dashboards enhance decision-making by clearly presenting key metrics, while strong communication practices ensure that security insights reach relevant stakeholders in an understandable format.
- Statistical and AI techniques, such as anomaly detection and predictive modeling, help analysts uncover patterns and detect potential threats, thus strengthening overall security posture.
- An integrated security analytics environment centralizes data and automates analysis, which provides a cohesive approach to threat management across the organization.
- Continuous improvement is essential for maintaining a relevant toolkit, with regular updates and adjustments ensuring the tools remain effective as security needs evolve.

Implementing a security metrics program

This chapter covers
- Designing a cybersecurity metrics program
- Building effective metrics dashboards
- Open source tools
- Analyzing and reporting to inform actionable decisions
- Common challenges and pitfalls and how to avoid them

Implementing an information security program is more than simply setting up defenses, checking boxes, and assuming everything is done. Organizations must continuously evaluate the effectiveness of security measures. Having data-driven insights and the ability to measure and analyze that data is the best way to make better, more informed decisions. The metrics discussed throughout this book will allow you to measure the performance of your information security program. In addition, it can help you identify weaknesses, optimize your defenses, and report to the C-level on your standing.

Chapter 3 discusses the importance of a well-designed cybersecurity metrics program. Here, I provide a repeatable and proven process using the METRICS (Measure, Evaluate, Threshold, Report, Improve, Communicate, and Sustain) methodology—a comprehensive guide for measuring and evaluating security performance to better align our efforts with business goals. This chapter presents the framework for building a sustainable and scalable metrics program.

In this chapter, we also discuss dashboards that provide real-time visibility of security programs' performance and how to choose the right tools for metric collection and visualization. These dashboards may facilitate informed decision-making, which drives continuous improvement in your organization.

By the end of this chapter, you will learn how to implement a metrics program, track performance, analyze and interpret results, report on those results to various stakeholders, and ultimately improve your organization's security maturity.

3.1 Introducing metrics program design

A structured metrics program allows companies to identify weaknesses, track improvements, and adjust their strategies based on real-time data. By measuring various security aspects, organizations can better align security efforts with broader business goals, thus transforming abstract security efforts into tangible performance indicators. Knowing how to analyze and report on this data will empower you to convey the story about your organization's security efforts in a way that is understandable for all levels—from technical staff to executives. This skill helps bridge the gap between technical security and operations, ultimately allowing you to justify investments, adjust resource allocation, and improve response strategies.

A well-designed security metrics program can boost an organization's overall security maturity. For instance, an organization might aim to improve its incident response times or reduce vulnerabilities across critical systems. These metrics don't just measure success, but they guide actions, showing whether security policies and tools are performing as expected. This benefit, in turn, helps the organization become more agile, capable of identifying and mitigating threats before they can cause significant damage.

3.1.1 Key components of a security metrics program

The first step in building a cybersecurity metrics program is to define its purpose. What are the organization's security goals? These could include reducing the number of successful attacks, improving response times, or ensuring compliance with industry regulations. Defining clear, measurable goals ensures that the program is aligned with broader business objectives. Goals should be specific, actionable, and tied directly to areas of risk or known security gaps.

Once the goals are clearly defined, the next step is selecting the appropriate metrics to track. Metrics should be meaningful and relevant, providing insights into specific areas of security performance. For example, tracking the number of detected threats alone may not provide enough insight—measuring the severity of those threats and the time taken to resolve them is essential. Selecting metrics tied to business-critical assets and operations will make the program more valuable.

Metrics are not static. A good program will include feedback loops that allow the organization to adapt based on the data collected. For example, if a particular vulnerability keeps resurfacing despite mitigation efforts, this could point to a deeper systemic problem that needs to be addressed. A continuous feedback loop allows organizations to refine their security strategies and improve their defenses.

Figure 3.1 shows the flow of a security metrics program with defined feedback loops.

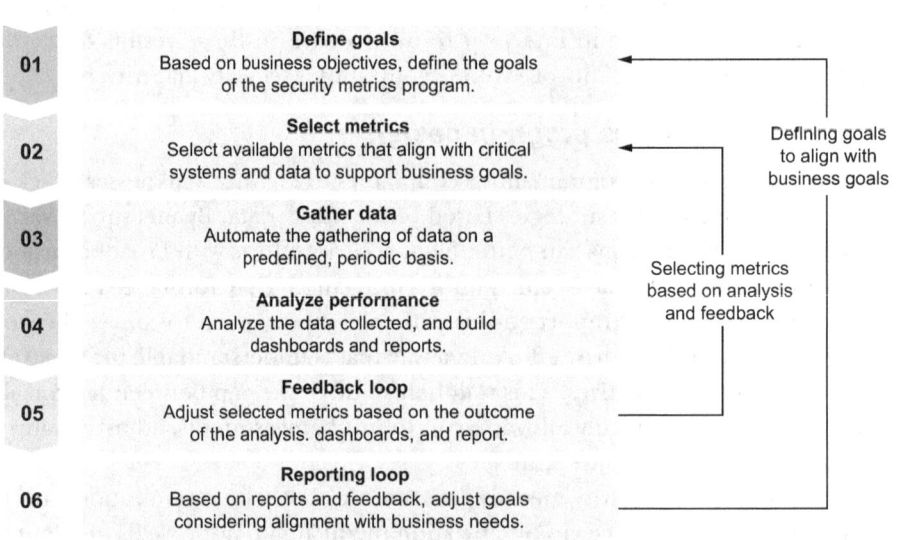

Figure 3.1 Security metrics program at a high level, showing key feedback loops

At a high level, we can see the feedback loops for selecting metrics and defining goals. This cyclical process is essential to maintaining an adaptive and proactive security posture. By consistently tracking key performance indicators, the organization can remain agile in its response to evolving threats, while demonstrating the tangible value of its security investments to stakeholders. As we move forward in this chapter, we will explore how to design this program step-by-step, ensuring it is robust, scalable, and tailored to your organization's specific needs.

3.2 METRICS methodology

The METRICS methodology offers a structured approach to designing, implementing, and maintaining a security metrics program. It provides a step-by-step guide for building an effective security metrics program that aligns with business goals and drives continuous improvement. Figure 3.2 shows the METRICS methodology.

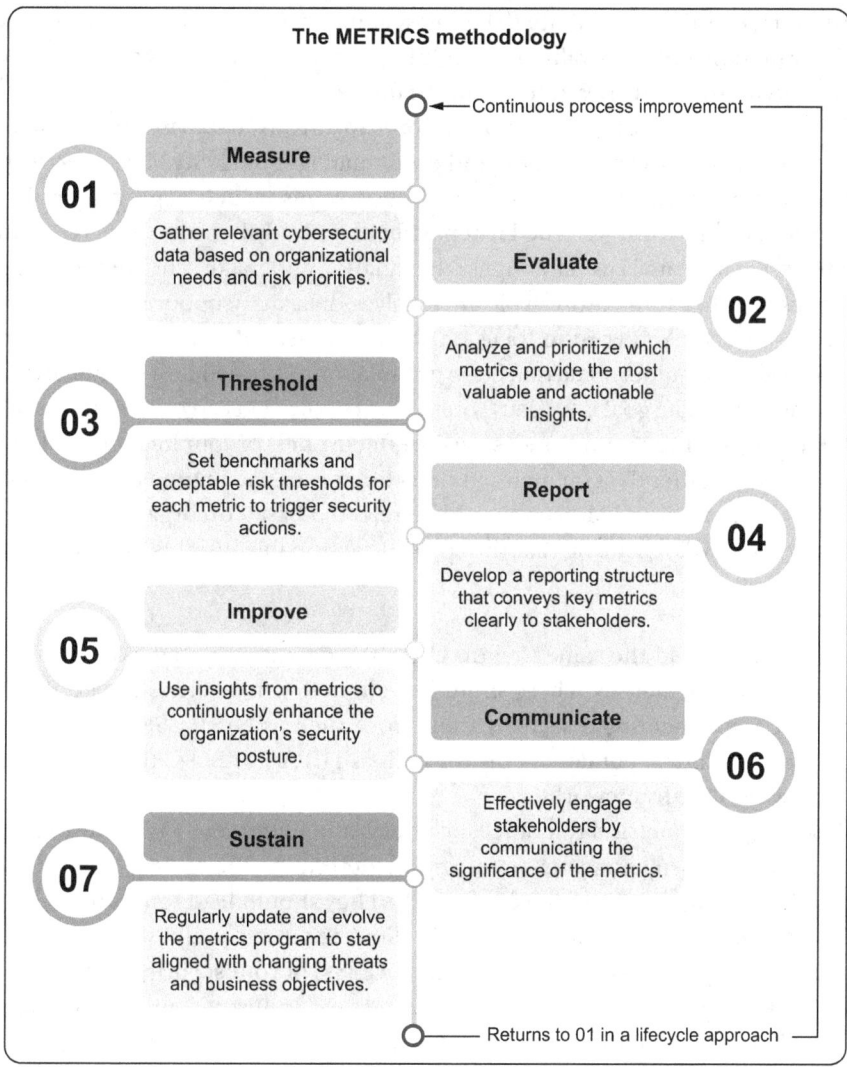

Figure 3.2 The METRICS methodology for designing, implementing, and sustaining a security metrics program

3.2.1 Measure

Good data is the foundation of a security metrics program. Organizations must determine what data is critical for measuring security performance. This task requires a deep understanding of key assets, threats, vulnerabilities, and security controls.

This data can come from various sources in the organization. Security tools such as firewalls, intrusion detection systems, and antivirus software can generate logs and alerts that can be collected for analysis. Incident management systems can generate alerts and feed information into ticketing systems, which can be enriched with supporting information and offer valuable insights. Network and system logs can provide information about user activities and system performance.

Storing and processing this information can involve databases or specialized platforms such as security information and event management (SIEMs) or security orchestration, automation, and response (SOARs) systems, which aggregate and correlate data from multiple sources. The IT department typically handles these responsibilities, and the security team is usually engaged to analyze and make sense of this data.

Choosing what to measure typically involves data that supports your organization's objectives directly. You want to focus on what matters and what can be directly aligned with business operations. Data that is too granular or unaligned with your goals may not be worth the effort. The goal is to focus your resources on what can offer significant benefits.

For example, if you want to measure the effectiveness of your incident response team, you'll need to gather data on incident detection times, mean time to respond (MTTR), and containment times. Metrics should be selected based on organizational needs and industry standards, ensuring that they provide actionable insights for decision-makers.

3.2.2 Evaluate

Not all metrics hold the same weight. Once the data is gathered, you should evaluate the most valuable metrics. These should be aligned with business goals and objectives. If you are implementing a security framework such as NIST CSF, ISO 27001, CIS, or HITRUST, or under regulatory control such as HIPAA or SOX, the metrics should be aligned with these frameworks.

Assessing your metric's relevance, accuracy, and alignment with your organization's objectives and risk management strategies to determine the value of a metric considers how it directly supports your business goals. They should lead to actionable outcomes. For instance, evaluating whether a metric allows for trend analysis over time will enable you to identify patterns and assess the effectiveness of your security measures. Consider whether the metric can be benchmarked against industry standards or past performance. This approach will provide context and aid in setting realistic targets.

For example, tracking the number of detected vulnerabilities may not be as insightful as tracking the number of vulnerabilities remediated within a specific time frame. It is desirable to evaluate each metric's relevance and ensure it offers clear, actionable insights that guide security decisions.

3.2.3 Threshold

Each security metric selected should have defined thresholds that indicate acceptable levels of risk. Thresholds act as benchmarks, helping security teams identify when action is needed. Furthermore, setting thresholds requires an understanding of the measured data's technical and business effect.

To determine appropriate thresholds and acceptable risks, teams often perform risk assessments that consider factors such as the organization's risk appetite, regulatory requirements, and historical data on security incidents. Engaging with stakeholders across the organization helps ensure that thresholds align with overall business objectives.

The ATLAS (Alert Threshold Lifecycle Assessment System) methodology, introduced in chapter 8, provides a structured approach to setting and evaluating thresholds. ATLAS assists teams in establishing initial thresholds based on data analysis and business priorities, monitoring their effectiveness over time and adjusting them in response to changes in the threat landscape or organizational needs.

For example, if you're measuring failed login attempts, setting a threshold at 10 failed attempts in 10 minutes may trigger an alert for potential brute-force attacks. Thresholds should be adaptable based on the evolving threat landscape and the organization's risk tolerance. See the ATLAS methodology in chapter 8 for more information on setting and evaluating thresholds.

3.2.4 Report

Reports ensure that metrics are communicated effectively across the organization, and they should be tailored to different audiences. Technical teams, executives, and regulatory bodies should all be informed in a language they understand. Each report should speak that specific language when communicating the analysis of metrics. Reports should be clear, concise, and visually appealing.

Including visual elements such as screenshots of dashboards and reports can greatly enhance understanding. For instance, a screenshot of a security dashboard might display key performance indicators (KPIs), such as the number of detected incidents over time, the status of vulnerability remediation efforts, or a real-time alert highlighting critical problems. Visual representations such as graphs, charts, and heat maps help stakeholders quickly grasp complex data and identify trends or areas that need attention.

By providing examples of how metrics are presented visually (figure 3.3), readers can see the practical application of reporting techniques. The examples reinforce the concepts discussed and offer guidance on designing effective reports. Incorporating screenshots into reports makes the data more tangible and allows stakeholders to better interpret and act on the provided information.

3.2.5 Improve

The goal of using the gathered data is to make better, more informed decisions that improve the organization's security posture. Metrics should not simply be static measurements but should drive security improvements.

Measuring improvements involves comparing current metrics against baseline data to assess the effectiveness of implemented changes. By establishing initial metric measurements before making any adjustments, you can create a reference point. For example, suppose metrics indicate that incident detection times are too long, and you invest in advanced threat detection tools or improve staff training. In that case, you should monitor the same metrics afterward to see whether detection times have decreased.

This report provides a summary of key security metrics collected during September 2023. The aim is to highlight critical areas affecting our organization's security posture and to recommend actions for improvement.

Data analysis

1. **Incident Response Metrics:**

Observation: While detection times are within our acceptable threshold of 45 minutes, the MTTR exceeds our target of 2 hours.

2. **Vulnerability management**

Observation: The correction rate is below our goal of 90%, indicating delays in addressing critical vulnerabilities.

3. **Failed login attempts**

Observation: This number exceeds our threshold and may suggest targeted brute-force attack attempts.

Recommendations

- **Improve incident response times:** Implement additional training and streamline procedures to reduce the MTTR to below 2 hours.
- **Enhance vulnerability corrective efforts:** Review and optimize the patch management process to ensure that at least 90% of critical vulnerabilities are remediated in the SLA.
- **Investigate failed login patterns:** Analyze the accounts with excessive failed login attempts to determine whether they are under attack, and consider enforcing multi-factor authentication for added security.

Figure 3.3 Example report showing some graphics that can be used to help drive the store behind the metrics

Setting specific, measurable targets or KPIs allows you to quantify the improvements. Continuous monitoring and analysis of these metrics provide tangible evidence of the effects of your security initiatives. Regularly reviewing these metrics helps identify whether the changes have effectively reduced risk and improved your security posture, or whether further adjustments are needed. This cyclical process warrants that the taken steps lead to real enhancements, enabling the organization to proactively adapt and evolve its security strategies.

3.2.6 Communicate

Clear communication keeps everyone in the organization informed about the security risks and steps being taken to mitigate them. Effective communication is essential for both technical teams and nontechnical stakeholders, including executives, board members, and regulators, and it ensures they understand the importance and effects of cybersecurity efforts. This means avoiding technical jargon and using visual representations such as graphs, charts, and dashboards that are easy to interpret for nontechnical audiences. Engaging stakeholders through regular updates is essential for ongoing support for the security program.

The appropriate teams in the organization—the IT department, security team, or a dedicated communications unit—should handle effective communication of cybersecurity responsibilities. All employees must stay informed through regular channels and be encouraged to report any suspicious activity they observe. Ongoing training and awareness programs ensure that everyone understands their role in maintaining security.

Here is how many organizations organize their communication responsibilities:

- The *chief information security officer (CISO)* or equivalent senior security leader often oversees the overall communication strategy related to cybersecurity. They are responsible for informing the executive team and the board of directors about the organization's security posture, significant risks, and strategic initiatives. The CISO ensures that security objectives align with business goals and that top-level stakeholders are aware of critical problems.
- *Security managers* and *team leads* are responsible for communicating detailed technical information to their teams and translating complex metrics into actionable insights for nontechnical departments. They act as liaisons between the technical staff and higher management, ensuring that critical information flows smoothly in both directions.
- The *security operations center (SOC)* analysts and other technical staff provide regular updates on security events, incidents, and metrics. They generate reports and dashboards highlighting key findings and trends, which are then shared with relevant stakeholders.
- *Corporate communications* or *public relations teams* may also be involved, especially when communication extends to external parties such as customers, partners, or regulators. In a security incident requiring public disclosure, these teams work closely with the security department to craft appropriate messages.

3.2.7 Sustain

A cybersecurity metrics program is not a one-time effort. It requires continuous updates and evolution. As new threats emerge and business goals change, the metrics must adapt. The sustain phase of the METRICS methodology ensures that the program remains relevant and effective.

This includes regularly revisiting the measured data, adjusting thresholds as necessary, and evolving reporting methods to capture new insights. Additionally, staying informed about industry trends, regulatory changes, and technological advancements helps sustain a resilient cybersecurity metrics program.

Organizations should typically revisit their metrics program on a regular cadence, such as quarterly or biannually. This reassessment allows analysts to evaluate the effectiveness of the metrics, thresholds, and reporting methods and keeps the focus on changing business goals and the evolving threat landscape. Significant events, such as a major security incident or the introduction of new technology, would require more immediate reviews.

Staying informed about industry trends, regulatory changes, and technological advancements is crucial for sustaining a resilient cybersecurity metrics program. Common resources to stay updated include subscribing to reputable cybersecurity news outlets such as Dark Reading or Krebs on Security, participating in professional organizations such as the Information Systems Security Association (ISSA or ISACA), and attending industry conferences such as RSA or BlackHat. Engaging with these resources facilitates anticipation of emerging threats and adapts your metrics program accordingly.

This ongoing commitment to monitoring and adjusting your cybersecurity metrics program ensures that it effectively addresses current risks. Regularly revisiting the data being measured, adjusting thresholds as necessary, and evolving reporting methods to capture new insights are all part of sustaining a robust cybersecurity posture in a constantly changing security environment.

3.3 Using the METRICS methodology example

Let's consider PharmaSecure, a life sciences company that produces pharmaceuticals and medical devices. PharmaSecure is bound by SOC2 requirements to maintain data privacy and security and HIPAA regulations to ensure patient data protection. As the company grows, a structured cybersecurity metrics program becomes critical to managing increasing incidents, ensuring compliance, and communicating risks effectively to stakeholders.

PharmaSecure's CISO has implemented the METRICS methodology to establish a robust cybersecurity metrics program. In the following sections, we walk through each step of the method using relevant data points for PharmaSecure to show how to implement this process effectively.

3.3.1 Step 1: Measure

The goal of this step is to capture security-related data points that reflect key compliance and operational risks.

EXAMPLE DATA

- Number of access control violations per month.
- Percentage of systems meeting patch compliance.
- Number of failed login attempts (related to SOC2).
- Frequency of encryption key rotations (related to HIPAA).
- Number of incidents involving patient data.

- Software License Compliance could be monitored, but it may not directly affect critical security objectives.

EXPLANATION

PharmaSecure begins by measuring key data points that align with SOC2 and HIPAA requirements. They collect detailed information on access control violations, patch compliance, and failed logins—critical for SOC2. For HIPAA, they track data incidents and encryption key management. These metrics provide a foundational view of the organization's security posture.

3.3.2 Step 2: Evaluate

The goal of this step is to determine the value of each metric and prioritize those that drive the most actionable insights.

EVALUATION EXAMPLE

- Access control violations may lead to unauthorized access, making them a high-priority metric.
- Encryption key rotations may be considered less frequent but critical for data integrity. While software license compliance is important from an operational standpoint, PharmaSecure determines that monitoring this metric does not significantly enhance its security posture or meet immediate compliance requirements.

EXPLANATION

PharmaSecure evaluates that access control violations represent the most significant risk to data breaches, particularly under SOC2. However, encryption key rotation under HIPAA has substantial business implications related to regulatory fines and patient trust. Both metrics are prioritized, clearly identifying the focus of corrective actions.

3.3.3 Step 3: Threshold setup

When defining thresholds and benchmarks for cybersecurity metrics, it is essential to balance security controls with operational flexibility. Establishing rigid limits may not always account for legitimate variations in user behavior. Instead of static thresholds, organizations should consider adaptive thresholds based on behavioral analytics. By integrating behavior-based analytics, cybersecurity policies remain effective and user-friendly, reducing unnecessary friction, while maintaining robust security controls.

THRESHOLDS EXAMPLE

- *Access control violations*—Maximum of five violations per month.
- *Patch compliance*—95% of all systems must be patched within 30 days of vulnerability disclosure.
- *Failed login attempts*—No more than three failed login attempts per user per session (before a temporary lockout is triggered).

EXPLANATION

Based on SOC2 and HIPAA requirements, PharmaSecure sets clear thresholds for each metric. These thresholds help determine when an action is necessary, such as increasing monitoring or locking down compromised accounts. The threshold-setting process clarifies acceptable risk levels for IT teams and executives.

Thresholds are determined by regulatory requirements, industry best practices, historical data, and the organization's risk tolerance. They are not arbitrary numbers but are carefully selected to balance security needs with practical operational considerations.

The threshold for access control violations (a maximum of five per month) is set after analyzing historical incident data and understanding the normal baseline of access control violations in the organization. PharmaSecure aims to promptly identify and address potential unauthorized access attempts without overburdening the security team with false positives by limiting violations to no more than five per month. This number is manageable and allows for swift action when the threshold is exceeded.

Patch compliance (95% within 30 days) is set as such because achieving 100% patch compliance is often challenging due to factors such as system availability requirements and compatibility problems. Setting the threshold at 95% is aligned with industry standards and demonstrates a strong commitment to security, while acknowledging operational realities. The 30-day window corresponds with common vulnerability management practices and regulatory expectations, ensuring timely remediation of security weaknesses.

Failed login attempts allow up to three failed login attempts per session before triggering a temporary lockout, a widely accepted security practice to prevent brute-force attacks. This threshold balances security and user convenience, reducing the risk of unauthorized access, while minimizing disruptions for legitimate users who may occasionally mistype passwords.

3.3.4 Step 4: Report

The goal of this step is to build a reporting system that communicates metrics to internal stakeholders and aligns with audit/compliance needs.

REPORTING EXAMPLE

- A quarterly SOC2 and HIPAA compliance report is generated.
- The report is segmented by business unit to track departmental compliance.
- A dashboard tracks real-time access control violations, patch status, and encryption key management.

EXPLANATION

PharmaSecure builds a dynamic reporting dashboard (see figure 3.4) that allows both security teams and C-suite executives to monitor real-time compliance status. The dashboard focuses on access control violations and patch compliance for SOC2, while addressing encryption key management for HIPAA. By visualizing these metrics, leaders can make more informed security decisions.

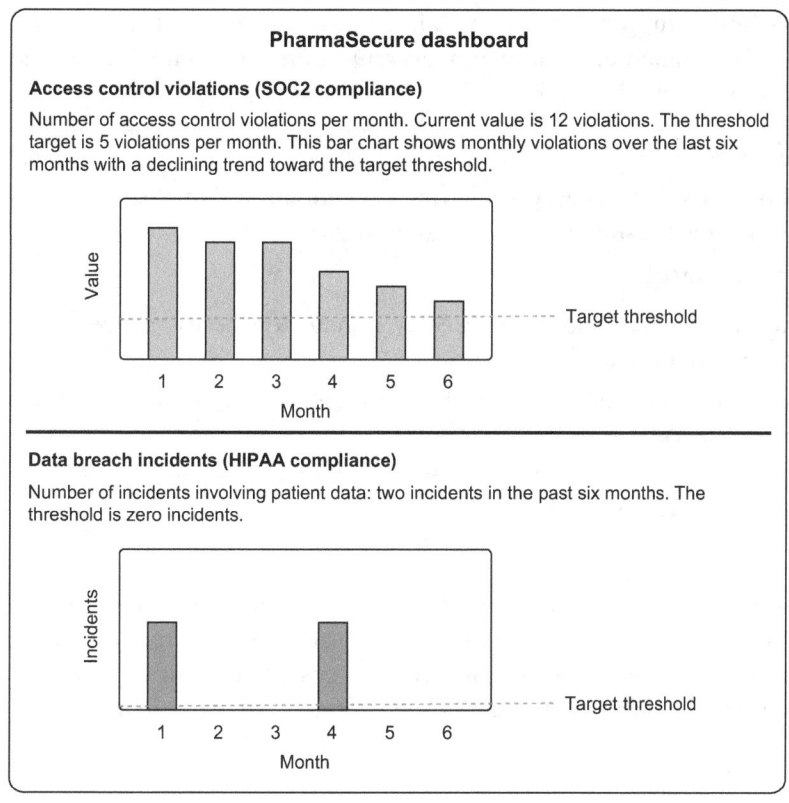

Figure 3.4 PharmaSecure example dashboard showing two metrics: access violations and data breach incidents.

3.3.5 Step 5: Improve

The goal of this step is to use data from the metrics program to drive security improvements and continuous compliance efforts.

IMPROVEMENT EXAMPLE

- PharmaSecure reduces access violations by implementing multifactor authentication (MFA) across critical systems.
- Patching timelines are improved by automating vulnerability scans and patch deployment.
- Encryption key rotations are now integrated into an automated schedule, reducing manual error.

EXPLANATION

After analyzing their initial metrics, PharmaSecure identifies areas for improvement. Implementing MFA reduces access violations, while automation accelerates patching timelines—important for SOC2 compliance. Key management is now automated for HIPAA, ensuring timely encryption practices. Over time, PharmaSecure refines its processes based on lessons learned.

3.3.6 Step 6: Communicate

The goal of this step is to ensure metrics are communicated clearly to internal and external stakeholders, including compliance auditors.

COMMUNICATION EXAMPLE

- The IT team communicates weekly updates on access control violations to department heads.
- Quarterly reports are shared with the executive team outlining trends and mitigation efforts.
- Annual reports are provided to external auditors as part of SOC2 and HIPAA compliance reviews.

EXPLANATION

PharmaSecure establishes a structured communication plan, where security metrics are reported on multiple levels: to department heads, the executive team, and external auditors. This transparent flow of information ensures that all key stakeholders are aware of the cybersecurity posture and progress toward improvement.

3.3.7 Step 7: Sustain

The goal of this step is to keep the metrics program aligned with evolving business and security needs.

SUSTAINMENT EXAMPLE

PharmaSecure reviews and updates its metrics annually to align with new threats and regulatory changes. The security team continuously monitors and adjusts thresholds based on real-time incident data.

EXPLANATION

To ensure long-term success, PharmaSecure regularly reviews its cybersecurity metrics program. The company ensures ongoing relevance by updating metrics in line with industry best practices and regulatory changes. As new threats emerge, the company adjusts thresholds and keeps the metrics program dynamic.

3.3.8 Exercise summary

In this exercise, PharmaSecure demonstrated how a life sciences company can implement the METRICS methodology to align its cybersecurity metrics with SOC2 and HIPAA compliance requirements. By measuring critical metrics, evaluating their value, and setting thresholds, PharmaSecure built a reporting structure that communicates risk. The company continuously improved its security posture and ensured sustained compliance through ongoing program updates.

3.4 Building a metrics dashboard

When designing a cybersecurity metrics dashboard, clarity, relevance, and accessibility are key principles that drive effectiveness. A well-designed dashboard ensures that users can quickly understand the most critical information, respond to emerging threats, and communicate essential security insights across different organizational levels. Typically, security teams build dashboards. A single pane of glass would be a great place to start tracking the essential metrics. A "single pane of glass" refers to a unified dashboard or interface that consolidates all relevant data, metrics, or system information into one view, allowing users to monitor and manage multiple systems or processes from a single point of access. In practice, there are many dashboards, each with a different focus and purpose. For example, a dashboard can provide real-time insights into the live analysis of networking traffic to identify any indicators of compromise. Or there may be a dashboard of collected metrics over a period that is reviewed weekly. These dashboards may or may not provide alerting capabilities.

Every metric on the dashboard must serve a purpose and be interpreted easily. Data should be presented in formats such as bar charts, pie charts, and line graphs that simplify analysis rather than complicate it. Avoid overwhelming the user with too many details on a single screen.

The dashboard must be accessible to all relevant stakeholders, regardless of their technical expertise. Board members, for instance, may need a simplified, high-level view of risk, while security analysts require detailed operational data. Accessibility also involves ensuring the dashboard is available in a secure, user-friendly format, whether that's through web access or via mobile applications.

3.4.1 Different dashboards for different stakeholders

Customizing dashboards to fit the needs of various stakeholders is critical in making them actionable. For example, a dashboard for CISOs would focus on high-level metrics such as the overall risk score, compliance status (e.g., HIPAA, SOC2), and top security incidents by severity, which provides an executive overview of the organization's cybersecurity posture.

Board members may need a simplified version focusing on business risk and financial effects. KPIs, such as the number of critical vulnerabilities, cost of recent incidents, and current compliance status with cybersecurity regulations should be included in an easily digestible format.

A more detailed dashboard is required for SOC analysts and incident responders. It should show real-time alerts, anomalous behavior detections, and breakdowns of threats per system or endpoint.

3.4.2 Security dashboard example

MedSecure, a life sciences company, recently experienced an access control incident in which unauthorized individuals gained access to confidential patient health information. Following the incident, the CISO and CEO both require a summary report with actionable insights tailored to their specific roles and needs.

The objective is to draft two executive summary reports: one for the CISO, focusing on technical and compliance-related details, and the other for the CEO, focusing on the business effects and high-level strategic insights. Both reports will describe the same incident and metrics, but in different lingos, suited to each audience.

EXECUTIVE SUMMARY REPORT FOR THE CISO

On September 12th, 2024, MedSecure detected an access control violation involving HIPAA-regulated data. The incident triggered a real-time alert after the system registered multiple failed login attempts, followed by unauthorized access to patient data stored in a restricted cloud environment.

Technical effects

- *Patch compliance*—92% of critical systems were patched within SOC2 and HIPAA compliance requirements. However, the vulnerable system was among the 8% that had missed a patch cycle.
- *Access control violations*—There were 15 violations, with failed authentication attempts preceding unauthorized access. The access management tool flagged the anomalous behavior, but the investigation revealed a configuration error that allowed access to sensitive data.
- *Incident response time (MTTR)*—The average response time was 3 hours, significantly above our target of 1 hour, highlighting delays in escalation and intervention. Further investigation revealed gaps in alert prioritization.

Corrective actions

- Immediate patching of vulnerable systems was conducted. All systems are now 100% compliant with patching requirements.
- Access control policies have been adjusted and the anomaly detection thresholds fine-tuned to reduce false negatives and prioritize critical violations better.
- Incident response times have improved following this event, with new automated escalations to shorten MTTR to under 1 hour.

Key metric results

- *HIPAA access control violations*—15 (pre-remediation); currently 0
- *Patch compliance*—Increased from 92% to 100%
- *MTTR*—Reduced from 3 hours to 1 hour

Next steps

- Continuous monitoring and weekly compliance audits will ensure HIPAA and SOC2 adherence.
- Ongoing testing of access control configurations should be conducted to ensure resilience against future attacks.

EXECUTIVE SUMMARY REPORT FOR THE CEO

On September 12th, 2024, MedSecure experienced a security incident that involved unauthorized access to protected patient data. The breach was detected quickly, and our response team worked to mitigate its effect. However, the incident highlighted vulnerabilities that have since been addressed.

Effects on business

- *Compliance risk*—One of our cloud systems, which had missed a critical patch, allowed unauthorized access to sensitive patient information. This posed a significant risk under HIPAA compliance guidelines. Remedial actions have been successfully implemented, and all systems are now fully compliant.
- *Financial risk*—While the incident was contained before any extensive damage occurred, a potential regulatory penalty remains. We are working with legal counsel to mitigate any fines or reputational damage.
- *Operational effects*—The incident caused minimal disruption, with a response time of 3 hours from detection to mitigation. Moving forward, response times have been cut down to 1 hour, significantly enhancing our ability to manage incidents in real time.

Strategic response

- We've increased system patching across all critical systems to 100% compliance, ensuring we meet HIPAA and SOC2 regulatory requirements.
- Our access control mechanisms have been overhauled to prevent similar incidents, and our cybersecurity team is continuously monitoring the system.
- This incident has reinforced our commitment to data security, and we have initiated further investments in automated security monitoring tools to prevent future breaches.

Key metric results

- *System patch compliance*—Achieved 100% compliance across all systems.
- *Incident response time*—Reduced from 3 hours to 1 hour.
- *Compliance risk mitigation*—Active steps are being taken to avoid regulatory penalties.

Next steps

Our focus remains on protecting patient data, while minimizing any business risks. As part of our long-term strategy, we invest in state-of-the-art security solutions and ensure that our response teams are equipped to handle future incidents swiftly and effectively.

Creating two distinct executive reports for the CISO and CEO emphasizes the importance of tailoring security insights to each role's needs and expectations. The CISO report highlights technical insights, compliance status, and immediate remediation actions. Meanwhile, the CEO's report focuses on the business and financial effects, along with high-level strategic responses.

3.5 Tools and technologies for metrics collection

There are various approaches to collecting cybersecurity metrics, each with its strengths depending on the data type required. Passive monitoring involves collecting data without actively probing the environment, relying on logs, network traffic, and endpoint monitoring. This method is suitable for detecting anomalies or monitoring ongoing processes in real-time without causing disruption. Active testing, such as penetration tests and vulnerability assessments, provides a more aggressive approach—simulating potential attacks or weaknesses in the system. External intelligence sources, such as threat intelligence feeds, enrich internal data with insights from global trends and real-time threat landscapes.

3.5.1 Open source tools for metrics collection

Several open source tools offer excellent capabilities for gathering, processing, and analyzing cybersecurity data. Some challenges include resource-intensive configurations and maintenance:

1. *Wazuh*—A powerful open source security platform that provides threat detection, integrity monitoring, and compliance analysis. It integrates seamlessly with Elasticsearch, Logstash, and Kibana (ELK Stack) for real-time data visualization and insights (see https://wazuh.com/).
2. *ELK Stack*—Elasticsearch, Logstash, and Kibana are widely used for aggregating logs, processing data, and visualizing metrics. The stack enables organizations to centralize data from various sources, perform searches, and generate dashboards for key metrics (see https://www.elastic.co/).
3. *OpenVAS*—An open source vulnerability scanning tool that helps identify security weaknesses in systems. It provides detailed reports on vulnerabilities, their severity, and suggestions for rectification, making it a vital tool in risk management (see https://openvas.org/).

3.5.2 Commercial tools for metrics collection

Commercial tools often come with built-in support, advanced features, and extensive integrations:

- *Splunk*—A popular platform for real-time data analytics. It offers extensive capabilities for log aggregation, threat detection, and reporting. Splunk provides customizable dashboards and integrates well with both on-premise and cloud-based environments (see https://www.splunk.com/).
- *Qualys*—A cloud-based security and compliance platform known for its comprehensive vulnerability management capabilities. It offers continuous scanning, monitoring, and reporting, focusing on automating compliance requirements (see https://www.qualys.com/).
- *Tenable*—A well-known platform for vulnerability management and network monitoring. Tenable's Nessus tool is widely used for vulnerability scanning, while

the Tenable.io platform provides additional threat intelligence and risk analysis capabilities (see https://www.tenable.com/).

3.5.3 Automation and integration

Automation is key to efficiently collecting and analyzing metrics. Most tools offer APIs or native integrations that enable organizations to automatically collect data, process it in real-time, and visualize it in dashboards. For instance, platforms such as Wazuh and ELK Stack offer seamless integration, allowing organizations to aggregate and analyze metrics from multiple sources without manual intervention. Similarly, commercial platforms such as Splunk and Tenable have automation frameworks that trigger alerts, generate reports, and even initiate responses based on predefined thresholds.

In my experience, choosing between open source and commercial tools often hinges on factors such as budget, technical expertise, and specific organizational needs. For example, I have worked with organizations that successfully implemented the ELK Stack for log management and metrics collection. They benefited from the cost savings and the ability to customize dashboards extensively. However, they also had dedicated staff with the technical skills to manage and maintain the system, which is essential for an open source solution.

Yet, you may have seen organizations opt for commercial tools such as Splunk because they needed a solution that could be deployed quickly, with robust support. The intuitive interface and comprehensive features allowed their teams to focus more on analyzing data rather than managing the tool itself. Although the cost was higher, they found value in the reduced administrative overhead and faster time to insight.

Figure 3.5 compares some of the more common tools available. Research like this can help you choose between closed and open source metrics collection tools.

3.5.4 Scripting for metrics collection

Scripting is the process of writing code to automate tasks that would otherwise be performed manually. It plays a crucial role in automating the collection and analysis of cybersecurity metrics, particularly in environments where metrics need to be gathered from multiple sources, such as Linux servers, databases, or network devices. Popular scripting languages such as Python, Bash, and PowerShell are widely used to automate these tasks. Each language has strengths, allowing system administrators and security teams to gather and process data efficiently.

PYTHON FOR METRICS COLLECTION

Python is one of the most popular languages for automating security tasks owing to its extensive libraries and ease of integrating various systems and databases. For example, you can use Python to gather system metrics such as CPU usage, disk space, and memory utilization, or to query a database for security logs and anomalies.

In the following listing, the `psutil` library gathers real-time data on CPU, memory, and disk usage. This data can be integrated into dashboards or reported for security analysis.

Comparison of close vs. open source metrics collection tools

Feature	Wazuh	ELK	OpenVAS	Splunk	Qualys	Tenable
Open source	YES	YES	YES	NO	NO	NO
Data collection	Real-time logs, file integrity intrusion	Centralized logging and analysis	Vulnerability scanning	Real-time data aggregation and analysis	Continuous scanning and vulnerability reporting	Vulnerability management and network monitoring
Threat detection	Anomaly detection, rule based	Customizable log analysis	Identifies vulnerabilities	Threat detection based on machine learning	Built-in threat detection and compliance monitoring	Advanced vulnerability and threat detection
Compliance	HIPAA, PCI DSS, and SOC2 compliance reporting	Customizable compliance monitoring	None	Built-in compliance reporting	Compliance automation	Comprehensive compliance reporting
Ease of use	Moderate	High	Moderate	High	High	High
Integration	Integrates with ELK, ElasticSearch	Easily integrates with various tools	Limited integrations	Extensive integrations with cloud and on-prem	Integrates with cloud and on-prem systems	Seamless integrations with third party
Cost	Free	Free	Free	Commercial licensing required	Subscription-based pricing	Subscription-based pricing
Customization	High	High	Low	High	Moderate	High

Figure 3.5 Comparison of open source solutions vs. commercial solutions for metrics collection (at the time of this writing)

Listing 3.1 Pulling system metrics from a Linux server using Python

```
import psutil                                    ◄─── Imports system monitoring library

# Collect CPU, Memory, and Disk usage data
cpu_usage = psutil.cpu_percent(interval=1)       ◄─── Gets CPU usage over 1 second
memory_usage = psutil.virtual_memory().percent   ◄─── Gets used memory percentage
disk_usage = psutil.disk_usage('/').percent      ◄─── Gets used disk percentage on root

# Print collected metrics
```

```
print(f"CPU Usage: {cpu_usage}%")
print(f"Memory Usage: {memory_usage}%")   ◁— Outputs metrics to console
print(f"Disk Usage: {disk_usage}%")
```

Here is the sample output:

```
CPU Usage: 31.1%
Memory Usage: 65.1%
Disk Usage: 34.5%
```

BASH FOR METRICS COLLECTION

Bash scripting is widely used for Linux systems. It's effective in environments where lightweight automation is required to pull metrics from servers or logs without the overhead of more complex languages. Bash scripts can automate tasks such as monitoring logs for suspicious activity or tracking system resource usage.

The following listing uses a Bash script to pull disk and CPU usage metrics. In this Bash script, the `top` command is used to extract CPU usage, and `df` is used to gather disk usage information. These values can be written to logs or integrated into a reporting system.

Listing 3.2 Pulling disk and CPU usage metrics (*modified to run in Jupyter Notebook*)

```bash
%%bash

# Check OS type
os_type=$(uname)                          ◁— Gets OS name

# Collect CPU usage based on OS
if [[ "$os_type" == "Linux" ]]; then
    cpu_usage=$(top -b -n1 | awk '/Cpu\(s\)/
        {print 100 - $8}')                ◁— Linux: CPU = 100 – idle
elif [[ "$os_type" == "Darwin" ]]; then   # macOS
    cpu_usage=$(ps -A -o %cpu | awk '{s+=$1} END
            {print s}')                   ◁— macOS: sum process CPU
else
    cpu_usage=$(vmstat 1 2 | tail -1 |
            awk '{print 100 - $15}')      ◁— Others: CPU via vmstat
fi

# Collect Disk Usage
disk_usage=$(df -h | grep '^/dev/' |
        awk '{ print $5 " " $1 }')        ◁— Disk % from /dev/ partitions

# Print collected metrics
echo "Operating System: $os_type"         ◁— Shows OS type
echo "CPU Usage: $cpu_usage%"             ◁— Shows CPU usage
echo "Disk Usage:"                        ◁— Disk usage label
echo "$disk_usage"                        ◁— Shows disk details
```

Here is the sample output:

```
Operating System: Darwin
CPU Usage: 177%
Disk Usage:
2% /dev/disk3s1s1
1% /dev/disk3s6
2% /dev/disk3s2
1% /dev/disk3s4
2% /dev/disk2s2
2% /dev/disk2s1
1% /dev/disk2s3
34% /dev/disk3s5
1% /dev/disk3s3
```

POWERSHELL FOR WINDOWS METRICS COLLECTION

For organizations operating Windows environments, PowerShell is the go-to scripting language. It is particularly useful for automating tasks related to active directory, security logs, and system performance on Windows servers.

In the following listing, PowerShell scripts allow administrators to pull metrics such as CPU load, memory utilization, and disk space. These scripts can be scheduled or triggered, based on security thresholds.

Listing 3.3 Collecting system performance metrics using PowerShell on Windows

```python
import subprocess                                    # Uses subprocess to run PowerShell
import json                                          # Uses json to parse results
import pandas as pd                                  # Uses pandas for DataFrame
from IPython.display import display                  # Uses display for notebook output

# PowerShell commands
cpu_cmd = "Get-WmiObject Win32_Processor | \
    Measure-Object -Property LoadPercentage -Average | \
    Select-Object -ExpandProperty Average"           # Gets CPU load avg
memory_cmd = "Get-WmiObject Win32_OperatingSystem | \
    Select-Object @{Name='FreeMemory';Expression={[math]::\
        round($_.FreePhysicalMemory/1MB,2)}},\
        TotalVisibleMemorySize | ConvertTo-Json -Compress"   # Gets memory stats
disk_cmd = "Get-WmiObject Win32_LogicalDisk -Filter \
    'DeviceID=\"C:\"' | Select-Object DeviceID,\
    @{Name='FreeSpaceGB';Expression={[math]::round\
        ($_.FreeSpace/1GB,2)}} | ConvertTo-Json -Compress"   # Gets disk stats

# Run PowerShell commands and capture output
cpu_usage = subprocess.run(["powershell", "-Command",         # Runs CPU command
    cpu_cmd], capture_output=True, text=True).stdout.strip()
    memory_output = subprocess.run(["powershell", "-Command", # Runs memory command
    memory_cmd], capture_output=True, text=True).stdout.strip()
disk_output = subprocess.run(["powershell", "-Command",
```

```
            disk_cmd], capture_output=True, text=True).stdout.strip()    ◄─┐ Runs disk
                                                                           │ command
# Parse JSON output
memory_usage = json.loads(memory_output) if memory_output else    ┐ Parses
    {"FreeMemory": "N/A", "TotalVisibleMemorySize": "N/A"}    ◄───┘ memory JSON
disk_usage = json.loads(disk_output) if disk_output else
    {"FreeSpaceGB": "N/A"}
                                      ◄───┐ Parses disk JSON
# Convert results into a DataFrame for Jupyter Notebook display
data = {                                                      ◄───┐ Builds
    "Metric": ["CPU Usage", "Free Memory (MB)", "Total Memory (MB)", │ metrics
    "Free Disk Space (GB)"], "Value": [cpu_usage + "%",              │ dict
    memory_usage.get("FreeMemory", "N/A"),
    memory_usage.get("TotalVisibleMemorySize", "N/A"),
    disk_usage.get("FreeSpaceGB", "N/A")]
}

df = pd.DataFrame(data)    ◄───┘ Converts to DataFrame

# Display DataFrame in Jupyter Notebook
display(df)             ◄───┐
                             │ Shows DataFrame
```

Here is the sample output:

```
    Metric                 Value
0   CPU Usage              8%
1   Free Memory (MB)       51.65
2   Total Memory (MB)      67016960
3   Free Disk Space (GB)   1617.3
```

Scripting languages such as Python, Bash, and PowerShell can be combined with open source tools such as Wazuh, ELK Stack, or OpenVAS to automate more complex tasks. For example, Python scripts can fetch vulnerability data from OpenVAS, process it, and report findings, while Bash can trigger scans or alerts based on server activity logs. By using scripting, security teams can ensure metrics collection is automated and scalable, enabling them to gather and process large volumes of data in real-time without manual intervention.

3.6 Common pitfalls in metrics programs

Understanding common pitfalls in a security metrics program aids in avoiding obstacles and improving its effectiveness. Quantitative metrics enables measuring of specific, countable elements using numerical statistics, or formulas. Examples include the percentage of incidents over a period, the number of vulnerabilities identified, or the average time to detect an incident. These measurements are important. However, an overreliance on numbers can sometimes obscure deeper insights. Focusing exclusively on numerical data may cause organizations to overlook qualitative factors such as employee behavior, threat actors' tactics, and other human elements that don't always present themselves in statistical reports.

3.6.1 Pitfall 1: Overreliance on quantitative metrics

For example, the metric mean time to detect (MTTD) can provide helpful information, but it does not explain why certain incidents were detected late or what human factors contributed to the delay. This overreliance on quantitative metrics can give a false sense of security if the context behind those numbers isn't identified and explored.

To avoid this pitfall, organizations should complement quantitative data with qualitative insights. For example, in a post-incident review, you can include interview information from the security team to understand how human factors, decision-making processes, or internal policies and procedures affected the incident. This balance between numerical data and contextual information can offer a more comprehensive view of an organization's security posture.

3.6.2 Pitfall 2: Misalignment with business goals

Another common reason metrics programs fail is that they don't align with an organization's broader business goals and objectives. For example, a company might focus heavily on patching low-priority vulnerabilities to improve its "vulnerability remediation rate." However, this metric may not reflect the critical areas where the business is most vulnerable to a breach, such as key financial systems or customer databases.

To avoid misaligning metrics to business objectives, it's important to ensure that metrics are tied directly to the organization's risk appetite and strategic goals. If the business is focused on safeguarding customer data to maintain trust, the metrics program should emphasize encryption, access controls, and incident response capabilities. For instance, a metric tracking how quickly customer data is secured after a potential breach would be far more valuable than simply counting all vulnerabilities patched.

3.6.3 Pitfall 3: Stagnation and complacency

Metric programs can become stagnant. Over time, organizations may continue to track data without thoroughly evaluating its relevance or adapting to changes in business needs or threat landscapes. This can lead to complacency, where metrics give the appearance of progress, but critical problems remain unnoticed, unaddressed, or unresolved. For example, a company may be satisfied with improving its average time to patch vulnerabilities. Still, if the threat landscape has shifted to more sophisticated attacks that exploit configuration errors, this metric will fail to address emerging risks. Failing to review and update the metrics program regularly could lead to missed opportunities for improvement.

To implement continuous improvement, organizations should periodically review metrics to reflect the evolving threat landscape, introduce new metrics when necessary to capture emerging risks, and incorporate feedback loops that allow for real-time adjustments based on performance. For example, setting up quarterly reviews of the metrics program with both security teams and business leaders can help identify outdated metrics and introduce more relevant ones. Metrics should be dynamic and adapt to the organization's current environment, rather than being treated as static performance measures.

By addressing these common pitfalls—balancing quantitative with qualitative data, aligning metrics with business goals, and providing continuous improvement—organizations can ensure that their cybersecurity metrics programs remain effective, actionable, and relevant.

Summary

- A structured metrics program is crucial for aligning security performance with business goals and improving decision-making.
- The METRICS (Measure, Evaluate, Threshold, Report, Improve, Communicate, and Sustain) methodology provides a framework for designing a comprehensive cybersecurity metrics program, focused on measurable and actionable data.
- A well-designed dashboard must include clear, relevant metrics, tailored to the needs of different stakeholders—from security teams to executive leadership.
- Various open source and commercial tools are available for effective metrics collection, monitoring, and analysis, each offering unique benefits.
- Continuous improvement is essential in a metrics program to ensure evolving threats are addressed and security posture remains robust.

Integrating metrics into business strategy

This chapter covers
- Aligning metrics with business strategy
- Interpreting metrics for stakeholders
- Communicating value to stakeholders
- Using metrics to inform strategic decisions

Metrics are often discussed in isolation, but they hold the most value when aligned with overarching business goals. This is when metrics become powerful tools for communicating risk, prioritizing resources, and justifying investments in cybersecurity initiatives.

Here, we shift the focus from merely tracking, analyzing, and reporting numbers to a guide for strategic decisions, and this chapter outlines the importance of aligning cybersecurity efforts not only to protect the organization but also to support its long-term objectives. Statistical analysis of these metrics will be used to extract meaningful insights that can guide business decisions. Effectively conveying the value of cybersecurity efforts is crucial for showing key stakeholders and executive leadership how metrics are used to quantify risk and security posture. This chapter provides actionable strategies for making your metrics a key part of your organization's business strategy.

4.1 Business alignment

Metrics bridge security efforts and business priorities, providing data that informs key business decisions. To align security with business growth, regulatory compliance, and customer trust, it is important to understand the organization's business model and key drivers of success. For example, in a healthcare organization, patient data security and HIPAA compliance are paramount to maintaining operational integrity and trust. In an e-commerce company, ensuring website uptime and protecting transaction data is critical for revenue generation and customer satisfaction. In each case, relevant security metrics should reflect the core needs of the business.

Once the business model and drivers are understood, carefully selecting the most appropriate metrics is key to reflecting security posture and business objectives. For example, a financial institution may focus on transaction fraud detection and regulatory audit success rates. A technology company might prioritize intellectual property protection metrics, while an online retailer might track website performance during peak shopping times. Table 4.1 shows some common industries and their key business objectives, summarizing how security metrics tie into core business priorities.

Table 4.1 Common industries with their key business objectives and associated security metrics

Industry	Business priorities	Relevant security metrics
Healthcare	Patient data security	Data breach incidents
	HIPAA compliance	HIPAA audit success rates
E-commerce	Website uptime	Uptime percentage
	Transaction data protection	Transaction fraud detection
Financial institutions	Regulatory compliance	Transaction fraud detection rates
	Fraud prevention	Audit success
Technology	Intellectual property protection	Data access control
		Intellectual property theft detection
Online retailer	Website performance	Website load times during peak traffic
	Customer data security	Data breach incidents

Each of the selected metrics is linked to a key business outcome. These metrics should resonate with leadership so that security can better communicate value. This enables security teams to become measurable organization components.

4.1.1 Business-aligned security metrics example

Consider a healthcare provider implementing security controls to ensure HIPAA compliance. A meaningful metric in this scenario might be data encryption compliance, which measures whether electronic health records (EHRs) are encrypted and whether encryption is consistently applied across storage, transmission, and backup systems. It could track compliance against industry standards such as FIPS 140-2, ensuring that sensitive patient data remains protected from unauthorized access. This metric directly ties to the business goal of maintaining regulatory compliance, avoiding hefty fines, and preserving patient trust.

Beyond compliance, failing to secure EHRs properly has significant consequences. A data breach in a healthcare setting not only leads to regulatory penalties but can also result in medical identity theft, operational disruptions, and loss of reputation, potentially causing patient attrition. For example, the 2015 Anthem breach exposed nearly 80 million patient records, which resulted in financial penalties and lawsuits that exceeded $115 million in settlements. This underscores the importance of aligning security metrics with compliance requirements and real-world business risks.

Similarly, a metric such as average time to patch critical vulnerabilities in financial services aligns directly with maintaining uptime and preventing breaches. A delay in applying security patches could expose customer financial data to cybercriminals, leading to regulatory action, financial losses, and reputational damage. Financial institutions can mitigate risks by tracking this metric and ensuring patches are applied within an acceptable timeframe, while maintaining trust and operational continuity. Effective security metrics should do more than track technical compliance—they must highlight business effects and drive decision-making that protects revenue, regulatory standing, and customer confidence.

These metrics provide actionable insights, influencing resource allocation and risk prioritization decisions. By using security metrics that reflect business priorities, security leaders can make a compelling case for investing in new technologies or processes.

4.1.2 Mapping metrics to business performance

Security key performance indicators (KPIs) should map to broader business performance indicators. For example, a KPI such as average incident response time may directly affect business continuity in a manufacturing company, where system downtimes can result in production delays and financial loss. Mapping security KPIs to business outcomes ensures that the cybersecurity function is not only defending against risks but also enabling the organization to meet its strategic objectives.

Business-aligned metrics help bridge the communication gap between security teams and executive leadership. When CISOs present metrics that illustrate how security contributes to reduced risk, operational efficiency, and customer trust, they can gain buy-in from decision-makers and align cybersecurity efforts with overall business success.

4.1.3 Supporting innovation with metrics

In some cases, aligning security with business goals also means supporting innovation. Consider a company launching a new product in a highly regulated industry such as pharmaceuticals. Metrics such as compliance readiness or third-party security risk can help leadership determine whether they are ready to move forward with the product launch, while maintaining compliance with industry regulations.

Security teams can play a proactive role in the business growth by integrating security metrics into product development and innovation processes. However, alignment often requires breaking down silos and improving communications across departments and teams. In many organizations, security teams, product development, and leadership may operate in isolation, which complicates the timely and effective flow of critical information.

To strengthen cross-functional collaboration between security, development, and leadership teams, organizations should go beyond routine meetings and foster joint ownership of security outcomes. Rather than treating security as a separate function, embedding security considerations into shared sprint planning and product roadmaps ensures that risk management becomes integral to development cycles.

One effective approach is to establish Security Champions within development teams—individuals who serve as liaisons between security and engineering, helping to bridge knowledge gaps and drive proactive security measures. Additionally, incorporating security as a standing agenda item in sprint reviews enables teams to track key metrics such as compliance readiness, vulnerability resolution timelines, and third-party risk exposure in real time.

Collaboration should also extend to the product organization, ensuring that security is embedded into product design from the start rather than treated as an afterthought. Using shared tools such as Jira to track security-related tasks, maintaining dedicated Slack or Teams channels for security discussions, and organizing periodic cross-functional tabletop exercises can help reinforce a culture of security across all teams. By integrating security into agile workflows, aligning security priorities with business objectives, and fostering shared accountability, organizations can ensure that security is not just a compliance checkbox but a fundamental part of the development process.

Another helpful strategy is using centralized metrics dashboards, where all relevant stakeholders can access real-time security readiness and compliance data. This transparency informs both security teams and product leaders with the same visibility into critical metrics that could affect product launches or innovation processes.

In addition to regular communication and transparency, aligning incentives across security, development, and leadership teams can also serve a powerful motivator. For instance, tying bonuses or performance evaluations to security milestones, such as meeting compliance standards or reducing vulnerabilities in production, can encourage teams to work collaboratively toward shared security objectives. When all departments have a stake in the success of security initiatives, it fosters a unified approach to risk management and product innovation.

Clearly outlining shared goals between security and product teams helps both departments understand how security metrics support business growth. For example, when launching a new product, security metrics such as compliance readiness can be tied to development milestones, making security a core part of the innovation process.

Secure coding practices help developers write resilient code that minimizes vulnerabilities from the outset. Code-scanning tools automate the detection of security flaws before deployment, thus reducing the risk of introducing exploitable weaknesses. Threat modeling ensures potential attack vectors are identified and mitigated early in the design phase. Additionally, third-party and open source software (OSS) library scanning is crucial, as many modern applications rely on external dependencies that could introduce security risks if not properly vetted. Organizations can proactively enhance their security posture, while maintaining development velocity by integrating these security measures into key milestones, such as design reviews, prototyping, and testing.

4.2 Security metrics alignment with business strategy exercise

Consider MediHealth, a mid-sized healthcare provider that faces the dual challenge of maintaining HIPAA compliance, while safeguarding sensitive patient information. The organization is looking to implement a security metrics program that aligns with its broader business objectives of regulatory compliance, operational continuity, and improving patient trust. MediHealth's leadership knows the need to invest in security but wants clear, measurable ways to track progress and effects.

Let's walk through selecting, designing, and mapping key security metrics for MediHealth's business goals to better understand how to choose meaningful metrics that reflect security requirements and business outcomes.

4.2.1 Step 1: Understanding MediHealth's business objectives

Start by defining the key objectives of MediHealth:

- *Regulatory compliance (HIPAA)*—MediHealth must comply with HIPAA regulations to avoid costly fines and maintain patient trust.
- *Operational continuity*—Any downtime could directly affect patient care, so ensuring continuous service is critical.
- *Patient trust*—Patients expect their medical information to remain secure, so MediHealth must prioritize protecting sensitive data.

These business objectives will drive the selection of metrics.

4.2.2 Step 2: Selecting key metrics

Let's select and define metrics for MediHealth. We choose five key security metrics that align with their business goals and document why it matters so that we tie each metric to specific business goals and objectives:

- *Data encryption compliance (regulatory compliance)*—Measures the percentage of sensitive patient records that are fully encrypted across all systems. Encryption is essential for HIPAA compliance, ensuring patient data is protected at rest and in transit.
- *Average time to detect breaches (operational continuity)*—Tracks how long it takes MediHealth to detect a potential data breach from the time it occurs. The faster the breach is detected, the lower the risk of compromised data, ensuring continuity of operations.
- *Average time to patch vulnerabilities (operational continuity)*—Monitors how quickly critical security patches are applied across systems. Unpatched systems are a major source of breaches, and timely patching is critical to maintaining uninterrupted operations.

- *Patient trust survey (patient trust)*—Measures patient confidence in the organization's ability to keep data secure through quarterly feedback surveys. Building patient trust is a long-term goal that requires consistent effort, and surveys directly measure how secure patients feel.
- *HIPAA audit success rate (regulatory compliance)*—Tracks the percentage of HIPAA compliance audits that MediHealth passes without any significant findings. Regular HIPAA audits are essential for maintaining regulatory compliance and avoiding fines or penalties.

4.2.3 Step 3: Mapping metrics to business goals

Table 4.2 shows MediHealth's chosen metrics and the business goals they are tied to.

Table 4.2 MediHealth's metrics tied to business goals

Metric	Business goal
Data encryption compliance	Regulatory compliance (HIPAA)
Average time to detect breaches	Operational continuity
Average time to patch vulnerabilities	Operational continuity
Patient trust survey	Patient trust
HIPAA audit success rate	Regulatory compliance (HIPAA)

4.2.4 Step 4: Measuring metrics

Table 4.3 shows the metrics' current value, target, and a description of why it matters.

Table 4.3 The MediHealth's metrics dashboard shows the current value, target value, and description of why it matters.

Metric	Value	Target	Description
Data encryption compliance	85%	100%	Measures the percentage of patient records and sensitive data encrypted in the system. This metric ensures that MediHealth's data is protected at rest and in transit.
Average time to detect breaches	4 hours	1 hour	Tracks the time between when a breach occurs and when MediHealth's monitoring systems detect it.
Average time to patch vulnerabilities	48 hours	24 hours	Measures how quickly security patches are applied to critical systems after discovering a vulnerability.
Patient trust survey	70%	85%	Quarterly survey assessing how secure patients feel about MediHealth's data protection measures.
HIPAA audit success rate	90%	95%	The percentage of internal and external audits that MediHealth passes with no significant findings related to HIPAA compliance.

4.2.5 Step 5: Communicating the Metrics

When communicating security metrics and reports, for example, to the CEO versus the CISO, the focus and depth of the message differ significantly. The CEO is primarily concerned with high-level business effects and how security affects overall business objectives (e.g., revenue, reputation, and regulatory compliance). The reports to the CEO should be concise, strategic, and focused on how security efforts support business growth, protect assets, and mitigate significant risks.

The CISO requires a more detailed, technically rich report focusing on operational details, such as the status of specific security controls, incident response metrics, and potential vulnerabilities. The CISO needs actionable insights to inform decision-making about resource alignment, risk management, and improving security posture.

EXECUTIVE SUMMARY TO THE CISO

Subject: Metrics Report on Cybersecurity Compliance and Risk Management

MediHealth has made notable progress in its security program, particularly in regulatory compliance and incident response times. Our current encryption compliance stands at 85%, and we intend to achieve full encryption coverage by the end of the next quarter. Vulnerability patching processes are improving, reducing the time it takes to patch critical systems from 48 to our target of 24 hours.

Key metrics

- *Data encryption compliance*—At 85% compliance, there is an immediate need to prioritize the remaining unencrypted data to ensure HIPAA requirements are fully met.
- *Average time to detect breaches*—We are currently detecting breaches within 4 hours but need to invest further in AI-driven threat detection tools to bring this time down to our target of 1 hour.
- *Average time to patch vulnerabilities*—The patching process is now within 48 hours, improving from previous cycles, but efforts must continue to meet the 24-hour target for critical vulnerabilities.
- *HIPAA audit success rate*—90% compliance in recent audits, focusing on pushing for 95% compliance through more robust internal auditing and system checks.
- *Patient trust survey*—Patient trust metrics currently sit at 70%, reflecting the public's concern about recent data breaches in the industry. This is a key area for improvement as we roll out additional security awareness initiatives.

Next steps

- Accelerate full data encryption across all systems to meet regulatory compliance goals.
- Continue the adoption of machine learning algorithms to reduce breach detection time.
- Focus on automating patch management to meet the 24-hour target for critical systems.

These efforts will not only help meet our compliance requirements but also improve the overall security posture of MediHealth.

EXECUTIVE SUMMARY TO THE CEO

Subject: Cybersecurity and Compliance Progress Report

MediHealth is making significant strides in securing patient data and meeting regulatory compliance requirements. Our current encryption compliance stands at 85%, and we are aiming for full compliance within the next few months. These efforts are critical as they support HIPAA regulations and our ongoing goal of safeguarding patient trust.

Key metrics

- *Data encryption*—We have encrypted 85% of patient data and are working toward 100% to ensure full HIPAA compliance and reduce the risk of data breaches.
- *Incident response*—We've reduced our detection time for potential security breaches from 6 to 4 hours. Investments in new technology will help further reduce this, which translates into faster responses to security threats and reduced operational risks.
- *Regulatory audits*—Our latest HIPAA audits show a 90% success rate. We aim to achieve a 95% success rate in the next cycle to ensure we continue to meet the necessary regulatory standards.
- *Patient trust*—Our patient trust survey shows a 70% satisfaction rate, which we're actively working on to improve through enhanced security communications and public awareness initiatives.

Business effects

The investments in encryption and faster incident detection directly contribute to the security of patient data, reinforcing our commitment to both regulatory compliance and customer trust. By continuing these efforts, we can mitigate the risk of costly breaches and maintain our standing as a leader in secure healthcare technology.

4.3 Security metric reporting

Executives such as board members and C-suite leaders focus on business effects, growth, and profitability. Communicating the value of cybersecurity metrics to these stakeholders who may reside outside the technical sphere requires a tailored approach. Translating technical metrics into meaningful business insights is important to demonstrate the return on investment of cybersecurity initiatives.

Often, cybersecurity metrics are seen as highly technical, making it difficult for nontechnical stakeholders to understand their full value and insights. To bridge this gap, cybersecurity leaders must learn to present metrics that resonate with business goals, such as cost savings, risk mitigation, and regulatory compliance. For example, instead of reporting the number of vulnerabilities detected, present how addressing these vulnerabilities reduced the potential for data breaches and saved the company from potential financial losses or legal penalties.

When presenting in a business context, it is essential to highlight the metrics' direct business effects. Metrics such as reduced downtime, faster incident response, or increased customer trust can build clear connections between security and business value.

4.3.1 Presenting metrics in executive reports

Executive reports should be concise, focus on high-level metrics, and tied to the company's strategic objectives. For example, instead of focusing on the technical details of malware detected, present metrics such as the number of incidents averted and tie this to cost savings, reduced operational downtime, or improved customer satisfaction.

Frame metrics based on their direct influence on operations, finance, and customer trust. For instance, show how risk reduction efforts have translated into cost savings by preventing costly breaches or downtime. Relate each cybersecurity metric to broader business objectives, such as regulatory compliance, operational efficiency, or growth.

Visuals such as graphs, pie charts, and executive summaries help simplify complex data and make it digestible for nontechnical audiences (see figures 4.1–4.3). When presenting metrics to stakeholders, focus on telling a story. For example, a presentation on reducing the organization's attack surface could begin by explaining the financial risks of having a large attack surface, followed by metrics showing how reducing this surface has lowered the likelihood of attacks. Always conclude by stating how these improvements align with business goals, such as profitability or market share.

EXAMPLE EXECUTIVE CYBERSECURITY REPORT

Executive cybersecurity report: Q3 2024

To: [CEO Name]
From: [CISO Name]
Date: [October 1, 2024]

Overview of cybersecurity posture

In Q3 2024, the organization's cybersecurity posture remained stable, with improvements in incident response times and compliance with key regulations. However, a few areas require attention, such as third-party risk management and patching delays.

Key metrics and indicators

- Incident response
  - *Mean time to detect (MTTD)*—45 minutes
  - *Mean time to respond (MTTR)*—1.5 hours
  - *Total security incidents*—12 (3 critical, 9 low)
  - *Incidents resolved within SLA*—92%

Security metric reporting

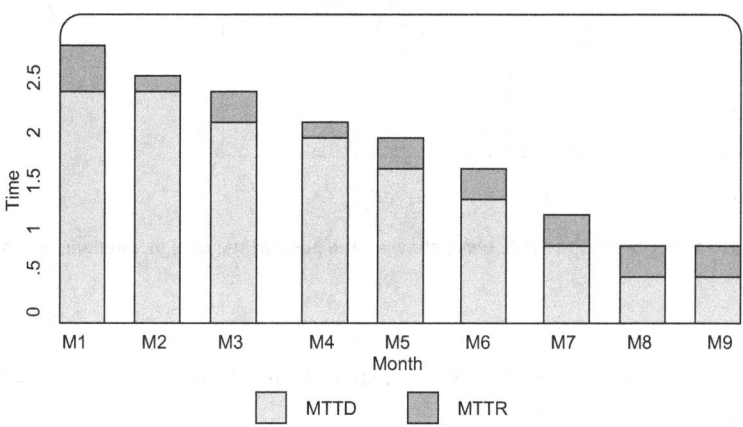

Figure 4.1 Incident response metrics over time (bar chart showing MTTD and MTTR)

- Compliance metrics
  - *HIPAA compliance*—98%
  - *PCI DSS compliance*—95%
  - *GDPR compliance*—96%

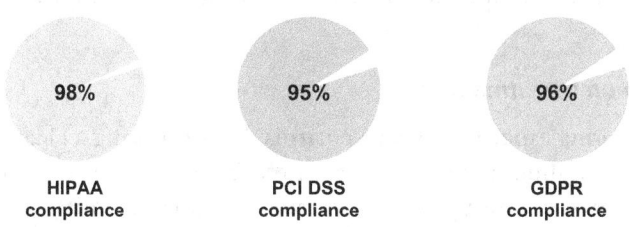

Figure 4.2 Compliance status by regulation (pie chart showing compliance percentages)

- Vulnerability management
  - *Total vulnerabilities identified*—240
  - *Critical vulnerabilities resolved within SLA*—85% (target: 90%)
  - *Patch compliance*—93% (target: 95%)

Key insights and recommendations
- *Third-party risk*—While internal security controls remain strong, we have identified an increased risk from third-party vendors. We recommend conducting

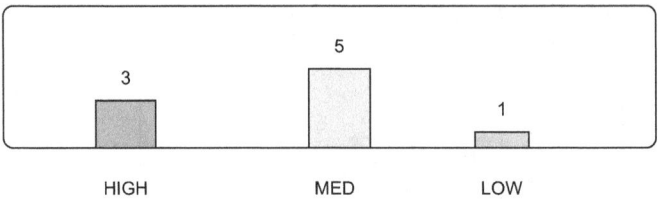

Figure 4.3 Vulnerability breakdown (bar chart showing the percentage of high, medium, and low vulnerabilities)

additional assessments for key third-party suppliers and implementing enhanced monitoring.
- *Patching delays*—The critical vulnerability patching rate remains below target. To ensure faster response times, we recommend additional automation in the patch management process.
- *Compliance improvement*—Compliance with major regulations such as HIPAA, PCI DSS, and GDPR remains strong, with small gaps noted in PCI DSS compliance. A focus on closing these gaps will ensure better preparedness for audits.

Upcoming focus areas for Q4 2024
- Enhance third-party risk management by onboarding new monitoring tools.
- Improve patching automation to meet our critical vulnerability SLA targets.
- Continue monitoring compliance metrics to sustain and improve current standings.

4.3.2 Demonstrating return on investment

One of the most challenging aspects of cybersecurity is demonstrating a clear *return on investment* (ROI). Unlike traditional investments, where financial returns are easier to calculate, cybersecurity investments prevent losses, rather than generating direct profits. To demonstrate ROI, you can show how security measures, such as patch management or endpoint protection, prevented potential incidents that could have resulted in financial losses.

The following example demonstrates how a $100,000 investment in a new intrusion detection system prevented a potential breach that could have cost the organization millions in fines, lawsuits, and lost business.

EXAMPLE SECURITY MEASURES AND ROI
The following measures were implemented:
- Intrusion detection system (IDS)
  - *Investment*—$100,000
  - *Prevention*—Avoided potential breach

- *Potential loss avoided*—$2 million (fines, legal fees, lost business)
- *ROI*—20x (cost savings from prevented breach)
- Patch management automation
  - *Investment*—$50,000
  - *Benefit*—Reduced vulnerability exposure by 30%; lowering the likelihood of an attack
  - *Potential loss avoided*—$500,000 (from potential exploitation of vulnerabilities)
  - *ROI*—10x (faster patching reduces risk and potential incident costs)
- AI-based threat detection
  - *Investment*—$150,000
  - *Benefit*—Reduced mean time to detect (MTTD) by 40%, enabling quicker incident response
  - *Time saved*—Reduced downtime by 4 hours per incident
  - *Potential savings*—$300,000 (from faster response and business continuity)
  - *ROI*—2x (cost saved in downtime and recovery)
- Endpoint protection solution
  - *Investment*—$75,000
  - *Prevention*—Blocked malware that could have compromised customer data
  - *Potential loss avoided*—$1 million (in reputational damage, customer trust, and legal fees)
  - *ROI*—13x (Prevention of major data breach)
- Compliance automation (HIPAA, PCI DSS)
  - *Investment*—$60,000
  - *Benefit*—Reduced the risk of noncompliance by 90%, avoiding regulatory fines
  - *Potential fines avoided*—$500,000
  - *ROI*—8x (reduction of noncompliance penalties)
- Summary of ROI Across Security Measures
  - *Total investment*—$435,000
  - *Total losses avoided*—$4.3 million

These examples convey how specific security investments translate into cost savings, improved efficiency, and reduced risk. Investments in security can reduce the risk of noncompliance penalties and avoid regulatory fines. Metrics can demonstrate how meeting compliance requirements has strengthened the company's competitive position in the market.

4.3.3 Communication strategies

Different stakeholders have varying concerns and priorities. While the CFO may be concerned with cost-effectiveness and ROI, the operations manager might prioritize system uptime and efficiency. Building a communication strategy requires tailoring the message for each audience. For example, you may highlight cost reductions and ROI for the finance team by demonstrating the savings achieved through preventive security measures. For operations teams, you may focus on metrics that show improvements in system uptime, operational efficiency, and faster incident response. For marketing teams, you may present how security efforts have enhanced brand reputation, customer trust, and compliance with industry standards, which can be used in marketing campaigns.

To communicate effectively with each stakeholder group, it is necessary to identify key metrics. Select metrics that are meaningful for each audience. For finance, this may be cost reductions. For operations, it could reduce downtime. Furthermore, use clear, nontechnical language and avoid technical jargon. For example, instead of "malware detection," use "prevented incidents" or "cost savings from breach prevention." In addition, use charts and visuals to make data easily understandable—for example, a pie chart showing the proportion of incidents detected versus incidents that impacted business operations.

STARTING THE CONVERSATION

Before any meaningful dialogue can occur, it's essential to understand the priorities of each stakeholder. To start these conversations effectively, first research and empathize with their goals. For example, a CFO is likely focused on cost management and risk mitigation, while an operations manager cares more about system uptime and efficiency. Begin the conversation by framing security in terms of their priorities:

- *For the CFO*—"I'd like to discuss how our security measures are providing a significant return on investment and reducing potential financial risks, particularly in light of recent data breaches in our industry."
- *For operations teams*—"I want to highlight how our improved incident response times have contributed to system uptime and operational efficiency, ensuring minimal disruptions."
- *For marketing teams*—"Our security efforts are directly enhancing customer trust and regulatory compliance, which can strengthen our brand reputation and be a key part of our messaging."

Starting the conversation with the stakeholders' goals in mind helps align cybersecurity as a value driver, not just a cost center.

NAVIGATING NAYSAYERS AND RESISTANCE

Not every stakeholder will immediately see the value in cybersecurity initiatives, especially if they haven't personally witnessed a breach or don't see a direct connection to their responsibilities. Here are some strategies for dealing with resistance or naysayers:

- *Relate security to business outcomes*—For stakeholders who might be skeptical about the value of cybersecurity investments, focus on how security affects their department's performance. For example, explain to a reluctant CFO how security investments have avoided potential losses that could disrupt revenue streams.

- *Use real-world examples*—Share industry case studies or recent high-profile breaches that impacted similar organizations. For instance, "Company X faced a major breach due to insufficient patch management, which resulted in $3 million in fines. Our current investments in automated patching have saved us from this kind of exposure."
- *Bridge the knowledge gap*—Avoid using technical jargon that might alienate non-technical stakeholders. Translate cybersecurity risks into business terms. Instead of saying, "Our malware detection system caught 10 threats," reframe it as, "We prevented 10 incidents that could have resulted in system downtime or data breaches, protecting us from potential losses."
- *Demonstrate value incrementally*—Show smaller, measurable wins over time. For example, demonstrate how a recent cybersecurity initiative reduced downtime by 15% or prevented a costly breach, even if these wins aren't immediately visible to all stakeholders.
- *Propose pilots or proofs of concept*—If someone remains resistant to larger investments, suggest starting with a smaller initiative demonstrating measurable success. For instance, pilot a specific security technology on a small scale and report on the effects before expanding.

TROUBLESHOOTING THE CONVERSATION

Challenges may arise when stakeholders have conflicting priorities or when cybersecurity initiatives are seen as hindrances to business agility or budgets. Here are some strategies for troubleshooting these conflicts:

- *Align security with business goals*—Continuously discuss how security initiatives align with business outcomes. For example, if the operations team is resistant to downtime caused by security updates, explain how those updates reduce the risk of extended downtime from a breach.
- *Anticipate budget concerns*—Be prepared to explain cost–benefit analyses and show that the cost of preventive security measures is far lower than the cost of a potential breach, regulatory fines, or reputational damage. Use concrete examples and data to illustrate this.
- *Involve stakeholders early*—To prevent pushback, involve key stakeholders in security planning early. Engaging them from the beginning fosters collaboration and helps ensure that security goals are integrated with objectives rather than seen as an afterthought.
- *Use cross-departmental champions*—If you encounter persistent resistance from one department, identify individuals from other departments who already understand the value of cybersecurity. Their support can help create momentum and influence reluctant stakeholders.

TAILORING COMMUNICATION TO DIFFERENT STAKEHOLDERS

Each department will resonate with different metrics, so choosing the correct data and framing is essential:

- *Finance team (CFO and financial controllers)*—Focus on ROI, cost savings, and risk mitigation. Use clear visuals, such as
  - A bar chart showing money saved through prevented incidents or compliance fines avoided
  - A line graph showing ROI on security investments over time
- *Operations team (IT and operations managers)*—Highlight system uptime, efficiency, and response times. Use visuals such as
  - A pie chart showing the proportion of incidents detected versus those affecting operations
  - A trend graph showing reductions in downtime over recent months
- *Marketing team (CMO, marketing leads)*—Emphasize brand reputation, customer trust, and compliance. Use charts such as
  - A bar chart comparing compliance improvements with industry benchmarks
  - A graph showing customer trust metrics over time and how security initiatives correlate with that
- *Executive team (CEO, board members)*—Provide a high-level overview focusing on overall risk reduction and alignment with business strategy. Use visuals such as
  - A heat map showing risks mitigated versus ongoing risks
  - A dashboard summarizing key metrics such as compliance, incident response times, and ROI

PROACTIVELY IMPROVING COMMUNICATION CHANNELS

To foster better communication in the long term, consider establishing regular updates or channels where security information is easily accessible:

- *Monthly or quarterly reports*—Schedule regular cybersecurity updates tailored for each group. For example, the finance team could receive a quarterly cost-savings report, while the operations team could get monthly updates on system efficiency improvements.
- *Dashboards*—Create live security dashboards accessible by key stakeholders. These dashboards can show tailored metrics for different teams in real time.
- *Workshops and training*—Organize workshops or executive briefings that focus on cybersecurity's role in supporting each department's objectives. This will help create ongoing dialogue and build understanding across departments.

Translating technical security investments into business-friendly language is critical for engaging executive stakeholders, especially when demonstrating the value of cybersecurity initiatives. Executives such as the CEO, CFO, and board members are primarily concerned with business outcomes, such as cost savings, risk reduction, regulatory compliance, and operational continuity.

For instance, instead of discussing the intricacies of AI-driven threat detection algorithms, you could explain how the system has reduced the risk of costly data breaches by identifying potential threats early and preventing ransomware attacks. Highlight measurable results, such as reduced security incidents, downtime avoided, or regulatory penalties averted due to HIPAA compliance. Use quantifiable data (e.g., how the $500,000 investment has prevented potential losses of $5 million) to show clear financial benefits. Additionally, emphasize improvements in operational continuity, illustrating how the system has ensured uninterrupted patient care by quickly mitigating cyber threats. These strategies help bridge the gap between technical investments and business outcomes, ensuring that key stakeholders clearly understand the value these initiatives bring to the organization.

By using these strategies to start, navigate, and troubleshoot conversations, you can ensure that your cybersecurity initiatives are well-communicated and aligned with the goals of different stakeholders, ultimately securing their support and engagement in the security strategy.

4.3.4 Metrics communication exercise

HealthSecure, a healthcare company that operates a series of hospitals and clinics, has recently invested $500,000 in implementing an advanced threat detection system powered by AI and machine learning. This was in response to growing cybersecurity threats, including data breaches and ransomware attacks, that put patient data and critical healthcare systems at risk. HealthSecure needs to improve its cybersecurity posture to maintain HIPAA compliance, protect patient data, and ensure operational continuity in the event of an attack.

The company is now preparing an executive presentation to showcase the ROI of this security investment to its board of directors, the CEO, and the CFO. The presentation must translate the technical aspects of the threat detection system into business-friendly language, while demonstrating measurable improvements.

SAMPLE PRESENTATION OUTLINE
Slide 1: Introduction & context
Title: Improving HealthSecure's Cybersecurity Posture with AI-Powered Threat Detection
Message: In response to escalating threats, HealthSecure invested $500,000 in advanced AI-driven threat detection to protect patient data and maintain uninterrupted operations. This presentation outlines the business effects of that investment.
Slide 2: Key metrics overview
Title: Key Metrics Driving Business Value
Message: The following key performance indicators (KPIs) demonstrate how the investment improved HealthSecure's overall security posture:

84 CHAPTER 4 *Integrating metrics into business strategy*

- *Incident response time reduction*—From 24 to 4 hours (6x faster)
- *Ransomware mitigation*—Zero successful ransomware attacks in the past year
- *HIPAA compliance*—100% HIPAA audit pass rate
- *Cost savings*—$2.5M in breach prevention (estimated cost if a breach had occurred)

Slide 3: Financial ROI (figure 4.4)
Title: Demonstrating financial ROI (figure 4.4)

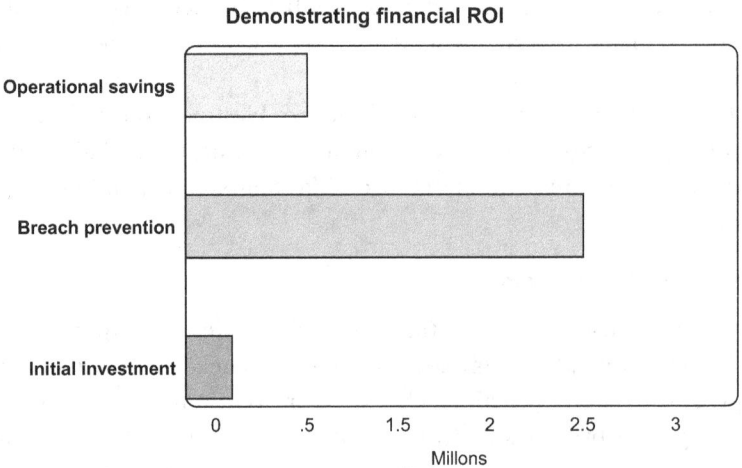

Figure 4.4 Example slide 3: Demonstrating financial ROI showing how $500,000 can have significant returns on investment.

Message

- *Initial investment*—$500,000 in an AI-driven threat detection system
- Cost savings:
  - *Breach prevention*—Estimated savings of $2.5M based on the cost of a potential breach (average healthcare breach cost: $9.2M)
  - *Operational efficiency*—Reduced downtime during security incidents saved an additional $500,000 in operational costs
- *Total ROI*—$2.5M (breach prevention) + $500,000 (operational savings) = $3M in total value for a $500,000 investment.

Slide 4: Operational effect (figure 4.5)
Title: Improved security & operational efficiency

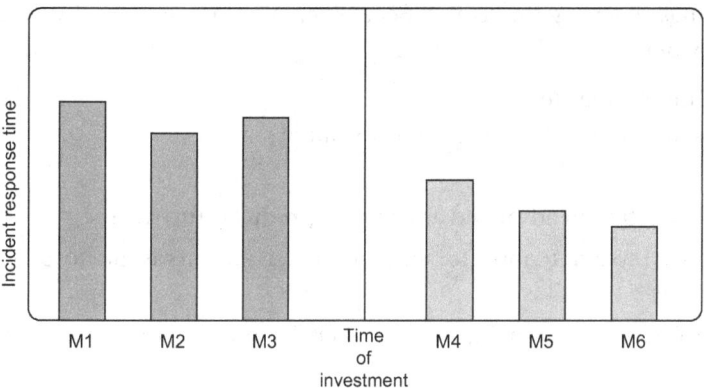

Figure 4.5 Example slide 4: Incident response time improvements before and after investment.

Message

- *Incident response time*—HealthSecure's ability to respond to security incidents improved from 24 hours to just 4 hours, minimizing disruption to healthcare services and safeguarding patient care.
- *System uptime*—By preventing ransomware and other cyber threats, the system ensured continuous system availability for 99.9% of the time, with no unplanned downtime impacting healthcare delivery.

Slide 5: Compliance and trust (figure 4.6)
Title: Maintaining HIPAA compliance & building trust

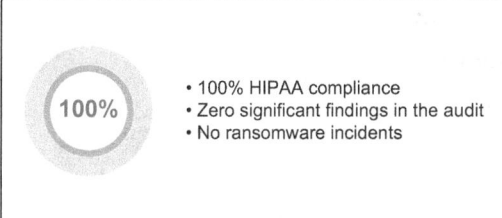

Figure 4.6 Example slide 5: Compliance and trust showing 100% compliance with HIPAA, no significant audit findings, and no ransomware incidents.

Message

- *HIPAA compliance*—The AI-driven threat detection system ensured full compliance with HIPAA regulations, which is critical to avoiding fines, protecting patient data, and maintaining trust.

- *Audit results*—All systems passed the latest compliance audits, with zero significant findings, ensuring that HealthSecure remains in good standing with regulators and patients.

Slide 6: Conclusion & next steps
Title: Next steps for continued security improvement
Message

- Continue investing in advanced analytics to predict future threats.
- Expand the AI system to monitor and secure new systems as the hospital network grows.
- Continue quarterly reporting of key security metrics to maintain executive visibility.

SAMPLE EXECUTIVE SUMMARY REPORT FOR CISO

HealthSecure—Executive Security Summary Report for Q3
Report prepared by: [CISO Name]
Focus area: AI-Powered Threat Detection System Implementation & ROI
Key metrics

- *Incident response time*—Reduced from 24 to 4 hours
- *Breach prevention*—0 successful ransomware attacks
- *System uptime*—99.9%
- *HIPAA compliance*—100% audit pass rate
- *Total investment*—$500,000
- *Estimated cost savings*—$3M ($2.5M in breach prevention, $500,000 in operational savings)
- *Security events detected*—150 per month
- *False positive reduction*—30%

SAMPLE EXECUTIVE SUMMARY REPORT FOR CEO

HealthSecure—CEO Security Update Q3
Report prepared by: [CISO Name]
Focus area: Demonstrating ROI from AI-Driven Security Investment
Financial overview

- *Investment*—$500,000 in AI-powered threat detection
- *ROI*—$3M ($2.5M from avoiding potential breaches, $500,000 in operational savings)
- *HIPAA compliance*—Fully compliant, ensuring no regulatory fines or reputational damage
- *Operational effects*—System uptime of 99.9%, ensuring patient care and data availability without interruptions.

Strategic Effect

- *Future proofing*—Protecting our digital infrastructure, while continuing to meet regulatory requirements.
- *Trust & brand protection*—Safeguarding patient data, maintaining trust, and upholding our reputation in the healthcare industry.

Summary

- Cybersecurity metrics are most effective when aligned with an organization's broader business goals.
- Presentation of metrics uncovers hidden trends and correlations, thus providing deeper insights into potential risks.
- Communicating the value of security metrics in business terms ensures that decision-makers see the ROI of security investments.
- A metrics-driven approach to security helps bridge the gap between technical teams and business leaders, fostering stronger collaboration.

Part 2

The metrics that matter

Chapters 5–9 are where the rubber meets the road. You'll get hands-on with specific metrics illuminating your organization's security posture. From monitoring user access and asset integrity to continuously detecting threats and effectively managing incidents, this section shows you which data points matter most and why. Think of part 2 as the heart of the book: the practical metrics driving informed decision-making, revealing vulnerabilities, and powering the everyday operations of a world-class security program.

Establishing the foundation

This chapter covers
- Implementing effective cybersecurity governance
- Roles and responsibilities in securing your organization's digital identity
- Risks associated with third-party vendors and supply chains

This chapter explores governance as a concept and examines identity in cybersecurity to determine which metrics can effectively measure these critical areas. A solid foundation rooted in an industry-trusted framework is essential for this analysis. Yet, with so many frameworks available, selecting the right one for your organization can feel overwhelming.

When starting in cybersecurity and conducting risk gap assessments, teams often need to investigate several frameworks to find the one that aligns with their processes and consistently delivers value. A well-chosen framework helps identify best practices and develop mitigation strategies to close identified gaps. To measure cybersecurity effectively, using a framework that resonates with your organization's specific needs and goals is essential. While frameworks differ in structure and terminology, their core concepts are consistent across the industry. This ensures that the principles discussed in this book remain applicable, regardless of your chosen framework.

This chapter demonstrates how these foundational concepts shape cybersecurity through practical examples and scenario-based learning, preparing your organization to meet future challenges confidently.

5.1 *Governance*

Governance refers to the internal policies, processes, and procedures, along with the organizational structure, with clearly defined roles and responsibilities used to manage an organization's cybersecurity program. It includes decision-making, accountability, and oversight that together ensure practices are aligned with organizational goals.

In the broader sense, governance is how authority is exercised and accountability is rendered for managing organizational risk. Policy development, oversight, regulations, and enforcement by responsible parties are important. Overall, the goals set forth in the governance section must ultimately support the organization's goals, safeguard assets, manage risks, and comply with laws and regulations.

Figure 5.1 illustrates how the concept of governance defines the objectives and scope for risk management and guides and approves policy development. Risk management, in turn, informs and updates policy development by identifying and assessing risk.

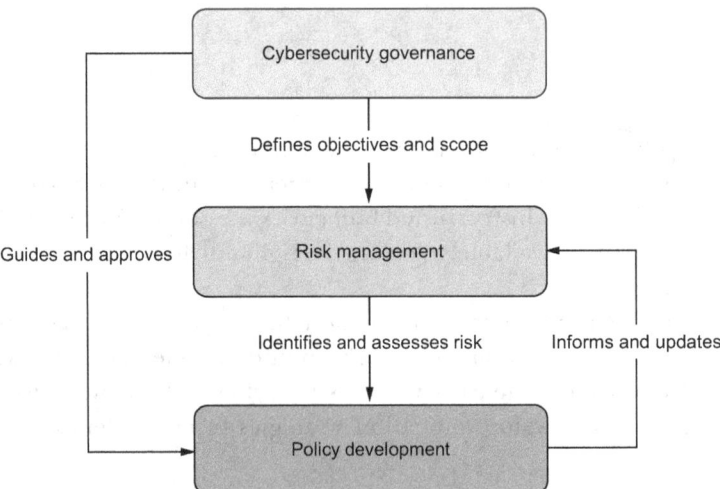

Figure 5.1 **The framework for establishing cybersecurity governance within an organization**

5.2 Organizational context

Understanding the organization's mission, objectives, and the board's expectations is fundamental to effective cybersecurity governance. What organizational context implies is that cybersecurity cannot exist in a vacuum; instead, it must be embedded within the company's broader strategy, ensuring that security efforts directly support business goals rather than being perceived as a roadblock.

When cybersecurity initiatives are misaligned with board expectations, organizations risk underfunding critical security measures or overinvesting in areas that do not directly mitigate the most pressing threats. For example, a board primarily concerned with regulatory compliance may push for excessive spending on compliance frameworks, while neglecting investments in proactive threat intelligence. Conversely, a board focused on cost-cutting may not allocate sufficient resources to security, leading to gaps that attackers can exploit.

One way to bridge this gap is by adopting a risk-based approach that translates cybersecurity into financial and operational terms. Security leaders must communicate how threats translate into business risks, using clear metrics that resonate with executives. For instance, instead of simply stating the number of phishing attempts blocked, security teams should demonstrate the potential financial effect of a successful attack and the return on investment (ROI) for security training programs that reduce employee susceptibility.

Another mitigation strategy is integrating cybersecurity into business risk assessments, prioritizing security risks alongside financial, operational, and reputational ones. This approach allows leadership to make informed decisions on security investments based on the organization's overall risk appetite. Additionally, regular board-level reporting that frames cybersecurity regarding business continuity, customer trust, and regulatory positioning can help ensure that security remains a strategic enabler rather than an afterthought. By proactively aligning cybersecurity efforts with the organization's core mission and leadership expectations, companies can create security programs that are well-funded, well-directed, and fully integrated into broader business strategies.

The organizational context of a company, as illustrated in figure 5.2, demonstrates how cybersecurity governance typically flows from the board of directors to executive leadership, including the chief information officer (CIO) and chief information security officer (CISO), and then down to policy development and risk management. This model accurately represents how cybersecurity oversight is structured in many organizations, particularly those with a strong regulatory or compliance-driven focus.

However, in product-driven organizations, security often operates as a peer function alongside engineering, product management, and operations rather than being strictly hierarchical under IT leadership. In such cases, security teams collaborate closely with development teams to integrate security by design rather than enforcing policies in a top-down manner. For example, in technology companies with agile development cycles, security teams work directly with product and engineering leads to ensure security controls are embedded within the software development life cycle. Security governance in this model is less about reporting structures and more about influence, partnership, and integration within cross-functional teams.

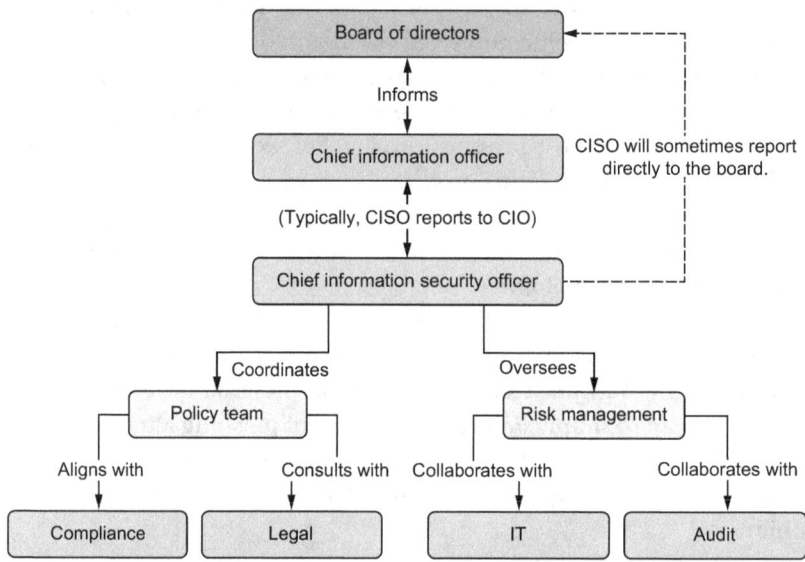

Figure 5.2 An example of aligning cybersecurity initiatives within the business environment and a typical reporting structure. CISOs most often report to the CIO. Also, the CISO will sometimes report directly to the board.

A great starting point for clearly defining your organizational context is the Baldrige Cybersecurity Excellence Builder, which is freely available on the National Institute of Standards and Technology (NIST) website (https://mng.bz/1Zr8). This tool provides exercises to help articulate your organization's purpose, mission, vision, and values. However, it is highly likely that your organization already has these elements documented. Before creating new definitions, the first step should always be to review and utilize what already exists.

Defining organizational context is not a solo effort—it requires collaboration across teams to ensure alignment with existing strategies and goals. In this section, we'll explore how to build on your current organizational context and refine it collaboratively, as shown in figure 5.3. This approach ensures the cybersecurity strategy aligns seamlessly with your organization's overarching mission and values.

An organization's mission, vision, and values shape its approach to cybersecurity. They are not just corporate slogans but guideposts that influence how security is integrated into the company culture. For example, a mission such as "to spread the power of optimism" compels a business to protect customer data earnestly, as trust is

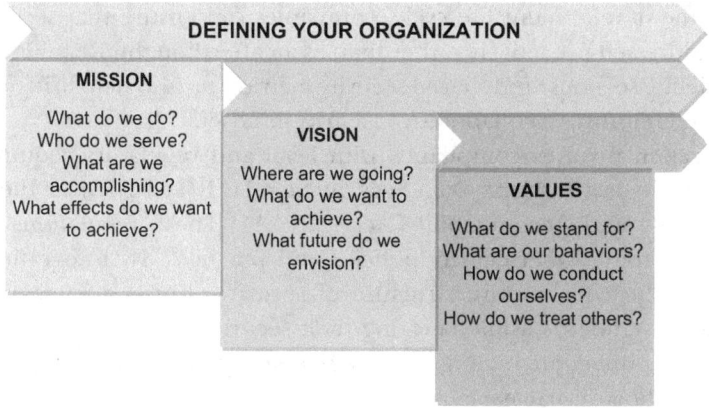

Figure 5.3 An organization's core beliefs and directional goals are foundational to shaping its cybersecurity policies and posture.

a cornerstone of optimism. This mission drives the company's cybersecurity policies, ensuring they are designed to uphold and reinforce that trust.

An organization's vision, perhaps a goal to empower individuals and businesses globally, implies a strong commitment to security measures that enable such empowerment. In cybersecurity, a vision such as this one translates into proactive defense systems and a culture of vigilance among staff.

Values are the compass by which a company navigates its ethical and operational decisions. In cybersecurity, values such as transparency and responsibility dictate that security practices are about defense and accountability to customers and stakeholders.

Understanding how teams collaborate across design, development, and testing phases provides valuable insight into the structure and implementation of security protocols. This collaboration ensures that key assets, such as proprietary processes or intellectual property, are safeguarded effectively. Security measures must be customized to address the unique risks associated with these critical assets.

However, effective cross-functional collaboration cannot be assumed. In many organizations, barriers such as siloed teams, competing priorities, and a lack of clear security ownership can hinder security integration into business processes. Development teams may prioritize speed and feature delivery, while security teams focus on risk reduction, which leads to friction when security requirements are perceived as slowing progress. Furthermore, a lack of security expertise within engineering teams can make implementing secure coding practices consistently difficult.

To overcome these challenges, organizations must foster a culture of shared responsibility for security, which includes establishing clear communication channels, integrating security into agile workflows, and embedding security champions within engineering and product teams. By shifting security from a standalone function to an integral part of the development life cycle, companies can ensure that security considerations are addressed proactively rather than as an afterthought. Regular training, joint threat modeling sessions, and shared security metrics can also help bridge the gap between teams and reinforce a collaborative security mindset.

This customization involves compliance with legal and regulatory requirements, such as the Payment Card Industry Data Security Standard (PCI DSS) or the Health Insurance Portability and Accountability Act (HIPAA). These regulations provide a framework for shaping cybersecurity policies and practices. By integrating these requirements into the collaborative structure of security efforts, organizations can uphold compliance standards, while tailoring their security strategies to mitigate distinct threats. This connection highlights how regulatory compliance supports and enhances the protection of vital assets.

5.2.1 Understanding the differences between mission, vision, and values

Once we become aware of our organizational context—the mission, vision, values, how our team functions, our critical assets, and our regulatory responsibilities—we can better develop a cybersecurity stance that's both robust and aligned with our business goals. This is as much about having a secure organization as having an organization that truly embodies and supports its mission and operations. Here are some examples of companies to illustrate the differences between mission, vision, and values.

HONEST TEA

Honest Tea is a sustainable beverage company, focused on offering organic, low-sugar teas that promote health and environmental consciousness:

- *Mission*—Create and encourage healthy and great-tasting organic beverages
- *Vision*—Mainstream healthful consumer beverages
- *Values*—Enforce sustainability, transparency, and social responsibility

From the cybersecurity perspective, Honest Tea's commitment to sustainability, transparency, and social responsibility translates into a cybersecurity approach that prioritizes protecting customer health data and proprietary formulas. Transparency in handling data breaches and proactive communication with stakeholders about cybersecurity measures reflect their core values and mission.

LIFE IS GOOD

Life is Good is a lifestyle brand centered on spreading optimism and positivity through casual apparel and philanthropic initiatives:

- *Mission*—Spread the power of optimism
- *Vision*—Mainstream optimism and positivity
- *Values*—Maintaining optimism, supporting community, and making positive changes

Spreading optimism and positivity means ensuring customers' interactions with Life is Good are secure and uplifting. The cybersecurity strategy here focuses on creating a safe digital environment that embodies optimism through resilience against cyber threats, safeguarding the community's data, and maintaining a positive brand reputation.

ACME TECH SOLUTIONS

Using Acme Tech Solutions as an example allows us to provide a relatable and adaptable scenario to illustrate key cybersecurity concepts:

- *Mission*—Simplify technology to enhance everyday life for small businesses and individuals
- *Vision*—Enable small businesses and individuals to use technology for maximum productivity and growth
- *Values*—Focusing on the customer, reliability, innovation, and community support

Acme Tech Solutions' mission to simplify technology for small businesses and individuals requires a robust commitment to cybersecurity. Acme ensures that technology remains a safe and empowering tool by focusing on innovative and reliable security solutions. Their community-focused approach tailors cybersecurity measures to the unique needs of small businesses, while emphasizing equal protection and privacy for all users.

5.2.2 Strategic objectives

Understanding how cybersecurity aligns with organizational strategy is critical for measuring its effectiveness. To do this, we can identify and track metrics that correlate with strategic objectives supported by cybersecurity initiatives. For instance, if a company sets a strategic objective to achieve HITRUST certification by a specific date, several cybersecurity initiatives, such as policy development and employee training, would support this goal.

In complex organizations, particularly those formed through mergers and acquisitions, measuring which business units have customized cybersecurity guidelines may be valuable. This metric helps assess progress toward unifying all business units under a cohesive set of policies and procedures.

Another potential metric is the level of employee cybersecurity awareness. By testing employees across the organization, it is possible to gauge their understanding of how cybersecurity integrates with broader organizational goals. While useful, this metric may be challenging to implement consistently due to resource or logistical constraints.

Metrics such as these fall into the category of potential metrics—valuable to track but less commonly used than direct or indirect metrics. They provide deeper insights into how cybersecurity supports organizational context and strategy, offering a broader view of its role in achieving business objectives.

5.2.3 Organizational metrics

Organizational metrics are critical in aligning cybersecurity efforts with strategic goals, assessing preparedness, and effectively allocating resources. These metrics provide insight into how cybersecurity integrates with broader business priorities and adapts to emerging challenges, such as the increasing influence of AI in cyber threats and defenses.

POTENTIAL ORGANIZATIONAL CONTEXT METRICS

Metrics in this category help evaluate how well cybersecurity aligns with an organization's strategic direction:

- *Number of strategic objectives aligned with cybersecurity initiatives*—This metric tracks how many strategic objectives incorporate cybersecurity. The intent is to align the importance of cybersecurity with the company's overall strategic direction. If, for example, a small healthcare provider company is looking to expand its offices to other locations, this metric evaluates how that would affect the importance of cybersecurity in terms of budgetary requirements.
- *Percentage of business units with customized security guidelines*—This metric measures how cybersecurity policies are tailored to specific business units or departments. Consider a pharma company that has recently merged with another company. It might want to evaluate the necessity of bringing all cybersecurity policies and procedures into a more homogeneous and holistic baseline to reduce expenditures for multiple, often duplicated, services.

DIRECT ORGANIZATIONAL CONTEXT METRICS

Direct metrics focus on quantifiable aspects of cybersecurity within the organization:

- *Employee cybersecurity awareness levels*—This metric is assessed via surveys or testing, and it indicates how well the organizational context of cybersecurity is understood across the company. It is a good measure to help adjust training for cybersecurity awareness to be effective, not just to check a box for compliance.
- *Cybersecurity budget as percentage of IT budget*—This metric is essential for maintaining an industry-accepted ratio of cybersecurity to IT budget allocation, ensuring that cybersecurity remains a top priority. At the time of this writing, we observe a range from 1% to 25%. Predictions estimate that the effects of AI on cybersecurity could push this ratio upward to 35%, making it the new norm.

AI's dual role as both a threat and a defense highlights the importance of balancing investments. For instance, attackers use AI to automate malware or create persuasive phishing attempts, while defenders use AI to automate threat detection and enhance incident response. By tracking cybersecurity budgets alongside other metrics, organizations can engage in data-driven discussions about financial commitments, ensuring they are prepared to address current and future challenges.

5.2.4 Organizational metrics exercise

David, the CEO of TechGuard Solutions, a medium-sized tech company, is determined to enhance his company's cybersecurity posture. Three years ago, TechGuard Solutions suffered a significant data breach that exposed sensitive customer data and intellectual property. The breach resulted from compromised credentials and a slow de-provisioning process for former employees. This incident caused not only financial losses, including regulatory fines and customer compensation, but also significant damage to the company's reputation, which led to a loss of customer trust and several canceled contracts.

Since then, the company has invested heavily in cybersecurity training and infrastructure, aiming to rebuild trust and strengthen defenses. Now, David wants to ensure these investments have delivered measurable improvements and that the company is prepared to handle future cybersecurity threats. He is particularly focused on ensuring all employees are well-trained to prevent similar incidents and that a substantial portion of the IT budget is dedicated to cybersecurity efforts, recognizing its critical role in safeguarding the company's assets and reputation.

On the left side of figure 5.4, David's organizational metrics are currently shown to be 75% for cybersecurity awareness training, with a current cybersecurity budget being 25% of the total IT budget.

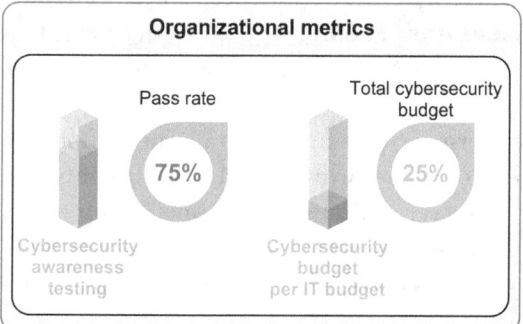 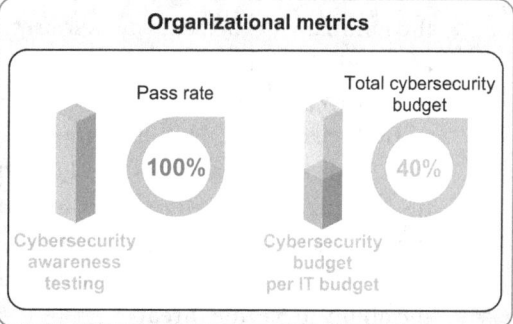

Figure 5.4 The left side shows TechGuard Solutions' organizational metrics dashboard before the focus on training and budget increases. Testing percentages show the overall pass rate from testing. The cybersecurity budget is the total cyber budget as a percentage of the total IT budget. Cybersecurity budgets are most often a percentage of the overall IT budget. The right side shows the organizational metrics dashboard after 3 years and the implementation of strategic training program improvements.

David must demonstrate to stakeholders that the following clear targets are being met and that the company is improving its security posture:

- *Cybersecurity awareness training*—Target 100% completion rate.
- *Cybersecurity budget*—Target 40% of the total IT budget.

On the right side, David's dashboard reveals several critical insights about TechGuard Solutions' cybersecurity efforts. First, the company has achieved a 100% completion rate for cybersecurity awareness training, indicating that all employees, contractors, and partners are now well-versed in handling potential cybersecurity threats. This improvement from the previous 75% completion rate demonstrates significant progress and a commitment to cybersecurity education.

Measuring behavioral change requires metrics that go beyond completion rates. For instance, post-training assessments could measure employees' ability to identify phishing attempts or respond appropriately to simulated cybersecurity incidents. Tracking metrics such as the number of reported phishing emails or reductions in policy violations can provide insights into whether training has effectively influenced behavior. By linking these metrics to training completion, organizations can assess the real-world effect of their cybersecurity education programs and refine them to drive meaningful change.

Allocating 40% of the total IT budget to cybersecurity underscores TechGuard Solutions' dedication to addressing security challenges. However, the value of spending alone does not guarantee an improved security posture. To ensure that this investment drives meaningful change, tracking the outcomes and effectiveness of the initiatives funded by this allocation is essential. Metrics such as the reduction in incident response times, the percentage of threats mitigated before escalation, or improvements in compliance audit results can provide a more accurate picture of how these funds strengthen the company's cybersecurity defenses. A data-driven approach ensures that resources are used efficiently and effectively, aligning spending with measurable improvements in security posture.

By focusing on these two metrics—cybersecurity awareness training completion rates and the allocation of the IT budget to cybersecurity—David gains insights into his company's commitment to security. However, without directly measuring actual threats, their frequency, or the company's response effectiveness, these metrics alone cannot fully demonstrate preparedness or prove a correlation between investment and the ability to handle threats.

To bridge this gap, David should incorporate threat-specific metrics into his analysis. For instance, tracking the number of detected and mitigated threats, response times to incidents, and reducing recurring vulnerabilities could provide a clearer picture of the company's readiness. Combining these operational metrics with the existing ones ensures a more comprehensive assessment of cybersecurity posture, allowing David to make a stronger, evidence-based case to stakeholders for continued investment and strategic focus on security.

5.3 *Risk management strategy*

A risk management strategy is essential for directing how an organization addresses cybersecurity risks. By clearly defining risk tolerance and appetite, an organization can tailor its risk management approach to minimize exposure or balance risk against potential rewards. Early establishment of risk decision-making and prioritization processes ensures the risk management strategy is effective and aligned with business objectives, fostering informed business decisions.

NIST provides a comprehensive guide on implementing a risk management framework called NIST RMF (https://mng.bz/Bzg8) as outlined in figure 5.5. As shown, iterative processes take place in a structured process design that helps organizations manage security and privacy in a repeatable manner. Following this flow, organizations are sure to consider cybersecurity in all phases of their life cycle. There is a heavy reference to preparation, where context, priorities, and criticality are defined to align with the company's mission and objectives.

Following the preparation stage, the RMF categorizes the information systems based on the risk classification of the CIA triad—confidentiality, integrity, and availability. This helps in selecting the appropriate security controls and ensures the organization considers its specific needs and risk posture, along with legal and regulatory considerations.

Once the controls are selected, the implementation phase begins. This phase is technical and also involves the documentation

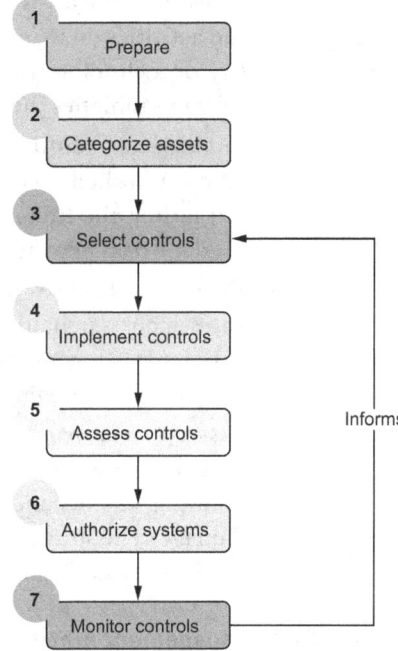

Figure 5.5 A risk management framework depicting a systematic process for identifying, assessing, and managing cybersecurity risks.

process. The effectiveness of the controls is assessed to ensure that they meet the expected risk reduction requirements.

The authorization phase is the critical decision point for owners to review, assess, and sign off on the implemented controls. This risk-based decision is key in defining residual risk—the risk that remains after mitigation efforts.

Continuous monitoring of security controls ensures that the risk level is maintained. This ongoing phase enables organizations to respond to changing and evolving threats, vulnerabilities, effects, and changes in business goals and strategies.

5.3.1 Risk mitigation

Mitigation in terms of cybersecurity aims to reduce the effects of identified risks. There is no way to eliminate risk. In risk management, we can choose how we respond to a specific risk. These response strategies are

- *Acceptance*—Acknowledging the risk's existence but deciding not to take any action to mitigate it. This decision is often made when the cost of the mitigation exceeds the potential risk reduction effects. The risk could also fall within the defined risk tolerance levels. A plan to monitor the risk is recommended to ensure that the risk does not exceed the acceptable limits.

- *Avoidance*—Involves removing the risk entirely. It can be done by discontinuing the activities or system that generated the risk or by changing the process, strategy, or technology that presented the risk. This method is most suitable for critical vulnerabilities that could threaten the organization's operations.
- *Transference*—Shifting the responsibility for the risk to a third party. Typically, this is accomplished via insurance policies or outsourcing. The risk is not eliminated, but rather, the financial effect is allocated to another entity. This is commonly used for risks beyond direct control.
- *Deterrence*—Focuses on discouraging threat actors. Usually done via legal measures such as penalties or by making known what security measures are in place to deter cybercriminals. However, the perceived difficulty of an attack could challenge some of the more egocentric hackers to try even harder.
- *Detection and response*—Not always categorized under mitigation. However, enhancing detection and response is a strategy to mitigate risk. It involves implementing systems and processes to identify and respond effectively to minimize damage. The strategy may include intrusion detection, regular security audits, or deploying a dedicated incident response team.

5.3.2 Risk management metrics

Risk management begins with some sort of evaluation, gap assessment, or other method to identify what needs to be done to bring the organization to the defined cybersecurity level. This assessment allows us to develop a risk register (RR) or *Plan of Action and Milestones (POAM) document*. Common data points in a POAM are the date discovered, a description of the risk, who needs to do what, and in what time frame.

What follows are some key metrics that we should be measuring. Each time a risk register review is conducted, we should document how many risks are *open*, how many have been *closed*, how many have *slipped*, and how many are *existing*. From here, we can track our progress and velocity of mitigation over time.

DIRECT RISK MANAGEMENT METRICS

These metrics help organizations evaluate and address risks effectively by providing measurable indicators of risk exposure:

- *Number of identified risks*—Measuring the number of risks currently identified and unresolved is used in conjunction with either time or severity. Knowing whether there is an increase or decrease in identified risks could help determine whether efforts are being effectively implemented to reduce risk. Measuring the severity of identified risks could help prioritize which risks should be addressed first. Typically, this would be the lowest effort and resources for the highest risk reduction.
- *Number of addressed risks*—The number of addressed risks can be compared to the number of identified risks, which shows how many have been mitigated.
- *Number of risks slipped*—Tracking the number of risks that have not been resolved by the due date can provide us with insight into how well we are addressing risks

promptly. The risk register can be examined further to determine the cause and realign resources to minimize it effectively.

DERIVED RISK MANAGEMENT METRICS

These metrics provide deeper insights by analyzing trends, correlations, and indirect risk indicators:

- *Percentage (or ratio) of identified to addressed risks*—By deriving a percentage of identified to addressed risks, we gain insight into the organization's effectiveness at mitigating identified risks. Over time, this could represent how reactive the organization is in addressing risks.
- *Risk treatment time to resolve*—This metric tracks the average time required to mitigate, accept, transfer, or avoid identified risks, offering valuable insights into the organization's ability to address risks effectively. Analyzing this metric over time can reveal important trends. For instance, if the time to address risks is consistently growing, it may indicate a lack of adequate resources, expertise, or tools, suggesting additional investment or process re-evaluation. However, if the time to resolve risks decreases, it could demonstrate improved efficiency in processes, better resource allocation, or enhanced team expertise. By continuously monitoring and evaluating this metric, organizations can address risks more effectively and identify opportunities for ongoing process improvement and strategic planning.

Indirect risk management metrics analyze secondary indicators rather than direct measurements, such as

- *Changes in cybersecurity insurance premiums related to cybersecurity incidents*—This metric tracks how the organization's risk posture, as reflected in insurance questionnaires and incident history, affects cybersecurity insurance premiums. It serves as a valuable indirect measure of risk management effectiveness and can contribute to estimating the return on investment in cybersecurity initiatives.
- *Number of cybersecurity incidents*—It is important to separately track the number of cybersecurity incidents as its own metric. Monitoring incident frequency over time gives you a clearer picture of risk trends and their direct effect. Combining these insights with changes in insurance premiums creates a more comprehensive view of how the organization's efforts influence risk management and financial outcomes. Separating the components ensures a more transparent and actionable understanding of the data.

5.3.3 Risk management metrics exercise

Imagine MedPharma Inc., a mid-sized pharmaceutical company, strives to enhance its cybersecurity posture due to increasing cyber threats targeting the healthcare industry. A couple of years ago, MedPharma experienced a data breach that exposed sensitive patient information. This breach prompted the company to adopt a robust RMF to prevent future incidents. The risk management dashboard at the time of the breach is shown on the left in figure 5.6.

Figure 5.6 The left side is an example of a risk management dashboard for MedPharma Inc. at the time of the breach several years ago. The risk register will contain the details of the risks. Tracking metrics helps depict the story of how well the organization is doing to reduce risk. The right is the risk management dashboard after focusing on reducing cybersecurity risks.

MedPharma needs to evaluate its status and determine areas for improvement with the following clearly defined targets to measure the effectiveness of its risk management efforts:

- Resolve 85% of identified risks.
- Address 90% of identified risks.
- Resolve 95% of risks within the target time to resolve.

After focusing on mitigating cybersecurity risks, the right side of figure 5.6 provides a clear overview of the company's progress in their mitigation efforts. The dashboard reveals that MedPharma has resolved 75% of all identified risks, showcasing significant strides in addressing vulnerabilities. However, evaluating the criticality of the unresolved 25% is crucial. If these include severe threats, MedPharma must prioritize mitigating these areas urgently to avoid potential breaches.

Additionally, 80% of all identified risks have been addressed, indicating that MedPharma has taken initial steps to understand and evaluate these risks. This is essential for long-term risk management. However, complete resolution may still be pending for some risks, particularly those involving third-party vendors or complex system integrations.

The metric showing that 90% of risks are resolved within the target time to resolve (TTR) is promising, suggesting that MedPharma's incident response team effectively manages most risks promptly. Nonetheless, striving for 100% resolution within the target TTR should be an ongoing goal. If they fall short of this target, it might be necessary to investigate the causes—be it resource constraints, process inefficiencies, or external dependencies—and implement improvements accordingly.

These specific metrics provide a snapshot of MedPharma's current risk management status, highlighting areas that require continuous monitoring and improvement. Using this dashboard, the company can make informed decisions and strategically allocate resources to enhance its cybersecurity resilience. MedPharma's efforts in risk management demonstrate a proactive approach to securing sensitive data and protecting the organization's reputation and operations.

5.4 Roles, responsibilities, and authorities

Clearly defined roles and responsibilities are crucial for effective governance of cybersecurity risks. However, in many organizations, we often see cybersecurity responsibilities being split or added to the duties of employees whose primary focus is not cybersecurity. For example, cybersecurity tasks might be assigned to IT team members in addition to their existing responsibilities. While this may seem efficient, it often leads to increased burnout and reduced effectiveness. Cybersecurity is a specialized field that requires dedicated focus and expertise, making it a full-time role rather than an ancillary duty.

Moreover, this practice can create ethical conflicts. For instance, budgetary restrictions may force compromises that hinder the balance between achieving organizational goals and adequately addressing cybersecurity risk targets. Organizations inadvertently expose themselves to greater risk by overburdening staff and underfunding cybersecurity. Clearly defining and resourcing cybersecurity roles ensures compliance and a stronger and more sustainable security posture.

Organizations must establish clear distinctions between IT and cybersecurity roles to ensure each can focus on their responsibilities, while collaborating effectively to support the organization's goals. Detailed documentation should define all aspects of cybersecurity management, including incident response, user access controls, compliance with laws and regulations, and maintaining required certifications. These clearly defined roles, responsibilities, and authorities serve as a reference for team members and the board, fostering consistency and enabling the development of an effective and cohesive cybersecurity program.

While certain positions center on cybersecurity, their responsibilities often intersect with broader organizational goals. For example, the chief information security officer (CISO) is a role that exemplifies this intersection. The CISO must balance the technical aspects of securing systems and data with the business' strategic objectives, which requires deep expertise in cybersecurity and the ability to communicate complex security concepts in ways that resonate with technical teams, business stakeholders, and financial leaders. By bridging these gaps, effective CISOs ensure cohesive strategies aligning cybersecurity initiatives with the company's overall objectives, thus enabling security and business growth.

5.4.1 Roles, responsibilities, and authorities metrics

This category is also one where we could find metrics to measure, but in practice, they will not yield any advantages that would outweigh the effort in collecting and maintaining metrics. We like practical metrics with high residual yield, and this will depend on your organizational needs.

POTENTIAL ROLES, RESPONSIBILITIES, AND AUTHORITIES METRICS

The following metrics help track cybersecurity governance, role clarity, and board meeting action item progress to ensure effective implementation and continuous improvement:

- *Number of roles with clearly defined cybersecurity responsibilities*—This would have to follow an evaluation of the organizational structure when planning out roles and responsibilities. These metrics would track your progress on clearly defining, documenting, and communicating these roles and responsibilities and serve as a metric for program implementation.
- *Board meeting action items open*—Following each board meeting, meeting minutes should highlight action items and identify who is responsible for completing those action items. For cybersecurity topics, we would typically track these within a POAM or other Risk Register to completion. This metric will help us track our progress on what needs to be done.
- *Board meeting action items close*—Target due dates are part of any POAM tracking and keeping metrics on how many action items were closed is a good measure of your progress.
- *Board meeting action items slipped*—If your target completion date is missed, tracking this metric will help you determine what resources are required or what changes are needed to close these items promptly.

DERIVED ROLES, RESPONSIBILITIES, AND AUTHORITIES METRICS

This type of metrics may provide insight into the progress and efficiency of cybersecurity-related board meeting action items:

- *Percentage of open vs. closed board meeting action items*—Tracking and reporting on your progress toward closing board meeting action items involving cybersecurity can help you report your progress to the team.
- *Percentage of on-time vs. slipped action items*—Tracking these metrics can help you determine your effectiveness and efficiency. To improve these numbers, you would discuss this with the key stakeholders to determine areas for improvement.

INDIRECT ROLES, RESPONSIBILITIES, AND AUTHORITIES METRICS

The following metric evaluates how well employees understand their cybersecurity responsibilities:

- *Employee satisfaction with cybersecurity role clarity*—Gathered through a survey, this metric can indicate how well employees understand their designated cybersecurity responsibilities and provide you with some insight into any required changes to ensure more effective training and awareness.

5.4.2 Roles and responsibilities metrics exercise

Let's consider TechSecure Solutions, a company specializing in developing advanced cybersecurity software. Recently, the management at TechSecure Solutions decided to enhance their internal cybersecurity awareness and accountability. To achieve this, they developed a comprehensive roles and responsibilities dashboard for monitoring key metrics related to organizational accountability and clarity in cybersecurity tasks.

On the right side of figure 5.7, the TechSecure Solutions roles and responsibilities dashboard shows areas of improvement before implementing more focused definitions of roles and responsibilities to improve accountability.

Figure 5.7 The left side shows TechSecure Solutions' roles and responsibilities dashboard before clearly defining roles and responsibilities to increase accountability. The right side shows the roles and responsibilities dashboard after clearly defining roles and responsibilities to increase accountability.

TechSecure Solutions experienced several cybersecurity incidents due to unclear responsibilities and lack of accountability. They set specific targets for improving their roles and responsibilities metrics to address this problem:

- Achieve 100% closure of action items from board meetings within a quarter.
- Ensure 100% of roles have clearly defined cybersecurity responsibilities.

In TechSecure Solutions' roles and responsibilities dashboard, several critical metrics are displayed that provide a comprehensive overview of the company's progress in enhancing organizational accountability and clarity in cybersecurity tasks. Initially, the company struggled with many open action items from board meetings, incomplete role definitions, and insufficient employee understanding of cybersecurity responsibilities.

The roles and responsibilities dashboard on the right in figure 5.7 reveals that 90% action items are currently open, indicating ongoing efforts to address and close those items. While it is typical to see less than 100% closure due to the varying complexity and time requirements of action items, a high number of open items may signal a need for better follow-up and prioritization. TechSecure Solutions aims to improve this metric to achieve timely completion and closure of action items.

The dashboard shows that 100% of roles within the company now have clearly defined responsibilities. This achievement is crucial as it eliminates ambiguities about task ownership and ensures every role is well understood and accounted for. Beyond assigning responsibilities, all open tasks must have a clearly defined owner. Designating ownership ensures no confusion about who is responsible for addressing specific tasks, preventing security gaps, enhancing accountability, and ensuring that actions are taken efficiently and effectively. Clear ownership drives execution and accountability across the organization, making it a cornerstone of effective cybersecurity management.

This dashboard also highlights that 97% of employees have been tested and achieved a passing grade in understanding their cybersecurity responsibilities. This metric indicates significant progress in educating employees about their roles in maintaining cybersecurity. While the company strives for 100% in this metric, realistically, some will fail the test and need to retake the course to pass. Achieving a high percentage of employee understanding ensures that everyone in the organization is aware of and capable of fulfilling their cybersecurity duties.

By tracking these metrics, TechSecure Solutions can ensure that all roles are clearly defined, responsibilities are well understood, and action items are actively managed and closed. This approach contributes to a robust and accountable cybersecurity culture, enhancing the company's overall security posture. Moving forward, TechSecure Solutions should continue monitoring these metrics, addressing any gaps promptly, and fostering a culture of continuous improvement to maintain and strengthen its cybersecurity efforts.

5.5 Policy, processes, and procedures

Developing policies, processes, and procedures guides the organization's cybersecurity activities, which requires a detailed and repeatable definition of all key cybersecurity activities. These documents serve as a playbook and reference point for all employees to help ensure consistent and effective implementation of cybersecurity throughout the organization.

The *policies* answer the question, "Why are we implementing the specific cybersecurity controls?" In policies, we define high-level statements that reflect the organization's goals, intentions, and principles. They set the overall objective and scope of the cybersecurity program. Policies establish the foundation of the cybersecurity program and help guide the development of processes and procedures. They also ensure compliance with legal and regulatory requirements.

Processes answer the question, "How are we implementing these specific cybersecurity controls?" We describe the steps, methods, and guides to implement the policies in the process. They are more detailed than policies but still relatively high level. They often contain flow charts, illustrations, or diagrams, ensuring high implementation consistency. Processes translate policies into actionable steps, helping coordinate resources and activities.

Procedures are step-by-step instructions on how a process is conducted. They are often at the operational level and should be able to be followed by any member of the team relevant to the task. Procedures describe what needs to be done, delegating responsibility, and how it should be done. They ensure tasks are conducted consistently, reducing variability and increasing reliability. Procedures also facilitate audit and compliance efforts by documenting how policies and processes are implemented.

While the specific policies and procedures required depend on your organization's industry, business, legal, and regulatory requirements, there are some very common policies and procedures that most companies will implement for a mature cybersecurity program, included in the following types of documentation:

- *Information security*—Provides a high-level approach to information security and outlines rules, guidelines, and responsibilities.
- *Acceptable use*—Outlines how employees can use organizational IT assets and systems, which usually includes internet/email and social media usage.
- *Access control*—Defines access permissions and restrictions to organizational data, and includes user and network access controls.
- *Password*—Defines the complexity, length, and usage of passwords throughout the organization and any recommended password management tools.
- *Change management*—Establishes a formal process for changing IT, software, and security systems, aiming to minimize any disruptions and/or effects when making changes.
- *Remote access*—Specifies approved methods and controls for remote/mobile access to organizational resources, and typically includes BYOD (bring your own device) and home network controls.
- *Incident response*—Defines the process for identifying, containing, and recovering from security incidents and helps minimize any damage or downtime when dealing with an event.
- *Disaster recovery*—Outlines the plans for restoring critical systems and data in the event of a significant incident. This document coordinates with the incident response and business continuity plans.
- *Business continuity*—Defines the strategy and procedures for maintaining essential business functions during and after a disaster. These documents ensure the organization can continue operations during and after a recovery event.

Keeping your documentation to a minimum is a key factor in maintaining manageability. It also helps reduce duplication of effort and keeps audit, legal, and regulatory control checks focused on a small set of documents. Some organizations prefer to have policies and procedures in separate documents, whereas others would prefer to keep them in one, where each document contains the policies and procedures together with standard operating procedures (SOPs) in separate documents. Whatever you decide, it is more important to keep things simple and what works for the organization and the team involved in documentation management.

5.5.1 *Policy, processes, and procedures metrics*

A large part of compliance comes down to documentation management. Implementing changes to documentation always seems to take longer than expected to make the changes, review them, and gather the appropriate signatures and authorizations. Then, depending on the document, you must communicate and disseminate these changes to key stakeholders or all employees. On average, we have seen documentation take about 3 months. When organizations have many policies, processes, and procedures, this can present a challenge.

Review documentation annually or whenever changes arise due to business needs, updated laws and regulations, or other requirements. Understanding how well you manage documentation is essential to staying ahead of challenges rather than falling behind and constantly playing catch-up. Spread reviews throughout the year to consistently update documents in smaller, more manageable chunks, ensuring the process remains efficient and effective.

DIRECT POLICY, PROCESS, AND PROCEDURE METRICS

These metrics help track compliance, efficiency, and overall program success:

- *Policies reviewed within time frame*—Tracking the number of policies reviewed and approved within the allocated time frame to remain compliant is a good indication of your resource capability to meet this requirement.
- *Policies that have missed their review window*—Tracking the number of policies past due for review and approval is a good metric to compare with past performance and/or a ratio of compliant versus noncompliant.
- *Time to update documentation*—This metric can help you better plan and change how often documents are updated, given the average time it takes to make, review, and approve the changes. You can use this metric to uncover trends that could lead you to adjust when, how, or what resources are required to reduce this to an acceptable level. Failing to update documentation promptly can have serious consequences, such as regulatory fines or failing certifications.

DERIVED POLICY, PROCESS, AND PROCEDURE METRICS

These metrics analyze trends, correlations, and secondary effects to provide deeper insights into policy and procedural outcome:

- *Ratio of compliant documents versus noncompliant documents*—Given this ratio, you can better determine where to focus on changes. Some possible considerations are whether you should move more difficult documents to another time frame, start your review process and extend the window to remain compliant, or implement a penalty for those holding up the process.
- *Ratio of reviewed documents that did not require significant change*—This metric can help determine which documents are more stable than others. Knowing this can lead to insights into better planning over the year to remain compliant. Perhaps you may want to move less significantly changed documents together as they tend to be processed more quickly.

INDIRECT POLICY, PROCESS, AND PROCEDURE METRICS

The following metric tracks employee cybersecurity policy violations, helping identify trends, evaluate training effectiveness, and highlight areas for improvement:

- *Number of employee violations of cybersecurity policies*—While the dashboard represents this metric as a percentage, it is crucial to clarify what is being measured. The percentage could reflect the proportion of employees committing violations relative to the total workforce or the change in violations compared to the previous period (increase or decrease). Additionally, analyzing whether the same individuals repeatedly violate policies or if the violations are widespread can provide valuable insights. These patterns can highlight areas where policies lack clarity, training needs improvement, or enforcement is inconsistent. Presenting this metric as a percentage ensures a clear, scalable comparison over time or across departments.

5.5.2 Policy, processes, and procedures metrics exercise

Let's consider MediHealth Solutions, a leading provider of healthcare management software. MediHealth has a robust policy and procedure management system to ensure compliance with industry regulations and internal standards. Recently, the company faced scrutiny during an audit, highlighting some areas needing improvement. In response, MediHealth implemented a comprehensive dashboard to monitor the status and effectiveness of its policies and procedures.

The left side of figure 5.8 shows a policy and procedure dashboard with some common metrics that tell a story about how well this organization was keeping up with maintaining policy and procedure updates. MediHealth Solutions discovered that some policies were outdated and that employee compliance with procedures was inconsistent.

MediHealth set the following clear targets to improve its metrics:

- Achieve a 100% completion rate for the annual document review process.
- Increase documentation compliance to 90% or above.
- Ensure all critical documents are reviewed promptly when regulations change.
- Maintain a 0% employee violation rate through continuous training and monitoring.

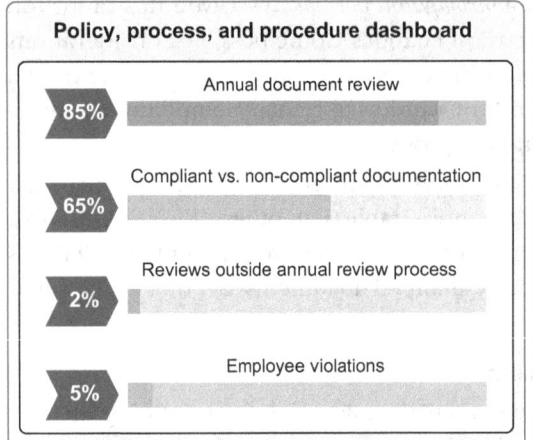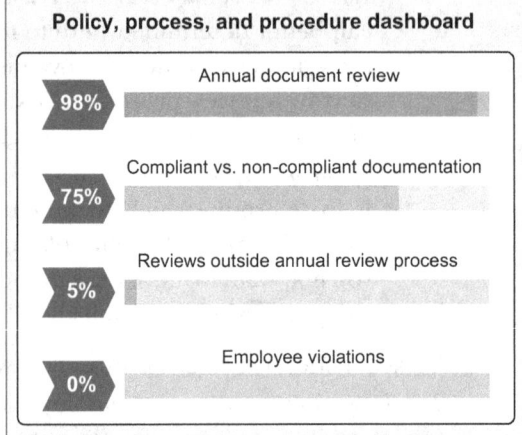

Figure 5.8 The left side shows an example policy and procedure dashboard for MediHealth Solutions depicting the need for policy and procedure improvements. On the right is the dashboard for MediHealth Solutions after implementing a formal document control process to update policies and procedures periodically.

On the right side of figure 5.8, the policy and procedure dashboard of MediHealth Solutions, several critical metrics provide a detailed insight into the company's adherence to internal and regulatory standards. Initially, the company struggled with outdated policies and inconsistent employee compliance, which were highlighted during an audit. The dashboard now reveals significant progress but also areas requiring further attention.

MediHealth has achieved a 98% completion rate for its annual document review process. This high percentage indicates that almost all policies and procedures have been reviewed within the past year. The slight fluctuation from 100% is normal and reflects the ongoing process of updating and approving documents. However, to achieve their target, MediHealth must focus on completing the review of the remaining 2%.

The 75% documentation compliance metric indicates that a significant portion of MediHealth's documentation is compliant, although there is room for improvement. Figure 5.8 also suggests that some policies may still be outdated or misaligned with current standards, posing a risk during audits such as SOC 2 type II. To enhance compliance and achieve their target of 90% or higher, MediHealth should investigate the root causes of these gaps.

It's also important to consider the relationship between this compliance metric and the documentation review rate. If the review rate is high but compliance remains below 100%, this could indicate that reviews are not leading to effective actions or that identified actions are not being completed. MediHealth should assess if the review process is sufficiently rigorous and are there any barriers to implementing necessary updates, ensuring reviews translate into tangible improvements in compliance.

The dashboard shows that 5% of documents have been reviewed outside the scheduled annual process. This metric demonstrates MediHealth's responsiveness to regulatory changes or internal process updates. It indicates the organization's adaptability to industry changes and regulatory requirements, ensuring that critical documents are promptly updated as needed.

The 0% employee violations metric strongly indicates that staff are well-trained and adhere to established policies and procedures, reflecting effective training programs and a culture of compliance. However, it's worth examining the relationship between this metric and others, such as employee training completion rates or documentation compliance. For instance, if training completion rates are high but violations were to increase, it could signal that training content isn't translating into behavioral change. Similarly, if compliance falls below 100%, it prompts concerns whether unclear policies or outdated procedures might eventually lead to an uptick in violations. Maintaining this metric requires enforcing policies and ensuring they are well understood, actionable, and supported through ongoing training and effective documentation management.

By tracking these specific metrics, MediHealth Solutions can maintain high compliance standards, improve its policy and procedure management, and robustly respond to regulatory requirements and internal standards. This example illustrates how specific metrics can provide actionable insights and guide continuous organizational improvement.

5.6 Oversight

Monitoring and evaluation of the effectiveness of cybersecurity strategies through regular assessment, audit, and review helps ensure measures are functioning as intended. Remaining compliant with laws and regulations is critical for many organizations that need to comply with strict federal and state laws and regulations. This oversight provides a mechanism for feedback and continuous improvement. Organizations can better adapt to respond to evolving threats, evolving business needs, and new changes of laws and regulations.

The essence of *oversight* is providing a clear view of how well the organization manages and mitigates cybersecurity risks. It is important to provide a gap check and assess performance at a high level, which fosters a culture of accountability and continuous process improvement. With cybersecurity threats in constant flux, businesses must adapt to industry shifts and evolving strategies, which necessitates diligent oversight.

Validating that cybersecurity practices are still aligned with the strategic direction of the organization's mission, values, and objectives is important for maintaining trust among stakeholders, requiring active engagement of senior management and the board of directors. The goal is to ensure that cybersecurity efforts are not siloed but integrated into the broader organizational strategy and risk management. And what is a better way to provide these indicators than by measuring and communicating them to key stakeholders?

Understanding governance is essential for any organization looking to implement a cybersecurity program. This understanding lays the groundwork for developing effective cybersecurity programs and the metrics to measure them. Now that we know what governance is, let's see how to best structure governance within an organization.

5.6.1 Governance structure

A *governance structure* is the framework that defines how an organization manages and enforces its policies, procedures, and overall security strategy. It outlines who holds authority, how decisions are made, and the processes by which accountability and communication are maintained. This structure ensures everyone understands their roles and responsibilities, enabling effective collaboration and alignment with organizational goals.

In cybersecurity, governance structures play a crucial role in implementing and enforcing policies and procedures. A well-defined structure clarifies authority, identifies decision-makers, and establishes the processes needed to adapt to changing circumstances. As we often say in the industry, it's essential to "swim in your lane." This means knowing your specific role, executing your responsibilities effectively, delegating tasks when necessary, and being adaptable when situations require adjustments.

To better understand and apply these concepts, we'll walk through a demonstration and exercise that illustrate the importance of governance structures in cybersecurity management.

5.6.2 Simulated governance structure

To demonstrate what a governance structure could look like, let's define a fictitious technology company—Acme Tech. This is a global company that offers cloud-based solutions. The governance structure in figure 5.9 is designed for clear accountability, efficient risk management, and effective decision-making.

BOARD OF DIRECTORS

The board of directors plays a crucial governance role in overseeing the organization's cybersecurity strategy. While traditionally the board governs and evaluates the CEO, who oversees C-suite roles such as the CIO, the governance of cybersecurity sometimes involves additional complexities. The CISO's reporting structure can vary, depending on the organization's hierarchy—some CISOs report directly to the CEO, others to the CIO, or even the CTO. This variability can affect how cybersecurity initiatives are prioritized and aligned with strategic goals.

The board's responsibility is to ensure that cybersecurity receives adequate resources and attention, particularly for protecting critical assets. They often evaluate the organization's cybersecurity program through the CEO's lens. However, wouldn't it be ideal if the board had access to clear metrics to evaluate these efforts effectively? By having measurable data on cybersecurity performance, the board can make more informed decisions, ensuring that cybersecurity strategies align with the organization's broader objectives and that performance is consistently monitored and improved.

CHIEF INFORMATION SECURITY OFFICER

The CISO is responsible for overseeing the cybersecurity strategy, ensuring compliance with policies and regulations, leading the cybersecurity teams, and communicating risk

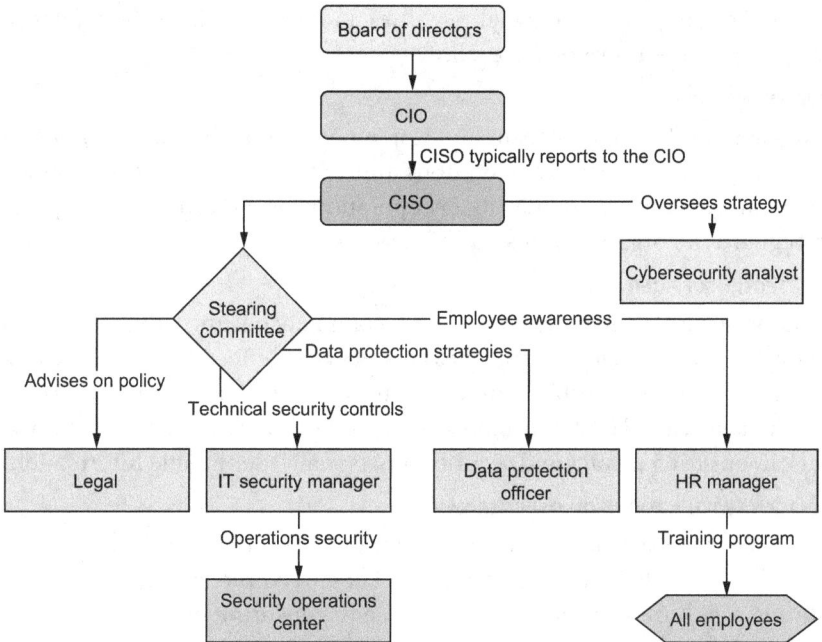

Figure 5.9 The governance structure of our example company, Acme Tech

to the board and executive management. Furthermore, the CISO bridges technology and management, ensuring business decisions and strategy are incorporated into cybersecurity.

CYBERSECURITY ANALYST

This position monitors security systems for threats and performs analysis, security audits, and assists with incident response and forensics. This position is sometimes fulfilled by a managed service provider. However, this role is challenging as cybersecurity analysts are the front-line defenders of the company's security posture. Identifying and mitigating threats are key to maintaining the security and privacy of critical assets.

CYBERSECURITY STEERING COMMITTEE

This group involves key stakeholders from various departments. IT, HR, legal, and finance all play a role in advising and contributing to policies, reviewing cybersecurity risk assessments, and approving key initiatives, which ensures cross-departmental coordination and communication, and facilitates a unified cybersecurity risk reduction approach across the organization.

LEGAL AND COMPLIANCE OFFICER

Legal and compliance officers advise on legal and regulatory requirements related to cybersecurity, contracts, agreements, and resulting implications. They ensure protection from legal and financial penalties and act to reduce the effects of reputational damage in the event of a breach.

IT SECURITY MANAGER

They manage the IT security team and implement the technical security controls. In addition, they oversee security operations and help respond to security incidents. IT security managers ensure the day-to-day operations of the cybersecurity program and help safeguard the organization's critical assets.

DATA PROTECTION OFFICER

The data protection officer (DPO) ensures compliance with data protection laws and regulations. DPOs manage the strategies and assess the effects on privacy, also serving as a point of contact for data subjects and regulatory bodies. They regularly coordinate with legal, compliance, and HR departments. This position is critical for maintaining integrity and trust by ensuring privacy and security of personally identifiable information (PII).

HR MANAGER (WITH A FOCUS ON CYBERSECURITY)

They manage cybersecurity awareness, training, recruitment, and background checks, and help develop policies and procedures related to employment. They play a key role in fostering a culture of cybersecurity awareness, ensuring all employees understand their roles and responsibilities.

5.6.3 Governance exercise

In figure 5.10, match the role with the responsibility. Keep in mind that this exercise is based on the most common roles and responsibilities, but in the real world, these roles and responsibilities will differ from one company to another, based on resources, the risk appetite of the organization, and their specific business goals. The answers are provided at the end of the chapter.

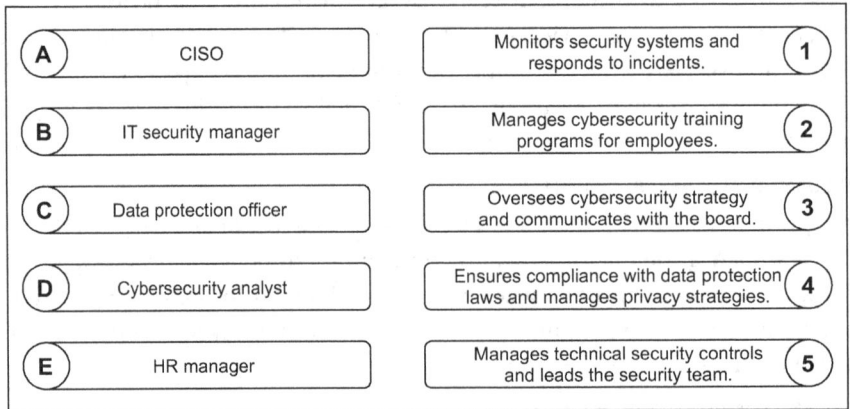

Figure 5.10 An interactive challenge to match various cybersecurity roles with their corresponding responsibilities

5.6.4 Oversight metrics

Oversight metrics are about validating that you are implementing due diligence and due care in your cybersecurity program. They track if you measured and followed up on the key metrics to assure stakeholders that you are properly monitoring and managing your cybersecurity risk. This is the case where we could create specific metrics for this purpose, but we would derive these metrics from other, more direct measurements. Some direct measurements would come from controls involving strategic planning and how those plans would affect cybersecurity.

Here are some examples of the derived oversight metrics:

- *Gap analysis between identified risks and existing controls*—We can review this metric quarterly based on how well we are closing the identified gaps. Incorporating stakeholder input into gap analysis allows organizations to move beyond reactive security measures and adopt a more holistic, risk-based approach to cybersecurity.
- *Performance problems with cybersecurity risk management*—As part of an annual review, tracking the number of cybersecurity-related employee performance problems can provide valuable insights into the effectiveness of the organization's cybersecurity risk management.

By "performance problems," we refer to incidents where employees' actions or inactions have led to cybersecurity vulnerabilities or breaches. This can include instances such as

- *Failure to follow protocols*—Employees who do not adhere to established cybersecurity policies and procedures, such as not using strong passwords, ignoring mandatory software updates, or mishandling sensitive data
- *Phishing susceptibility*—Instances where employees fall victim to phishing attacks, either by clicking on malicious links or providing sensitive information in response to fraudulent emails
- *Insufficient incident response*—Situations in which employees fail to appropriately respond to or report cybersecurity incidents promptly, leading to increased risk or effect of the threat
- *Completion of security training*—Employees not participating in or not completing required cybersecurity training and awareness programs, which results in a lack of understanding and vigilance regarding potential threats.

By identifying and analyzing these performance problems, organizations can make informed decisions on where to focus their efforts to improve cybersecurity risk management. This might include

- *Enhanced training programs*—Developing more comprehensive and engaging training sessions to ensure all employees know and understand the importance of cybersecurity protocols

- *Awareness campaigns*—Implementing regular cybersecurity awareness campaigns to keep cybersecurity top of mind for all employees
- *Policy updates*—Reviewing and updating cybersecurity policies to address common performance problems and reinforce the importance of compliance
- *Improved monitoring and feedback*—Establishing better monitoring systems to quickly identify and address performance problems, coupled with constructive feedback to employees to help them improve.

Tracking employee performance problems related to cybersecurity can help organizations pinpoint weaknesses in their cybersecurity risk management strategies and implement targeted measures to enhance overall security. One useful metric in this context is the *number of adjustments made due to performance problems*, which tracks the frequency of adjustments made to address cybersecurity performance. Over time, this number should decrease, indicating that we are becoming more efficient at avoiding changes due to performance problems.

5.6.5 Oversight metrics exercise

Let's consider TechGuardian Solutions, a mid-sized cybersecurity firm specializing in providing tailored cybersecurity solutions to various industries. The company has identified several risks to existing controls through regular assessments and gap analyses. To ensure continuous improvement and maintain a robust cybersecurity posture, TechGuardian Solutions has implemented specific metrics to track its progress. The left side of figure 5.11 shows a gap analysis dashboard that TechGuardian Solutions is using to measure its risks.

Following their risk assessment, TechGuardian Solutions found that the following several critical vulnerabilities needed immediate attention:

- Achieve 90% coverage in gap analysis within the next quarter.
- Reduce the number of performance problems related to cybersecurity by 50%.
- Ensure all identified gaps are addressed within the set time frame to maintain a proactive cybersecurity stance.

On the right side of figure 5.11, TechGuardian Solutions has implemented a gap analysis dashboard to measure their risks and track progress in identifying vulnerabilities. Initially, the company had a gap analysis coverage of 60%, highlighting a need for increased visibility into its cybersecurity posture. After implementing targeted strategies, they have improved this coverage to 85%, nearing their target of 90%. This improvement reflects enhanced visibility and a stronger ability to identify gaps in their security controls. However, while identifying gaps is a critical first step, this metric does not directly address whether the gaps have been effectively mitigated. TechGuardian should thus pair this metric with additional data that tracks the resolution and closure of identified vulnerabilities to ensure progress.

The dashboard also reveals a reduction in the number of cybersecurity performance problems, from 20 incidents per quarter to 10. This decrease suggests that

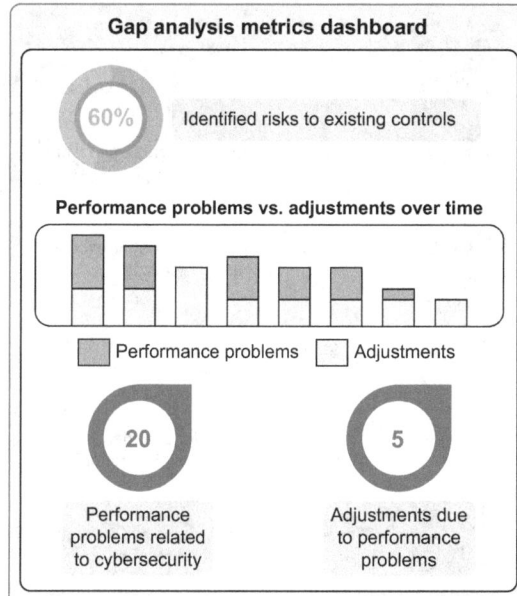 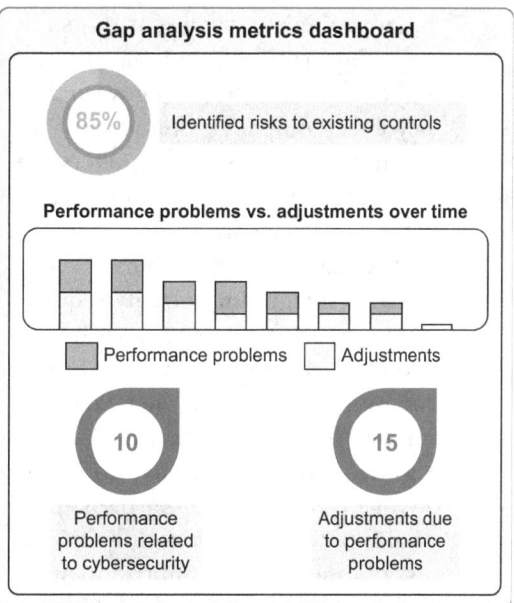

Figure 5.11 The left side shows TechGuardian Solutions' gap analysis metrics dashboard before implementing a continuous improvement program. The right side shows the gap analysis metrics dashboard after implementing the program and tracking metrics over time.

TechGuardian Solutions' efforts to enhance its cybersecurity measures are paying off, leading to fewer incidents that could compromise its systems. However, the company should continue monitoring these metrics to ensure sustained improvement and strive to achieve even lower numbers.

The number of adjustments made due to performance problems has increased from 5 to 15 per quarter. This increase indicates a proactive approach to managing and resolving problems as they arise. By making more adjustments, TechGuardian Solutions is continuously refining its processes and controls, ensuring that any identified problems are promptly addressed and mitigated.

These specific metrics provide a snapshot of TechGuardian Solutions' current oversight status, highlighting areas that require continuous monitoring and improvement. Using this dashboard, the company can make informed decisions and strategically allocate resources to enhance its cybersecurity resilience. The example illustrates how specific metrics can provide actionable insights and guide continuous organizational improvement.

5.7 Cybersecurity supply chain risk management

A *supply chain* encompasses the network of vendors, suppliers, and partners that provide goods or services to an organization. In today's globalized environment, supply chains introduce unique vulnerabilities that must be considered as part of an organization's cybersecurity strategy. This category emphasizes the importance of extending governance beyond company boundaries to ensure all vendors and suppliers are well-vetted and adhere to the organization's cybersecurity standards.

Managing supply chain risk involves integrating security requirements into contracts, conducting thorough risk assessments, and implementing methods to evaluate compliance and mitigate vulnerabilities. As shown in figure 5.12, the complexity of properly managing the supply chain becomes evident. Identifying risks, implementing mitigation strategies, and monitoring their effectiveness can be a daunting but essential task to protect organizational assets.

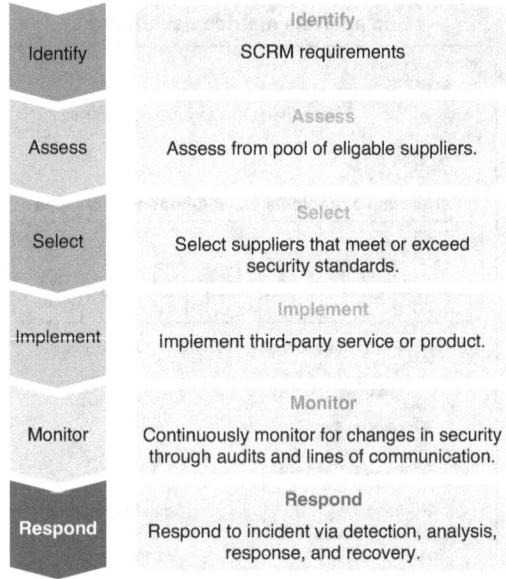

Figure 5.12 The process of securing an organization's supply chain

With the increasing complexity of global supply chains and the increase in cyberattacks and data breaches, *supply chain risk management* (SCRM) has become a focus area for many organizations. New laws and regulations focus on all companies in the supply chain sharing the responsibility for a cyberattack, including fines and other legal ramifications. Recent executive orders and updates to laws and regulations have put the responsibility on all organizations to properly evaluate third-party entities.

5.7.1 Supply chain risk management practices

SCRM best practices provide a structured methodology for identifying, assessing, and mitigating risks across the supply chain. These practices are widely applicable, offering organizations across industries—whether healthcare, finance, or government—a universal approach to protecting sensitive information. By adopting SCRM methodologies, organizations can create a consistent framework that ensures robust cybersecurity measures are in place throughout their supply chain.

Identifying and prioritizing third-party relationships involves creating a catalog of all third-party providers, contractors, suppliers, vendors, and partners. Assessing the criticality and sensitivity of the data exchanged with these third parties can help prioritize risk management efforts. A healthcare provider would prioritize vendors handling patient data, while a financial company may prioritize third parties accessing sensitive bank account information.

Organizations must specify their security requirements to ensure alignment with third-party data handling. Ensuring third parties adhere to internal policy and procedures is part of the due diligence and due care required by companies dealing with highly sensitive information. In the financial and healthcare industries, SCRM requires implementing a combination of controls, such as defining minimum encryption standards and ensuring proper access control methods. These measures are critical across industries to safeguard sensitive data and maintain compliance with regulatory requirements.

THIRD-PARTY ASSESSMENTS

These assessments evaluate the security posture and alignment of third-party vendors with internal policies and procedures. Certifications such as HITRUST, SOC2, or ISO 27001 can be validated in lieu of a comprehensive security questionnaire. As an example of this type of assessment, a retail company may assess a supplier's defenses to mitigate risks of supply chain interruptions.

CONTRACTS AND SERVICE AGREEMENTS

Contracts and service agreements clearly state security expectations and incident handling procedures. They include the right to audit the vendor's security measures to ensure ongoing compliance. As an example, a technology company may require software providers to follow strict policies for patching and updates.

CONTINUOUS MONITORING STRATEGIES

Continuous monitoring should be implemented to adapt to emerging threats and ensure third-party compliance. While automation plays a critical role in streamlining monitoring efforts, an overreliance on automated tools without human oversight can lead to missed risks and false assumptions about security effectiveness. For example, in the energy sector, monitoring the security of smart grid suppliers helps prevent service disruptions.

INCIDENT RESPONSE COORDINATION

Incident response plans are to be coordinated with third parties to ensure preparedness and effective recovery from incidents. For example, a government agency might collaborate with its cloud providers to respond to potential data breaches.

ANNUAL REVIEW AND UPDATES

Review and update third-party risk management practices at least annually to address changing threats and business needs. Reassess third-party relationships regularly to ensure continued alignment and effectiveness.

EMPLOYEE EDUCATION AND AWARENESS

Train employees to reduce risks associated with third-party entities. For example, an educational institution may train staff to use third-party online learning platforms securely to minimize risks.

5.7.2 Cybersecurity supply chain risk management metrics

When collecting metrics on third-party entities, it is good practice to separate these based on criticality. Typically, we would only focus on critical third-party entities.

However, there have been numerous instances where a seemingly benign third-party entity allowed for a much more severe cybersecurity breach. The recommendation is to track all third parties, but track metrics based on criticality, which can then be combined for a complete picture.

DIRECT SCRM METRICS

These metrics provide quantifiable data to evaluate an organization's supply chain security, resilience, and compliance, offering clear data to assess risks and enhance mitigation efforts:

- *Number of third-party entities*—The total number of third parties that the organization is currently doing business with. This metric is used in conjunction with other metrics to better illustrate the magnitude of third-party risk management.
- *Number of evaluated third-party entities*—Measuring how many third parties have been fully evaluated against the organization's defined security and privacy standards gives insight into how well the organization is keeping pace with properly vetting third-party entities. If you fall behind, this could help determine whether you need more resources or it is a temporary spike given recent changes.
- *Number of third-party incidents per year*—Tracking the frequency of security-related incidents from third parties is essential for identifying vendors requiring more frequent security evaluations. If a specific vendor demonstrates increased incidents, it may signal the need to consider alternatives with a better track record to reduce risk. However, it is important to note that third parties may not always have a legal obligation to disclose incidents, depending on the industry or jurisdiction.

    For example, in healthcare, a Business Associate Agreement (BAA) under HIPAA requires third parties (business associates) to notify their covered entities of breaches involving protected health information. In other industries, similar contractual agreements should clearly outline the reporting requirements for security incidents.

    To mitigate this potential gap in visibility, organizations should include incident notification clauses in vendor agreements and establish robust monitoring and auditing practices to detect and trace incidents that may have originated from third-party vendors. This ensures transparency and allows for a proactive approach to third-party risk management.

DERIVED SCRM METRICS

The ratio of fully compliant third-party entities that meet or exceed the organization's defined security and privacy requirements is a good metric to help you determine the effectiveness of your third-party risk management process. Your goal would be 100%, but this evaluation may take time, especially in case of a vulnerability that is difficult to patch properly.

INDIRECT SCRM METRICS

If you can determine a method to aggregate scores from regular cybersecurity audits of third-party entities, it would help indicate their security posture, give you further insight into overall performance for risk reduction, and provide focus areas for further investigation.

5.7.3 Supply chain risk management metrics exercise

David's chain of produce stores, Foodie Fruits, has been a leading supplier of fruits and vegetables for years. Recently, customer demand for more exotic selections has increased, prompting David to consider working with a new third-party vendor. However, David is concerned about the robustness of his current cybersecurity measures. To address this, he evaluates the risk management practices associated with his existing third-party vendors to ensure they are sufficient before taking on a new vendor. The left side of figure 5.13 shows an example supply chain risk management dashboard illustrating some problems involving delayed compliance and inconsistent adherence to security standards.

Figure 5.13 On the left, Foodie Fruits' third-party supply chain risk dashboard indicates problems with delayed compliance and inconsistent adherence to security standards. On the right, the dashboard shows improvements in compliance and adherence to security standards.

Foodie Fruits has encountered several challenges with its third-party vendors, including delayed compliance and inconsistent adherence to security standards. David wants to ensure that these problems are resolved to protect his business from potential cybersecurity threats by setting the following targets:

- Achieve 100% compliance with security standards among third-party vendors.
- Improve the annual review process to achieve at least 90% completion.
- Ensure that 90% of third-party vendors are compliant when audited.

On the right side of figure 5.13, the third-party risk dashboard shows that nearly all third parties comply with Foodie Fruits' security standards, but the compliance rate is still not 100%. This discrepancy might be due to a delay in processing or a vendor working to close a compliance gap. David needs to investigate these cases further to ensure full compliance.

The dashboard shows that only 75% of annual reviews are completed, suggesting that Foodie Fruits may lack the necessary resources to keep up with the review process. This can indicate that additional staffing or process improvements are needed to manage the reviews more efficiently.

Only 80% of third-party vendors were compliant when audited. This could highlight a lapse in the third-party vendor review process or suggest that the frequency of audits needs to be increased to keep up with changing factors. Foodie Fruits can ensure a more consistent and reliable supply chain security posture by addressing these problems.

The third-party audit scores metric provides an overall assessment of the compliance and security posture of third-party vendors based on periodic audits. Higher scores indicate better compliance and security practices, while lower scores suggest areas needing improvement. Monitoring these scores helps identify vendors that may require additional support or corrective actions to meet Foodie Fruits' security requirements.

By focusing on these specific metrics, David can gain valuable insights into the effectiveness of his supply chain risk management efforts. This enables him to make informed decisions about resource allocation, process improvements, and vendor management, ultimately enhancing Foodie Fruits' overall cybersecurity resilience.

5.8 Governance metrics

Now that we have a clear understanding of governance and its categories, we can develop our direct and indirect metrics to see how measured cybersecurity can be used to make informed decisions. Keep in mind that while we could develop metrics for just about anything, not everything is worth tracking, and we want to maximize our time-to-benefit ratio and focus on what matters. To that end, we will focus on proven, industry best-practiced metrics. We will break down each category and discuss what metrics make the most sense and why. Then we can continue our journey as we delve deeper into other functions and categories and see how we can obtain more derived metrics for decision making.

5.9 Answer to exercise 5.6.3

Figure 5.14 shows the answers for our exercise in section 5.6.3, matching the role with the corresponding responsibility.

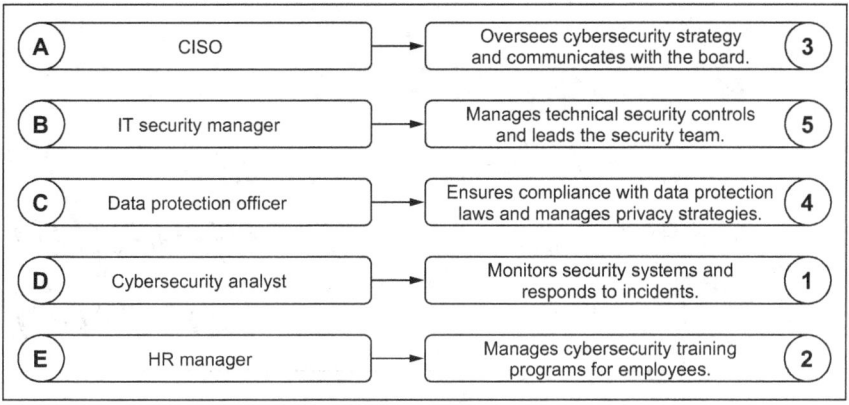

Figure 5.14 Answers to exercise in figure 5.10.

Summary

- Risk management involves defining acceptable risk levels and decision-making processes.
- Supply chain risk management ensures that external partners adhere to cybersecurity standards.
- Roles and responsibilities must be delineated to balance IT and security needs.
- Regular oversight, through assessment and audit, ensures continuous cybersecurity improvement.
- Risk assessments are crucial to understanding and mitigating organizational risks.
- Policies and procedures provide a structured approach to implementing and enforcing cybersecurity practices, which ensures consistency and compliance across the organization.

Foundations of cyber risk

This chapter covers
- Fundamentals of access management
- Evaluating and prioritizing risks
- Continuous refinement of security measures

A strong cybersecurity framework starts with a clear understanding of an organization's assets, possible risks, and how to continuously improve security measures. This chapter explores the critical aspects of asset management, risk evaluation, and security enhancement, providing a structured approach to identifying and mitigating threats before they affect business operations.

Asset management is the backbone of cybersecurity strategy, granting organizations clear visibility into their systems, data, and dependencies. Effective protection is nearly impossible without awareness of existing assets. This includes everything from hardware and software inventories to cloud resources and third-party dependencies.

Risk assessment complements asset management by evaluating the vulnerabilities, threats, and potential business effects of security incidents. Understanding the likelihood and consequences of various cyber threats allows organizations to prioritize security investments and allocate resources effectively. A structured risk assessment process ensures that security efforts align with business objectives, regulatory requirements, and evolving threat landscapes.

Beyond risk assessment, continuous improvement is vital in maintaining a resilient cybersecurity posture. Cyber threats are constantly evolving, and static security measures quickly become outdated. By employing data-driven security metrics, organizations can refine their strategies, measure the effectiveness of existing controls, and implement targeted improvements over time.

This chapter covers the fundamentals of asset management, risk evaluation, and continuous security enhancement. It also discusses the importance of proactive risk mitigation and how organizations can adapt their security frameworks to keep pace with emerging threats. Through real-world examples and best practices, the chapter illustrates how a structured security assessment and improvement approach can significantly reduce risk exposure and enhance overall cybersecurity resilience.

6.1 Identify

Knowing what you have is the prerequisite for knowing how to protect it. This information is essential for the initial phase of establishing a comprehensive cybersecurity strategy. Once you know what assets you have in your environment, do all of them need the same protection? This is the second question that needs to be answered as a foundational information-gathering exercise. Not every asset is critical. This is the groundwork completed in the identify function.

In cybersecurity, "identity" encompasses the following two primary categories:

- *Organizational assets*—These include physical hardware, software systems, data repositories, and intellectual property. Each asset has its own identity in the organization's ecosystem.
- *Individual identities*—These refer to the digital representations of people within your system, such as employees, contractors, customers, or other users interacting with your organizational assets. Each identity carries its own set of access rights, permissions, and potential security risks.

With this distinction in mind, the identity function in cybersecurity involves

- *Asset identification*—Cataloging all organizational assets described in the original text
- *Identity management*—Mapping out all individual identities that have access to your systems, as well as their roles and their levels of access
- *Relationship mapping*—Understanding how individual identities interact with organizational assets

Addressing both organizational assets and individual identities creates a more comprehensive picture of your cybersecurity landscape. This dual focus allows for more nuanced risk assessment and targeted protection strategies.

In the initial phase, it is necessary to understand which organizational assets require heightened protection and why. This step involves cataloging assets, systems, and data. The goal is to understand the business context of each asset and identify the potential cybersecurity effects of threats to better assess the overall risk landscape, which will help you prioritize your activities, allocate resources more effectively, and design cybersecurity solutions to specific needs and challenges based on the criticality of your assets.

6.2 Asset management

Asset management is a daunting task that is often overlooked. It involves systematically identifying, classifying, and administering organizational assets throughout their life cycle, which includes physical devices, systems, software applications, data, and intellectual property.

There are five phases of an asset life cycle, as shown in figure 6.1. Each stage of the asset life cycle must be carefully addressed to uphold the appropriate levels of security and privacy, aligned with the assets' sensitivity and importance.

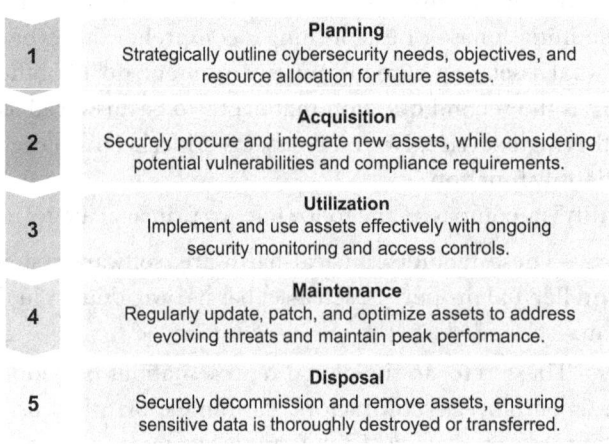

Figure 6.1 Managing cybersecurity risk in all life cycle phases—from conception to destruction

Organizations should outline the necessary specifications and security requirements during the planning stage or the acquisition of new assets. This approach ensures that future acquisitions align with the cybersecurity policies and business objectives. During the planning phase, you would define the roles and responsibilities associated with the asset, conduct a risk assessment to understand potential cybersecurity risks, and establish a set of security controls and compliance requirements the asset should adhere to.

When procuring an asset, to prevent vulnerabilities, organizations must verify it meets the specifications outlined in the planning phase. This step includes validating off-the-shelf products, which ensures custom assets are designed and developed following secure coding practices, as well as assessing third-party vendors and suppliers for security compliance.

When deploying an asset within the organization, its usage must align with established security standards to maintain the security integrity. Properly configuring assets, instantiating access controls, and training users are key utilization aspects. Key considerations include meeting least privilege principles, monitoring usage to detect unauthorized access or malicious activity, and training users on security best practices. The principle of least privilege states that only the minimum authority is given to users to use the asset. For example, a laptop user does not need to be an administrator who could install possibly malicious software.

During the maintenance phase, it is necessary to update, patch, audit, and address vulnerabilities regularly. These functions present potential attack vectors, such as installing a patch that did not come from the software's authorized distributor. Reviewing and adjusting security controls to maintain baseline requirements is another important aspect of the maintenance phase.

Disposing of assets marks the end of the asset life cycle. Disposal must also be carried out securely to ensure sensitive information cannot be recovered. This would include wiping or physically destroying the asset, making sure software and digital records are unrecoverable, and properly documenting the disposal process for compliance and audit purposes.

6.2.1 Asset management metrics

Asset management metrics are good indicators of an organization's inventory and risk profile. By measuring and analyzing these metrics, organizations can prioritize their security efforts, allocate resources efficiently, and maintain accurate records, which can help minimize the risk of downtime or data breaches and improve overall cybersecurity resilience.

DIRECT ASSET MANAGEMENT METRICS

Direct asset management metrics are used to evaluate the following:

- *Critical hardware assets*—Essential physical devices such as servers, firewalls, or medical equipment (i.e., the hardware you need to run your business, without which functional operation would be impossible). For example, an MRI machine would be considered a critical hardware asset to an imaging clinic because it stores and processes sensitive patient data.
- *Critical software assets*—The number of vital applications, such as databases, operating systems, or software, that process your orders, handle confidential information, or are crucial to business activities. A financial organization trading platform may be considered critical due to the sensitive financial data and processing of stock sales.
- *Total hardware assets*—All critical and noncritical hardware assets, including computers, printers, and other peripherals.
- *Total software assets*—All critical and noncritical software assets approved for use as part of daily operations.

DERIVED ASSET MANAGEMENT METRICS

These types of metrics include

- *Ratio of critical to total hardware assets*—Indicates the proportion of critical hardware assets compared to the total inventory. A company with 100 total hardware assets and 30 critical assets has a ratio of 30%.
- *Ratio of critical to total software assets*—Indicates the percentage of critical to total software assets. For an organization with 500 total software assets and 150 critical assets, the ratio is 30%.

6.2.2 Asset management metrics exercise

Let's consider TechMed Solutions, a leading provider of innovative medical technology solutions. They supply hospitals and clinics with cutting-edge equipment and software to manage patient data and support critical medical procedures. Recently, TechMed Solutions has been focusing on enhancing its cybersecurity posture to protect sensitive patient information and ensure the continuous operation of its critical systems.

TechMed Solutions has implemented a comprehensive asset management strategy to monitor and protect their hardware and software assets. By doing so, they aim to minimize downtime, prevent data breaches, and ensure that their medical devices and software are always up-to-date and secure. On the left side of figure 6.2, TechMed Solutions' asset management dashboard provides a clear overview of their hardware and software assets.

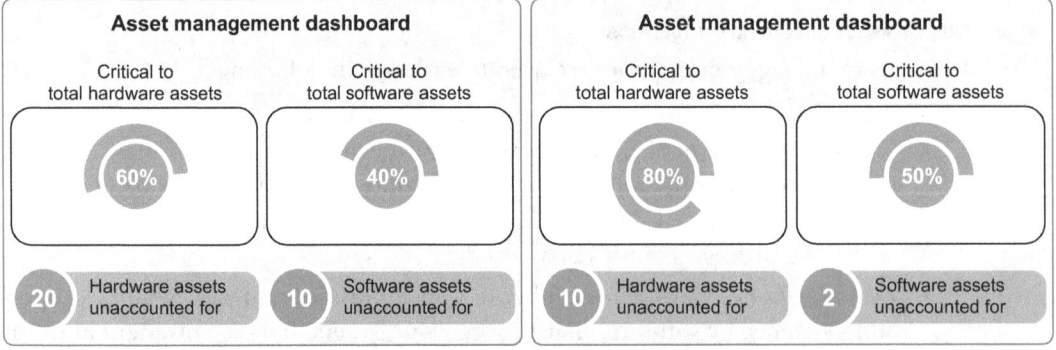

Figure 6.2 The left side shows TechMed Solutions' asset management dashboard before managing hardware and software assets. The right side shows the dashboard after implementing hardware and software asset management.

TechMed Solutions faced a significant challenge last year when an outdated piece of equipment caused a critical system failure, affecting patient care. To prevent such incidents, they have set specific targets:

- Achieve 100% accountability for all hardware and software assets.
- Ensure that 90% of hardware assets and 70% of software assets are classified as critical.
- Reduce the number of unaccounted assets to zero.

On the right side of figure 6.2, TechMed Solutions' asset management dashboard provides a clear overview of their hardware and software assets. The dashboard reveals that 80% of their hardware assets are classified as critical. This high percentage highlights the importance of focusing cybersecurity efforts on these essential systems to maintain operational integrity and patient safety. Additionally, 50% of their software assets are considered critical, indicating a balanced approach to managing and securing critical and non-critical software to ensure comprehensive protection across the organization.

To achieve these improvements, TechMed Solutions conducted an inventory audit to warrant complete accountability of all assets. They implemented automated asset-tracking tools that enabled real-time hardware and software monitoring, which significantly reduced the likelihood of unaccounted assets. Additionally, they classified assets based on criticality and focused on securing those deemed most vital. This move involved updating and patching critical systems regularly and establishing clear protocols for managing noncritical assets. Regular audits and reviews of asset management practices were also instituted to ensure that all systems remained up-to-date and secure, ultimately improving the organization's overall cybersecurity posture.

The dashboard also shows that 10 hardware systems and two software assets are unaccounted for, which is a red flag for TechMed Solutions. These unaccounted assets need to be promptly investigated and located, as they can pose significant security risks if not updated, patched, or properly secured. By continuously monitoring these metrics, TechMed Solutions can make informed decisions about resource allocation, risk management, and security measures, ultimately enhancing their cybersecurity resilience and protecting sensitive patient data.

TechMed Solutions should prioritize securing 80% of critical hardware assets and 50% of critical software assets to maintain operational integrity. Investigating and accounting for the untracked 10 hardware systems and two software assets is crucial for closing potential security gaps. Regular audits and updates of the asset management dashboard will guarantee ongoing protection and help maintain cybersecurity resilience.

6.3 Risk assessments

To properly identify, analyze, and evaluate organizational risks, we need a framework or methodology to ensure consistency and repeatability. A proactive approach to risk identification and handling is important to help inform and guide cybersecurity decision-making. Risk assessments identify risks, potential threats, and vulnerabilities, and determine the likelihood, exploitability, and effects of these risks. This information conveys what mitigation controls would be best to implement, as well as their priority, and it helps identify any residual risks. Most industry best practices for conducting risk assessments follow a similar methodology, but here we will take a closer look at NIST's 800-30 guide for conducting risk assessments.

6.3.1 NIST 800-30: Guide for conducting risk assessments

Figure 6.3 shows that NIST 800-30 steps are using a widely adopted framework for conducting and reporting on risk assessments. Risk assessments can be done on a product, a change, a new implementation, critical assets, office locations, data centers, or the organization. Setting the scope of the risk assessment is key to focusing the efforts of the risk assessment so you don't encounter scope creep, where you start to analyze one area, but end up analyzing attached systems and cloud the results. Along with detailing the scope of the risk assessment, you must clearly define the assets associated with the scope. Assets should define the boundaries, systems, and data. All of this is done during the preparation phase.

Once we know what we are focused on, we can define the potential threats and events that introduce risk. It's essential to avoid "Hollywood" threats—those exaggerated, sensational scenarios—and instead focus on realistic, current, and potential threats relevant to your organization.

This book does not cover identifying threats or conducting a complete threat assessment. For readers interested in learning these foundational skills, resources such as NIST's Cybersecurity Framework or the MITRE ATT&CK Framework provide excellent guidance on identifying and understanding potential threats.

Next, you need to determine the vulnerabilities. This can be done programmatically via software analysis and comparison with known vulnerabilities using Common Vulnerabilities and Exposures (CVEs; https://cve.org), a comprehensive list of all known vulnerabilities compiled worldwide. Here you can find many details about CVEs, including recommendations on how to address them.

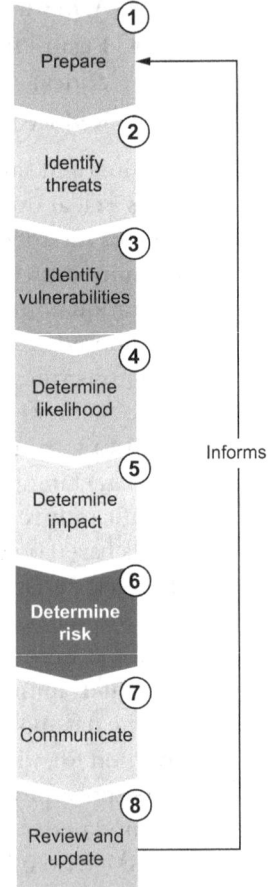

Figure 6.3 Guide for conducting risk assessments

Not all vulnerabilities for all organizations have a CVE. However, they are widely recognized and provide a comprehensive database of known vulnerabilities for publicly reported software and hardware. They primarily focus on vulnerabilities in widely used systems and applications, leaving some organization-specific or proprietary vulnerabilities unaddressed. For example, vulnerabilities in custom-built software, internal systems, or niche platforms may not have a CVE entry.

In addition to using CVEs, organizations should conduct internal vulnerability assessments to identify problems specific to their environments. Tools such as penetration testing, source code analysis, and configuration reviews complement CVE-based assessments by uncovering vulnerabilities that may not be publicly cataloged. Combining CVE resources with these methods ensures a more holistic approach to identifying and mitigating vulnerabilities.

Once you have an idea of the threat and any vulnerabilities, you can better determine the likelihood of occurrence. You could use the Common Vulnerability Scoring System (CVSS; https://www.first.org/cvss), which assigns a number from 1 to 10, based on the CVE severity. However, it should be used only as a guide. Not every CVSS for a known CVE will be a one-to-one translation in your environment. Perhaps you have compensating controls (i.e., controls implemented to reduce the risk of exposure) or perhaps you have layered security (i.e., more than one control in place, making it more difficult to exploit.) Determining the likelihood of occurrence may depend on the velocity of vulnerability. In other words, has an exploit been developed and published, thereby increasing the chances of vulnerability being exploited? For more info, you can refer to the Exploit Prediction Scoring System (EPSS; https://www.first.org/epss/). This system provides an estimate of the likelihood that vulnerability will be exploited in the wild.

Using CVSS can indeed be complex as it involves analyzing multiple factors to assess the severity and potential effect of vulnerabilities. To gain a deeper understanding and learn how to apply CVSS effectively, you can explore the resources and documentation available on the official CVSS website at https://www.first.org/cvss. This site provides comprehensive guides, examples, and tools for calculating CVSS scores.

Many cybersecurity training platforms, such as SANS Institute (https://www.sans.org/) and Cybrary (https://www.cybrary.it/), also offer courses and tutorials specifically covering vulnerability scoring and risk assessment methodologies. For hands-on practice, using vulnerability management tools such as Nessus, Qualys, or Rapid7 InsightVM can provide real-world experience using CVSS as part of a broader risk assessment strategy.

The last piece of the formula for risk is impact. The *impact* is possible damage if a threat actor exploits a vulnerability to realize a threat. By knowing this, you can determine your risk: Risk = Likelihood x Impact. But wait, how do we measure these values? Typically, you would use either a qualitative or a quantitative method to measure them. Qualitative methods involve educated guesses based on expert judgment, historical data, and experience, often translating them into numbers within a matrix for easier comparison and decision-making, as shown in figure 6.4. However, quantitative methods use numerical data and statistical models to provide a more precise measurement of risk. This can include detailed financial analysis, probability distributions, and other statistical techniques to quantify both likelihood and impact more rigorously.

The idea is to stay within an acceptable range, such as medium or low. For example, if your likelihood of an incident is medium and the impact is high, your risk would be high. If your likelihood is critical and your impact is negligible, your resulting risk would still be high. Finally, if your likelihood is low and the impact is low, your resulting

Risk		Impact				
		Critical	High	Medium	Low	Negligible
Likelihood	Critical	C	C	C	H	H
	High	C	H	H	M	M
	Medium	H	H	M	M	L
	Low	H	M	M	L	L
	Negligible	M	L	L	N	N

Figure 6.4 Visualizing threat likelihood and impact for effective risk management

risk would be negligible. You don't have to use this specific matrix—design one that best fits your organizational needs and context, considering qualitative insights and quantitative data for a comprehensive risk assessment.

6.3.2 Risk assessment metrics

Risk assessment metrics provide a structured approach to evaluating cybersecurity risks across various scopes—including software, operations, office environments—and infrastructure. While certain metrics can be universally applied across all risk categories, context matters when assessing vulnerabilities, particularly in software and hardware environments.

One common pitfall in risk assessments is overreliance on CVSS scores. While CVSS provides a standardized way to assess severity, it does not account for exploitability or business effects. Not every vulnerability with a high CVSS score should be classified as high risk in your environment. Prioritization must consider real-world exploitability and the potential effect on business operations to avoid unnecessary correction efforts on low-risk vulnerabilities, while missing critical threats.

To improve prioritization, organizations should incorporate:

- *Exploit Prediction Scoring System (EPSS)*—This system provides a probability score that estimates the likelihood of a vulnerability being exploited in the wild. By using EPSS, security teams can focus on vulnerabilities that pose an immediate and real risk, rather than just those with a high CVSS score.
- *Threat intelligence feeds*—Correlating vulnerabilities with active threat intelligence (e.g., known exploits in the MITRE ATT&CK framework) helps determine whether attackers are currently targeting a vulnerability.
- *Business impact analysis*—A vulnerability in a mission-critical system (e.g., a production database) should be prioritized over an equally severe problem in

a low-risk test environment. Business context should always guide corrective efforts.

- *Compensating controls assessment*—A high-risk vulnerability in a system protected by network segmentation, strict access controls, and monitoring may pose less immediate risk than a moderate vulnerability in an exposed external-facing system.

By shifting from a CVSS-only approach to a risk-based prioritization strategy, organizations can more effectively allocate resources, reduce risk exposure, and prevent wasting time on vulnerabilities that are unlikely to be exploited, while ensuring truly critical threats are addressed first.

DIRECT RISK ASSESSMENT METRICS (VULNERABILITIES)

We can run risk assessments on many different scopes, including software, operations, offices, infrastructures, and so on. Some metrics in this category can be universal for all types of risk. However, when dealing with vulnerabilities, typically in software and hardware, a few metrics can be beneficial in defining context. Not every vulnerability with a high CVSS score should necessarily be considered high risk in your environment.

When researching and evaluating CVE, you would typically want to mitigate the scores that are the least difficult or expensive to implement with the highest risk reduction. Figure 6.5 illustrates that the risks that fall in the darker square—high-risk level with low effort/cost, are the risks we should prioritize.

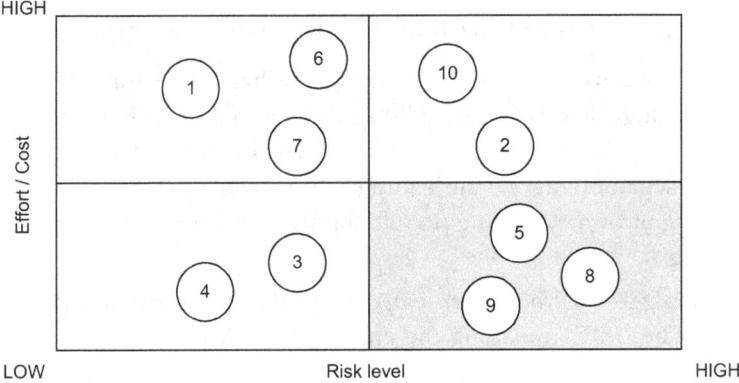

Figure 6.5 The vulnerabilities in the darker area are the ones that represent the lowest effort/cost vs. the highest risk level. These are the vulnerabilities that should be addressed as a priority.

These types of metrics include

- *Common Vulnerability Scoring System (CVSS)*—An open standard for assessing the severity of computer system vulnerabilities. It provides a numerical score ranging from 0 to 10, with higher scores indicating greater severity. CVSS scores are based on factors such as attack vectors, attack complexity, required privileges, and effects on confidentiality, integrity, and availability.

- *EPSS exposure*—These ratings assess the potential effects and likelihood of specific threats or vulnerabilities affecting an organization's assets or systems. They help prioritize correction efforts based on the level of risk exposure.
- *Mean time to detect (MTTD)*—Measures the average time to identify and detect a security incident or breach. Lower MTTD indicates better security monitoring and detection capabilities.
- *Mean time to respond (MTTR)*—Measures the average time to respond to and mitigate a detected security incident. Lower MTTR reflects more efficient incident response processes.
- *Mean time to contain (MTTC)*—The average time it takes an organization to contain an incident, limiting its effect on the system or data. Shorter times indicate more effective management of incidents, while longer times show room for improvement.
- *Mean time to report (MTTR)*—The time it takes to report a cybersecurity incident to relevant authorities or stakeholders. Shorter times indicate a quick response, while longer times would indicate better communication methods are required.

DERIVED RISK ASSESSMENT METRICS

Annual loss expectancy (ALE) is a key metric used to quantify an organization's expected financial loss due to a specific risk or threat. It is calculated as

$$ALE = \text{Single loss expectancy (SLE)} \times \text{Annual rate of occurrence (ARO)}$$

Understanding the exposure factor (EF) is critical when calculating ALE because it directly affects the single loss expectancy (SLE) calculation. The EF represents the percentage of an asset's value that would be lost if a specific security incident occurred. The overall risk calculation may be misleading without accurately assessing EF, leading to underestimating or overestimating potential losses. To determine EF properly, consider the following:

- *Extent of damage*—If a cyberattack leads to total data loss without backup recovery, the EF may be 100% (meaning the entire asset is lost). If a ransomware attack only disrupts operations for a short period, but no permanent data loss occurs, the EF may be much lower.
- *Asset type and recoverability*—A customer database might have a higher EF than an individual workstation, because losing customer data could lead to severe financial and reputational damage, while a workstation can be easily replaced.
- *Mitigation factors*—The presence of redundancies, backups, and compensating security controls can reduce EF. For example, an encrypted laptop stolen from an employee may have an EF of 10% rather than 100%, because encryption prevents data exposure.

To calculate ALE, it is necessary to identify the asset first and determine its value (asset value or AV). Next, we determine the EF as the percentage of AV that would be lost in an incident. ARO represents the estimated likelihood of a security incident or threat event occurring in one year. To calculate ARO, we need to determine the number of expected incidents per year and express the ARO as a decimal between 0 and 1. The formula for ARO is

$$ARO = \text{Number of incidents} / \text{Year}$$

For example, if the expected number of incidents per year = 0.5 (once every two years), then the ARO = 0.5 / 1 = 0.5. You would then calculate the SLE as

$$SLE = AV \times EF$$

The key challenges in calculating SLE and ARO include accurately estimating asset values and exposure factors, obtaining reliable historical data on security incidents and their frequency, accounting for uncertainty and unpredictable events that may influence the likelihood of occurrence, and ensuring the data and assumptions used are up-to-date and representative of the organization's risk profile. By determining the SLE and ARO, organizations can calculate the ALE, a critical metric for quantifying and managing information security risks.

Here is an example use case. Consider a financial organization called ACME Trading, which has a critical web application that processes online transactions. The application is supported by two redundant servers to ensure high availability. If one server goes down, the other can handle the transactions. If the transaction rate increases, both servers can handle increased traffic. However, an advanced persistent threat (APT) group has targeted this application and is issuing a denial of service (DoS) attack by flooding the server with requests. This causes the one server to crash.

We have a service-level agreement with our customer that our services will be available 99.9% of the time. This incident will cause a 0.1% decrease in availability.

ACME Trading knows the SLE could be the revenue lost during server downtime, customer dissatisfaction, and potential reputational damage. They estimate the cost of a single hour of downtime at $100,000.

ACME Trading also knows that historical data indicates that a similar DoS attack will occur on average once every two years, so the ARO would be 0.5 incidents per year. By calculating the SLE and ARO, we can calculate the ALE, which would be $100,000 x 0.5 = $50,000:

- *Risk exposure score (RES)*—Combines the likelihood of a threat event occurring with its potential effects or consequences. It helps organizations prioritize their security efforts based on the level of risk exposure.
- *Residual risk*—Measures the risk that remains after implementing risk mitigation measures or controls. It represents the level of risk an organization is willing to accept or unable to eliminate.

- *Single loss expectancy (SLE)*—The estimated monetary loss from a single security incident or threat event.
- *Annual rate of occurrence (ARO)*—The estimated likelihood of a security incident or threat event occurring within one year.
- *Annualized loss expectancy (ALE)*—Calculates the expected financial loss owing to a particular risk over one year. It considers the potential loss magnitude (single loss exposure), the probability of the risk occurring, and the frequency of occurrence.

6.3.3 Risk assessment metrics exercise

Three years ago, TechMed Solutions, a leading provider of innovative medical technology solutions, faced significant cybersecurity challenges. During an industry-wide rise in healthcare cyberattacks, an initial audit revealed substantial gaps in their cybersecurity framework, highlighting the need for a comprehensive risk assessment strategy. The company struggled with numerous critical vulnerabilities and inefficiencies in its response times, leading to a heightened risk of data breaches and operational disruptions. Recognizing the urgent need for improvement, TechMed Solutions implemented a detailed risk assessment dashboard to monitor and manage vulnerabilities within its flagship software. The left side of figure 6.6 shows TechMed Solutions' risk assessment metrics before implementing a detailed risk assessment management program.

TechMed Solutions set specific targets for each metric to measure their progress effectively. The targets were defined as follows:

- *Critical vulnerabilities*—Target reduction to below 10
- *High vulnerabilities*—Target reduction to below 25
- *Medium vulnerabilities*—Target reduction to below 20
- *Low vulnerabilities*—Target reduction to below 15
- *Informational vulnerabilities*—Target reduction to below 30
- *MTTD (mean time to detect)*—Target set to 6 hours or less
- *MTTR (mean time to respond)*—Target set to 2 hours or less
- *MTTC (mean time to contain)*—Target set to 1 hour or less
- *MTTR (mean time to report)*—Target set to 2 hours or less

The right side of figure 6.6 shows TechMed Solutions' metrics after implementing a risk management program. The significant reduction in vulnerabilities, particularly critical and high ones, demonstrates that TechMed Solutions' focused patch management and risk mitigation efforts have paid off. However, the 20 high vulnerabilities still require prioritized action to maintain robust security.

The improved mean time in hours reflects better incident detection and response processes. The MTTD of 6 hours and MTTC of 1 hour are commendable, indicating swift identification and containment of incidents. Although improved, the MTTR of 2

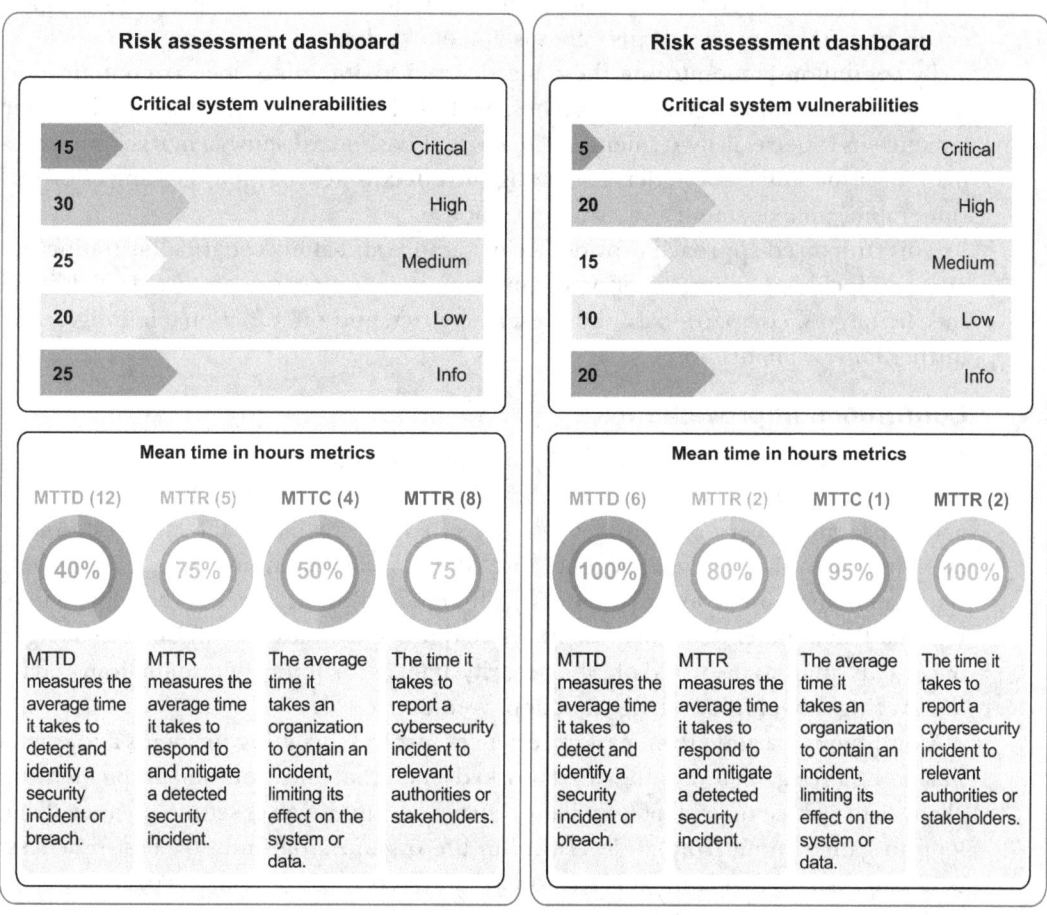

Figure 6.6 On the left, the TechMed risk assessment dashboard before the risk management program is implemented. In this figure, the bottom metrics are displayed as a percentage to indicate the percentage of incidents that were within the predefined target of hours. For example, 40% of the incidents were detected within the 12-hour target detection time. On the right, the risk assessment dashboard after implementing the risk management program.

hours still falls short of the desired 100% target. This metric suggests a need for further streamlining response protocols to ensure all incidents are mitigated promptly.

To achieve these improvements, TechMed Solutions began implementing a patch management program to address critical and high vulnerabilities, focusing on timely updates and coordination with software vendors. They also enhanced their incident detection and response protocols by deploying automated monitoring tools, allowing faster identification and containment of threats. The company invested in continuous training for its security team to ensure quick and accurate incident response, contributing to the reduction in MTTD, MTTC, and MTTR metrics. These efforts were complemented by regular reviews and adjustments to their risk management strategies, ensuring that the improvements were sustained over time.

By continuously monitoring these metrics and maintaining open communication with software vendors for timely patches, TechMed Solutions can sustain and further enhance its cybersecurity resilience. The current dashboard shows a marked improvement over the initial audit, demonstrating the effectiveness of their ongoing efforts in vulnerability management and incident response.

This structured approach provides a clear before-and-after scenario, illustrating the effect of TechMed Solutions' efforts to improve its cybersecurity posture. It highlights specific targets, compares past and present metrics, and offers actionable insights for further improvements.

6.4 Continuous improvement

Cybersecurity is not a static field. It requires ongoing adaptation and refinement. Continuous improvement aims to establish and maintain a cycle of evaluating, learning, and enhancing cybersecurity practices. The cybersecurity landscape changes rapidly, even more so with the advent of generative AI. It is a cat-and-mouse game of red teams (attackers) and blue teams (defenders), ebbing and flowing in a never-ending game. It is said that as defenders, we must always be right, and attackers only need to be right once. This sums up the world of cybersecurity. It takes fortitude, determination, and an unwavering thirst for knowledge and improvement.

Continuous learning from past experiences involves analyzing incidents and events that went wrong, determining what worked and what did not, and implementing changes to reduce the risk of a similar occurrence. This involves setting up a feedback loop to gather input from all levels within the organization, industry best practices, benchmarks, and regulatory updates to stay informed and have a means of adapting.

This could include updating policy and procedures, implementing new or updated controls, or developing new teams to better manage cybersecurity risks. A large part of this involves measuring performance, which can help you make better decisions about where to focus your resources.

Training and awareness are key aspects of this effort toward continuous improvement. Organizations should conduct regular reviews and use risk assessments to identify and manage risk and focus on areas of improvement, training, and awareness. This is a cultural as well as a technical implementation.

6.4.1 Continuous improvement metrics

Here, we focus on metrics that gauge the progressive enhancement of an organization's cybersecurity practices. These continuous improvement metrics measure the ongoing development and refinement of security strategies, ensuring that these strategies adapt to emerging threats and organizational changes. By tracking these metrics, organizations can gain insight into strengths and areas for growth, fostering an environment of perpetual advancement. This section explores the key metrics organizations can use to track their continuous improvement efforts in cybersecurity, thus providing a clear pathway for sustained development in their security posture.

DIRECT CONTINUOUS IMPROVEMENT METRICS

These metrics involve

- *Security awareness and training metrics*—Measure the effectiveness of security awareness and training programs, such as the percentage of employees trained, the frequency of training sessions, and the results of phishing simulations.
- *Percentage of employees trained*—It should be implemented within the first months of employment as part of onboarding and then annually after that. Keeping track of this metric will ensure that you don't fall behind, and when you are not at 100%, you can focus on full compliance.
- *Phishing simulation results*—This metric can assess the effectiveness of your phishing simulations, where mock emails are sent to employees, and you receive data on how many emails were marked spam, how many were opened, how many were clicked, and how many employees placed compromising data as requested by the simulation. It should be implemented quarterly, with mandatory retraining on any failure. In addition, the retraining should be conducted in the event of an employee failing the phishing simulation.
- *Security control effectiveness*—These metrics assess the performance and effectiveness of implemented security controls, such as the percentage of systems with up-to-date antivirus software, the effectiveness of firewalls in blocking malicious traffic, and the coverage of data encryption.
- *Percentage of systems with up-to-date antivirus software*—Typically, this metric would be automated so that all machines are mandated to install, run, update, and scan periodically to ensure that you catch any malware or viruses promptly. However, we have seen instances where people delay updates. This metric can help you enforce 100% compliance.
- *Firewall effectiveness*—Firewall rules should be reviewed, and log analysis for suspicious behavior should be done quarterly. If you have continuous system monitoring via an SIEM or SOAR, you may validate this more often when dealing with alerts. SIEM is a security information and event management tool that alerts you when suspicious behavior is detected. A SOAR is a security orchestration, automation, and response system that can be used to act immediately rather than send an alert for further investigation.
- *Data encryption coverage*—With system baselining, encryption should be mandatory and turned on by default, with the user unable to disable or remove this protection. You should strive for 100% compliance with this metric. Tracking it can alert you to any machine that falls outside this goal. We have seen in the news more than one occasion of laptops being left or stolen with sensitive information on the drive that was compromised.

- *Compliance metrics*—Measure an organization's compliance with relevant security standards, regulations, and best practices, such as the percentage of systems compliant with security baselines, the number of audit findings resolved, and the time to achieve compliance.
- *Number of audit findings resolved*—This metric can help you remain compliant with laws and regulations and any certifications you may have. You want to ensure all audit findings are resolved within a reasonable time frame. Tracking the success rate with this metric can help you stay on track.
- *Time to achieve compliance*—Tracks how long it takes for an organization to comply with relevant security standards, regulations, or best practices. It is a general metric that can help you report on how effective your team has been in achieving these goals.
- *Continuous improvement metrics*—Evaluate the overall effectiveness of an organization's continuous improvement processes, such as the number of security process improvements implemented, the time to implement improvements, and the measurable effects of improvements on security posture.
- *Number of security process improvements implemented*—Another tool to report achievements over a given period, which can help reflect the commitment to ongoing improvement.
- *Time to implement improvements*—Reflects the improvement process by tracking security control implementation over a period and/or in response to emerging threats.
- *Measurable effects of improvements on security posture*—The quantifiable effect which security process improvements have on the overall security posture, reflecting the value of continuous improvement efforts.

6.5 Identity metrics exercise

Let's revisit our financial company, Acme Trading, and analyze their identity cybersecurity dashboard presented in figure 6.7. The dashboard reveals that Acme Trading has a critical hardware asset ratio of 25%, indicating that a quarter of their hardware assets are deemed critical to their operations. It is essential to ensure that the budget allocated for securing these critical assets is sufficient. The dashboard would typically also include a detailed table listing all assets, with information on their location, usage, and criticality.

The critical software ratio stands at 33%, suggesting that Acme Trading has either increased its total software inventory or decreased the use of critical software. This metric provides insight into the software landscape and helps plan security measures accordingly.

Regarding vulnerabilities, the dashboard shows an increase, with a current count of 15 vulnerabilities, out of which 2 have high EPSS scores. These high-EPSS vulnerabilities should be prioritized for resolution. Using the risk level graph, we observe that

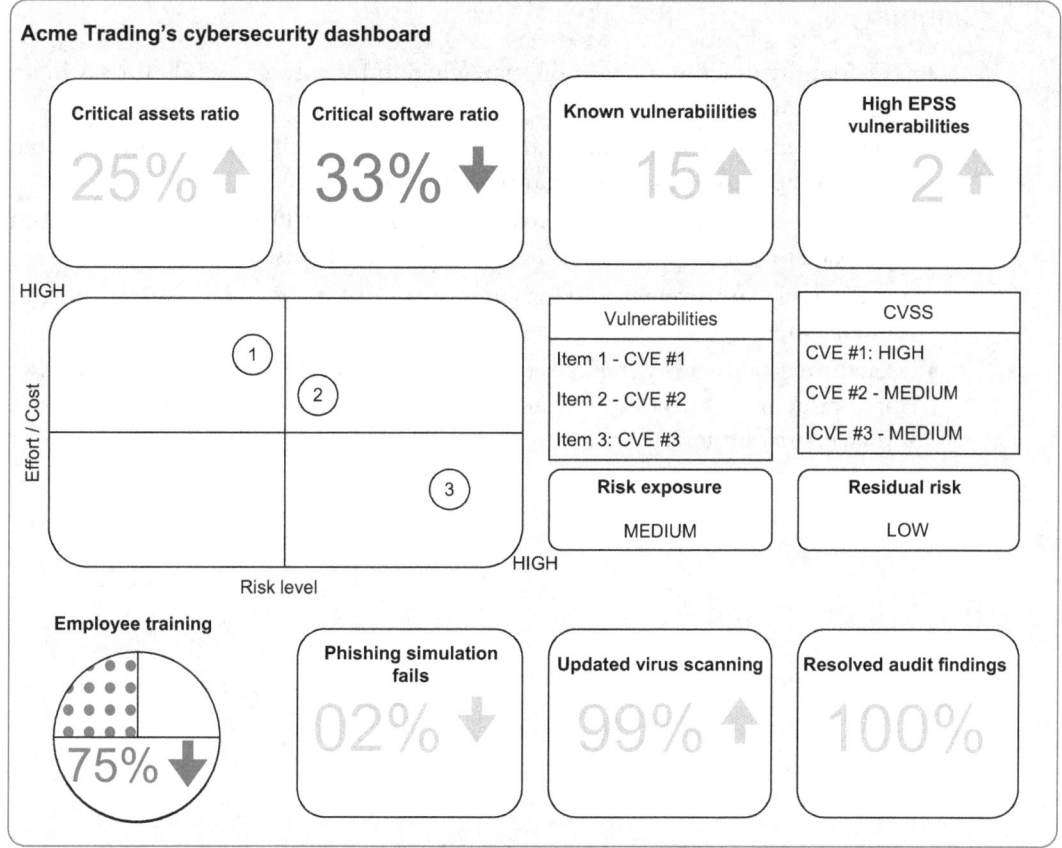

Figure 6.7 Acme Trading's identity cybersecurity dashboard

although CVE #3 has a medium CVSS score; it poses the highest risk and requires the least effort to mitigate. Addressing this vulnerability first can significantly reduce overall risk exposure, leaving only a medium residual risk. Tracking trends in vulnerability counts and correction times is essential to assess the effectiveness of ongoing security measures.

In the continuous improvement section, employee training completion has dropped to 75%, indicating that some employees have not completed mandatory training. Investigating and addressing this gap is crucial to achieving a 100% training completion rate. The phishing simulation failure rate is down to 2%, which, while not perfect, shows a positive trend. Implementing mandatory retraining can reduce this rate further, thus enhancing email security awareness.

The virus scanning metric is at 99% and improving, and 100% of audit findings have been resolved. Having these metrics in a single dashboard provides a comprehensive view of Acme Trading's cybersecurity posture, aiding in reporting and improving its security efforts and maturity.

Summary

- The identity function focuses on managing and securing assets and risks in an organization.
- Comprehensive risk assessments are conducted to identify and mitigate potential vulnerabilities and threats to organizational security.
- Adopting guidelines such as those from NIST 800-30 provides a structured approach to conducting comprehensive risk assessments.
- Continuous improvement in cybersecurity involves regular evaluation and enhancement of security measures and practices.
- A mature cybersecurity stance requires integrating identity management, asset management, risk assessment, and continuous improvement into a cohesive cybersecurity strategy.

Protecting your assets

This chapter covers
- Identity and credential access management
- The role of training in cybersecurity risk management
- Best practices for data confidentiality and integrity
- Resilience and security in technology infrastructure

Imagine your company data as a vault filled with gold. Data security is like a high-tech security system for that vault. It uses multiple layers of protection to keep the gold (data) safe from anyone who tries to steal it.

First, there are strict rules about who can enter the vault (access control). Then there are alarms, cameras, and even laser grids (firewalls, antivirus) to stop anyone who tries to break in. But what about the people who already have access (employees)? They need to be trained like security guards to spot suspicious activity (security awareness training).

Data security isn't a one-time thing, either. The security system needs regular updates and maintenance to stay ahead of new threats. Just like a vault wouldn't use outdated locks, your data security needs to be constantly improved.

In short, data security is a comprehensive strategy that protects your valuable information at every step, from when it's stored (data at rest) to when it's being used. Let's dive deeper and see how each security system layer works!

7.1 Identity management, authentication, and access control

Identity management (IdM) is a foundational process in which organizations manage individuals' identification, authentication, and authorization to access data, systems, and resources. It encompasses not only the policies and procedures but also the technologies required to ensure the right individuals have the appropriate access at the right times, in the right locations, and for the right reasons. IdM serves as a digital gatekeeper, ensuring that critical assets are accessible only to those with clear permissions.

The identity life cycle management (ILM) in table 7.1 is the core approach to managing user identities throughout their lifespan. ILM includes creating of an identity when an employee is onboarded, managing changes to that identity as the employee's role evolves, and ultimately deactivating that identity when the employee is offboarded. ILM ensures access privileges are accurately granted and promptly revoked when no longer required. This life cycle management maintains control over who has access to the company resources, thus minimizing the risks of insider threats and maintaining regulatory compliance.

Table 7.1 Stages of identity life cycle management

Create user	Assign access	Provision identity	Manage identity	Offboard identity
Document roles and attributes. Align onboarding exceptions.	Create an access matrix. Define attributes. Create a cadence of review.	Understand the best route for each resource. Use SAML, SCIM, LDAP, agents, and APIs. Map attributes downstream.	Define the standard method of access. Collaborate with department leaders. Log and document changes.	Use a centralized directory. Schedule suspensions to revoke access.

Centralized identity management systems are necessary to streamline and secure the identity management process. These systems provide a single reference point for managing identities across the organization. In addition, the systems are integrated with various directories, databases, and applications. By centralizing identity management, organizations can enforce consistent access policies, reduce administrative overhead, and provide a single source of truth for auditing and compliance. These systems can scale with the organizational needs and respond to user changes, roles, access requirements, or organizational and technology changes. A centralized approach to IdM enables secure and efficient business operations, allowing organizations to keep pace with changes.

7.1.1 Authentication

Authentication mechanisms are required to verify the identity of users, services, or hardware before granting access. These mechanisms involve traditional passwords, biometrics, and new passwordless technologies. Passwordless technologies are slow to adopt, although there is a significant push in the cybersecurity community for more alignment with zero trust architecture, which includes passwordless technologies. Each has its own level of security and user experience.

Password-based authentication has been the most used digital identity verification for decades. Despite its popularity, passwords have significant vulnerabilities, such as theft, phishing attacks, or brute force cracking. Passwords are also known for their common usage and usage across accounts. For example, "123456," "Abc123," and "password123" have shown up as the most used passwords over the last decade. Not only do users still use these common and very weak passwords, but they also use them across multiple accounts. So, if a cybercriminal obtains your social media account password, they can now access your bank and/or credit card account. While passwords are familiar and cost-effective, they often require complementary authentication methods to be secure.

Token-based authentication can include hardware or software tokens that generate a code that users must provide in addition to their password. This is called *multi-factor authentication* (MFA) or *two-factor authentication* (2FA). Context-aware MFA adapts based on factors such as user behavior, location, or device, thus enhancing both security and usability. Hardware tokens such as FOBs (frequent operations button—a small physical device used for authenticating a user's identity) or smart cards provide a physical object that generates a unique code, while software tokens replicate this functionality in an app or user's device. This is an added layer of security as these generated codes are time-sensitive and difficult to replicate.

Biometric authentication uses unique physiological characteristics to identify individuals, such as fingerprints, facial recognition, or retinal scans. The method provides a high level of security as these unique characteristics are difficult to duplicate. However, biometrics raises concerns around privacy and requires special handling for sensitive biometric data. Biometric authentication is commonly used with passwords as another form of MFA.

MFA has proven effective in preventing many account-compromised attacks. It requires a combination of "something you know," such as a password, with "something you have," such as a time-sensitive code, or with "something you are," such as biometric data.

Each authentication mechanism has its context, benefits, and potential drawbacks. The choice should be guided by the level of risk that is associated with the asset being protected. Other considerations, such as user experience and resources available for implementing and maintaining, should be evaluated when deciding which to use. A mix of these mechanisms can be deployed to achieve security and accessibility, while remaining functional for legitimate users.

7.1.2 Access control

Access control mechanisms are required to determine how users interact with a system and what resources they can access. Implemented through various models, each is designed to fit different organizational needs and security requirements.

DISCRETIONARY ACCESS CONTROL

Discretionary access control (DAC) is the most flexible model, where the resource owner decides on the access rights. This model allows users to control resources they have been given authority over, and they can grant access permissions to other users at their discretion. This model is used in environments where collaboration and information sharing are prioritized, but it is vulnerable to poor human decisions.

MANDATORY ACCESS CONTROL

Mandatory access control (MAC) is a stricter model in which access rights are regulated based on centralized policies and cannot be changed by a user. Under MAC, every object (e.g., files, directories, or systems) and every subject (e.g., users or processes) is assigned classification labels. Access is allowed or denied based on these labels. This model is commonly used in environments that require high security, such as military or government systems.

ROLE-BASED ACCESS CONTROL

Role-based access control (RBAC) limits system access to authorized users based on their role in the organization. System administrators define roles and give rights and permissions. RBAC simplifies management ensuring that users have access only to the information necessary to perform their role. RBAC is a popular choice for many organizations where roles and responsibilities are clearly defined.

ATTRIBUTE-BASED ACCESS CONTROL

Attribute-based access control (ABAC) defines access rights based on a set of policies that use attributes of users, the system, and the environment. These attributes can include user details such as age or role, while resource attributes can include the type of information or factors such as the time of access. ABAC provides high granularity and flexibility, making this model more dynamic and context-aware than other models.

Table 7.2 compares access control models based on restrictiveness, control, flexibility, the policy maker, and various advantages and disadvantages.

Each model lends itself to the "principle of least privilege," which states that users should be granted the minimum level of access required to perform their duties. This helps minimize the chance of accidental or malicious data breaches because users cannot access information unrelated to their roles. It also limits the damage if a user's credentials are compromised.

Implementing the least privilege across an organization requires planning and regular review to adapt to changes in roles and responsibilities. RBAC and ABAC offer more

Table 7.2 Unique features of different access controls models

	DAC	MAC	RBAC	ABAC
Restrictiveness	Low	High	Medium	Medium
Control	High	Low	Medium	Medium
Flexibility	Low	Low	High	High
Policy maker	Owner	System	Roles	Attributes
Advantages	Easy privilege configuration	Highly secure	Supports large enterprises Mitigates damage to data	Automated trust negotiation Improves on RBAC
Disadvantages	Low storage capacity Unauthorized privileges can be granted	Low storage capacity Unable to modify security levels	Privileges depend on role	Requires investigation for defining attributes relevant to authorization decisions

flexibility and precision for dynamic organizations. Each model mitigates the risk of unauthorized access to critical data and systems and maintains a strong security posture.

7.1.3 Identity and credential management

The primary objective of identity and credential management is to ensure that access rights are securely associated with verified identities. This process begins with identity verification, which confirms an individual's claimed identity, involving collecting and validating identity information. For example, this could mean verifying a user's details against a government-issued ID or an HR database during onboarding.

Once an identity is verified, credential issuance follows. This is where the organization provides the individual with the necessary elements, such as a username and password, security token, or digital certificate, to authorize their access to data or systems. The strength of the credentials depends on the security level. For more sensitive data, stronger credentials are needed, such as cryptographic keys or MFA mandates.

7.1.4 Context-based identity proofing and credential binding

When managing identities, organizations can use context-based identity proofing and credential binding to factor in the context of user interactions. This is important in organizations where access needs are changed often, based on conditions or attributes.

Going beyond static verification at the time of onboarding, context-based system identity proofing continuously assesses the validity of a user's claimed identity by analyzing a range of situational data points. For example, if a user typically logs in during work hours from a specific location, a login attempt that deviates significantly from this pattern may trigger additional verification steps.

Associating the verification process with specific devices or behaviors, such as commonly used devices or IP addresses, is context binding. By binding credentials to context, organizations can enhance security, while maintaining usability. For example, a user may not need to provide a second set of authentication factors when accessing a system from a known secure geolocation but would require a second set of authentication factors when accessing the system from outside the country when traveling.

This method is useful for adapting to various risk levels and providing a custom-designed user experience. It can offer stronger security when needed and avoid unnecessary friction for user experience in low-risk situations. This method's adaptability is key to managing evolving risk without impeding organizational productivity.

7.1.5 User, service, and hardware authentication

Sometimes, a three-part process to ensure security throughout an organization's operations is valuable. This is where user, service, and hardware authentication come into play. Here, authorization is extended beyond individuals to encompass services and hardware components integral to the integrity of the IT systems.

For services, authentication is about verifying any interservice communications to prevent unauthorized data access or manipulation. For example, a web service may need to authenticate an API call from another service before it responds with sensitive information. This process uses tokens or certificates rather than traditional user credentials.

Hardware authentication includes validating devices that connect to an organization's network. This could involve verifying a machine's MAC address or using TPM chips to ensure the device is authorized and has not been compromised. A MAC address is an acronym for *media access control* address, a unique 12-digit hexadecimal number assigned to each device connected to a network. A TPM chip is short for *trusted platform module*, a secure crypto processor designed to carry out cryptographic operations used to improve the security of your system.

These layers of authentication work together to secure an environment where trust is established at every touchpoint, minimizing the potential attack surface and protecting against internal and external threats.

7.1.6 Identity assertion, protection, conveyance, and verification

Single sign-on (SSO) and federated identities are used for identity assertion, protection, conveyance, and verification to manage identities across different systems and platforms. In this respect, conveyance is the transfer of this identity to other systems that accept the SSO identity assertion.

SSO allows users to authenticate once and gain access to multiple systems without having to re-enter credentials. This enhances user convenience and reduces the risk of password fatigue, where users may be overwhelmed with numerous passwords, contributing to weak password practices. SSO solutions rely on secure token services that issue a token to users after a successful initial authentication. These tokens are then used to access other services.

Figure 7.1 shows a user accessing domain 1. This request is redirected to the SSO domain, which, once authenticated, retrieves the token from the authentication server. The server returns the token to the user, which is typically saved as a cookie. This token can then be used for subsequent access to approved domains, such as domain 2, domain 3, and domain 4, without the need to reauthenticate for each domain.

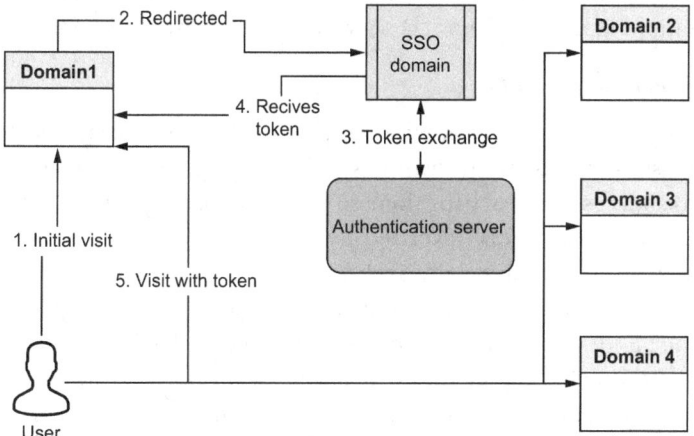

Figure 7.1 An example of a single sign-on (SSO) process.

Federated identities go further than SSO by allowing systems to trust identities managed by other domains. For example, a user's identity verified by their home organization can be used to access services provided by a partner organization. This is done by using standards such as SAML, which is short for security assertion markup language and is a standardized method to tell external applications and services that users are who they say they are. Figure 7.2 presents a simplified scenario of federated access such as SSO. A user attempts to access domain 1 but is redirected to the identity provider, which provides a token for authorized access once the user is authenticated. This token can be used for any authorized domain.

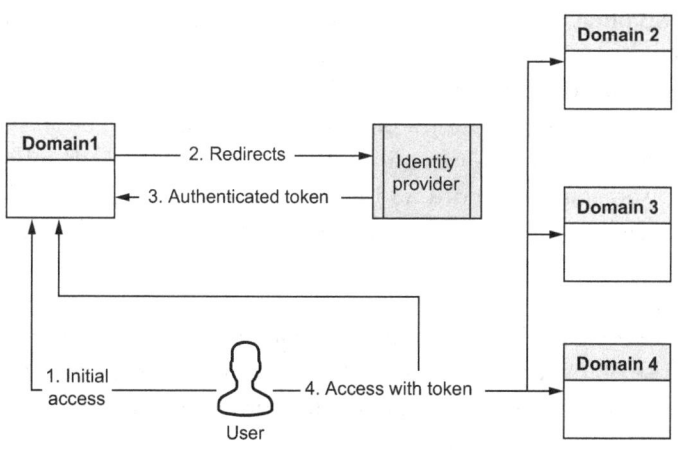

Figure 7.2 Federated identities require a user to be authenticated at their home organization, after which separate security domains use SAML to verify that they can trust and accept user identities from one another.

SSO and federated identity scenarios protect identity assertions and ensure they have not been tampered with, improperly conveyed, or falsely verified. These are robust mechanisms put in place to encrypt and sign assertions, and the verification processes are designed to rigorously check protection before granting access. By using these methods, organizations can streamline access, while keeping strict protections in place.

7.1.7 Access permissions management

Access permissions management plays a key role in protecting assets by serving as a regulatory mechanism that ensures individuals within an organization can access only information and resources necessary for their role. Policy-based access control is structured so that access to resources is governed by policies, and it typically reflects the organization's broader security objectives and compliance requirements.

Access control involves defining clear policies that dictate who has permission to access specific data and under what circumstances. This clarification is enforced through access control technologies that rely on a comprehensive understanding of user roles, data sensitivity, and the potential effects of unauthorized access. The principle of least privilege is central to this approach, granting permissions only when required for users to perform their duties. The challenge is enforcing these policies with the ability to dynamically manage and adjust permissions as roles or business needs change. Regular audits of these controls are essential for maintaining security and ensuring permissions remain appropriate over time.

7.1.8 Physical access controls

Cybersecurity often focuses on technological controls. However, physical access controls are just as important in companies that may still have paper copies of data or on-premises servers and data centers. Physical access controls pose a risk as they can lead to potential data theft, vandalism, or introduce hardware-based threats such as USB drops. A *USB drop* is a type of threat where a threat actor loads malicious programs onto a USB drive and drops them in a public location. A user unaware of malicious programs on the USB plugs it into a company system and releases the malware. Sometimes, small computers can be plugged into data centers to intercept sensitive data transmissions and/or copy data from protected drives.

Physical access controls range from traditional locks to biometric entry systems to prevent unauthorized access. These entry and exit protections are often combined with closed-circuit security systems to record and monitor any activity. Logs of electronic entry to protected rooms are saved and audited to ensure that only authorized personnel have access.

Visitor logs, escort policies, and surveillance systems complement physical barriers to creating a multilayered security approach. They combine physical and security controls to reduce the risk of unauthorized access. These controls must be proportional to the assessed risk and regularly tested and updated to evolve with changing business and threat landscapes.

7.1.9 Types of security controls

Security controls are categorized based on their function to ensure a comprehensive approach to risk management in an organization. Physical, technical, and administrative controls can be classified as preventive, detective, or corrective.

Physical controls are tangible security measures that protect assets and personnel from physical threats. *Technical security controls* are logical, in that they apply security measures with technology rather than with physical security measures. *Administrative controls* consist of policies, procedures, and regulatory compliance measures.

Preventative controls aim to avoid or deter threats from unauthorized access and consist of fences, firewalls, or background checks. Detective control functions seek to identify potential threats, such as cameras, intrusion detection systems, or auditing access logs. Corrective control functions are intended to repair any damage, such as reissuing access cards, patching vulnerabilities, or implementing an incident response plan.

Figure 7.3 shows an example of security controls and their control functions.

		Control functions		
		Preventive	Detective	Corrective
Types of security controls	Physical controls	• Fences • Gates • Locks	• CCTV • Surveillance cameras	• Repair physical damage • Reissue access cards
	Technical controls	• Firewalls • Intrusion prevention systems • MFA • Antivirus	• Intrusion detection systems • Honeypots	• Vulnerability patching • Reboot system • Quarantine virus
	Administrative controls	• On-boarding and off-boarding policies • Separation of duties • Data classification	• Review access rights • Audit logs	• Business continuity plan • Incident response plan • Disaster recovery plan

Figure 7.3 Security controls can be categorized by their type and by their function.

Understanding the control functions helps organizations balance the layered security model to ensure that proper protections are in place to maximize the benefit, while minimizing the cost of protecting critical assets.

7.1.10 Identity management, authentication, and access control metrics

For identity management, authentication, and access control, the metrics we collect directly reflect our system's integrity and user management efficiency. For discussion purposes, a *false positive* occurs when a security system incorrectly identifies benign activity as a threat, leading to unnecessary alerts or actions (e.g., blocking a legitimate user's login attempt). A *false negative* happens when a real security threat is missed, allowing malicious activity to go undetected (e.g., failing to flag a phishing email as suspicious).

DIRECT METRICS

- *Number of identity and credential management-related incidents per year*—Tallies incidents stemming from compromised credentials or identity management failures, providing a straightforward measure of the effects of such events.
- *Time to provision and de-provision user access*—Measures the efficiency of adding or removing access rights, with quicker times typically indicating more efficient identity-management processes.
- *Success rate of authentication*—This percentage reflects the number of successful authentications against all attempts, giving insights into the reliability of the authentication system.
- *Failure rate of authentication*—Conversely, this metric indicates potential problems with either security or user experience if the failure rate is high.
- *Number of problems found during identity validation audit*—A count of discrepancies or problems identified during audits, indicating the soundness of the identity verification process.
- *Number of incidents of unauthorized physical access*—A count of physical breaches, which can reveal the effectiveness of physical security controls.

DERIVED METRICS

- *Ratio of success versus failure of authentication attempts*—Offers a comparative analysis of successful versus failed attempts to access resources.
- *Mean time to respond to authentication anomalies*—Indicates the responsiveness of the security team in addressing authentication problems, with a shorter time suggesting a more agile response capability.
- *Effectiveness of physical access controls and monitoring systems*—Derived from various data points and assesses how well physical barriers and surveillance deter or detect unauthorized access.

7.1.11 Identity and access management dashboard exercise

Two years ago, ACME Corporation, a global technology firm, faced significant security challenges related to identity and access management (IAM). An internal audit revealed numerous access problems, lengthy provisioning and de-provisioning times, and frequent authentication failures. These problems strained the IT team and posed severe security risks. Consequently, ACME implemented a new IAM system and set specific targets to enhance its security. The left side of figure 7.4 shows ACME Corps' identity and access management metrics before improvements in their IAM practices.

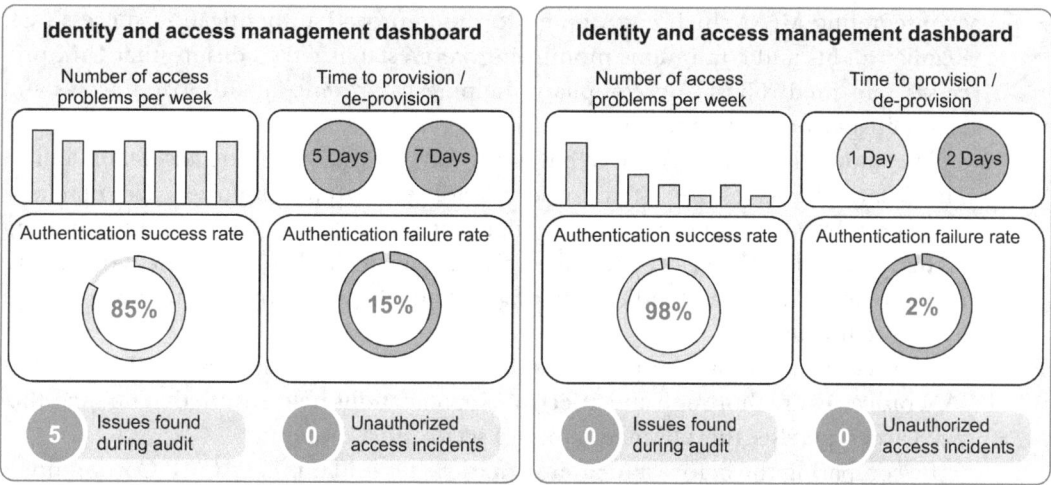

Figure 7.4 The left shows ACME Corp's identity and access management metrics before IAM improvements. On the right are the identity and access management metrics after IAM improvements.

ACME Corporation set the following targets for their IAM metrics:

- *Access problems per week*—Reduce access problems by 50% during the first year.
- *Time to provision users*—Target set to less than one day.
- *Time to de-provision users*—Target set to less than one day.
- *Authentication success rate*—Aim for a success rate greater than 95%.
- *Audit problems*—Strive for zero problems found during audits.

The IAM dashboard on the right side of figure 7.4 shows the results of a current audit. It reveals several critical metrics that provide insight into ACME's security operations. The downward trend in the number of access problems per week, now reduced to 10, indicates that ACME's IAM efforts effectively lessen these problems, suggesting improved security practices. This reduction allows the IT team to focus on more strategic tasks rather than constantly addressing access problems.

The time to provision new users has been reduced to one day, meeting the target and ensuring new employees can start working without delay. However, the time to de-provision users, although improved to two days, still exceeds the target. ACME should further reduce this time to minimize the risk of unauthorized access after an employee leaves the company. Addressing this problem might involve automating more aspects of the de-provisioning process or streamlining the approval workflow.

ACME Corporation focused on refining its IAM processes to achieve these improvements. They implemented automated tools to streamline user provisioning and de-provisioning, significantly reducing manual intervention and approval bottlenecks. Additionally, ACME invested in training their IT staff to improve the efficiency and accuracy of user access management. They also enhanced their authentication systems by integrating MFA, which contributed to the improved authentication success rate. Regular audits and continuous monitoring were established to ensure that IAM processes remained robust and compliant, helping to prevent unauthorized access and maintain a secure environment.

The authentication success rate has improved to 95%, within the acceptable range. This balance indicates the system is user-friendly enough to minimize accidental lockouts and robust enough to detect potential brute-force attacks. Consistent monitoring of this metric will help ensure the system remains secure and user-friendly. If the failure rate were to spike, it could indicate an ongoing attack, prompting further investigation by the security team.

The dashboard shows no problems during recent audits, suggesting that ACME's IAM processes are thorough and effective. Regular audits help ensure that no unauthorized access persists, thereby maintaining a secure environment.

By comparing the before and after scenarios, it is evident that ACME Corporation's new IAM system has significantly improved its security posture. However, continuous monitoring and adjustments are necessary to maintain and further enhance these gains. This structured approach provides a clear before-and-after scenario, illustrating the effects of ACME Corporation's efforts to improve its IAM practices.

7.2 Awareness and training

Security is part of everyone's job. Organizations must ensure all employees have cybersecurity knowledge to perform their duties and reduce risk. Specific cybersecurity training is provided so that employees can perform their cybersecurity-related tasks, and cybersecurity awareness training is provided for all employees so that the knowledge of preventing cybersecurity events is well understood by all.

Cybersecurity awareness is crucial to navigating the digital landscape safely. Regular training, at least annually, highlights the nature of cyber threats, the importance of adhering to security policies, and best practices for incident reporting. Shorter training sessions at shorter intervals are becoming increasingly popular. For example, some organizations will conduct 15-minute sessions every month rather than an hour of training annually. This approach helps keep security at the forefront and enables organizations to update their training to relevant and new security threats.

In addition to awareness training, cybersecurity training should be relevant to an employee's position so they can relate what they have learned to their specific job role. Targeted training should be used to build skills in the latest security protocols. For example, developers should be versed in secure coding practices, and administrators should be proficient in system security measures. By providing awareness and specific cybersecurity training to employees, organizations can embed a culture of security into their core values, reinforcing a shared responsibility among employees.

7.2.1 Awareness and training metrics

In the domain of awareness and training, our metrics shed light on the effectiveness and penetration of our training programs.

DIRECT METRICS

- *Number of different types of training*—Reflects the breadth of training initiatives addressing various aspects of cybersecurity
- *Training completions for each type of training*—Provides a count of how many individuals have completed each training, an indicator of organizational coverage
- *Testing scores for each training type*—Reveals the effectiveness of training material in imparting necessary knowledge and skills

DERIVED METRICS

- *Pre- and post-training assessment improvements*—Measures the knowledge gained due to training sessions
- *Number of employees retrained on failure*—Indicates the necessity for additional training efforts and can highlight areas where training may be initially ineffective
- *Number of repeat failures after training*—A critical metric for assessing whether training outcomes translate into improved practical performance

INDIRECT METRICS

- *Cybersecurity incident reduction following training*—Connects training efforts to a tangible outcome of reduced incidents, indicating long-term effectiveness

7.2.2 Awareness and training metrics exercise

The left side of figure 7.5 indicates that ACME Corporation faced significant challenges with employee cybersecurity awareness three years ago. An internal audit revealed that many employees were not adequately trained in recognizing and responding to cyber threats, leading to several near-miss incidents. To address this problem, ACME launched a comprehensive cybersecurity training program, setting specific targets to ensure all employees were well-versed in the latest cybersecurity trends and protocols.

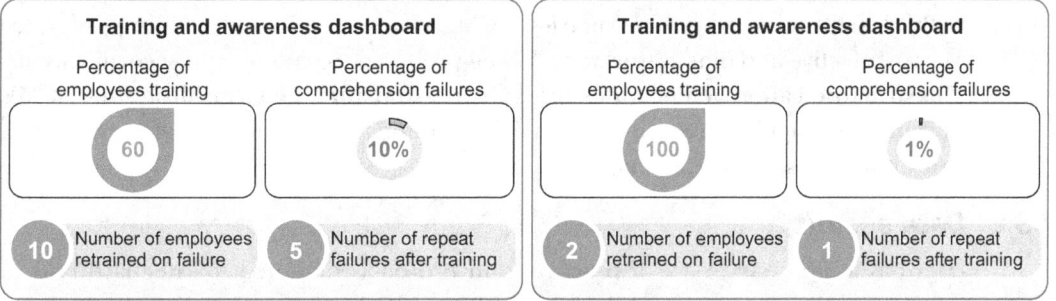

Figure 7.5 The left side shows the review of training and awareness metrics before implementing a comprehensive training program. The right side shows the improvements after implementing the training program.

ACME Corporation set the following targets for their training and awareness metrics:

- *Employee training completion rate*—100% participation in mandatory training.
- *Comprehension rate*—Less than 2% failure rate.
- *Retraining rate*—Aim for minimal retraining to address and reduce initial failures.
- *Repeat offender rate*—Ensure persistent failures are addressed promptly with policies including potential sanctions.

On the right side of figure 7.5, we observe ACME Corporation's awareness and training metrics as they stand now, reflecting the effects of their comprehensive training program. The dashboard indicates that 100% of all employees have completed the mandatory training. This significant achievement ensures all staff members are informed about the latest cybersecurity trends and attack patterns. Maintaining this level of participation is crucial for keeping the workforce vigilant in identifying and reporting problems. If this number begins to drop, ACME may need to introduce incentives or enforcement measures to ensure compliance with the training requirements.

The comprehension metric shows a 1% failure rate, which is deemed acceptable for ACME. This low failure rate indicates that the training program effectively transfers the necessary knowledge to employees. However, each organization must define an acceptable failure rate that balances effective knowledge transfer with the evolving nature of cybersecurity threats. As cyberattacks become increasingly sophisticated, setting a realistic and achievable goal for comprehension is essential to ensure employees are well-prepared.

The metrics for employees retrained after a failure and repeat training for those who failed multiple times are within ACME's policy limits. This indicates that the training program effectively addresses initial failures and improves employee understanding. Should these numbers rise, it would be necessary to investigate the underlying causes, such as changes in training content or employee engagement levels. Additionally, the company should enforce its policies regarding repeat offenders, which might include sanctions and termination for persistent failures. This approach guarantees that all employees understand the importance of cybersecurity and take the necessary steps to protect the organization.

By closely monitoring these metrics, ACME can ensure that its training programs remain effective and that its workforce is well-prepared to handle cybersecurity threats. This structured approach provides a clear before-and-after scenario, illustrating ACME Corporation's significant improvement in its training and awareness efforts, enhancing its overall cybersecurity resilience.

7.3 Data security

Data has a life cycle. A set of practices and protocols designed to safeguard critical information is recommended during this life cycle. Data security refers to the measures an organization implements to safeguard critical information, ensuring its confidentiality, integrity, and availability remain intact.

7.3.1 Data at rest

Data stored on physical media is called "data at rest." It includes on-premises servers, cloud storage, and off-site backups. Protecting data at rest involves encryption protocols that render data unreadable without the proper decryption keys. Access controls are in place to prevent unauthorized data retrieval, and regular integrity checks are done to detect any unauthorized modifications, which ensures the security of the data even if the physical security is breached.

Encryption is used to obfuscate data, and there are two types of encryptions—symmetric and asymmetric. *Symmetric encryption* uses the same key to encrypt and decrypt data, while *asymmetric encryption* uses a pair of public and private keys. In asymmetric encryption, if someone wants to send you encrypted data, they use your public key to encrypt it, and you use your private key to decrypt it. The private key is used to decrypt and sign data and is never shared. The public key encrypts data and verifies signatures, which can be shared.

ENCRYPTION ALGORITHMS AND THEIR LIFESPAN

Not all encryption algorithms are created equal. Over time, as computational power increases and vulnerabilities are discovered, some algorithms may become obsolete or breakable. For example, only TLS v1.2 and above are considered secure at the time of this writing. Older versions, such as TLS v1.1 and below, are now deemed susceptible to attacks due to known methods of cracking these encryption methods. It's critical to stay updated with the latest, secure encryption protocols to ensure data protection.

THE ROLE OF TLS IN SECURE COMMUNICATION

Transport layer security (TLS) is the primary encryption mechanism used across the internet. It is employed in protocols such as HTTPS to ensure secure communication between a user's device and a server. TLS helps maintain the integrity and privacy of data exchanged, preventing eavesdropping and tampering during transmission. Ensuring that only the latest versions of TLS (v1.2 and later) are used is crucial in protecting sensitive information during online transactions.

IMPORTANCE OF HASHING ALGORITHMS

Just as encryption algorithms require attention, so do hash algorithms, which are used to verify data integrity. Hash functions create a fixed-length output, known as a hash, from any given input. A key property of hash algorithms is the avalanche effect, where even a small change in the input causes a significantly different hash value. This property is vital because it ensures that data remains secure and that any alteration to the input will be evident in the hash.

PROTECTING DATA INTEGRITY WITH HASH FUNCTIONS

The primary goal of a hash algorithm is to prevent alterations to the original data. Since any slight change in the input results in a drastically different output, it becomes nearly impossible for attackers to predict or replicate the original data from the hash. This feature makes hashing algorithms essential for ensuring that data remains unchanged and secure from tampering, especially when storing passwords or verifying data integrity. Older hash algorithms, such as MD5 or SHA-1, were historically used to verify that a software download is genuine and untampered with by comparing the publisher's provided hash value with the hash value generated from the downloaded file. However, it is important to emphasize that these algorithms are no longer considered secure and should not be used in any modern security context. Advances in computational power have made it possible to exploit vulnerabilities in these algorithms, rendering them susceptible to attacks such as collisions, where two different inputs produce the same hash value. Given the current capabilities of modern CPUs, the speed differences between outdated algorithms such SHA-1 and more secure alternatives such as SHA-256 are negligible. Therefore, it is imperative to use robust, up-to-date hash algorithms such as SHA-256 to ensure the integrity and security of data. MD5 and SHA-1 should be avoided entirely and considered obsolete for any security-related purposes.

For modern and secure hashing needs, consider using the following algorithms:

- *SHA-256*—Provides a high level of security and is widely used in various applications
- *SHA-384*—Offers even stronger security with a longer hash output
- *SHA-512*—Provides the highest level of security among the SHA-2 family with the longest hash output
- *SHA-3*—Released in 2015, it provides a modern alternative to the SHA-2 family with enhanced security features

7.3.2 Data in transit

When transmitting data from one system to another, it is considered "data in transit." Once the data leaves one system to travel to another, it can be intercepted along the many paths to its destination. Protecting this data requires encryption during transmission using security protocols such as TLS or VPNs in combination with endpoint authentication. TLS is a cryptographic protocol that protects internet communications. VPNs are Virtual Private Networks that establish an end-to-end encrypted connection from one host to another via a private tunnel. VPNs even mask your IP address and will sidestep firewalls as they cannot read data inside the encrypted tunnel.

By securing data in transit, organizations can prevent eavesdropping and ensure that data received at the endpoint is complete and unaltered. This approach also prevents the theft of this data, as the encryption protections will prevent access to the data, even if copied.

7.3.3 Data in use

When applications process data or when being accessed by users, it is considered "data in use." Protecting this data usage relies on application-level encryption and stringent access controls. Data in use encryption is more difficult to implement, and depending on other protections in place, is sometimes foregone to increase data-processing speeds since encryption and decryption take time.

Special care needs to be considered for all types of encryption use, as there is a balance that needs to be maintained. Security is critical, but not to the point where it hinders the application's functionality or otherwise jeopardizes the organization's goals.

7.3.4 Data backup and recovery

Creating, protecting, testing, and maintaining backups are especially important today. Ransomware is a common cyber-attack method where cybercriminals encrypt data until a ransom is paid. Paying these ransoms only perpetuates the profitability of these attacks, contributing to proliferation of ransomware and making it the number one attack method (Verizon 2024 DBIR).

Like ransomware, crypto extortion involves cybercriminals stealing sensitive data and threatening to release or sell it on the dark web unless a ransom is paid. To mitigate this risk, organizations should focus on preventing data breaches through strong access controls, encryption, and continuous monitoring for suspicious activity. While a robust backup and restore program is vital for recovery in case of a ransomware attack, it does not directly address the extortion aspect. Instead, focusing on proactive threat detection and response strategies is key to preventing these types of attacks from succeeding in the first place.

Backups should be encrypted at rest and while in transit to prevent the backup procedure itself from being a point of compromise. Testing and setting proper *recovery time objectives* (RTOs) and *recovery point objectives* (RPOs) are essential. RTO is the amount of time needed to restore backups to full system functionality. RPO is the amount of data loss the organization can afford to lose in terms of time.

Having clear RTOs and RPOs is crucial for recovering from cyberattacks. RTO helps prioritize resources and ensure critical systems are revived swiftly. RPO guides how often backups are made, ensuring you have the most recent data to restore. Setting these objectives allows you to respond to cyberattacks efficiently, minimizing downtime and data loss.

7.3.5 Data security metrics

Data security metrics quantify the safeguarding of our most crucial asset—data.

DIRECT METRICS

- *Number of encrypted vs. nonencrypted systems*—Overviews how well sensitive data is protected. However, data classification should also be considered to ensure that systems with sensitive information are prioritized for encryption, while nonsensitive systems may not require the same level of protection.
- *Number of defunct encryption methods*—Highlights outdated encryption methods that may expose systems to vulnerabilities. Regularly updating encryption protocols is critical for maintaining data security.

- *Incidents per period*—Tracks the frequency of security incidents over a defined period, helping identify trends and areas where the organization's security posture needs improvement. This can include breaches, unauthorized access, or data leaks, regardless of whether encryption existed.
- *Successful backups and backup tests*—Verifies the reliability of the organization's data recovery processes. Regular backup testing ensures that data can be restored in case of an incident. However, backup data should also be classified and encrypted according to sensitivity.

DERIVED METRICS

- *Ratio of encrypted to nonencrypted systems*—Offers a percentage-based perspective on the organization's data protection efforts
- *Ratio of incidents to data breaches*—Helps determine the severity and effect of security incidents on data confidentiality and integrity
- *RPO and RTO compliance rates for data backups*—Measures how effectively the organization meets its targeted recovery objectives

7.3.6 Data security metrics exercise

On the left side of figure 7.6, we examine SecureTech Solutions, a data security firm that discovered vulnerabilities in its data protection practices during a recent internal audit. The audit highlighted that a significant portion of their systems were not encrypted, posing a risk of data breaches. Additionally, the company faced challenges in meeting its backup and recovery objectives. To address these problems, SecureTech Solutions set clear targets to enhance its data security measures, aiming for full encryption compliance and improved backup and recovery processes.

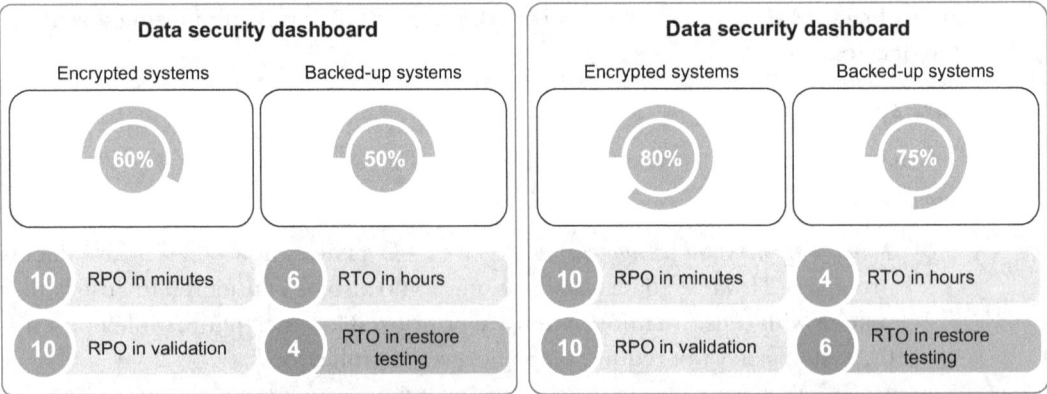

Figure 7.6 The left side shows the Secure Tech data security dashboard before implementing data protection practices. The right side shows the situation after implementing these practices.

SecureTech Solutions established the following targets:

- *Encryption compliance*—Achieve 100% encryption of all systems.
- *Backup systems compliance*—Ensure 100% of critical systems are backed up regularly.
- *RPO compliance*—Maintain current compliance.
- *RTO compliance*—Reduce recovery time to meet the 4-hour target.

The right side of figure 7.6 shows data security metrics for SecureTech Solutions after implementing data protection practices. These metrics provide critical insights into the company's current security posture. The dashboard reveals that 20% of the systems are not encrypted, falling short of the company's mandatory full disk encryption policy. This represents a significant security risk, requiring immediate action to identify and secure the noncompliant systems. Ensuring that all systems are encrypted is vital for protecting sensitive data from potential breaches.

To improve its data security metrics, SecureTech Solutions took a systematic approach by prioritizing encryption and backup compliance. They implemented a phased encryption plan that first targeted the most vulnerable systems, gradually expanding until all systems were fully encrypted.

In deciding which systems were most vulnerable, SecureTech Solutions conducted a risk assessment to identify systems that stored or processed sensitive data, such as personal information, financial records, or intellectual property. They also considered systems with known security weaknesses, outdated encryption methods, or high exposure to external threats. By evaluating these factors, SecureTech could prioritize systems that posed the most significant risk to the organization and focus its resources on securing those first. This approach allowed them to progressively strengthen their security posture, while addressing the highest risks first.

To address the backup shortfall, SecureTech enhanced its backup procedures by automating the process, ensuring regular and consistent backups of all critical systems. Additionally, they introduced more frequent testing of backup systems to guarantee data integrity and availability. SecureTech also focused on refining its recovery processes by streamlining the workflows involved in system recovery, reducing the recovery time objective RTO to align with the company's 4-hour target. Through continuous monitoring and adjustments, SecureTech improved its data security posture significantly.

The backup systems metric shows that only 75% of the critical systems are backed up, which is below the company's goal. SecureTech Solutions' policy mandates that all critical systems be backed up regularly and tested to ensure data integrity and availability. This shortfall indicates a need for an investigation to identify the reasons behind the gap and implement corrective measures. Achieving full compliance with backup policies is essential to make sure data is available and secure in case of a system failure or cyberattack.

While SecureTech Solutions is meeting its RPO targets, there is a discrepancy in the RTO. The company aims for a 4-hour recovery time, but the current metric shows a deviation, indicating a longer recovery period. This variance could be temporary; however, it necessitates a thorough investigation to determine the root cause and apply necessary corrections. Ensuring that the RTO aligns with the target is crucial for maintaining business continuity and minimizing downtime.

By addressing these discrepancies and continuously monitoring these metrics, SecureTech Solutions can enhance its data security measures, ensuring robust protection for its systems and data. The before-and-after comparison highlights significant improvements in encryption and backup compliance, with further efforts necessary to achieve full targets. This structured approach demonstrates how specific metrics can drive informed decisions and improve cybersecurity resilience.

7.4 Configuration management

Systems require a baseline to establish and maintain standard configurations. Regularly updating these configurations can address vulnerabilities and changes in compliance. Automated tools are sometimes used to manage and track configurations for unauthorized changes.

7.4.1 Software maintenance

Patch management is key to software maintenance; timely testing and implementation of changes are needed to ensure the reliability of software components. End-of-life and non-supported older software pose a risk and should be considered when replacement and upgrades are required. Organizations need to establish a process for safely and securely transitioning from old software to new software versions or migrating to entirely new components.

7.4.2 Hardware maintenance

Hardware must also be managed and protected. Conducting regular inspections and maintenance to ensure reliability and replacing outdated or vulnerable hardware components are essential for maintaining security standards. Safely decommissioning and disposing of hardware that is no longer in use is part of this planning. Upgrading and replacing hardware is essential to prevent outdated or vulnerable systems from becoming security liabilities for the organization.

7.4.3 Log maintenance

Generation, storage, and analysis of logs are important for continuous monitoring and are used for incident response or forensics. Capturing and storing logs must be done securely and be tamper evident to prevent cybercriminals from manipulating logs to hide their tracks. Regularly reviewing logs for signs of security incidents and/or policy violations is important as part of due diligence. Integrating log data with security information and event management (SIEM) systems allows real-time analysis and alerting.

7.4.4 Unauthorized software prevention

Preventing the installation and execution of unauthorized software reduces the risk of malware infections and data breaches. Organizations should enforce application whitelisting policies and only allow approved software to be installed on systems. Limiting the administrative privilege to install software adds another layer of protection. Endpoint protection solutions can block unauthorized applications. Users should be trained to recognize and avoid installing unapproved software.

7.4.5 Secure software development

If organizations have in-house software development as part of their business operations, integrating secure software development practices is required for designing, building, and maintaining secure code and applications. Figure 7.7 shows how the process includes embedding security into every stage of the software development life cycle (SDLC). Regular code reviews and testing are needed to identify and resolve vulnerabilities before they are exposed in production. Organizations should monitor the performance of security controls embedded in software throughout its life cycle—from birth to death.

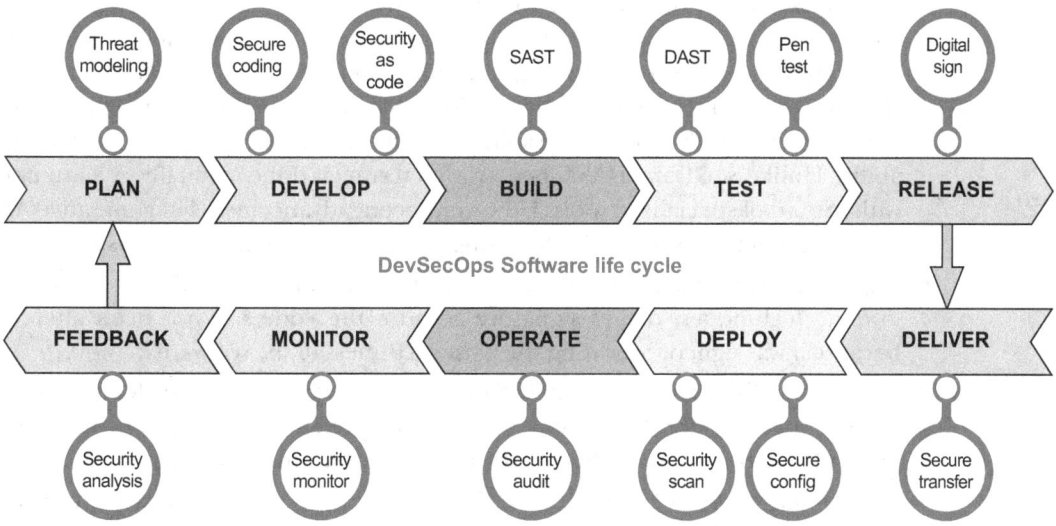

Figure 7.7 An overview of how security is integrated into each SDLC phase, highlighting critical security tasks associated with planning, development, testing, deployment, and maintenance stages.

Let's take a deeper look at each of these security controls:

- *Threat modeling* is a process that allows development teams to identify, predict, and define potential threats and determine required mitigating measures to counteract these risks. By considering potential threat actors and their attack vectors, development teams can proactively design a system more resilient to attacks.

- *Secure coding practices* require writing software that guards against the introduction of security vulnerabilities. This involves following coding standards which prioritize security and avoid common coding vulnerabilities that attackers could exploit. For example, input validation is a common attack vector, and developers can code not to allow any input types except approved ones.
- *Security as code* reflects the shift toward automation in security practices, where security measures are defined and implemented throughout the code. This approach allows security configurations to be version controlled, automatically deployed, and consistently applied across all environments.
- *Static application security testing* (SAST) and *dynamic application security testing* (DAST) are complementary testing methods used to uncover vulnerabilities. SAST is like proofreading the code before it is run. Programs can automate the process, or a code review can be done manually. SAST is code-aware and can pinpoint the line of code that requires correction. DAST, however, is automated and conducted while the code is running. DAST can uncover run-time vulnerabilities, but further analysis would need to be done to find the line of code that requires correction, since DAST only tests the executable.
- *Penetration testing* involves hiring an ethical hacker to execute approved cyberattacks on software systems to identify and address security weaknesses. There is little difference between what a penetration tester would do and what an actual hacker would do. However, a penetration tester has permission and will do no harm. They will only uncover the ability to harm, so developers can fix the vulnerability. Unlike SAST and DAST, penetration testing is done manually by a human with the aid of specialized tools. However, recent advancements in generative AI have lent themselves to semi-automating penetration testing and analysis.
- *Digital signatures* maintain software integrity and authenticity. By using cryptographic techniques, digital signatures ensure the code has not been altered because it was signed, providing the trustworthiness of the software deployed.
- *Transferring the data security via TLS* or other encrypted data transfer methods ensures that software deployment is not intercepted and manipulated. The program's functionality when dealing with data transfer must also be encrypted.
- *Secure configurations* of software and the underlying systems are needed to protect against attacks that exploit default or weak configurations. Changing default passwords for the admin is a typical example. Creating gold images as standard configurations helps prevent system misconfiguration so that whenever a system is created, it is done so with approved and vetted security configurations following best practices. This is called system hardening and includes turning off unused ports and applying the principle of least privilege to access controls.
- *Regular security scanning and auditing* can be automated to continuously monitor systems for vulnerabilities. These routines provide a more in-depth review of

security practices and compliance regulations. Ongoing security monitoring can alert the incident response team to investigate further. Some automated security monitoring systems can orchestrate and take immediate action following patterns and playbooks. This way, when a known pattern is detected, the system can respond immediately to rectify and then issue an alert for further investigation. These are SOAR (security orchestration, automation, and response) systems.

- *Security analysis* is done on all data gathered from various security practices and evaluated to understand the effectiveness of the security measures. This analysis can inform security practices, allowing for continuous process improvement. The practices are shared among all who participate in the development process.

7.4.6 Platform metrics

Platform metrics evaluate the hardware and software security underpinning our organization's operations.

DIRECT METRICS

- *Deviation from baseline security configurations*—Tracks unauthorized changes that could expose the system to risk
- *Software patch management numbers per frequency*—Indicate the rate at which security updates are applied
- *Number of unauthorized software installations*—Measures control over software installations to prevent malware introduction

DERIVED METRICS

- *Average time to rectify security configurations*—Gauges the agility of the response to identified configuration problems
- *Mean time to update software*—Reflects the efficiency of the patch management process

INDIRECT METRICS

- *System uptime*—The total time a system has been running uninterrupted.
- *System resource usage*—Tracking system variables such as memory, CPU, GPU, and storage space over time helps you identify patterns of high usage, such as time of year or during special events.

7.4.7 Platform security metrics exercise

The left side of figure 7.8 presents the platform security metrics for our example company, SecureNet Inc., a mid-sized tech firm specializing in cloud-based solutions. Before SecureNet implemented the new monitoring strategy, they experienced several security incidents due to unauthorized software installations and system misconfigurations. These incidents led to frequent system downtimes and increased the risk of data breaches. The average time to rectify misconfigurations was 30 minutes, and system updates often took more than an hour. Their system uptime was below the industry standard of 98%, and system resource usage frequently spiked, indicating possible security breaches.

To address these challenges, SecureNet implemented a comprehensive platform security strategy. The goal was to ensure that all systems adhere to policy-defined images, improve response times for addressing misconfigurations and updates, and maintain high system uptime and stability.

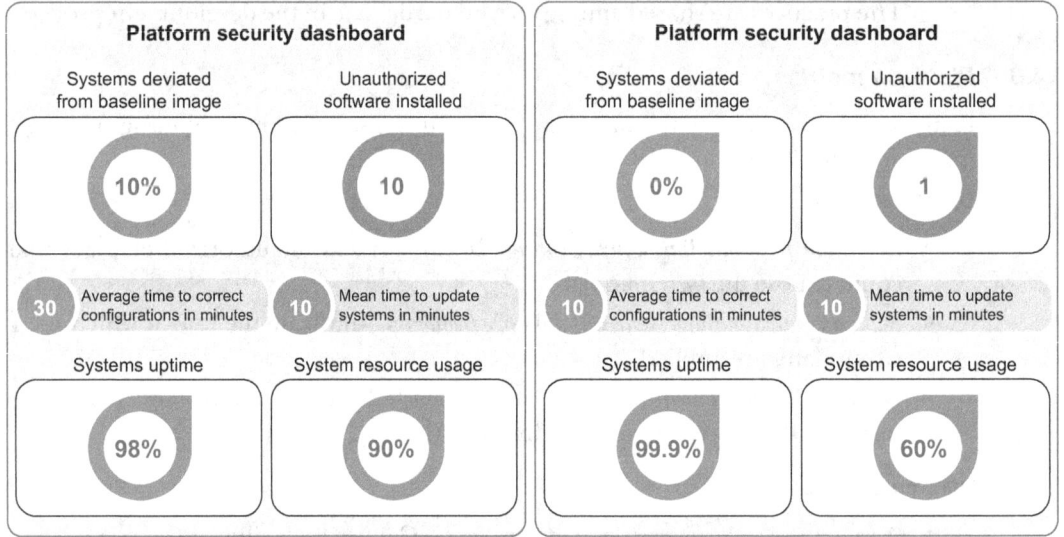

Figure 7.8 The left side shows the SecureNet Inc. platform security dashboard before implementing the new security monitoring strategy. The situation after implementing the new strategy is presented on the right.

SecureNet Inc. set the following targets:

- *Systems deviated from baseline image*—0%
- *Unauthorized software installed*—0 incidents
- *Average time to repair configurations*—10 minutes
- *Mean time to update systems*—10 minutes
- *Systems uptime*—99.9%
- *System resource usage*—Maintain below 70% to ensure stability and detect anomalies quickly.

After implementing the new platform security monitoring strategy, SecureNet Inc. saw significant improvements across all key metrics. The right side of figure 7.8 shows the systems deviated from the baseline image dropped to 0%, ensuring all systems adhered strictly to approved configurations and reducing the risk of security vulnerabilities.

They reported only one instance of unauthorized software installation, which was promptly documented and resolved, demonstrating improved monitoring and incident response capabilities. The average time to repair misconfigurations decreased to 10 minutes, highlighting the efficiency and effectiveness of their incident management process. Similarly, system updates were now completed in 10 minutes, keeping systems secure with minimal downtime. The system uptime improved to 99.9%, meeting their target and ensuring high availability and reliability of their services. Additionally, system resource usage stabilized at 60%, well below the 70% threshold, which indicates efficient system operations and proactive anomaly detection.

To maintain the achieved metrics, SecureNet Inc. should continue to enforce strict configuration management policies to keep the systems' deviation rate at zero. Additionally, addressing a single unauthorized software installation should involve continuous monitoring and periodic employee training to ensure such incidents do not recur, aiming for zero incidents. The improved times for remediation and updates suggest that streamlined processes are effective; these should be regularly reviewed and optimized to maintain efficiency. System uptime can be preserved by scheduling maintenance during off-peak hours and reinforcing infrastructure resilience. Finally, consistent analysis of system resource use will enable early detection of potential threats, ensuring the systems remain stable and secure.

7.5 SDLC testing exercise

In figure 7.9, line up the appropriate testing methods with the phases of the SDLC. The answer is provided at the end of the chapter.

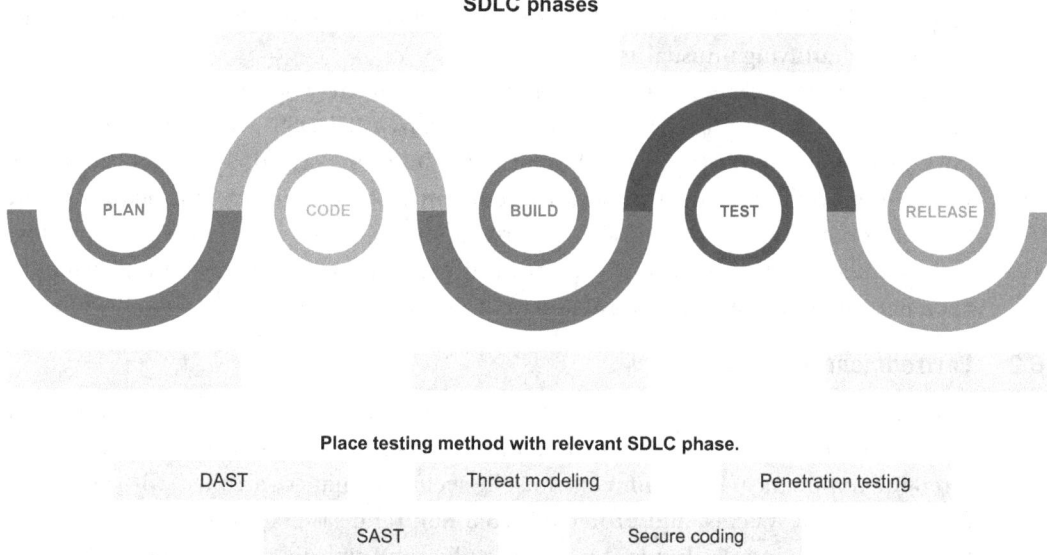

Figure 7.9 Exercise: Match the testing method with the SDLC phase.

7.6 Technology infrastructure resilience

Security architecture and networks also need protection. Protection protocols include protection against attacks and the flexibility to adapt to surges of usage. Networks consist of many connected devices, and organizations must ensure that there are no weak links in the chain.

7.6.1 Networks

Layered defenses are essential for protecting networks. These include defenses such as firewalls, intrusion detection and prevention systems, and access controls. Updating, maintaining, and responding to threats are duties that require routine work. Wireless networks should always be encrypted to avoid eavesdropping and should have proper network configurations. In addition, networks should segment data and systems to prevent attackers from moving from one system to another. For example, a guest connected to the wireless system should not be visible in the office production environment.

Network segmentation enhances security and performance by controlling traffic flow between segments and by limiting the reach of potential breaches. In traditional IT infrastructures, network segmentation may be as simple as separating public-facing web servers from internal networks containing sensitive data. In complex and cloud-based environments, segmentation may include more granular divisions, such as segmenting different departments or user groups, to control access and reduce the risk of lateral movement of an attacker in the network. Implementing network segmentation consists of the use of firewalls, *virtual local area networks* (VLANs), and *access control lists* (ACLs) that enforce policies stating which devices and users can communicate across the network. Monitoring tools help provide insights into network traffic patterns and can aid in identifying unusual activities.

Regulatory requirements and best practices support network segmentation, such as the Payment Card Industry Data Security Standard (PCI DSS), which mandates network segmentation to protect cardholder data. Only authorized personnel can access sensitive information. Effective network segmentation requires careful planning and balancing security with accessibility. Over-segmented networks may be too complex, and so hinder legitimate business activities, affecting user experience and satisfaction. Each network must be custom designed to fit the needs of the specific organization.

7.6.2 Environmental threats

Networks are not immune to physical threats. Server rooms, data centers, and even cloud-based networks all have an element of physical security that needs to be monitored for compliance. Environments must be secure, climate controlled, with adequate fire suppression systems, and protected from natural disasters through strategic location or construction. Redundant power supplies and uninterruptible supplies (UPS) with backup generators help guard against power outages.

7.6.3 Resilience mechanisms

Redundant systems, failover systems, and load balancing are all part of resilience mechanisms, ensuring the availability of critical data. Regular drills and tests are standard, such as fire drills, where mock problems are presented to confirm everyone knows their roles, responsibilities, and required actions.

7.6.4 Resource capacity

Maintaining sufficient hardware is crucial for supporting business growth and preventing limitations in data storage or processing capacity. Capacity planning and stress testing help predict and manage loads, allowing organizations to scale resources as needed. Cloud-based solutions offer elastic scaling capabilities and provide an additional buffer to accommodate unexpected spikes in demand. Cloud-based solutions are attractive because of their pay-on-demand cost structure, so organizations will only pay for what is used rather than purchasing a permanent system to accommodate a temporary spike in demand.

To enhance resilience, organizations must anticipate potential points of failure and proactively implement strategies to mitigate risks. This requires a combination of technical, environmental, and capacity planning to align security measures with the organization's risk appetite and business continuity plans. Ongoing risk assessments help uncover vulnerabilities, ensuring security strategies remain adaptive and responsive to emerging threats.

In real-world scenarios, challenges such as securing hybrid cloud environments and managing third-party dependencies can significantly affect resilience. For example, organizations using both on-premises and cloud-based infrastructure must ensure consistent security policies across both environments, while addressing risks such as misconfigurations and unauthorized access. Similarly, reliance on third-party vendors introduces supply chain risks that can disrupt operations if not properly managed.

Building resilience in these contexts requires continuous monitoring, redundant controls, and incident response plans that account for external dependencies. Organizations should also conduct regular tabletop exercises to test their response strategies and validate their ability to recover from disruptions effectively. By integrating resilience into every aspect of cybersecurity planning, businesses can better withstand and recover from evolving threats.

7.7 Protection metrics

Protection mechanisms relate to the comprehensive defensive measures discussed throughout this chapter. These mechanisms encompass IAM controls, data security protocols, platform security measures, and the application of encryption and backup policies. Each of these elements plays a critical role in maintaining organizational assets' integrity, confidentiality, and availability.

Analyzing the metrics tied to these protection mechanisms provides valuable insights into their operational effectiveness and overall security performance. For instance, IAM metrics such as time to provision and de-provision users or authentication success rates indicate the success of controls function. Data security metrics, including encryption compliance and backup success rates, reveal the robustness of data protection strategies. Furthermore, platform security metrics, such as system deviation from baseline configurations and unauthorized software installation incidents, help assess the resilience of the organization's infrastructure.

To enhance this assessment, organizations should incorporate drift detection tools that continuously monitor for configuration changes. These tools provide real-time visibility into deviations from security baselines, allowing teams to detect and remediate unauthorized changes before they lead to security incidents. By integrating drift detection into security monitoring, organizations can proactively maintain compliance, prevent misconfigurations from introducing vulnerabilities, and ensure that security policies remain consistently enforced across all systems.

7.8 Answer to exercise from section 7.5

Figure 7.10 shows the answers to exercise from section 7.5, matching the testing method with the relevant SDLC phase.

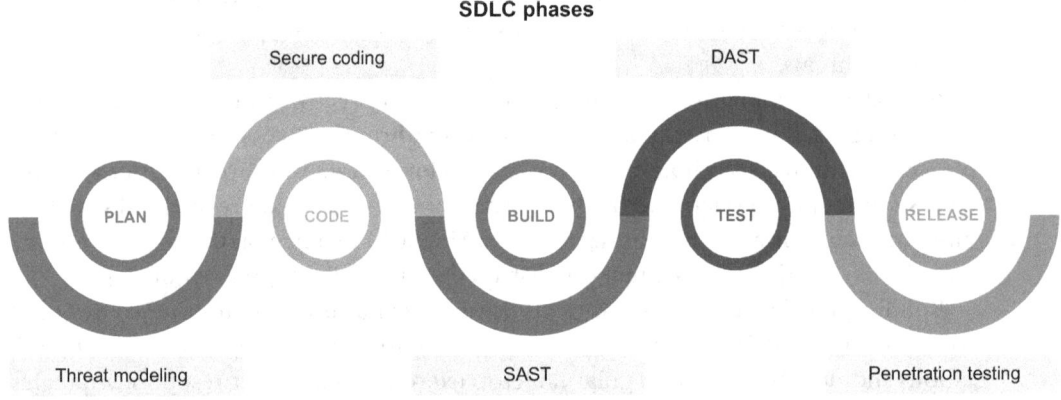

Figure 7.10 Answers to exercise from section 7.5.

Summary

- Identity and access metrics measure how well users are managed and authenticated.
- Authentication success and failure rates highlight security and user access reliability.
- Training metrics track the scope and effectiveness of cybersecurity education programs.

- Data security is evaluated by tracking encryption use and incident response success.
- Metrics for platform security assess the maintenance and response to software vulnerabilities.
- Resilience in infrastructure is measured by incident responses and system availability.

Continuous threat detection

This chapter covers
- Implementing continuous monitoring system
- Using open source solutions for continuous threat detection
- The process of Information Security Continuous Monitoring
- Alert threshold life cycle assessment systems
- Strategies for continuous monitoring

The ability to detect and respond to threats in real time is critical to cybersecurity. Continuous threat detection is a proactive measure for safeguarding an organization's data and assets against cyber threats. Phishing attacks and ransomware continuously threaten the cyber landscape. If not detected and addressed promptly, these threats can have severe implications.

This chapter discusses the details of continuous threat detection, offering guidelines on how to implement monitoring systems. We explore continuous threat detection using open source tools such as Wazuh (https://www.wazuh.com) to enhance detection capabilities, ensuring that even the most subtle anomalies are identified and addressed. By understanding and applying the right metrics, cybersecurity professionals can better evaluate the effectiveness of their threat detection systems and make better, more informed decisions to bolster their defenses.

We also look at real-world scenarios and case studies to illustrate how continuous monitoring can be effectively integrated into different organizational contexts. By the end of this chapter, you will clearly understand how to set up and manage a continuous threat detection program, interpret the data collected, and use it to enhance your organization's security posture.

8.1 Implementing continuous threat monitoring systems

According to National Institute of Standards and Technology (NIST) guidelines, particularly those outlined in NIST SP 800-137, continuous monitoring involves defining scope and strategy, defining metrics, collecting data, analyzing information, and responding to threats. This cyclical process provides organizations with a clear understanding of their security posture, enabling them to make informed decisions based on real-time data.

Figure 8.1 illustrates the overall method recommended by NIST for Information Security Continuous Monitoring (ISCM) for federal information systems and organizations. This framework emphasizes integrating continuous monitoring into an organization's security strategy.

Figure 8.1 NIST 800-137 Information Security Continuous Monitoring for Federal Information Systems and Organizations describes the steps for implementing ISCM in organizations.

To implement an effective continuous threat monitoring system, several key components must be considered. These include data collection mechanisms, data analysis tools, threat detection systems, and automated response mechanisms. Each component ensures that threats are detected and addressed promptly.

Sensors and data collection mechanisms form the first line of defense in a continuous monitoring system. These sensors can be deployed across various network parts, including endpoints, servers, and network devices. They collect data on a wide range of activities, such as network traffic, system logs, and application behavior. This data provides the raw information needed to detect potential threats.

Automated response mechanisms are crucial for making sure that threats are addressed as quickly as possible. These mechanisms can automatically trigger predefined actions when a threat is detected, such as isolating affected systems, blocking malicious IP addresses, or alerting the security team. Automation helps reduce the time it takes to respond to threats, thereby minimizing the potential effects on the organization.

Setting up a continuous monitoring system involves several steps. First, it is necessary to define the scope of the monitoring program, including which systems and networks will be monitored. Next, the necessary sensors and data collection mechanisms, such as Wazuh, are to be employed. Once the sensors are in place, the data analysis and threat detection tools are configured to process the collected data. Finally, automated response mechanisms should be established to address threats promptly.

Integration with existing security infrastructure is also essential. Continuous monitoring systems should complement and enhance other security measures, such as firewalls, intrusion detection systems, and endpoint protection solutions. Organizations can create a more comprehensive and effective security strategy by integrating continuous monitoring with these existing tools.

The following sections present the detailed steps of the NIST SP 800-137 framework, focusing on defining strategy, establishing architecture, implementing data collection and analysis, and responding to findings. We use Wazuh as an example of how to practically apply these concepts and provide a deeper understanding of continuous threat monitoring in real-world scenarios.

8.1.1 Defining strategy

The first step in establishing an ISCM program is to define a clear strategy. The step involves setting the program's scope and objectives, determining risk tolerance, and establishing visibility into assets, vulnerabilities, and threats. This ISCM strategy should align with the organization's mission and business objectives.

Understanding and defining risk tolerance involves determining the level of risk the organization is willing to accept. In defining risk tolerance, you also define the threshold for action. This approach helps guide the prioritization of monitoring activities and the allocation of resources.

Maintaining an updated inventory of hardware and software assets will help determine which critical assets need continuous monitoring. Once defined, your critical assets can be scanned for known vulnerabilities, threats, or anomalous behavior, which assists in assessing the potential effects of their mission. Knowing which asset's compromise would have the most significant effect on the organization's operations, mission, and objectives keeps your security focused on what matters.

8.1.2 Establishing architecture, implementing data collection, and analysis

Establishing an architecture for continuous monitoring involves determining the metrics to be monitored, the frequency of monitoring and assessment activities, and the reporting mechanisms. With the architecture in place, the next step is *implementing the continuous monitoring system and collecting security data,* which involves deploying sensors and agents across the network to gather data on various aspects of the IT environment. Security data should cover network traffic, system logs, application activity, and user behavior. This data is then used for continuous monitoring, regular assessments, and stakeholder reporting.

The collected data needs to be *analyzed* to identify potential security incidents and assess the effectiveness of security controls. This step involves determining the appropriate response to detected threats, supporting the data with contextual information, and reporting findings to relevant stakeholders. Analysis should be thorough, employing automated tools and manual inspection to identify patterns and anomalies. Reports generated should provide actionable insights and clear recommendations for mitigating identified risks.

8.1.3 Responding to findings

Responding to the analysis' findings is crucial for mitigating risks and improving the organization's security posture. This involves taking technical, management, and operational actions to address identified vulnerabilities and threats.

Mitigation involves applying specific actions to reduce the likelihood or effects of identified risks. From a technical perspective, it might include applying security patches to software vulnerabilities, updating system configurations to strengthen defenses, or deploying advanced security tools to detect and prevent threats. For instance, if a vulnerability is discovered in a critical system, the technical team would prioritize patching this vulnerability to prevent exploitation by attackers.

From a management standpoint, mitigation could involve regular employee training sessions to raise awareness about cybersecurity best practices and emerging threats. Such approach guarantees the workforce is knowledgeable and vigilant, thus reducing the risk of human error—often a significant factor in security breaches. Additionally, management might review and update security policies and procedures to align with the latest industry standards and regulations, ensuring the organization's security posture remains robust.

Operationally, mitigation includes implementing and refining security processes that support the organization's daily activities. This might involve establishing incident response protocols, regularly testing backup systems, and conducting drills to ensure readiness in case of a security incident. Integrating security measures into everyday operations allows the organization to respond swiftly and effectively to potential threats, minimizing disruption and damage.

Transferring risk involves shifting the responsibility for a particular risk to another entity, often through purchasing cybersecurity insurance or outsourcing certain security functions to a specialized third-party provider. For example, an organization might transfer the risk of data breaches by purchasing an insurance policy that covers the costs associated with a breach, including legal fees, notification expenses, and recovery efforts.

Risk avoidance involves making choices that prevent a threat from emerging, which might involve discontinuing certain high-risk activities, choosing not to use specific technologies known to have vulnerabilities, or opting out of markets with high threat levels. For instance, an organization might decide not to engage in online financial transactions if it determines that the associated cyber risks are too high and cannot be adequately mitigated or transferred.

Accepting or rejecting risk requires a thorough risk assessment to determine the potential effect and threat likelihood. If the risk is deemed acceptable, the organization might take no further action beyond monitoring the situation. This approach is often chosen when the cost of mitigation, transfer, or avoidance outweighs the potential detrimental effects of the risk. Conversely, rejecting a risk means deciding it cannot be tolerated under any circumstances, prompting immediate action to eliminate the threat.

These response actions are critical in a comprehensive risk management strategy, and they enable organizations to make informed decisions based on their risk tolerance and the potential effect on their operations. Organizations can maintain a balanced and resilient security posture by effectively eliminating risks through mitigation, transfer, avoidance, or acceptance, safeguarding their assets and ensuring business continuity.

8.2 Open source alternative to continuous threat detection

Wazuh is an excellent example of a powerful open source security monitoring platform that integrates with various systems to provide comprehensive, continuous monitoring capabilities. Designed to detect intrusions, analyze vulnerabilities, monitor compliance, and provide real-time security insights, Wazuh aligns well with continuous monitoring needs. It can be installed on a single server or scaled across multiple nodes, collecting information from systems and assets via agents installed on endpoints. These agents send data to a centralized Wazuh server, where it is analyzed and presented via a single dashboard interface.

One of Wazuh's core features is its ability to provide real-time threat detection by continuously monitoring system logs, network traffic, and file integrity. Its robust rule-based engine identifies suspicious activities and generates alerts for potential security incidents. For instance, it can detect unusual login attempts, unauthorized file modifications, and unexpected network connections, critical for early threat identification and mitigation.

Wazuh also excels in vulnerability detection and management. It can scan systems for known vulnerabilities, assess their severity, and provide actionable insights for corrective action. This warrants that systems are not left exposed to known vulnerabilities that could be exploited by attackers.

Compliance with industry standards and regulations is another important aspect of cybersecurity. Wazuh offers compliance monitoring capabilities that help organizations adhere to regulatory requirements such as PCI DSS, GDPR, and HIPAA. It provides reports and dashboards that illustrate compliance status, making it easier for organizations to demonstrate their adherence to regulatory standards.

File integrity monitoring is another key feature of Wazuh—it tracks changes to critical system files and directories, determining that any unauthorized modifications are detected and reported. This capability is essential for identifying potential breaches and ensuring the integrity of sensitive data.

Wazuh also incorporates an intrusion detection system that monitors network traffic and system logs for signs of malicious activity. By analyzing data from multiple sources, Wazuh can identify complex attack patterns and provide early warnings of potential intrusions, helping organizations respond swiftly and effectively to emerging threats.

8.3 Continuous monitoring metrics

Here I provide some real-world examples of metrics that can be used, given what we understand how to implement an ISCM program:

- *Ransomware detection metrics*—Track the total number of unique file extensions being modified or encrypted from file servers, critical systems, and endpoints
- *Command and control (C2) beaconing*—Tracks the total number of files modified or encrypted within a specific period from assigned sources
- *Crypto-mining detection metrics*—Measure average CPU or GPU utilization within a specific period
- *Data exfiltration detection metrics*—Track the total bytes transferred from specific network segments or critical servers within a particular period
- *External/unknown IP communication over north/south*—Measures connections to external IP addresses originating from the assigned source(s)
- *Malware communication detection*—Tracks the destination IP addresses or domains of outgoing connections from endpoints, critical servers, or network segments
- *Signature-based threats*—Track the number of connections to malicious hosts within a specific period
- *Brute-force attack detection metrics*—Track failed login events or authentication failures from authentication servers, VPN gateways, or critical systems
- *Distributed denial of service (DDoS) attack detection metrics*—Track the total packets or bytes per second from internet-facing network segments or critical servers

8.3.1 Continuous monitoring metrics exercise

Let's consider the left side of figure 8.2, the continuous monitoring dashboard for SecureTech Solutions, a prominent provider of cybersecurity services. Despite having a robust threat detection system, the sheer volume of alerts, many of which are false positives, has been hampering their efficiency. This inefficiency has led to delayed responses and increased risk exposure. To address this problem, SecureTech has implemented a refined methodology to optimize its alert thresholds and enhance monitoring capabilities.

Before implementing the new methodology, the metrics dashboard showed several alarming metrics. The total number of unique file extensions being modified or encrypted was detected at 50, indicating potential ransomware activities. A high volume of file modifications accompanied this, with 2,000 files being encrypted in a single day. Additionally, the average CPU utilization across 10 servers was a staggering 95%, suggesting possible crypto-mining activities. The total bytes transferred from critical servers within an hour amounted to 500GB, highlighting potential data exfiltration risks. Moreover, the number of failed login events on the main authentication server was alarmingly high, with 6,000 failed attempts within a 5-minute interval, indicating possible brute-force attacks.

After six months of implementing the refined methodology, SecureTech Solutions achieved significant improvements in its metrics. The right side of figure 8.2 shows that the total number of unique file extensions being modified or encrypted has been reduced to 10, reflecting improved detection and filtering of ransomware activities. Similarly, the number of files modified or encrypted in a single day decreased to 500, indicating improved identification and isolation of suspicious activities.

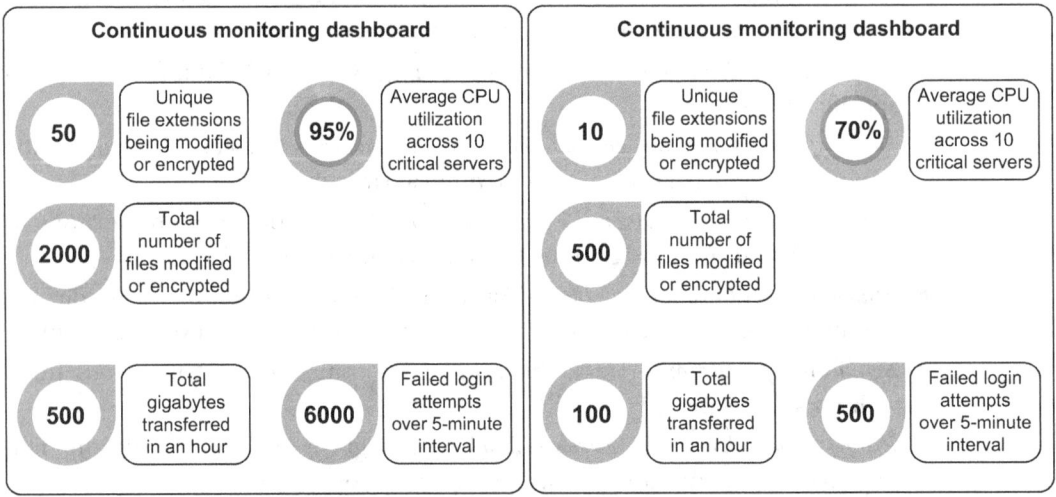

Figure 8.2 The left side shows SecureTech's initial continuous monitoring metrics on their example dashboard. On the right are the improved numbers 6 months after analysis and corrections.

To achieve these improvements, SecureTech Solutions revisited its alert configuration and fine-tuned its detection thresholds by analyzing historical data to set more precise parameters. They implemented more granular logging and integrated behavioral analytics to distinguish between normal and suspicious activities. Additionally, they enhanced their data loss prevention strategies. They incorporated more robust user behavior analytics to effectively detect and mitigate potential threats, resulting in reduced false positives and more focused threat detection.

To make these improvements, SecureTech Solutions took a systematic approach by revisiting their configuration and thresholds and reviewing existing rules. Adjustments based on this analysis help differentiate between genuine threats and benign activities. The organization implemented a more granular logging strategy, allowing for more precise identification of unusual file modifications and encryption activities. SecureTech also introduced more robust user behavior analytics (UBA) to identify and flag suspicious login attempts. These activities, along with more robust data loss prevention mechanisms, enabled SecureTech Solutions to enhance their metrics dashboard, aligning it with their measurement goals.

The average CPU utilization across the 10 servers stabilized at 70%, suggesting that crypto-mining activities had been effectively mitigated. The total bytes transferred from critical servers in an hour dropped to 100GB, demonstrating better control and monitoring of data transfers. Additionally, the number of failed login events on the main authentication server was reduced to 500 within a 5-minute interval, indicating enhanced detection and prevention of brute-force attacks.

The refined thresholds and enhanced monitoring capabilities enabled SecureTech to focus on genuine threats, reducing the number of false positives. By setting more accurate thresholds for unusual file encryption activities, they could concentrate their efforts on genuine ransomware threats. The improved detection and mitigation of crypto-mining activities resulted in a significant reduction in average CPU utilization across servers. Monitoring and analyzing data transfer patterns helped the company detect and prevent unauthorized data exfiltration, leading to a substantial decrease in total bytes transferred. Better anomaly detection mechanisms allowed the security team to identify and block brute-force attacks more efficiently, reducing the number of failed login events.

This case study illustrates the practical application of a refined methodology in continuous threat detection, providing valuable insights into its effectiveness in a real-world scenario. By continuously improving its monitoring processes and refining alert thresholds, SecureTech Solutions enhanced its overall threat detection and response capabilities, reducing alert fatigue and increasing the efficiency of its security team. By using Alert Threshold Lifecycle Assessment System (ATLAS), organizations can create an effective continuous monitoring architecture that reduces alert fatigue and enhances overall security efficiency.

8.4 Understanding ATLAS

This section will introduce the Alert Threshold Lifecycle Assessment System, a methodology I developed to address alert fatigue in network monitoring systems. While ATLAS offers a systematic approach to fine-tuning alert thresholds, it's not the only method available. Feel free to adapt or choose another system that best fits your organization's needs. ALTAS is currently being developed as an open source SaaS application. It is important to remember that ATLAS is a methodology and does not require an application.

ATLAS is designed to combat the problem of alert fatigue, where analysts are overwhelmed by the volume of alerts, leading to desensitization and potential oversight of critical alerts. Figure 8.3 illustrates the ATLAS methodology.

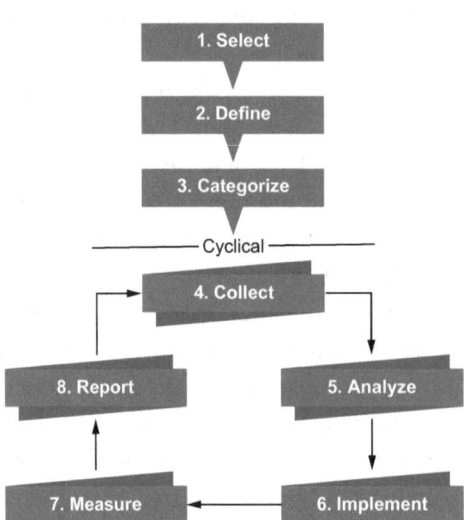

Figure 8.3 ATLAS defines a method to set appropriate thresholds for alerts to reduce fatigue.

8.4.1 ATLAS methodology

By implementing ATLAS, organizations can systematically select, define, assess, and set alert thresholds, significantly reducing false positives and enhancing overall alert management. Let's take a closer look at each of the ATLAS steps.

SELECT

The first step in the ATLAS methodology is to identify the alert to be added. It's recommended to start with the simplest forms of alerts and systematically add more. Some companies roll out an initial batch of alerts that can easily overwhelm analysts and contribute to alert fatigue. The alert name should indicate a meaningful description. Avoid cryptic alert names such as PROD1AL2 or similar. This is the *what* of the alert.

DEFINE

Next, take the time to properly define the alert. Provide a short description of what you are monitoring, what you hope to achieve by tracking this alert, and how it contributes to the information and security program. This is the *why* of the alert.

CATEGORIZE

In ATLAS, we define three major categories of alerts:

- *Zero tolerance alerts*—These alerts are notified immediately upon triggering. They are strictly prohibited alerts; even a single event should be investigated. For example, access to the system from a known bad actor's IP or access from a restricted geographical location.
- *Policy violation alerts*—These alerts have thresholds set by policy and are generated when there is a breach or violation of these predefined thresholds. For example, an alert on the number of failed password attempts before lockout, such as triggering on the third attempt.
- *Anomaly detection alerts*—These alerts are based on statistical analysis of analyzed behavior. They typically follow a cyclical approach to provide continuous process improvement. Examples include data leakage, configuration change, malware detection, behavior anomaly, traffic anomaly, resource consumption, and account privilege alerts.

COLLECT

Once an anomaly detection alert has been defined, specific logs must be collected for analysis. For instance, you may want to collect all the data throughput for the past six months or as long as you have maintained logs. This data collection is crucial for establishing a baseline and identifying deviations.

ANALYZE

ATLAS uses five types of statistical analysis for comparison: weekly percentiles, weekly mean, standard deviation (simple, moving average, and log-transformed), slide positivity rate (if false-positive data is available), and the slope of weekly data on a log scale. These analyses help identify patterns and deviations that may indicate potential threats. In later chapters, we will dive deeper into statistical analysis and the use of AI in metric analysis.

IMPLEMENT

Once the analysis is complete and documented, outliers are typically chosen by specifying thresholds such as Mean + 2 x Standard Deviation. Anything above this threshold should be considered an anomaly requiring investigation. This implementation phase ensures that only significant deviations trigger alerts, reducing the likelihood of false positives.

MEASURE

After implementation, it is essential to document any false positives and review the data to determine whether thresholds need to be adjusted. Continuous measurement and adjustment help refine the alert thresholds over time.

REPORT

Each step of the ATLAS process should be documented in a spreadsheet and maintained as a living document for historical reference and continuous process improvement. This documentation provides a clear trail of changes and helps audit and refine the process.

8.4.2 Review and update

The final step in the ISCM process is regularly reviewing and updating the continuous monitoring program. This ensures the ISCM strategy remains aligned with the organization's evolving needs and threat landscape.

Regular reviews and updates help refine the ISCM strategy; improve the relevance and accuracy of metrics; and enhance overall visibility into assets, vulnerabilities, and threats. This continuous improvement process strengthens the organization's resilience against cybersecurity incidents.

8.4.3 ATLAS benefits

There are many benefits to using a methodology such as ATLAS:

- *Enhanced analyst efficiency*—It enables analysts to prioritize actual threats, which leads to quicker detection and mitigation. This efficiency reduces the time spent chasing false leads, allowing analysts to focus on more strategic tasks.
- *Increased effectiveness*—By setting appropriate thresholds, ATLAS improves the accuracy of alerts, enabling faster and more targeted incident responses.
- *Cost savings*—While implementing ATLAS requires an upfront investment in time, resources, and planning, the long-term savings from reduced man–hours spent on false positives, quicker incident resolutions, and potentially avoided breaches can outweigh the initial costs.
- *Scalability*—Using ATLAS ensures that your alert management system can scale accordingly as your network grows without significant additional infrastructure investments.
- *Real-time collaboration*—A SaaS platform facilitates real-time collaboration among teams, making sharing insights, alert statuses, and collaborating on incident responses easier. This collaborative approach enhances the overall efficiency of the security operations center (SOC). However, the thresholds set and utilized by ATLAS can be tracked in a simple spreadsheet or other methods.
- *Improved compliance*—By consistently and accurately managing alerts, ATLAS helps ensure a more robust compliance posture, potentially reducing risks of regulatory penalties or breaches.

8.5 Determining valid threat detections

False rejection rate (FRR), false acceptance rate (FAR), and equal error rate (EER) are key metrics when monitoring access to key systems. These metrics play a significant role in evaluating the performance and reliability of security systems, particularly those involving biometric authentication and anomaly detection.

8.5.1 False rejection rate

The FRR measures the frequency with which the security system incorrectly denies legitimate access attempts. A high FRR can lead to user frustration and operational inefficiencies, as genuine users are repeatedly blocked from accessing necessary resources. In continuous monitoring systems, a high FRR might indicate overly stringent thresholds, where normal behavior is often flagged as suspicious, leading to unnecessary alerts and potentially ignoring genuine threats due to alert fatigue.

Imagine SecureTech Solutions has implemented a new biometric access control system. Initially, they notice a high FRR, with many employees unable to access their workstations despite being authorized. This scenario highlights the importance of balancing security with usability. To address high FRR, SecureTech might need to adjust its biometric matching algorithms to better distinguish between genuine users and potential threats without compromising security.

8.5.2 False acceptance rate

The FAR, on the other hand, measures how often unauthorized access attempts are mistakenly granted. A high FAR poses significant security risks, as attackers or unauthorized users can access sensitive information or critical systems. In the context of continuous monitoring, a high FAR would mean that many potentially harmful activities are not flagged, leaving the organization vulnerable to undetected threats.

For instance, consider the initial deployment of an anomaly detection system at SecureTech Solutions. If the FAR is high, it could mean that the system allows numerous unauthorized data transfers or access attempts to go unnoticed. This scenario underscores the need for precise calibration of detection algorithms to ensure that malicious activities are accurately identified and addressed.

8.5.3 Equal error rate

The EER is a critical metric representing the point at which the FRR and FAR are equal. It serves as a balanced measure of the system's overall accuracy. The lower the EER, the more reliable the system is at distinguishing between legitimate and illegitimate activities. Achieving a low EER involves fine-tuning the system to minimize both false rejections and false acceptances, thus ensuring optimal performance.

Figure 8.4 shows that SecureTech Solutions achieves a low EER with their continuous monitoring and biometric systems, which means they have successfully balanced security and usability. This would involve iterative testing and adjustment, using real-world data to refine the system's sensitivity and specificity.

Understanding and optimizing FRR, FAR, and EER are pivotal in enhancing the effectiveness of security systems. These metrics provide insights into the system's reliability and ability to accurately differentiate between legitimate and illegitimate actions. Organizations like SecureTech Solutions can ensure robust security, while maintaining operational efficiency and user satisfaction by continuously monitoring and adjusting these rates.

8.5.4 FRR, FAR, and EER metrics

Balancing between minimizing false rejections and false acceptances is a significant challenge. Finding the equal error rate can help measure the system's overall accuracy. Let's discuss further how to optimize these numbers to ensure a seamless and user-friendly experience. Here are some metrics that can help in this delicate balancing act.

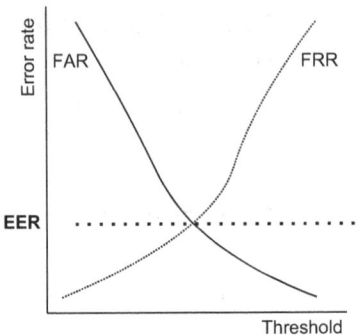

Figure 8.4 This graph illustrates the relationship between the false accept rate (FAR) and false reject rate (FRR) as a function of the threshold setting in a security system. The equal error rate (EER) is the point at which the FAR and FRR are equal, indicating the threshold where the probability of false acceptances is equal to the probability of false rejections.

FRR METRICS

- *Number of false rejections per day/week/month*—Tracks the number of legitimate access attempts incorrectly rejected by the system
- *False rejection rate percentage*—Calculates the percentage of legitimate access attempts that were falsely rejected out of the total access attempts

FAR METRICS

- *Number of false acceptances per day/week/month*—Tracks the number of unauthorized access attempts incorrectly accepted by the system
- *False acceptance rate percentage*—Calculates the percentage of unauthorized access attempts that were falsely accepted out of the total access attempts

EER METRICS

- *Equal error rate value*—Represents the point at which the FRR and FAR are equal. It is a critical value that indicates the accuracy of the biometric or authentication system

8.5.5 FRR, FAR, and ERR exercise

As seen on the left side of figure 8.5, DataSecure Inc., a financial services company, has been experiencing problems with its biometric authentication system. Employees and clients have reported frequent difficulties accessing the system due to high false rejection rates. At the same time, security teams have noticed a worrying number of false acceptances, indicating potential security breaches. The company thoroughly reviews and improves its authentication system to address these problems. The high numbers in these metrics indicate significant problems with false rejections and acceptances, resulting in user frustration and potential security vulnerabilities.

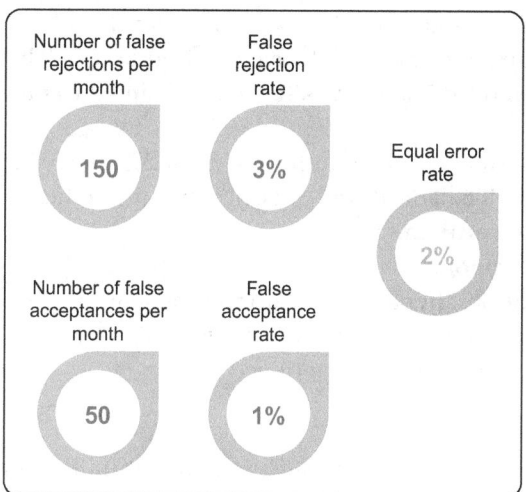 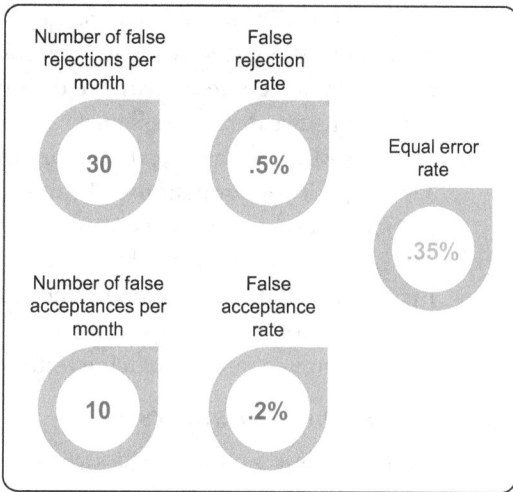

Figure 8.5 The left side shows DataSecure, Inc. FRR, FAR, and EES dashboard before implementing improvements. The right side shows improvements after reducing both false rejection and false acceptance rates.

By applying system enhancements and recalibrations, the right side shows DataSecure Inc. was able to reduce both the false rejection and false acceptance rates. The number of false rejections decreased from 150 to 30 per month, making the system much friendlier for users and reducing frustration among employees and clients. The false rejection rate percentage also dropped from 3% to 0.5%, indicating a more reliable authentication process.

To achieve this goal, DataSecure Inc. began by analyzing the biometric authentication system's performance data, focusing on both the false rejection and false acceptance rates. They recalibrated the biometric system thresholds to balance security and usability, adjusting sensitivity settings to better distinguish between legitimate users and potential intruders. Additionally, they introduced advanced machine learning algorithms to enhance the accuracy of user identification and reduce error rates. By continuously monitoring these metrics and making iterative adjustments, they were able to significantly improve both the security and user experience, leading to a much lower rate of false rejections and acceptances.

To achieve these improvements, DataSecure Inc. analyzed the biometric system's error patterns. They focused on recalibrating the sensitivity thresholds to strike a better balance between security and usability. The team also integrated advanced machine learning algorithms, which helped refine the system's ability to differentiate between legitimate users and potential threats. Continuous monitoring and iterative adjustments based on real-time data allowed them to progressively lower both the false rejection and false acceptance rates. This approach ensured the system became more reliable, reducing user frustration and enhancing overall security.

The number of false acceptances decreased from 50 to 10 per month, greatly enhancing the system's security by minimizing the risk of unauthorized access. The false acceptance rate percentage dropped from 1% to 0.2%, further securing the company's sensitive data and systems.

The EER value, a critical measure of system accuracy, improved from 2% to 0.35%. This significant reduction indicates a well-balanced and highly accurate biometric authentication system that ensures both security and usability.

The improvements in these metrics demonstrate the effectiveness of DataSecure Inc.'s system enhancements and recalibrations. By closely monitoring and adjusting the authentication system, the company was able to achieve a much lower false rejection and acceptance rate, enhancing both security and user experience.

8.6 Adverse event analysis

Adverse event analysis is the process of investigating unusual activities or indicators that could signify a security incident. The primary goal is identifying whether these events are benign anomalies or genuine security threats. This analysis helps understand the root cause of incidents, the effectiveness of existing security controls, and the necessary actions to prevent future occurrences.

Anomalies are deviations from normal behavior. *Indicators of Compromise* (IoCs) are pieces of evidence demonstrating a potential security breach. They need to be analyzed to determine whether they pose a risk. We need to establish event characterization, which involves categorizing events based on their severity, type, and potential effect on the organization. Root cause analysis involves identifying the underlying reasons for the occurrence of adverse events to address these problems and prevent recurrence.

8.6.1 Adverse event analysis metrics

Several metrics can be used to analyze adverse events effectively. These metrics help quantify the analysis process, track improvements, and ensure that the organization's security posture remains strong.

DIRECT METRICS

- *Time to detect (TTD)*—Measures the time taken to identify an adverse event after it occurs. A shorter TTD indicates a more efficient detection system.
- *Time to respond (TTR)*—Tracks the time between detecting an event and initiating a response. A shorter TTR is crucial for minimizing the effects of security incidents.
- *Event volume*—Measures the total number of adverse events detected within a specific period. It helps understand the overall threat landscape and the effectiveness of detection mechanisms.

DERIVED METRICS

- *False positive rate*—Calculates the percentage of alerts incorrectly identified as threats. Reducing false positives is essential for improving threat detection accuracy and reducing alert fatigue.

- *Incident classification accuracy*—Evaluates the accuracy with which events are categorized into different severity levels. Accurate classification ensures appropriate response and resource allocation.
- *Root cause resolution rate*—Tracks the percentage of identified root causes that have been addressed and resolved. A higher resolution rate indicates effective vulnerability mitigation.

8.6.2 Adverse event analysis metrics exercise

Let's consider a case study of SecureData Inc., which recently enhanced its adverse event analysis capabilities. SecureData Inc. is a mid-sized enterprise specializing in data management solutions. Due to high false positive rates and inefficient event analysis processes, it has been facing challenges with alert fatigue and delayed incident responses. The dashboard on the left in figure 8.6 represents the situation before they enhanced their adverse event analysis.

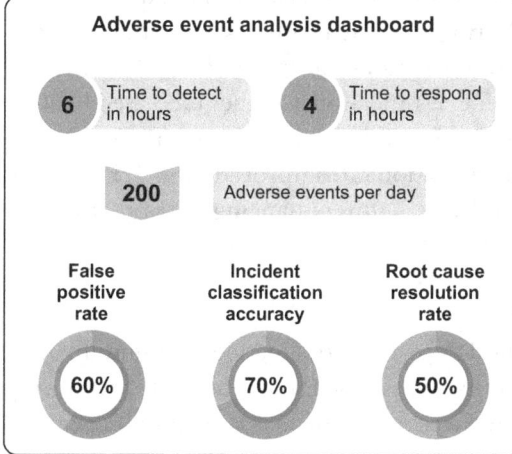
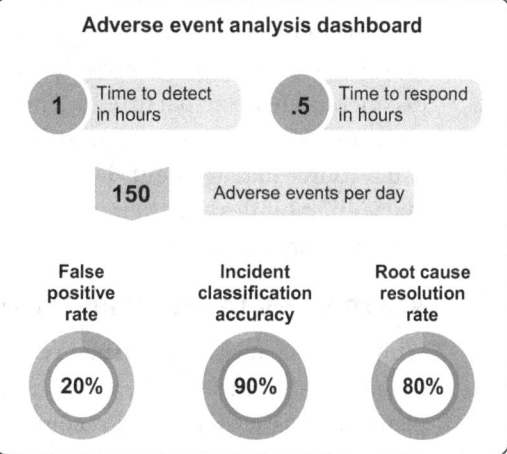

Figure 8.6 The left side shows the adverse event analysis dashboard before implementing enhancements. The right side shows the dashboard after implementing enhancements.

SecureData Inc.'s dashboard revealed problems in its threat detection and response metrics. TTD was high at 6 hours, indicating substantial delays in identifying potential threats. The TTR was lengthy, taking 4 hours to initiate a response after detecting an incident. The event volume was substantial, with 200 adverse events being reported daily. This high volume was exacerbated by a 60% FPR, overwhelming analysts with numerous irrelevant alerts. The incident classification accuracy stood at 70%, meaning a significant portion of events were not being accurately categorized, leading to potential mismanagement of resources. Additionally, the root cause resolution rate was at a low 50%, reflecting inefficiencies in addressing and mitigating the underlying causes of incidents.

On the right side of figure 8.6 is the situation after implementing a more robust adverse event analysis framework, which shows a notable improvement across all metrics. To achieve these improvements, SecureData Inc. began by revising their event analysis tools and processes. They implemented advanced filtering techniques that allowed the system to more accurately distinguish between legitimate threats and false positives, significantly reducing irrelevant alerts. The company also incorporated enhanced event correlation methods and machine learning algorithms, which contributed to faster and more precise threat detection and response. Additionally, SecureData Inc. refined its incident classification criteria, improving the accuracy and efficiency of resource allocation and response efforts. To bolster their root cause analysis, they introduced more rigorous investigative tools and procedures, leading to a higher resolution rate of underlying problems and further strengthening their overall security posture.

TTD was reduced to 1 hour, demonstrating a more efficient detection system capable of identifying threats much faster. TTR improved to just 30 minutes, allowing for rapid initiation of responses to incidents. The event volume stabilized at 150 adverse events per day, indicating better control and filtering of events to focus on genuinely relevant threats. The FPR decreased to 20%, reducing alert fatigue and enabling analysts to concentrate on actual threats. The incident classification accuracy increased to 90%, ensuring that events were accurately categorized, and facilitating appropriate response and resource management. The root cause resolution rate improved to 80%, indicating that vulnerabilities were being effectively addressed, thus enhancing the organization's overall security posture.

8.7 Alternatives to ATLAS and Wazuh

While ATLAS provides a structured methodology for reducing alert fatigue through optimized alert thresholds, and Wazuh offers a robust open source security monitoring platform, it is important to recognize that these solutions may not suit all organizational needs. Here are some alternatives you can consider for ATLAS:

- *MITRE ATT&CK® framework*—This framework can complement or substitute ATLAS by providing a comprehensive knowledge base of adversarial tactics and techniques. It helps organizations prioritize alerts based on identified threats relevant to their environment.
- *CIS Critical Security Controls (CIS controls)*—These controls can be used to develop prioritized alert mechanisms by focusing on critical areas such as access control, vulnerability management, and monitoring.
- *Risk-based alerting with SIEM tools*—Tools such as Splunk or QRadar have integrated capabilities to establish dynamic alert thresholds based on the severity and context of threats. They allow for more granular customization and automation compared to static threshold models.

Here are some alternatives to consider for Wazuh:

- *Elastic Security (ELK Stack)*—This highly scalable alternative offers advanced threat detection, visualization, and alerting capabilities. It integrates seamlessly with existing Elastic Stack deployments.
- *AlienVault OSSIM*—An open-source SIEM solution that, in addition to alerting, provides essential features for security monitoring, such as threat detection, asset discovery, and event correlation.
- *Graylog*—Known for its robust log management capabilities, Graylog supports security operations through real-time alerts, anomaly detection, and integrations with external threat intelligence feeds.
- *Commercial SIEMs*—For organizations with more extensive resources, commercial options such Splunk, Microsoft Sentinel, or IBM QRadar can offer more advanced functionality, including automated response, machine learning-based anomaly detection, and better scalability.

Summary

- Implementing continuous threat monitoring systems is crucial for maintaining a proactive security posture.
- Defining a strategy involves setting clear risk tolerance levels and ensuring comprehensive visibility over assets and vulnerabilities.
- Responding to findings requires timely and effective mitigation strategies to address detected threats.
- Open source solutions such as Wazuh offer powerful tools for continuous threat detection and monitoring, integrating seamlessly with existing infrastructure.
- Establishing a robust architecture for continuous monitoring includes defining key metrics, determining appropriate monitoring frequencies, and setting up reliable reporting mechanisms.
- Effective implementation and data collection are vital for maintaining an up-to-date security posture and ensuring prompt threat detection.
- Thorough analysis and reporting of collected data help in understanding and responding to security incidents effectively.
- The ATLAS methodology enhances alert thresholds and reduces alert fatigue, thus improving overall incident response efficiency.
- Determining valid threat detections involves balancing false rejection, false acceptance, and equal error rates to maintain system accuracy.
- Adverse event analysis helps address potential threats fast and improve the overall security strategy.

Incident management and recovery

This chapter covers
- Incident management in cybersecurity
- Evaluating and improving incident response
- Techniques for effective incident analysis
- Strategies for reporting and communicating incidents
- Methods for incident mitigation and recovery

Incident management is a cornerstone of any cybersecurity strategy, enabling organizations to address and recover from cyber threats. Managing incidents swiftly and accurately often defines whether threat remains minor or spirals into a major breach. This chapter focuses on responding to and recovering from incidents using proven methodologies and a systematic approach that is both efficient and repeatable.

We investigate the steps necessary to build a comprehensive incident management plan—from the initial detection of a security event to its resolution and communication with stakeholders. Each section provides practical insights and metrics to help organizations assess and improve their incident response capabilities. By the end of this chapter, you will learn how to develop an effective incident management process, analyze incidents to prevent future occurrences, and verify that your organization is prepared to respond to any cybersecurity threat.

9.1 Incident management

Incident management is a systematic approach to detecting, responding to, and recovering from cybersecurity incidents. It is designed with the primary objective of minimizing the effects of incidents on the organization. Incident management must be able to preserve continuity of your business operations and safeguard its assets. A well-defined and tested incident management plan is critical in effectively managing and mitigating the consequences of cybersecurity breaches.

Effective incident response plans are based on a balanced approach between proactive and reactive measures. Proactive measures focus on anticipating potential threats and implementing safeguards to prevent incidents from occurring, which includes deploying security controls, conducting threat hunting, enforcing access restrictions, and running continuous vulnerability assessments. Reactive measures, however, focus on mitigating damage and restoring normal operations once an incident has occurred. They include containment, forensic investigation, remediation, and post-incident reviews to strengthen future defenses.

A hybrid approach blends proactive and reactive strategies for faster detection and response. For example, automated threat detection using AI-driven anomaly recognition can proactively identify suspicious activities before they escalate. This feature can be paired with immediate containment actions, such as isolating compromised endpoints or blocking suspicious IP addresses in real time. Deception technology, such as honeypots, proactively lures attackers into controlled environments, while simultaneously triggering automated incident response mechanisms. Endpoint detection and response (EDR) solutions use continuous monitoring to detect abnormal behavior and trigger automatic responses, such as rolling back malicious changes or quarantining infected systems. Combining automated threat detection with rapid containment empowers organizations to significantly reduce dwell time, limit the effects of security incidents, and continuously refine their security posture.

A strong change management process is key to maintaining an effective security posture. Engineering teams might inadvertently introduce vulnerabilities without sufficient oversight and compliance, such as exposing sensitive data without proper authentication or authorization. For instance, if a system changes without involving the necessary stakeholders, a security threat and risk assessment (STRA) may not be conducted, thus leading to an undetected flaw in the live environment. This type of oversight increases the risk of security incidents and emphasizes the need for stringent approval workflows, security testing, and documentation before deploying any changes.

Additionally, security teams must differentiate between a breach and a potential breach assessment. A *breach* refers to confirmed unauthorized access or data compromise, requiring immediate response and mitigation. On the other hand, a *potential breach assessment* involves evaluating security gaps or misconfigurations that could be exploited but have not yet resulted in an incident. Conducting regular assessments, security audits, and penetration tests helps identify these potential threats early, preventing them from escalating into full-scale security breaches.

Most incident response plan frameworks have similar steps, which will be discussed in detail in the following sections. You also want to add steps that we feel are often missed but are critical to a successful incident response plan. Figure 9.1 introduces a comprehensive incident response framework that includes 10 critical steps: planning and preparation, testing, detection and documentation, triage, notification and communication, containment, evidence gathering and forensic analysis, eradication, recovery, and post-incident and lessons learned. Each step is vital in enabling a robust and effective incident management process.

Figure 9.1 Steps to develop a comprehensive incident response plan

The foundation of any successful incident management strategy is thorough planning and preparation. This involves developing and documenting an *incident response plan*

(IRP) that outlines the procedures and protocols to follow in the event of an incident. Key elements of planning and preparation include defining roles and responsibilities, identifying critical assets, and establishing communication channels. Regular training and awareness programs for staff ensure that everyone understands their role in incident response, which helps minimize confusion and delays during an actual incident.

An IRP should not be a static, one-time document created and then forgotten. Instead, it must be a living document—regularly reviewed, updated, and refined to reflect evolving threats, organizational changes, and lessons learned from previous incidents. The IRP should be as detailed as necessary to be practical and actionable, ensuring it serves as a functional playbook rather than a compliance-driven formality.

An IRP is only as strong as its adoption and usability. Security teams should integrate the IRP into their daily workflows, treating it like any other long-term strategic project. Regular tabletop exercises, incident simulations, and continuous feedback loops ensure the plan remains relevant, scalable, and aligned with the organization's risk landscape. The goal is not to create documentation for its own sake, but to establish a flexible and adaptive framework that enables swift, coordinated, and effective incident response.

Let's now examine some key steps in the incident response framework to better understand how to implement and measure the IRP effectiveness.

9.2 Planning and preparation

This is the foundational step for ensuring your organization is ready to respond to cybersecurity incidents efficiently. A well-prepared IRP minimizes damage, reduces recovery time, and helps maintain business continuity. The primary objective of planning and preparation is to establish a structured approach to managing incidents. This involves creating detailed response procedures, assembling the *incident response team* (IRT), and verifying that all resources and support structures are in place. Proper planning enables organizations to identify potential threats early, assess their effects, and mitigate damage.

The first step in this phase is to define the IRP scope and objectives, which involves understanding the organization's needs and tailoring the IRP to address those requirements. You can't guard each asset all the time, so you must categorize and prioritize the critical business functionality to define precisely what is required for minimal business operations and focus your IRP within this scope. Key considerations include the data types the organization handles, the potential effects of different incidents, and regulatory requirements.

The next step in planning and preparation is defining the IRT. This team is responsible for executing the IRP and managing all aspects of the incident response. The IRT should include representatives from various IT, legal, communications, and executive management departments. Each member of the IRT should have clearly defined roles and responsibilities that cover all the critical IRP aspects. Each member should also have at least three methods of communication at their disposal to cover any incident.

Furthermore, each member should have a fallback person assigned if either the communications or the availability of the primary IRT member is compromised.

Training and awareness are also integral parts of planning and preparation. All employees should know the organization's IRP and understand their role in the process. Regular training sessions and simulated incident response exercises can help reinforce this knowledge and verify that everyone is prepared to act swiftly in the event of an incident.

The final element of planning is defining the communication plan. This is critical for managing an incident, maintaining stakeholder trust, and confirming regulatory compliance. This communication plan should outline how information will be shared internally and externally, who is responsible for communications, and what information can be disclosed.

Once the planning and preparation are completed, the scope is defined, the IRT is developed, and the communication plan is defined, the next step in the IRP is testing. Let's look at how to test an IRP.

9.3 Testing an IRP

Testing should be done before an IRP is placed into practice and redone periodically, at least annually. Testing confirms that the IRP is practical, effective, and well-understood by all key stakeholders. One of the most effective methods for testing the IRP is accomplished via tabletop exercises. These exercises mimic real-world scenarios, allowing the IRT to practice their response procedures and identify any gaps or weaknesses in the plan so organizations can make adjustments before an incident.

During a tabletop exercise, a facilitator presents a hypothetical incident scenario. These are discussion-based sessions where team members gather and walk through various IRP aspects. These sessions focus on the decision-making process and coordination among team members. The exercises help evaluate the plan, improve team coordination, and identify areas for improvement. Most often, the facilitator is the CISO or other cybersecurity manager or analyst.

Here is an outline of an effective tabletop exercise:

- *Defining objectives*—The first step in conducting a tabletop exercise is to define its objectives, such as evaluating specific procedures, testing communication strategies, or identifying gaps in the IRP. Clear objectives help focus on the exercise and ensure that it addresses the most critical aspects of the IRP.
- *Developing scenarios*—Next, create realistic and relevant scenarios that reflect potential threats to your organization. Scenarios should be detailed and cover various types of incidents, such as data breaches, ransomware attacks, or insider threats. The scenarios should evolve in complexity to test different IRP aspects. While working on the scenarios, you should inject additional challenges to simulate the complexity of incidents in the real world.
- *Assembling the team*—Gather the incident response team and any other stakeholders involved in the incident response process. This includes representatives

from IT, legal, communications, management, and any external partners. Ensure that each participant understands their role in the exercise. Participation in the tabletop exercise should be a mandatory requirement for everyone on the IRT.
- *Facilitate the exercise*—The facilitator plays a crucial role in guiding the exercise. They present the scenario, lead the discussion, and keep the exercise on track. The facilitator should encourage participation, ask probing questions, and provide feedback for a thorough evaluation of the IRP.
- *Document the exercise*—Assign a scribe to document the exercise, including the decisions, actions taken, and any identified problems or gaps. Detailed documentation helps capture lessons learned and provides a reference for improving the IRP.
- *Debriefing and analyzing*—Conduct a debriefing session after the exercise to discuss the outcomes and gather participant feedback. Analyze the results to identify strengths and weaknesses in the IRP. Focus on areas where the team struggled, communication breakdowns, or any procedures that need refinement.
- *Developing action plans*—Based on the analysis, develop action plans to address any identified problems. This may involve updating the IRP, providing additional training, or implementing new tools and technologies. It should also be confirmed that these action plans are documented and assigned to specific team members for follow-up.
- *Repeating and refining*—Conduct tabletop exercises regularly to keep the IRP current and effective. Each exercise should build on the lessons learned from previous sessions, continuously improving the organization's incident response capabilities. The minimum recommended periodicity of tabletop exercises is annual.

Most companies have an annual tabletop exercise. It is highly recommended that CEOs participate in these exercises to ensure that they understand how the company responds to an incident and what role they play in the process.

9.3.1 Tabletop exercise example

Here, we explore how a tabletop exercise is practically designed and implemented through a real-world scenario:

OBJECTIVE

Test the incident response team's ability to handle a data breach involving sensitive customer information and evaluate the effectiveness of the communication and containment procedures.

BACKGROUND

SecureTech Solutions, a mid-sized cybersecurity firm, has recently detected unusual activity on its network. The company holds sensitive customer information, including financial data and personally identifiable information (PII).

PARTICIPANTS

Incident response team (IRT) includes

- IT support staff
- Legal department
- Communications/Public relations
- Management
- External partners (if applicable)

INITIAL SCENARIO SETUP

- *Day 1: Incident detection (9:00 AM)*—The IT support staff detects unusual network traffic originating from a critical server containing customer data. Initial analysis suggests potential unauthorized access.
- Discussion points
  - How will the team confirm the breach?
  - What initial steps will be taken to contain the potential breach?
  - Who needs to be informed at this stage?

INJECTION POINT 1: ESCALATION

- *Day 2: Incident escalation (10:00 AM)*—While investigating the breach, the IRT discovers that the attacker has encrypted a significant portion of the customer data, demanding a ransom for the decryption key.
- Discussion points
  - What is the organization's policy on ransomware demands?
  - How will the team handle the encrypted data?
  - What additional containment measures should be implemented?
  - How will the team communicate this escalation to internal and external stakeholders?

INJECTION POINT 2: ADDITIONAL COMPLICATION

- *Day 3: Public disclosure (2:00 PM)*—A journalist contacts the PR department, claiming to have information about the breach and asking for a comment. This adds pressure on the organization to manage public perception and media inquiries.
- Discussion points
  - How should the PR team respond to the journalist's inquiry?
  - What steps should be taken to prepare a public statement?
  - How will the communication strategy change in light of potential public disclosure?
  - How will the organization manage potential customer concerns and legal implications?

FINAL PHASE: RESOLUTION AND RECOVERY

- *Day 4: Recovery and lessons learned (4 PM)*—The IRT manages to restore the encrypted data from backups, and the network is secured. The team begins recovering from the incident, including a thorough review and improvement of security measures.
- Discussion points
  - What steps are necessary to guarantee a complete recovery from the breach?
  - How will the team document the incident and the response efforts?
  - What long-term measures will be implemented to prevent future incidents?
  - How will the team conduct a post-incident review and lessons learned session?

Tabletop exercises are designed with your company's business objectives in mind. Each is custom designed to play out potential incidents relevant to your business. Many cybersecurity frameworks mandate that at least one setup covers a ransomware scenario.

9.3.2 Tabletop exercise metrics

There are some quantifiable metrics we can use to measure the effectiveness of the tabletop exercises. As always, we evaluate the possibilities and determine what is most important for your team and the organization. Never record metrics for the sake of having data. Instead, determine the reason for collecting metrics and what story these measurements will help you tell.

To quantitatively measure the effectiveness of the tabletop exercise, you can use a combination of performance indicators and participant feedback. Here are some metrics that can be represented with numbers.

PROCEDURE ADHERENCE METRICS

- *Adherence to incident response plan*—Measures the percentage of steps followed correctly according to the incident response plan
- *Deviation instances*—Counts the instances where the team deviated from the established incident response procedures

GAP AND WEAKNESS IDENTIFICATION METRICS

- *Number of gaps identified*—Counts the gaps or weaknesses identified during the exercise
- *Severity of gaps*—Measures the percentage of identified gaps classified as high, medium, or low severity

PARTICIPANT FEEDBACK METRICS

- *Feedback score*—Collects numerical feedback scores (e.g., on a scale from 1 to 10) from participants on the realism, relevance, and overall effectiveness of the exercise

- *Improvement suggestions*—Counts the number of improvement suggestions provided by participants

TRAINING EFFECTIVENESS METRICS

- *Knowledge retention rate*—Measures the percentage of participants correctly recalling and applying the incident response procedures during the exercise
- *Skill improvement rate*—Measures the percentage of participants who improve their incident response skills compared to previous exercises

9.3.3 Table for tabletop exercise evaluation sample

Figure 9.2 shows an example of the collected tabletop metrics that aim to quantify the exercise's effectiveness. Each metric has a target value, an actual value, and the corresponding correction action required to close the gaps.

Metric	Target	Value	Notes
Procedure adherence (%)	100	95	Minor deviations; closer adherence required
Deviation instances	0	3	Investigate reasons for deviations
Gaps identified	0	4	Identify and address gaps
Severity of gaps (high/medium/low)	0/0/0	2/1/1	Focus on high-severity gaps
Feedback score (1–10)	8	7.5	Overall positive, but there is room for improvement
Improvement suggestions	0	5	Implement feasible suggestions
Knowledge retention rate (%)	100	90	Reinforce training where needed
Skill improvement rate (%)	100	85	Continue skill-development efforts

Figure 9.2 Tabletop exercise example metrics table with target values, actual values, and corrective actions based on metrics

9.4 Detection and documentation

Effective detection ensures that incidents are identified promptly, minimizing potential damage. Thorough documentation provides a detailed account of the incident from start to finish, facilitating comprehensive post-incident analysis and lessons learned. These steps are combined into step 3 to remember that any detection must be documented. This can provide useful information on how well your threat detection is performing, as covered in previous chapters. You can then use ATLAS or other means to collect false acceptance rate (FAR) and false rejection rate (FRR) metrics to fine-tune your detection process and minimize unnecessary work.

Incident identification is the first step in responding to an anomaly. It involves monitoring systems for *Indicators of Compromise* (IoCs) and unusual activities that could signal a security incident. Utilizing automated tools such as intrusion detection systems (IDS), security information and event management (SIEM) systems, and continuous monitoring solutions such as Wazuh helps detect these threats.

When an incident is detected, it must be logged accurately and comprehensively. This log serves as the primary record of the incident and is essential for tracking the incident's life cycle.

Key elements to include in the incident log are

- *Date and time of detection*—Records when the incident was detected to help trace the timeline.
- *Incident identifier*—Assigns a unique identifier to each incident for easy tracking and reference.
- *Source of detection*—Identifies the tool or system that detected the incident (e.g., IDS, SIEM, firewall).
- *Description of incident*—Provides a brief yet detailed description of the suspected incident.
- *Affected systems*—Lists all systems and assets affected by the incident.
- *Initial severity assessment*—Assesses the initial severity level (e.g., low, medium, high, critical).
- *Severity*—Typically, you should use a three- or five-tier severity tag. High, med, and low are commonly used in three-tier systems. However, you can use a five-tier solution, such as informational, low, moderate, high, and critical, for more granularity.
- *Chain of custody*—Each time an incident is updated with additional information, enriched with forensic or other data, or changed in status or severity, the person making the update, date, and time should be recorded. This log of events should not be editable and can be used for review, audit, or regulatory purposes.

For instance, if a SIEM system detects multiple failed login attempts on a server, this should be logged immediately with all relevant details, including the IP addresses involved, the specific accounts targeted, and the time frame of the attempts.

Once an incident is identified and logged, it must be prioritized and categorized to guarantee an appropriate and timely response. This task involves assessing its potential effects and urgency. Factors to consider include

- *Effects*—The potential damage the incident could cause to systems, data, and business operations
- *Urgency*—How quickly the incident must be addressed to prevent further damage
- *Scope*—The extent of the incident, including the number of affected systems and the breadth of the compromise

Incidents can be categorized into malware infections, phishing attacks, unauthorized access, data breaches, and denial-of-service attacks. Each category may have specific response protocols and prioritization criteria.

9.4.1 Three-tier severity model

In a three-tier severity model, incidents are categorized as low, medium, or high severity. This model provides a straightforward way to prioritize incidents based on their potential effects and urgency:

- *Low severity*—Incidents that pose minimal risk and can be addressed without significant urgency. Examples include minor policy violations, low-severity malware, and isolated phishing attempts. These incidents may require standard procedures and routine checks without immediate escalation.
- *Medium severity*—Incidents that have a moderate effect and require timely attention but are not immediately critical. This could include unauthorized access attempts that are detected early, suspicious but nondisruptive network activity, and malware that has been contained but needs further investigation.
- *High severity*—Incidents that pose a significant threat to the organization and require immediate response. Examples include data breaches, widespread malware infections, and successful unauthorized access to critical systems. These incidents demand rapid action and significant resource allocation to contain and mitigate.

9.4.2 Five-tier severity model

A five-tier severity model provides a more granular approach, allowing for finer distinctions between different levels of threat and urgency. This model is often preferred in larger organizations with complex IT environments. Low, mid, and high are the same as in the three-tier system, but the five-tier model includes two other categories—one at the low end (informational) and one at the high end (critical):

- *Informational*—Incidents that are not necessarily harmful but should be logged for record-keeping and potential future analysis. These could include routine scans or minor policy violations that do not pose an immediate threat.
- *Low, medium, and high*—Same as in the three-tier severity model.
- *Critical*—Incidents representing a severe and imminent threat to the organization's operations, data, or reputation. This level requires an all-hands-on-deck

approach, with rapid response and escalation to senior management and possibly external authorities.

9.4.3 Changing severity over time

As an incident progresses through the incident response life cycle, its severity level may change based on new information and analysis. Initially, an incident might be tagged as moderate due to limited information. As the investigation unfolds and more data is gathered, the severity may be escalated to high or critical if the incident's effects are found to be more severe than initially thought. Conversely, an incident initially assessed as high severity may be downgraded if it is less damaging than expected.

9.4.4 Practical example of incident documentation

A well-documented incident record is crucial for effective incident management. What follows is a practical example and template that can be used to document an incident thoroughly.

DETAILED INCIDENT REPORT TEMPLATE
Incident identifier: INC-2024-001
Date and time of detection: 2024-07-24, 10:15 AM
Source of detection: Wazuh SIEM
Description of incident: Multiple failed login attempts were detected on the primary database server. The attempts originated from an external IP address and targeted the admin account.
Affected systems: Primary database server (DB01)
Initial severity assessment: Moderate
Detection details: At 10:15 AM, Wazuh SIEM detected 5,000 failed login attempts within a 5-minute interval on the primary database server.
Source IP: 192.168.1.100
Targeted account: admin

- Incident identification
  - *Indicators of compromise*—Unusual spike in failed login attempts
  - *Detection tool*—Wazuh SIEM
- Incident analysis
  - *Initial analysis*—The IP address 192.168.1.100 is flagged in threat intelligence databases as associated with known malicious activity.
  - *Impact assessment*—High potential risk of unauthorized access to sensitive data.
- Containment and eradication
  - Containment actions—Blocked the source IP address at the firewall.
  - Eradication actions—Reset the admin account password and review server access logs for any other suspicious activity.

- Evidence gathering and forensic analysis
  - *Collected evidence*—SIEM logs, firewall logs, and access logs from the database server
  - *Forensic analysis*—Ongoing to determine if there was any successful breach before blocking the IP
- Recovery
  - *Recovery actions*—Implemented additional monitoring on the database server and conducted a full security audit of the affected systems.
  - *System restoration*—Confirmed that no unauthorized access occurred.
- Notification and communication
  - *Internal notification*—Notified the IT security team and senior management
  - *External notification*—Not required as no data breach occurred
- Post-incident review
  - *Lessons learned*—Need to enhance monitoring rules to detect and respond to brute-force attacks more quickly.
  - *Action items*—Review and update incident response protocols, implement additional login attempt thresholds, and schedule regular security training for the IT team.
- Chain of custody
  - Log entry created by John Doe, IT Security Analyst
  - Log entry reviewed by Jane Smith, IT Security Manager
  - Forensic evidence collected by Forensic Team

9.4.5 Chain of custody

Maintaining a clear chain of custody is vital for preserving the integrity of the evidence collected during an incident. This task involves documenting who handled the evidence, when it was collected, and any changes or transfers in custody, which makes sure that the evidence remains admissible in legal proceedings and supports the accuracy of the post-incident analysis.

9.4.6 Incident management metrics

These metrics provide quantifiable insights into how quickly and efficiently incidents are detected, identified, and addressed, allowing organizations to fine-tune their processes and reduce their overall risk exposure. By tracking these metrics, it is possible to identify bottlenecks, measure the edicts of your response strategies, and demonstrate the value of your security initiatives to stakeholders.

DIRECT METRICS

- *Incident detection time (IDT)*—Measures the average time taken to detect an incident from the moment it occurs. This metric helps in understanding how quickly the system can identify potential threats and incidents.

- *Number of incidents detected*—Tracks the total number of security incidents detected within a specific time frame. This metric provides insight into the volume of potential threats the system encounters.

DERIVED METRICS

- *Mean time to detect incident (MTTD-I)*—The average time taken from an incident to its detection.
- *Mean time to identify incident (MTTI-I)*—The average time taken from the detection of an incident to its identification as a legitimate threat. This metric assesses the efficiency of the initial incident response process.

9.4.7 Incident management metrics exercise

Let's consider SecureNet Inc., a medium-sized financial services company that has recently enhanced its incident response plan to improve its cybersecurity posture. By implementing the 10-step IRP framework and introducing several key metrics, SecureNet Inc. aims to measure and improve its incident detection and response capabilities.

Once SecureNet Inc. was able to determine its goals for these metrics, it could focus on improving them. Prior to implementing the enhanced IRP, they struggled with high incident detection times and slow identification of legitimate threats. As shown in figure 9.3, initial dashboard metrics indicated significant delays in both detection and identification, leading to prolonged exposure to potential threats. The right side of the figure shows significant improvements in incident response metrics following the implementation of the enhanced incident response plan and introducing the 10-step IRP framework.

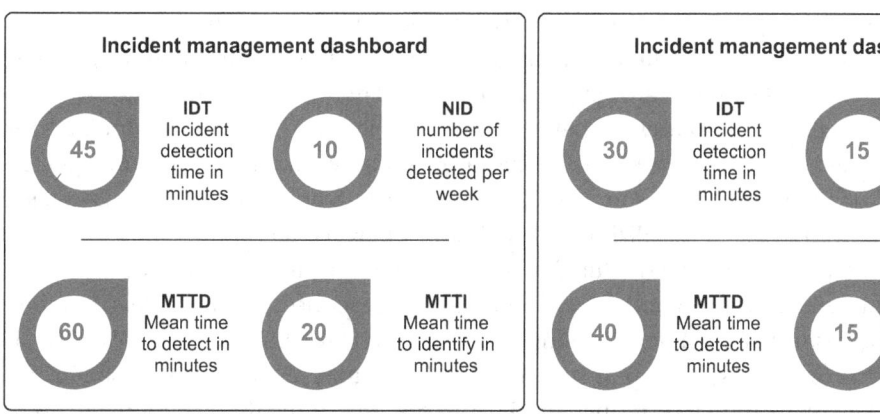

Figure 9.3 The left side shows the SecureNet Inc. incident management dashboard before implementing the enhanced IRP and introducing the 10-step IRP framework. The right side illustrates the situation after implementing the plan and introducing the framework.

By refining the monitoring tools and increasing the sensitivity of detection mechanisms, SecureNet significantly reduced the IDT from 45 to 30 minutes. This improvement indicates that potential threats are being identified more quickly, allowing faster response times.

The increased number of detected incidents from 10 to 15 per week suggests that enhanced monitoring capabilities are more effective at identifying potential threats. This increase is not necessarily a negative indicator; instead, it shows that monitoring tools are more sensitive and capable of detecting a wider range of threats.

The reduction in TTD reflects improved efficiency in the detection process, which reduced this metric from 60 to 40 minutes. SecureNet's efforts to streamline monitoring and introduce automated detection mechanisms have resulted in quicker incident identification.

The decreased MTTI from 20 to 15 minutes highlights the effectiveness of enhanced analysis tools and improved training of the incident response team. Faster identification of legitimate threats means that the team can respond faster and mitigate potential damage.

9.5 Incident triage and analysis

The incident analysis and triage phases involve meticulously examining the details of the incident to understand its nature, scope, and effects. Proper incident analysis not only helps address the current incident but also aids in preventing future occurrences by identifying vulnerabilities and improving security measures.

Incident analysis begins immediately after the detection and initial documentation of the incident. The primary objectives are to determine the cause of the incident, understand how it unfolded, and assess the extent of its effects. This process typically involves several key steps.

First, we must collect the initial set of all relevant data related to the incident, which includes system logs, network traffic data, security tool alerts, and other pertinent information. Tools such as Wazuh, an open source security monitoring platform, can be invaluable for collecting and organizing this data. Then we must correlate and analyze the collected data to identify patterns and correlations. This involves looking for IoCs, such as unusual network traffic, unauthorized access attempts, and unexpected changes to system files. Open source tools such as Elastic Stack (Elasticsearch, Logstash, and Kibana) can help in visualizing and analyzing log data effectively.

We must also reconstruct the timeline of the incident. This timeline should include the initial detection, subsequent activities, and any responses taken. A clear timeline helps understand the events' sequence and identify the root cause. Tools such as Timesketch or Autopsy are open source forensic analysis tools that can assist in this process. Finally, we assess the influence. Here we can determine the scope and effects of the incident and evaluate which systems and data were affected, the extent of any data breaches, and the potential business and operational effects. This assessment helps prioritize response efforts and allocate resources effectively.

Various methods and tools can be employed to conduct thorough incident analysis:

- *Log analysis*—System and network logs are analyzed to identify unusual activities and potential indicators of compromise. Tools such as Wazuh, Graylog, and the Elastic Stack are commonly used for log analysis.
- *Network traffic analysis*—Network traffic is monitored and analyzed to detect suspicious patterns and potential threats. Tools such as Wireshark (https://www.wireshark.org/), Zeek (https://zeek.org/), formerly Bro, and Suricata (https://suricata.io/) can provide deep insights into network activities.
- *File integrity monitoring (FIM)*—Changes to critical system files are monitored for unauthorized modifications. Wazuh (https://wazuh.com/) provides robust FIM capabilities, alerting administrators to any unexpected changes.
- *Malware analysis*—Malicious software is analyzed to understand its behavior, origin, and potential effects. Tools such as YARA (https://yara.readthedocs.io/en/latest/) can perform in-depth malware analysis. YARA, playfully dubbed "Yet Another Ridiculous Acronym," is a framework dedicated to large-scale pattern matching, where rules are its cornerstone.
- *Forensic analysis*—Conducts a detailed examination of digital evidence to uncover hidden threats and understand the incident's mechanics. Open source forensic tools such as Autopsy (https://www.autopsy.com/) and The Sleuth Kit (https://www.sleuthkit.org/) can be valuable in this phase.
- *Root cause analysis*—Involves a systematic process for identifying the underlying cause of an incident.
- *Data collection*—Gathers all relevant information related to the incident. The collected data is then analyzed to identify patterns and potential causes. During this stage, techniques such as the Five Whys are often employed to drill down to the root cause by repeatedly asking why a problem occurred until the root cause is uncovered. This iterative questioning helps peel back layers of symptoms to reveal the core problem.
- *Root cause identification*—Determination of the primary factor that led to the incident. This could be due to vulnerability, misconfiguration, or an exploit used by an attacker. Identifying the root cause is essential for addressing the problem rather than treating symptoms.
- *Corrective actions*—Developed and implemented to address the root cause and prevent future incidents. The measures are designed to eliminate identified vulnerabilities or weaknesses, enhancing the overall security posture and reducing the likelihood of recurrence. Organizations can effectively respond to and learn from incidents by following this structured approach, continually improving their security practices.

The listed methods and tools are suggested to conduct a thorough investigation. However, your company may have specialized software that covers some or all of these. Not every organization has the budget or resources to automate or delegate these responsibilities to a third-party or *managed service provider* (MSP). You can use this list to check off items, verifying that you have the key information to document in your incident response.

9.5.1 Case study: Financial institution data breach

Let's consider a case study involving a data breach at a financial institution. This example will illustrate the incident analysis process in a real-world scenario:

- *Incident overview*—A financial institution detected unusual network traffic originating from an internal server. Initial investigation revealed that sensitive customer data had been exfiltrated to an external IP address. The institution immediately initiated its incident response plan.
- *Data collection*—Using Wazuh and the Elastic Stack, the security team collected system logs, network traffic data, and alerts from various security tools. They also retrieved access logs from the affected server and firewall logs to trace the data exfiltration path.
- *Correlation and analysis*—The analysis revealed multiple unauthorized login attempts from an external IP address. Correlating these logs with network traffic data showed a significant volume of data transferred to this IP. Further investigation identified a phishing email that compromised an employee's credentials, allowing the attacker to access the server.
- *Timeline reconstruction*—The team constructed a detailed timeline, from receiving the phishing email, the subsequent login attempts, and the eventual data exfiltration. This timeline helped in understanding the attack's progression and identifying points of failure in the security defenses.
- *Outcome assessment*—The assessment showed that the personal information of over 10,000 customers had been compromised. The breach had significant implications for the institution's reputation and regulatory compliance.
- *Root cause identification*—The root cause analysis identified the phishing email as the initial entry point. The lack of MFA for remote access was a critical vulnerability that allowed the attacker to exploit the compromised credentials.
- *Corrective actions*—The institution implemented MFA for all remote access points, enhanced email filtering to detect phishing attempts, and conducted organization-wide training on recognizing phishing emails. They also upgraded their network monitoring tools to improve detection capabilities.

9.5.2 Incident metrics

Incident metrics offer a detailed view of the incident response life cycle, providing insights into how incidents are analyzed, classified, and resolved. By tracking incident analysis metrics, you can evaluate the efficiency and thoroughness of your incident investigation processes, ensuring that all relevant information is captured and analyzed promptly.

RESPONSE TIME METRICS

- *Incident detection time*—Measures the time from the initial detection of unusual activity to the confirmation of a breach
- *Containment time*—Measures the time to contain the breach after detection
- *Resolution time*—Measures the total time to fully resolve the incident from detection to recovery

COMMUNICATION METRICS

- *Internal communication time*—Measures the time to notify internal stakeholders after incident detection
- *External communication time*—Measures the time taken to communicate with external stakeholders, such as customers and the media
- *Number of communication errors*—Counts the communication errors or miscommunications during the exercise. Miscommunication refers to any failure to deliver or understand information correctly, leading to confusion or incorrect actions during the exercise.

EFFECTIVENESS OF RESPONSE METRICS

- *Number of containment actions taken*—Counts the successful containment actions
- *Number of recovery actions completed*—Counts the recovery actions completed
- *Success rate of mitigation actions*—Measures the percentage of mitigation actions that effectively reduced the effects of the incident

9.5.3 Incident metrics exercise

The left side of figure 9.4 shows SecureTech Solutions, a prominent cybersecurity firm, actively working to enhance its incident analysis processes. Despite having an incident detection system, the company has experienced high false positive rates, prolonged root cause analysis times, and recurring incidents. To address these problems, SecureTech Solutions has implemented several key metrics to measure and improve the efficiency of its incident analysis.

Initially, SecureTech's dashboard reflected some concerning metrics. The FPR was at 45%, indicating that nearly half of the alerts were incorrectly flagged as incidents, contributing to alert fatigue among analysts. The root cause analysis time (RCAT) averaged 12 hours, demonstrating the difficulty in swiftly pinpointing the root causes of incidents. The incident re-occurrence rate (IRR) showed that the same types of incidents were re-occurring at a rate of 20%, highlighting persistent problems that needed

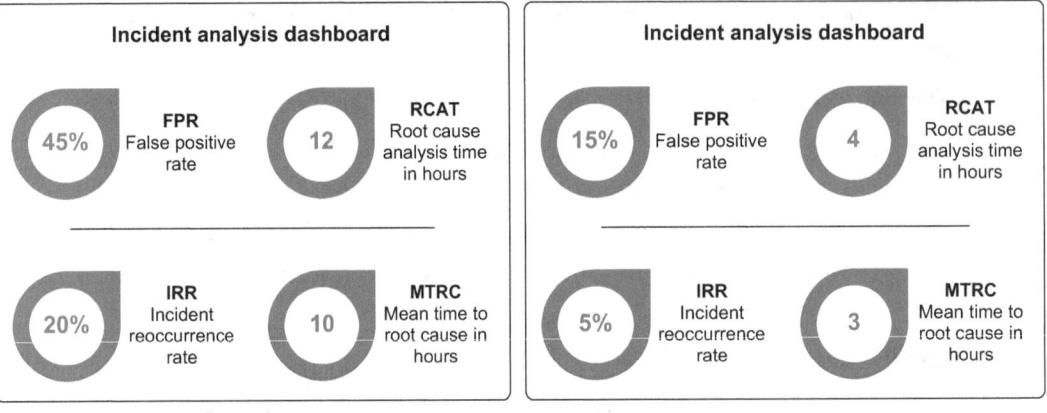

Figure 9.4 The left side shows SecureTech's incident analysis dashboard before improving the incident management process. The right side shows the dashboard after improvements.

addressing. The mean time to root cause was 10 hours, not within their acceptable risk boundaries.

On the right side of figure 9.4, we can see SecureTech's improvements after implementing targeted changes based on these metrics. The updated dashboard showed significant progress.

The FPR decreased to 15%, thanks to better tuning of detection algorithms and improved initial incident triage processes. The RCAT was reduced to 4 hours on average, reflecting the enhanced efficiency in incident analysis workflows. The IRR dropped to 5%, indicating successful measures to address and rectify the root causes of recurring incidents. The mean time to root cause was reduced to 3 hours.

9.5.4 Incident metrics table

Figure 9.5 is an example of a table that would be derived from an incident analysis periodically. These exercises help determine the current value and deviation from the target values to help cybersecurity professionals document analysis and correction plans.

9.6 Notification and communication

The sooner relevant parties are informed, the faster they can take appropriate actions to contain and mitigate the incident. The notification process should be triggered as soon as an incident is identified. Initial notifications might provide a high-level overview of the situation, with more detailed updates as further information becomes available.

Clear and concise notifications should include essential details such as the nature of the incident, the systems affected, potential effects, and steps being taken to address the problem. Avoid technical jargon that could confuse nontechnical stakeholders; instead, provide information in a way that is understandable to all recipients.

Metric	Target	Value	Notes
Incident detection time (minutes)	10	15	Exceeded target; faster detection required.
Containment time (minutes)	30	25	Met target: effective containment strategy implemented.
Resolution time (hours)	4	5	Slightly over target: review recovery steps
Internal communication time (minutes)	5	7	Improve internal notification process
External communication time (minutes)	15	20	Review external communication protocol
Communication errors	0	2	Address communication errors
Containment actions taken	0	5	Count of actions executed
Recovery actions completed	0	4	Ensure all recovery steps are completed
Mitigation success rate (%)	100	90	Evaluate unsuccessful mitigation actions

Figure 9.5 Incident metrics table showing an example of target, values, and notes that would govern corrective actions

For instance, an initial notification to senior management might read: "We have identified a potential security incident affecting our customer database. Our IT team is currently investigating the scope and effects. We will provide further updates as more information becomes available. Immediate actions have been taken to contain the problem and protect data integrity."

Regular updates are essential to inform stakeholders of the incident's progression and the response efforts. These updates should detail what has been discovered, actions taken, any changes in the incident's severity, and the next steps. Transparent communication helps maintain trust and demonstrates that the organization is actively managing the situation.

Communication channels should be pre-established and tested regularly to confirm they function effectively during an incident. This includes keeping contact lists up to date so that communication tools (e.g., email, phone, and messaging systems) are reliable and backup methods are available in case primary channels fail.

Legal and regulatory requirements must be adhered to when notifying external parties. Different jurisdictions may have specific mandates on how and when incidents must be reported, particularly if they involve personal data breaches. Understanding and incorporating these requirements into the incident response plan enables compliance and avoids potential legal repercussions.

Post-incident, a debrief should be conducted to review the communication process. This review helps identify what worked well and what could be improved, so that the organization can continuously enhance its communication strategies for future incidents. Documenting these lessons learned and integrating them into training and exercises will prepare the team for more effective communication in subsequent incidents.

9.7 Containing validated incidents

Containment limits the damage caused by a cybersecurity incident and prevents further compromise. Effective containment strategies help isolate the affected systems, reduce the effect on the organization, and provide a controlled environment for further analysis and remediation.

The first step in containment is to identify the extent of the incident. This involves determining which systems and data have been affected and assessing the potential spread of the threat. A thorough understanding of the scope of the incident is essential for selecting the appropriate containment strategy. There are two main types of containment: short and long term.

Short-term containment focuses on immediate actions to prevent the incident from escalating. This can include isolating affected systems from the network, blocking malicious IP addresses, disabling compromised accounts, and stopping any ongoing malicious processes. For instance, if a ransomware attack is detected, the security team might disconnect the infected systems from the network to prevent the ransomware from spreading to other devices. Short-term containment aims to quickly stop the attack and mitigate immediate threats without disrupting business operations more than necessary.

Long-term containment involves more comprehensive measures to address the root cause of the incident and verify that the threat is fully eradicated. This phase includes applying security patches, reconfiguring network settings, strengthening access controls, and conducting a thorough investigation to identify and remove any remaining vulnerabilities. Long-term containment often requires coordination with various departments within the organization, including IT, legal, and management, to validate that all aspects of the incident are addressed.

There are preventative containment strategies, such as the use of network segmentation. Organizations can limit the spread of malware and other threats by dividing the network into smaller, isolated segments. If an incident occurs in one segment, it can be contained within that segment, preventing it from affecting the entire network. This approach helps contain the incident and makes it easier to monitor and manage network traffic.

Another preventative containment measure is the deployment of honeypots, decoy systems designed to lure attackers and detect malicious activities. Honeypots can provide valuable insights into attackers' tactics and techniques, helping security teams develop more effective containment and mitigation strategies for actual incidents. By diverting attackers to these decoy systems, organizations can protect their actual assets and gain valuable intelligence on potential threats. Keep in mind that honeypots require careful configuration and monitoring to avoid becoming attack vectors themselves.

The incident response team must keep all relevant stakeholders informed about the actions being taken and any changes in the incident's status. This approach enables everyone to be aware of the situation and take appropriate measures to support the containment efforts. Clear and timely communication helps prevent confusion and provides a coordinated response across the organization.

Every action taken during the containment phase should be thoroughly documented, including the steps taken, the tools used, and the results achieved. This documentation serves as a valuable reference in post-incident analysis and helps identify areas for improvement in the IRP. Organizations can learn from each incident by maintaining detailed records and enhancing their containment strategies for future incidents.

9.8 Evidence gathering and forensic analysis

Evidence gathering and forensic analysis are supported by reliable data and intended to uncover an incident's details, identify attackers, and prepare for legal proceedings. What sets this step apart in the incident response process is the forensic approach used to secure the scene and conduct an in-depth examination of the affected systems. This phase involves specialized forensic techniques to preserve evidence and uncover hidden data.

One of the key components of forensic analysis is validating and preserving the incident scene. Unlike previous phases, where real-time analysis is prioritized, forensic analysis focuses on securing compromised systems to prevent further contamination. Securing the scene involves isolating systems and validating that no further interaction can alter the state of the affected environment. This step prioritizes that the evidence remains intact for forensic examination.

The use of advanced tools that go beyond regular log analysis is specific to forensic analysis. Disk imaging, for example, is often employed to create a bit-level copy of storage devices, preserving not only the files in use but also deleted data, hidden partitions, and unallocated space. This approach allows analysts to retrieve critical data that might otherwise be missed. Another key forensic technique is memory analysis, which captures volatile data from system memory, helping identify malware or processes that may have run without a trace on the hard drive.

Network forensics can also be employed to trace back anomalous network behaviors during the incident. This can involve reconstructing packets to identify data exfiltration attempts or tracing lateral movement across the network. This step is important when sophisticated attackers attempt to cover their tracks.

While the fundamental steps of gathering evidence and maintaining the chain of custody remain consistent throughout the process, forensic analysis distinguishes itself through these advanced methodologies. These techniques are vital to building a comprehensive understanding of the incident and supporting any legal actions that may follow.

9.9 Eradication of incidents

Once we have completed our investigation, we must remove the root cause of an incident and validate that the threat is eliminated from the organization's environment. This step goes beyond temporary fixes and isolation and addresses the underlying vulnerability that allowed the incident to occur in the first place.

The first step in the eradication process is to identify all compromised systems and components within the organization's environment, which requires a comprehensive assessment to verify that no remnants of the threat remain. For example, scanning all systems for malware signatures, malicious files, and any unauthorized changes to configurations and settings is essential if the incident involves malware. Tools such as anti-malware software, network scanning utilities, and specialized forensic tools are commonly used to perform these tasks.

Once all compromised elements are identified, the next step is to remove the malicious components. This could mean deleting or replacing infected files, cleaning infected systems, or restoring systems from backup. Even the smallest remnant of the incident could lead to reinfection.

After eradication, the focus moves toward patching vulnerabilities and improving security measures to prevent similar incidents. This could involve applying security patches, updating software and firmware, reconfiguring firewalls and security policies, or enhancing access controls. Once eradiated, systems must be validated.

Consider a practical example involving a phishing attack that led to a malware infection. After containing the incident by isolating the affected systems, the incident response team would begin the eradication process by scanning all endpoints for the malware. They would identify and remove the malicious files from all infected systems using advanced anti-malware tools. They would also examine email logs and identify any other potential victims who received the phishing email but had not yet been compromised.

The team would then analyze how the malware exploited vulnerabilities to infiltrate the network. Suppose the analysis reveals the malware exploited an unpatched vulnerability in the company's email server software. In that case, they would apply the necessary patches to the email server and other systems with similar vulnerabilities. Additionally, they would implement enhanced email filtering and phishing protection measures to reduce the likelihood of similar attacks in the future.

Documentation throughout the eradication process is crucial. Detailed records of all actions taken should be maintained, including system scans, files removed, patches applied, and configurations changed. This documentation helps with post-incident analysis and provides a valuable reference for handling future incidents. As you can see, documentation is a critical component at every step of the IRP. This documentation could be used for forensic review, validation, or compliance with regulatory requirements.

9.9.1 Incident response metrics

Incident response metrics help evaluate the timeliness and effectiveness of incident response actions. By tracking these metrics, organizations can identify bottlenecks, streamline their incident response processes, and ensure that their security measures are effective and efficient in minimizing the effects of security breaches.

DERIVED METRICS

- *Mean time to contain incident (MTTC-I)*—The average time to contain an incident after it has been identified. This metric evaluates the speed and effectiveness of the incident containment process.
- *Mean time to remediate incident (MTTR-I)*—The average time to fully remediate an incident, including all necessary repairs and mitigation efforts. This metric helps in understanding the overall effectiveness of the incident response process.
- *Incident response success rate incident (IRSR-I)*—The percentage of incidents that were successfully mitigated and did not result in further security breaches. This metric indicates the effectiveness of the response efforts.

CyberSecure Solutions, a medium-sized cybersecurity firm, recently encountered several security incidents that highlighted the need for improved incident response strategies. Over the past year, the company has struggled with prolonged incident containment and recovery times, leading to significant downtime and potential data loss (figure 9.6).

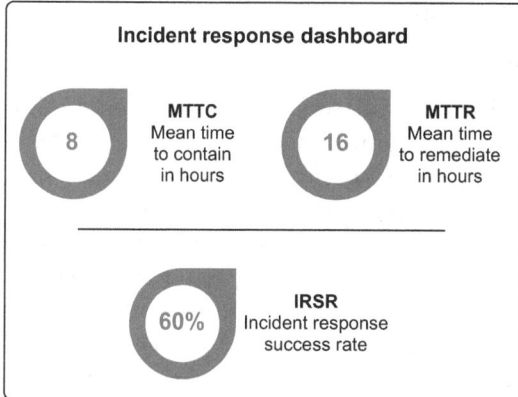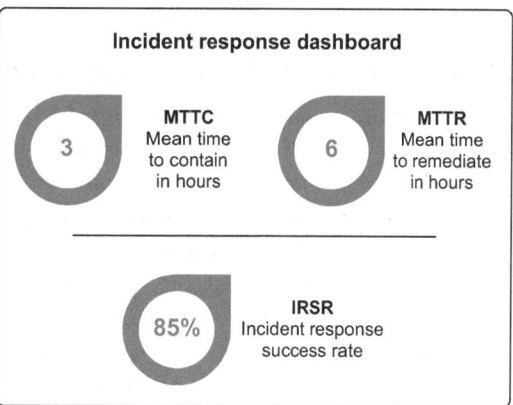

Figure 9.6 On the left side, CyberSecure Solutions' incident response dashboard is shown before implementing incident response strategies and process improvements. The right side shows the incident response dashboard after the implementation of these strategies and improvements.

To address these problems, CyberSecure Solutions implemented a comprehensive incident response plan and tracked specific metrics to gauge their effectiveness. These metrics indicated that it took an average of 8 hours to contain an incident, during which the threat could spread and cause further damage. The recovery time was longer, averaging 16 hours to restore normal operations. The incident response success rate was only 60%, meaning that 40% of incidents significantly affected the organization.

The right side of figure 9.6 shows CyberSecure Solutions after six months of refining their incident response strategies and processes, indicating significant improvements. These improvements resulted from several key changes. The containment time was reduced to an average of 3 hours, meaning threats were neutralized more quickly, minimizing their potential effects. The recovery time was reduced to 6 hours, allowing the company to resume normal operations much faster. The incident response success rate increased to 85%, indicating that most incidents were handled effectively with minimal disruption.

9.10 Recovering to operational status

Communication is key during the recovery phase. Keep all key stakeholders informed about the status of the recovery efforts, the estimated timeline for complete restoration, and any potential impacts on business operations. Effective communication helps manage expectations and provides transparency throughout the recovery process. This includes regular updates to executives, IT staff, and affected business units.

Post-recovery validation and documentation is the final step in the recovery phase. This involves reviewing the entire incident response process, assessing the effectiveness of the recovery efforts, and documenting any lessons learned. This documentation is valuable for improving the IRP and enhancing the organization's overall incident response capabilities. After each incident, the lessons learned can be folded back into the IRP as part of the continuous improvement process.

9.11 Post-incident and lessons learned

Communication details should be listed within the IRP to establish a communication plan that outlines the roles, responsibilities, and communication channels for all stakeholders. This plan should detail who will communicate with executives, IT staff, business units, customers, and external parties such as regulators or the media.

A data breach scenario illustrates a practical example of incident recovery communication. During the recovery phase, the incident response team would provide regular updates to executives, IT staff, and affected business units, informing them of the progress to secure and restore compromised systems. They would also communicate with customers and regulators, providing transparent and timely information about the breach, the steps to address it, and any measures to prevent future incidents.

Effective communication involves not only providing information but also listening to and responding to feedback. Engaging with stakeholders, addressing their concerns, and incorporating their feedback into the recovery process can help build trust and improve the overall effectiveness of the recovery efforts.

9.11.1 Incident reporting and communication metrics

This section introduces key metrics to measure the effectiveness of incident reporting and communication. They help organizations refine their communication strategies, enhance stakeholder trust, and confirm regulatory compliance during incident management.

DERIVED METRICS

- *Incident communication time (ICT)*—Measures the average time to communicate an incident to all relevant stakeholders, including internal teams and external partners. This metric assesses the efficiency of the communication process during incidents.
- *Stakeholder satisfaction rate (SSR)*—The percentage of stakeholders satisfied with the incident reporting and communication process. This metric can be gathered through surveys and feedback mechanisms.
- *Compliance reporting rate (CRR)*—The frequency and accuracy with which incidents are reported to regulatory bodies and compliance agencies. This metric ensures that the organization adheres to necessary legal and regulatory requirements.

9.11.2 Incident reporting and communication metrics exercise

XYZ Healthcare, a leading provider of health services, has recently encountered challenges in its incident reporting and communication processes. During several incidents, there were delays in informing stakeholders, resulting in confusion and inefficient incident management. The organization struggled to meet compliance reporting requirements on time, which put it at risk of regulatory penalties.

The reporting and communication metrics highlighted significant communication delays, dissatisfaction among stakeholders, and a need for better adherence to regulatory reporting requirements. To address these problems, XYZ Healthcare decided to implement metrics to improve its incident reporting and communication processes. The right side of figure 9.7 shows the outcome of their targeted improvements.

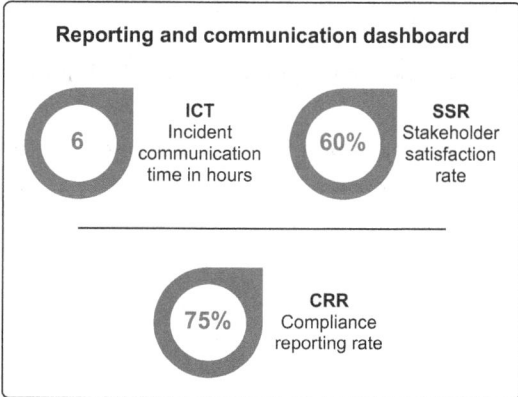 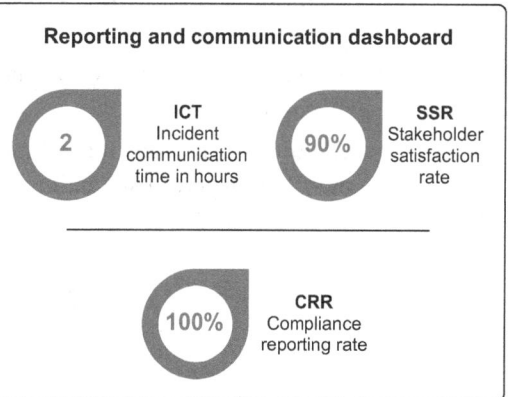

Figure 9.7 The left side shows XYZ Healthcare reporting and communication metrics before implementing their process improvement plan. The right side shows the metrics after making improvements.

By implementing a streamlined communication protocol and utilizing automated notification systems, XYZ Healthcare significantly reduced the time it took to inform stakeholders about incidents. This improvement verified that all relevant parties were quickly aware of incidents, which enabled a coordinated and efficient response.

The increased satisfaction rates indicated stakeholders appreciated the timely and accurate information during incidents. Regular feedback from stakeholders was used to refine the communication processes further, ensuring that their needs and expectations were met.

Integrating compliance requirements into the incident management system improved compliance reporting. Automated reminders and checklists ensured that all necessary reports were completed correctly and on time, reducing the risk of regulatory penalties.

Through these targeted improvements, XYZ Healthcare enhanced its incident reporting and communication processes, which led to more efficient incident management, higher stakeholder trust, and better compliance with regulatory requirements.

Summary

- Effective incident management involves planning, preparation, and detailed incident identification and logging.
- Thorough incident analysis identifies the root cause and aids in preventing future occurrences.
- Prompt and clear communication during incidents ensures that all stakeholders are informed and regulatory requirements are met.
- Containment strategies help in isolating and mitigating the effects of incidents quickly.
- Evidence gathering and forensic analysis are critical for understanding incidents and preparing for legal or regulatory actions.
- Eradication focuses on removing the cause of the incident and recurrence prevention.
- A well-executed recovery plan restores normal operations and minimizes downtime.
- Continuous monitoring and improvement through metrics are essential for maintaining a robust incident response framework.

Part 3

Beyond the basics: Advanced analytics, machine learning, and AI

Chapters 10–13 take you to a more sophisticated territory. After establishing a solid metrics practice in the first two parts, you'll explore advanced cyber analytics that push your data beyond simple dashboards. You'll learn how statistical methods can uncover hidden insights and how machine learning can automate pattern recognition in large-scale environments. Finally, you'll see how generative AI opens new frontiers in threat detection, anomaly spotting, and even predictive modeling of future attacks. By the end of this section, you'll be ready to harness cutting-edge technologies that turn security metrics into proactive, intelligence-driven cyber defense.

Advanced cybersecurity metrics

This chapter covers
- The role of advanced cybersecurity metrics
- AI and predictive analytics in cybersecurity
- Using advanced metrics
- Data-driven approaches for proactive cybersecurity management

The cybersecurity landscape has evolved rapidly with advancements in technology. One of the most effective recent changes is the availability of generative and agentic AI. These technologies offer more sophisticated approaches to cybersecurity. Traditional metrics remain a cornerstone for measuring information security programs. Still, we must balance the cat-and-mouse game of defender (blue team) versus attacker (red team). Advanced cybersecurity metrics provide a richer, more nuanced insight into what is taking place within your organization. The purpose is to help define what is happening, understanding the underlying reasons, determining the key actors, and anticipating future developments.

A key difference between traditional and advanced metrics is the latter's ability to reflect on current and past events, but also to predict and forecast future events, such as threats and vulnerabilities. In this chapter, we use artificial intelligence and predictive analytics to offer these prescriptive insights. This data-driven foresight is where advanced metrics offer a strategic advantage.

Through machine learning systems, we can detect patterns and anomalies in massive datasets that would be daunting and time-consuming for a human to analyze manually. For example, AI can correlate seemingly unrelated events to detect subtle indicators of compromise, flagging a potential threat before it escalates into a full-scale attack. By understanding trends and patterns in past data, security teams can estimate the likelihood of specific threats and take preemptive actions.

This chapter explores more advanced metrics that you can incorporate into your cybersecurity strategy to fortify defenses, enhance data-driven decision-making, and improve your organization's overall security posture. While we will touch on AI topics, we will save the deep dive into statistics and AI topics for later.

10.1 Risk exposure and predictive analysis

The ability to anticipate and mitigate risk is essential for a good cybersecurity defense strategy. Traditional cybersecurity metrics rely on incidents after they have occurred. However, we can use predictive analytics to build a risk model that helps organizations become more proactive in their approach.

Predictive analytics uses statistical algorithms, machine learning, and data analysis techniques to identify patterns in data and make informed predictions about future events. In cybersecurity, this involves building models that forecast potential security incidents based on historical data, threat intelligence, and current vulnerabilities. These models allow organizations to move beyond traditional reactive approaches and become more proactive in their defenses.

To successfully implement predictive analytics, cybersecurity teams need the right tools and expertise. Commonly used tools include open source platforms such as Wazuh, which integrate machine learning capabilities, as well as more specialized software such as Splunk (for data aggregation and analysis) and Python (for custom machine learning algorithms). These tools allow organizations to collect, process, and analyze large datasets, transforming raw information into actionable insights. Some of the questions to consider include

- Given the technical complexity, does any of your training address problems with application security in languages that aren't memory safe?
- We have an internal learning platform we utilize for training. Is it possible to integrate SafeStack into this platform? If so, what information do we need to determine compatibility?
- If we need to add additional licenses after our initial agreement, how would those licenses be priced?

- Are users licensed individually, or are we purchasing generic seats for access to the platform?
- Is there a requirement to use Rocket Lab branding to participate in the Horizons program?
- Is it possible to purchase the training separately from the service or a perpetual license?
- You mentioned training focused on requirements such as National Institute of Standards and Technology. We're currently working toward NIST 800-171 compliance. Can you give us more information on how your training will help us achieve compliance with the requirements in that document?

Analysis, clustering, and anomaly detection are essential. Familiarity with tools such as Python's `scikit-learn` or TensorFlow will also be valuable for developing custom models tailored to the organization's specific risk landscape.

Building a strong predictive analytics capability requires close collaboration between cybersecurity teams, data scientists, and senior leadership to ensure that the chosen metrics and models align with the organization's overall risk management strategy.

10.2 Risk exposure and predictive metrics

Risk exposure refers to the potential for loss or damage an organization faces due to existing vulnerabilities or emerging threats. Organizations can prioritize their resources by understanding the factors that contribute to risk. These factors often include the presence of unpatched vulnerabilities, the likelihood of a specific type of attack, and the potential effect on critical systems.

A key challenge in assessing risk exposure is the dynamic nature of vulnerabilities and threats. A vulnerability that is considered low risk may, in fact, be high risk given a new exploitation method. For instance, a buffer overflow vulnerability that was previously thought to be difficult to exploit could become critical if a new method that allows for remote code execution with minimal privileges is found. Continuously monitoring and reassessing risk exposure in real time gives organizations an advantage over periodic risk evaluation.

Predictive analytics allow cybersecurity teams to forecast potential threats based on historical data, behavioral patterns, and current threat intelligence. We can analyze past incidents and use statistical techniques to estimate the likelihood of future attacks. Understanding risk scores and threat forecasts, such as risk exposure index (REI) and predictive threat index (PTI), helps assess current events and anticipate future ones:

- The REI quantifies an organization's overall risk based on a combination of factors, such as the number of vulnerabilities, the likelihood of exploitation, and the potential effect on the business. This index gives decision-makers a clear picture of their current risk landscape and can guide investments in security improvements.

- The PTI employs historical attack data, threat intelligence, and real-time monitoring to estimate the probability of future incidents. This metric allows organizations to focus their defenses on the most likely attack vectors, improving resource allocation and response readiness.

The following sections discuss these indexes in more depth.

10.2.1 Risk exposure index

Traditional metrics often focus on static or historical data, such as incident reports or post-event analysis. In contrast, the REI uses predictive analytics and AI to provide a forward-looking measure of risk, quantifying an organization's exposure based on vulnerabilities, threat intelligence, and business effects. By combining real-time data and predictive modeling, the REI allows organizations to anticipate potential threats and proactively mitigate risks before they materialize.

The REI quantifies an organization's exposure to risks based on several factors. This index is calculated by considering

- *Number of vulnerabilities*—The more vulnerabilities in the system, the higher the exposure risk. The number of vulnerabilities is typically calculated based on scans or reports generated by vulnerability management tools such as Qualys, Nessus, or open source alternatives such as OpenVAS. These tools assess your systems for known vulnerabilities, often using a database of Common Vulnerabilities and Exposures (CVEs). Each scan returns a list of vulnerabilities detected across your assets. You can track this number over time, by system, or by asset group, and classify vulnerabilities based on their severity and exploitability.
- *Severity of vulnerabilities*—Not all vulnerabilities are equal. High-severity vulnerabilities pose more risk than low-severity ones. Vulnerabilities are often classified using a standardized scoring system such as the Common Vulnerability Scoring System (CVSS). This system scores vulnerabilities on a scale from 0 to 10, with a higher score indicating a more severe vulnerability. A low-severity vulnerability might involve minor information disclosure, while a high-severity vulnerability could enable remote code execution (RCE), which gives attackers control over the system. Typically, vulnerabilities are classified as:
  - *Low severity*—CVSS scores from 0.1 to 3.9
  - *Medium severity*—CVSS scores from 4.0 to 6.9
  - *High severity*—CVSS scores from 7.0 to 8.9
  - *Critical severity*—CVSS scores from 9.0 to 10.0
- *Likelihood of exploitation*—Some vulnerabilities are more likely to be exploited due to the availability of known exploits or because attackers are actively targeting them.
- *Effects*—The potential business effects if a vulnerability is exploited, such as data breaches, financial losses, or operational downtime.

The REI is calculated as the total value score over the total number of assets multiplied by the business impact factor. Equation 10.1 is a basic formula for calculating REI, which looks like this:

$$\text{REI} = \frac{\text{Total Vulnerability Score}}{\text{Total Number of Assets} \times \text{Business Impact Factor}} \quad (10.1)$$

where

- The *total vulnerability score* can be a sum of vulnerability scores based on severity (e.g., CVSS scores).
- The *business impact factor* assigns weight to the impact based on the criticality of assets and the business functions they support.

Let's apply equation 10.1 in an example:

- *Total vulnerability score*—Sum of vulnerability scores across all assets. Suppose you have five critical vulnerabilities, each with a CVSS score of 9, so your total score would be $5 \times 9 = 45$.
- *Total number of assets*—Let's say you have 20 critical assets.
- *Business impact factor*—Let's assume a high business impact factor of 2.5, indicating that your critical assets support key business functions.

Now apply the formula as in equation 10.2:

$$\text{REI} = \frac{45}{20} \times 2.5 = 5.625 \quad (10.2)$$

A REI of 5.625 suggests moderate risk exposure, and you would need to monitor this metric over time to gauge the effectiveness of risk mitigation measures.

10.2.2 Predictive threat index

Rather than relying solely on past incidents, *predictive threat index* (PTI) uses historical data, threat intelligence feeds, and machine learning algorithms to forecast the likelihood of future attacks. This metric applies sophisticated techniques to model potential threats and assess risk based on evolving patterns and behavior, offering organizations the ability to make proactive security decisions.

AI and predictive analytics identify trends, detect anomalies, and continuously learn from new data. This allows the system to evolve in real time, adjusting its risk assessments as new information becomes available, making it far more dynamic and forward-looking compared to basic metrics. The predictive threat index estimates the likelihood of future threats based on past incident data, threat intelligence feeds, and other historical data:

- *Historical attack data*—By analyzing previous incidents (such as malware attacks or breaches), an organization can estimate how often certain threats are likely to recur.
- *Threat intelligence*—Gather intelligence from sources like open threat-sharing communities (e.g., MITRE ATT&CK, Open Threat Exchange) to predict new or emerging threats.
- *Current vulnerabilities*—Active vulnerabilities in the network can increase the probability of future attacks.

Predictive threat index is calculated as the number of incidents multiplied by the threat likelihood divided by the total assets. Equation 10.3 is a basic formula for PTI:

$$\text{PTI} = \frac{\text{Previous Incidents} \times \text{Threat Likelihood}}{\text{Total Assets}} \qquad (10.3)$$

where

- *Threat likelihood* is based on how frequently a particular threat or attack vector is observed in threat intelligence feeds.

For example, SecureTech has experienced 15 malware attacks over the past year. Threat intelligence data shows that, based on recent trends, the likelihood of malware attacks affecting the industry has increased to 30%. SecureTech is currently managing a network with 200 critical assets.

Using these numbers, we can plug them into equation 10.4:

$$\text{PTI} = \frac{15 \times 0.30}{200} = \frac{4.5}{200} = 0.0225 \qquad (10.4)$$

This PTI value of 0.0225 (or 2.25%) suggests that, based on historical data and threat intelligence, SecureTech is 2.25% likely to encounter a malware attack in the near future. This information helps the security team prioritize resources and preemptively strengthen defenses, such as deploying malware detection and protection tools on the most vulnerable assets.

10.2.3 Risk exposure and predictive metrics exercise

SecureNet Inc., a medium-sized financial services company, has struggled with frequent malware attacks and data breaches over the past year. These incidents have highlighted weaknesses in its ability to anticipate and respond to evolving threats. To address these challenges, SecureNet Inc. has decided to implement predictive analytics to enhance its risk management strategy. They set specific goals to improve their overall risk posture by implementing the risk exposure and predictive threat indexes as key metrics.

The initial dashboard on the left in figure 10.1 shows SecureNet Inc.'s cybersecurity posture before introducing predictive analytics. The company's REI is alarmingly high, sitting at 80%, due to numerous unpatched vulnerabilities, weak incident response, and high-risk systems. Based on historical data and current threat intelligence, the PTI indicates a 60% likelihood of a malware attack in the next six months. Additionally, the company has seen an average of 50 malware-related incidents per month, and its current response time to incidents is 12 hours, leaving them highly vulnerable to further attacks.

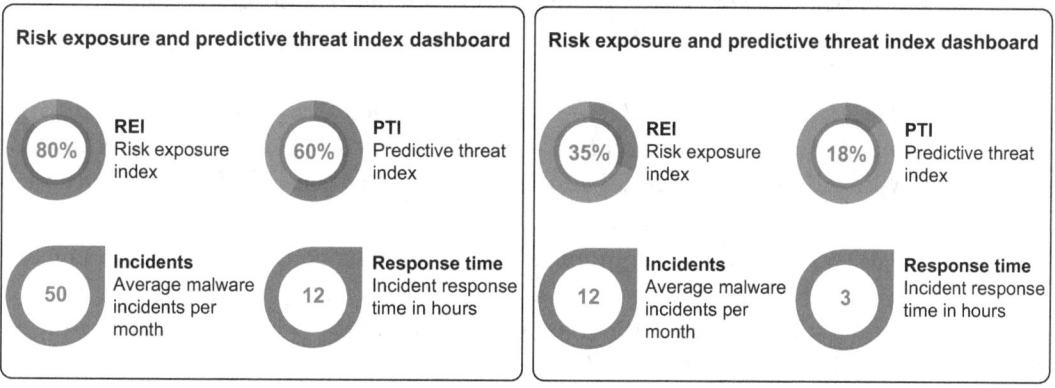

Figure 10.1 The left side shows risk exposure and predictive analytics before implementing improvements. The right side shows the situation afterward.

SecureNet Inc. has set the following targets for its metrics:

- *REI*—Reduce to below 40%
- *PTI*—Reduce to below 20%
- *Average malware incidents per month*—Reduce to 15
- *Incident response time*—Reduce to 4 hours

To achieve the desired improvements, SecureNet Inc. began by prioritizing the patching of vulnerabilities that had the highest risk exposure. They used predictive analytics to anticipate which vulnerabilities were most likely to be targeted based on past attack patterns. SecureNet also introduced machine learning algorithms to monitor network traffic and user behavior, helping to detect potential malware infections before they could spread. This proactive approach allowed them to reduce their REI significantly, while improving their response times to incidents.

The right side of figure 10.1 indicates that SecureNet Inc. saw significant improvements across all metrics after six months of implementing a predictive analytics-based approach.

The REI decreased to 35%, reflecting a reduction in unpatched vulnerabilities and a stronger focus on addressing high-risk systems. The PTI fell to 18%, indicating a much lower likelihood of future malware incidents. The average number of malware incidents per month dropped to 12, and the response time to incidents improved dramatically, decreasing to an average of 3 hours.

10.2.4 Using open source tools to calculate REI and PTI

Fortunately, there are open source tools and methods that automate the calculation of these metrics, making it easier for organizations without sophisticated resources to track their risk exposure and predict future threats:

- *OpenVAS*—An open source vulnerability scanner that integrates with CVSS scoring, helping you quantify vulnerabilities and calculate REI based on vulnerability data (https://openvas.org/).
- *Elastic Stack (formerly ELK)*—Combines Elasticsearch, Logstash, and Kibana, which can be used to process historical incident data, perform predictive analysis, and visualize both REI and PTI metrics in a dashboard (https://www.elastic.co/elastic-stack).
- *Wazuh*—Provides security monitoring and threat detection, as well as predictive analytics capabilities through integration with machine learning models and threat intelligence feeds. Wazuh can help build the predictive models required for PTI calculations (https://wazuh.com/)
- *Cortex and TheHive*—Open source threat intelligence platforms that aggregate, correlate, and analyze threat data to help determine the likelihood of future attacks, which is crucial for calculating the PTI (https://strangebee.com/).

10.2.5 How cybersecurity teams work together with open source solutions

To clarify how these open source tools can be used in practice, it's essential to consider how cybersecurity teams can implement them, even without extensive resources. Here is just one of many scenarios your organization could implement using these open source tools.

OpenVAS is an open source vulnerability scanner that integrates with the CVSS. Teams can run regular vulnerability scans using OpenVAS to calculate the REI. After the scan, OpenVAS provides detailed reports of vulnerabilities found on the system, including their CVSS scores, which can be directly used to calculate the REI by summing the severity of the vulnerabilities.

For teams to manage this task, security analysts or system administrators usually run these scans. They are responsible for scheduling routine scans, reviewing vulnerability reports, and integrating the results into the organization's vulnerability management program. Many of these tools have dashboards that can simplify the visualization of critical vulnerabilities across the organization's assets.

Elastic Stack, which includes Elasticsearch, Logstash, and Kibana, allows teams to collect, process, and visualize data in a comprehensive dashboard. For calculating REI and PTI, teams can collect historical incident data (e.g., past attacks, vulnerability reports, or threat intelligence feeds) and analyze patterns using Elasticsearch. Kibana is then used to create visual dashboards that show key metrics such as risk scores and threat likelihood.

Security teams or data analysts would manage this process. They would set up data ingestion pipelines, configure dashboards, and run queries in Elasticsearch to detect patterns in incidents or threats over time. Elastic Stack's predictive analytics capabilities allow teams to forecast potential attacks based on the collected data.

Wazuh offers security monitoring, threat detection, and integration with machine learning models. Using Wazuh, teams can monitor network activity, detect potential threats in real-time, and even run predictive models to estimate the likelihood of attacks, thus directly supporting PTI calculation.

Wazuh's integration with threat intelligence enables predictive analytics by correlating current system events with known threat patterns, helping teams predict potential attack vectors. Security analysts or engineers typically manage this tool by configuring alerts and thresholds that align with the organization's risk tolerance and monitoring for anomalous behavior.

Cortex and TheHive are specialized platforms for threat intelligence analysis. Cortex automates the collection and enrichment of threat data, while TheHive helps manage incident response as a ticketing system with enrichment features. Both platforms help gather data about new and emerging threats, essential for calculating PTI.

Threat analysts or security teams would manage Cortex and TheHive by configuring integrations with external threat intelligence feeds. They would use these platforms to assess which threats are relevant to their environment, automate analysis workflows, and integrate the results into risk prediction models.

In smaller organizations, a single cybersecurity team might manage all these tools—from setup to monitoring and analysis. In larger organizations, responsibilities might be divided across teams—vulnerability management teams handling OpenVAS, data analytics teams using Elastic Stack, and incident response teams using Wazuh and Cortex. For predictive analytics, data scientists might collaborate with the security team to build machine learning models.

10.3 Advanced threat detection

Another critical focal point for cybersecurity is threat detection. Being able to quickly respond to malicious activity is important, and measuring this is a great way to ensure that you are maximizing your resources. Advanced threat detection builds on the concepts of risk exposure and predictive analytics by applying real-time monitoring and AI-driven models to proactively identify and mitigate potential threats before they fully materialize.

While traditional methods of threat detection (e.g., signature-based approaches) typically rely on established patterns, advanced threat detection goes a step further by using anomaly detection and predictive analytics. This allows for the identification of threats that deviate from the norm, even if they don't match known attack signatures. In this section, we focus on metrics that allow your organization to measure the accuracy and efficiency of threat detection.

10.3.1 Anomaly detection

Anomaly detection involves identifying patterns of behavior that deviate from the expected norm. In cybersecurity, anomalies often signify a potential threat such as unauthorized access, data exfiltration, or malware activity. Distinguishing legitimate behavior from actual threats can be challenging. For example, while working with a financial services company, we identified a sudden spike in file transfers between internal systems. Normally, the systems communicate regularly with moderate traffic levels, but this spike indicated a possible unauthorized data exfiltration attempt. We could trace this activity to an insider threat and prevent a significant breach using advanced anomaly detection models.

In another case, during the monitoring of a large e-commerce company, we observed irregular login patterns from multiple geographic regions within a very short time frame. Although the company had a global user base, these logins deviated from the usual user behavior. The anomaly detection system flagged this as suspicious, leading us to investigate further and uncover a botnet-driven brute force attack that had just begun. Early detection allowed us to implement mitigations before customer accounts were compromised.

Anomalous behavior detection can involve complex algorithms that continuously monitor network traffic, system performance, and user behavior to determine potential security risks. The goal is to minimize false positives, while focusing on disallowing genuine threats to go undetected.

ANOMALOUS BEHAVIOR DETECTION RATE

The anomalous behavior detection rate (ABDR) measures the success rate of threat detection systems, allowing cybersecurity analysts to fine-tune detection algorithms to improve accuracy. Specifically, it measures the proportion of true anomalies detected against the total number of abnormal behaviors identified by the system.

At a high level, the ABDR works by assessing the detection system's ability to distinguish between normal and abnormal activity. The system constantly monitors baseline behaviors (e.g., typical network traffic, user logins, and file transfers), creating a model of what normal looks like for the organization. Any deviations from this baseline, such as unusual login patterns or unexpected data transfers, are flagged as anomalies.

This process typically involves integrating machine learning models, which continuously learn and adapt to new patterns of normal behavior, improving detection accuracy over time. By measuring ABDR, security analysts can evaluate the detection system's performance and identify areas for further adjustment.

10.3.2 Time to predict

AI has affected nearly every corner of cybersecurity with a significant shift in predictive threat detection. These predictive capabilities help prevent attacks such as ransomware, where early detection can stop an attack before encryption occurs. For example,

AI models can simultaneously analyze user behavior, network traffic, and system activities to recognize deviations that might indicate an emerging threat, such as a ransomware attack. By identifying patterns that correlate with known threats but are not yet fully realized, AI systems can predict an attack before it reaches critical stages, such as file encryption in ransomware cases.

How quickly can an AI-based system forecast a potential threat? Shorter prediction times allow organizations to take preemptive actions, reducing the effects of an attack or preventing it entirely. This metric reflects the effectiveness of AI models in processing real-time data, analyzing trends, and making informed predictions that enable organizations to take preemptive actions. A shorter time to predict (TTP) means the AI system is performing well, offering faster threat identification and reducing the window for potential damage.

TTP is typically calculated by analyzing when the AI system starts receiving data (e.g., network logs, user behavior patterns, traffic anomalies) and when it identifies a potential threat with sufficient confidence to prompt action. Essentially, it's the time from when an anomaly first becomes detectable until the system predicts a possible attack.

To calculate TTP, as shown in equation 10.5, you would measure

- *Data ingestion start time*—The moment the AI system begins processing relevant data
- *Prediction time*—The point when the system generates a prediction based on patterns or anomalies

$$\text{TTP} = \text{Prediction Time} - \text{Data Ingestion Start Time} \qquad (10.5)$$

Several AI-powered cybersecurity tools focus on reducing TTP by processing real-time data and predicting threats based on historical attack patterns, behaviors, and threat intelligence:

- *Elastic Stack (formerly ELK)*—By integrating machine learning, Elastic Stack processes data and logs to identify anomalies and predict threats. It continuously learns from historical data, improving its TTP over time.
- *Wazuh*—Integrates with machine learning algorithms and threat intelligence to monitor and predict threats in real time, significantly reducing the time it takes to identify potential attacks.
- *Splunk*—Through its machine learning and anomaly detection capabilities, Splunk analyzes vast amounts of data from across the network and security infrastructure, helping shorten TTP by quickly predicting potential threats.
- *Cortex XDR*—By using behavioral analytics and AI-driven models, Cortex XDR predicts threats across endpoints, networks, and cloud environments. It automates detection and predictive analysis, reducing TTP and improving the response window.

10.3.3 Dynamic risk scoring

Static, point-in-time risk assessments have great value to organizations. However, the buzzword in cybersecurity for post-generative AI is *continuous*. For organizations to adapt in real time, continuously updating risk scores as new information becomes available is key.

Dynamic risk scoring (DRS) assigns a real-time risk score to every asset, user, or event in the system based on multiple factors, such as current vulnerabilities, threat intelligence, and real-time monitored activities. This score changes dynamically, based on various inputs, such as current vulnerabilities, real-time activities, and threat intelligence feeds. It is critical for environments where the threat landscape constantly evolves, enabling security teams to make fast, informed decisions to mitigate risks.

For example, if an employee's device begins communicating with an unfamiliar IP address or shows unusual login attempts, its risk score might increase, triggering further investigation or preemptive isolation of the device. DRS is vital in environments where the threat landscape constantly evolves, and decisions must be made on the fly.

DRS uses a weighted model that evaluates several risk factors to assign a real-time risk score. The formula typically involves multiple inputs:

- *Current vulnerabilities*—The number and severity of known vulnerabilities in the asset. This can be informed by vulnerability scanners such as OpenVAS, which give scores based on the CVSS.
- *Threat intelligence*—Real-time feeds provide information on active threats, such as IP addresses known for malicious activities or trending attacks. Sources such as MITRE ATT&CK and AlienVault Open Threat Exchange (OTX) can provide such intelligence.
- *Monitored activities*—Real-time system activities, including unusual login attempts, high traffic volumes, file transfers, or connections to unfamiliar or blacklisted IPs. Behavior analytics tools can flag suspicious activities that raise the risk score.
- *Contextual factors*—The criticality of the asset to the business. For example, a vulnerability on a critical server will result in a higher risk score than the same vulnerability on a non-critical system.

Equation 10.6 shows a dynamic risk score example formula:

$$\text{DRS} = (\text{Vulnerability Severity} \times \text{Threat Intelligence Weight}) + (\text{Monitored Anomalies} \times \text{Asset Criticality}) \tag{10.6}$$

If a user's device starts communicating with an unfamiliar IP, that asset's risk score increases in real-time. The organization can then take immediate action, such as isolating or flagging the device for further investigation. By continuously updating the risk score based on real-time data, DRS enables organizations to respond faster and more effectively to potential threats. Here are some open source examples of where we would pull this information from:

- *Splunk*—Through its Enterprise Security suite, Splunk offers real-time risk-based alerting by analyzing vulnerabilities, monitored activities, and user behavior. Splunk uses predefined thresholds and real-time data to dynamically adjust risk scores across the environment.
- *Wazuh*—This open source security platform integrates with various tools, providing real-time monitoring, vulnerability assessment, and risk scoring for assets and users. Wazuh can calculate dynamic risk scores by using logs, threat intelligence, and anomaly detection.
- *Elastic Stack*—With machine learning capabilities, Elastic Stack can analyze event data and provide dynamic risk scoring based on detected anomalies, threat intelligence integration, and asset importance.
- *Cortex XSOAR*—This tool automates the risk scoring process by correlating real-time alerts with asset vulnerability data, enabling security teams to focus on high-risk threats.

10.3.4 Advanced threat detection metric exercise

Let's consider SecureShield, a large financial institution that recently implemented an AI-powered threat detection system. Before the system's implementation, SecureShield had several problems identifying *advanced persistent threats* (APTs), and its response time to potential threats was slow. The company decided to be more proactive and integrated machine learning-based anomaly detection and predictive threat intelligence into its security operations.

Some common AI models and systems that can be integrated into cybersecurity operations include

- *Machine learning algorithms*—Systems such as random forests, support vector machines (SVM), and neural networks can be trained to detect patterns in network traffic or user behavior that signal potential security threats. These models can help detect anomalies, such as APTs, by learning from historical data and recognizing deviations from typical behavior.
- *Deep learning*—More advanced models, such as convolutional neural networks (CNNs) or recurrent neural networks (RNNs), can process large datasets in real time. Deep learning models are particularly effective in detecting subtle anomalies, such as lateral movement within a network, that might indicate an ongoing breach.
- *Natural language processing (NLP)*—AI models using NLP can analyze logs, emails, or threat reports to identify and classify emerging threats. For instance, AI can review threat intelligence feeds in real time, categorizing and flagging known threat vectors.
- *Open-source tools such as OpenAI's GPT models or Wazuh*—These can help analyze threat intelligence, improve anomaly detection, and make predictions about

234 CHAPTER 10 *Advanced cybersecurity metrics*

potential future attacks. Wazuh's integration of machine learning for anomaly detection makes it a practical tool for security teams.

By using these models, SecureShield can automate the detection of threats such as APTs and reduce response times by predicting potential vulnerabilities based on historical threat patterns. This proactive approach ensures that threat detection becomes more accurate and quicker, improving the overall security posture of the organization.

The left side of figure 10.2 shows how SecureShield struggled with a low anomalous behavior detection rate of 65%. Many anomalies were going undetected, and the system was overwhelmed with false positives.

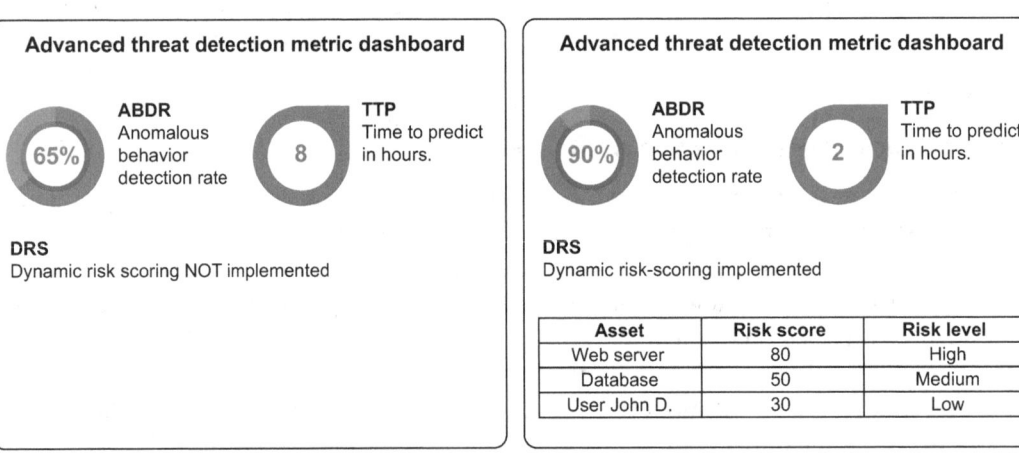

Figure 10.2 The left side shows the advanced threat detection metric dashboard for SecureShield before implementing improvements. On the right is the metrics after implementing dynamic risk scoring with anomaly detection and real-time threat intelligence feeds.

SecureShield's time to predict metric was also high, with the system taking an average of 8 hours to predict threats. This gave attackers enough time to infiltrate systems undetected. Their dynamic risk scoring was nonexistent, leaving them with a static risk assessment model that failed to adjust based on real-time threat activities.

To achieve improvements, SecureShield fine-tuned its anomaly detection algorithms to better differentiate between normal and abnormal behavior patterns, which reduced false positives and increased the detection rate. They also integrated real-time threat intelligence feeds to enable faster predictions, lowering the TTP. Finally, SecureShield shifted to an adaptive risk scoring model that continuously updates based on the latest threat data, which allowed them to adjust their defenses dynamically. We can see the results of these changes on the right in figure 10.2, showing a marked improvement in their advanced threat detection metrics dashboard.

Their ABDR rose to 90%, showing a significant reduction in missed anomalies and more precise threat detection. Their TTP dropped from 8 to 2 hours, giving the security response analysts time to respond to potential threats before they escalated. The introduction of DRS allowed them to respond more effectively in real time, with risk scores adapting dynamically as threats evolved. SecureShield can now adjust their response efforts based on real-time data, which improved their overall security posture.

10.4 Effectiveness of AI in cybersecurity

AI is a tool that brings advanced capabilities to threat detection, response, and prediction. The effectiveness of these capabilities must also be measured to validate that their contributions lead to tangible improvements. We touched on false-positive and false-negative metrics in chapter 8. Both metrics present risks. However, false positives are particularly burdensome and often lead to fatigue that desensitizes analysts to real threats. The challenge lies in striking the right balance between catching actual threats (true positives) and minimizing false positives.

Some of the widely used AI tools and platforms in cybersecurity include

- *IBM Watson for Cybersecurity*—Uses natural language processing to analyze structured and unstructured security data, making threat identification faster and more comprehensive.
- *Cortex XDR by Palo Alto Networks*—This platform uses machine learning to provide continuous threat detection and automated response to incidents across networks and endpoints.
- *Darktrace*—This AI-driven tool uses machine learning to model normal network behavior and identify anomalies in real time, allowing it to detect unknown threats and APTs.

The AI workflow fits into the traditional cybersecurity process at various points, including

- *Data collection*—AI systems continuously ingest data from logs, network traffic, and endpoint activity.
- *Threat detection*—Machine learning models analyze this data for anomalies or patterns indicative of malicious activity.
- *Response automation*—AI systems can automate the response to certain threats, such as quarantining infected devices or blocking malicious traffic.
- *Learning and feedback*—AI models improve over time by learning from incidents and user feedback.

10.4.1 False-positive suppression rate

AI systems that use machine learning models are designed to suppress false positives by learning from historical data and improving the accuracy of their decisions over time. They analyze behavior patterns across large datasets, flagging anomalies while filtering out known benign activities. AI-driven systems can adapt as the nature of cyberthreats changes, becoming more effective at recognizing legitimate versus suspicious activity.

False positive suppression rate (FPSR) measures how effectively AI-driven cybersecurity systems reduce false positives. This is important because a high rate of false positives leads to wasted time and resources and increases the risk of overlooking real threats due to alert fatigue.

The FPSR is calculated as the percentage reduction in false positives after AI has been implemented compared to before AI-driven detection was in place. If an organization initially faced 1,000 false positives per month and the number decreased to 200 after AI implementation, the FPSR would be 80%.

An example scenario would involve a company experiencing a high volume of false positives from its intrusion detection system (IDS). After integrating an AI-based solution, the organization notices a significant reduction in false positives, allowing the security team to focus on more pressing problems, such as responding to actual threats.

10.4.2 AI-based decision accuracy rate

AI-based decision accuracy rate (AI-DA) measures the trustworthiness of AI-based systems. If the AI system consistently achieves high decision accuracy, it indicates that the model is well-calibrated and can be trusted to assist in making decisions that protect organizational assets.

AI-DA assesses the precision with which AI systems identify genuine cybersecurity threats. AI models make decisions based on analyzing behavioral patterns, threat intelligence, and anomaly detection. The AI-DA metric helps evaluate how often the system makes the correct decision, either identifying a true positive (genuine threat) or a true negative (benign activity), and rejecting false positives and negatives.

AI-DA is typically calculated by dividing the number of correct decisions the AI system makes (true positives and true negatives) by the total number of decisions made (true positives, true negatives, false positives, and false negatives). For instance, if the AI system correctly flagged 900 true positives and true negatives out of 1,000 total decisions, its AI-DA score would be 90%. This accuracy rate should improve over time as the AI model receives more data and is fine-tuned.

AI's role in cybersecurity extends beyond just detecting threats. It helps automate processes, reduce human error, and augment human decision-making capabilities. To truly assess AI's influence, organizations need to track the following:

- *Reduction in incident response time*—AI systems can automatically flag and sometimes respond to incidents in real time, which significantly reduces the time it takes human analysts to identify and address potential threats.
- *Alert prioritization*—AI assists in organizing and ranking alerts by risk severity, thus helping analysts focus on the most critical incidents first.
- *Threat intelligence integration*—AI can process and analyze external threat intelligence data, helping organizations stay ahead of emerging threats.

Consider a financial institution using an AI-powered threat detection system. The AI system analyzes behavioral patterns and network traffic in real time. After a month of monitoring, the AI detected and correctly flagged 500 true positives (malicious activities) and 400 true negatives (normal activities) out of 1,000 incidents analyzed. Additionally, the system produced 50 false positives and 50 false negatives, where genuine threats were missed or benign activities were incorrectly flagged.

In this scenario, equation 10.7 shows how to calculate AI-DA as 90%, calculated as the number of correct decisions (900) divided by the total number of decisions (1,000) multiplied by 100 to obtain the percentage:

$$\text{AIDA} = \frac{900(\text{Correct Decisions})}{1000(\text{Total Decisions})} \times 100 = 90\% \qquad (10.7)$$

10.4.3 Effectiveness of AI in cybersecurity exercise

Let's consider DataGuard Solutions, a mid-sized enterprise struggling with alert fatigue and inefficiency in its incident response process. Before integrating an AI-based system, security analysts were overwhelmed by many false positives daily, which led to missed threats and delayed responses. The left side of figure 10.3 shows these metrics before implementing the AI-based system.

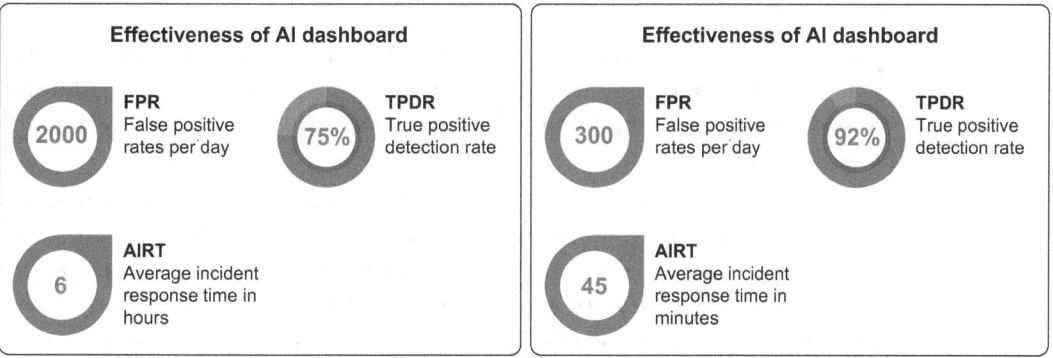

Figure 10.3 The left side shows the effectiveness of the AI dashboard, presenting daily false positive rates, true positive detection rates, and the average incident response time. On the right is its effectiveness after implementing an AI-driven solution.

DataGuard Solutions set targets for less than 500 false positives daily, a true positive detection rate of 90%, and an average incident response time of 1 hour. To achieve these goals, they implemented an AI-driven anomaly detection system, integrated with real-time threat intelligence feeds. By continuously learning from new data, the AI model refined its ability to identify benign behaviors, drastically reducing false positives. Simultaneously, the AI system began categorizing and prioritizing incidents based on risk, enabling security teams to focus their efforts on the most critical threats, leading to faster response times and more accurate threat detection. The right side of figure 10.3 shows their metrics dashboard after implementing these improvements.

By incorporating metrics such as FPR and AI-DA, DataGuard successfully used AI to streamline its security operations, improve decision accuracy, and reduce the cognitive load on its human analysts. The exercise demonstrates how organizations can measure the tangible effects of AI in cybersecurity.

10.5 Cloud and network threat management

Threat management typically involves cloud and network security as organizations increasingly rely on cloud and/or hybrid environments. The challenge of securing cloud and network activities grows more complex. Some advanced metrics can provide deeper insights into threat detection and surface management in cloud and network environments.

10.5.1 Cloud threat detection

Monitoring threats in the cloud requires focusing on several unique factors that differ from traditional network systems. A sudden spike in data egress from a cloud storage service could signal an insider attack or misconfigured storage permission. Standard threat detection systems may not be fully equipped to handle the dynamic nature of cloud infrastructure, where new workloads are continuously spun up and torn down.

CLOUD-SPECIFIC EXAMPLE 1

- *Data egress spikes*—A sudden increase in outbound traffic from cloud storage could indicate a misconfigured storage bucket or an insider threat. Traditional systems might not flag this because they are more attuned to packet-level anomalies within a static network.
- *Comparison*—In traditional networks, threat detection focuses on monitoring network devices (e.g., firewalls, switches) for irregular traffic patterns. However, cloud systems require monitoring for more abstract patterns such as unexpected data transfers from cloud storage accounts or API usage anomalies. Cloud-native detection systems often use tools such as AWS GuardDuty or Azure Security Center, which are built to monitor such data-specific anomalies.

CLOUD-SPECIFIC EXAMPLE 2

- *Workload dynamism*—In cloud environments, new virtual machines and containers are spun up and terminated rapidly. This dynamism requires detection methods that adapt to the ephemeral nature of workloads and the elastic scaling of resources. Traditional systems, designed for static infrastructure, may struggle with this.
- *Comparison*—Traditional network monitoring tools tend to assume a stable number of hosts or devices. In contrast, cloud-based monitoring tools such as Wazuh

and Elastic Stack focus on continuous integration and adaptation, using lightweight agents and API-driven data collection to monitor the ever-changing cloud workloads. Cloud systems need to detect when a new workload is potentially misconfigured or compromised immediately after deployment.

CLOUD-SPECIFIC EXAMPLE 3

- *Shared responsibility*—Cloud environments follow a shared responsibility model, where the cloud provider secures the infrastructure and the customer secures the data and workloads. This division means that threat detection in cloud systems must focus on securing configurations (e.g., permissions on cloud storage buckets or encryption policies) that traditional systems may not prioritize.
- *Comparison*—In traditional data centers, the company owns and manages all layers of security. However, in cloud environments, services such as AWS Config or Azure Policy help organizations ensure that their configurations adhere to security policies, focusing on compliance and cloud-specific risks such as insecure IAM roles or misconfigured security groups.

10.5.2 Cloud threat detection accuracy

Cloud threat detection accuracy (CTDA) evaluates the effectiveness of threat detection specifically tailored to cloud environments such as top providers—Amazon Web Services (AWS), Microsoft Azure, or Google Cloud Platform (GCP). Each cloud platform has its own associated tools to collect this information if implemented. However, many companies will implement another software solution integrated with these cloud service providers.

The CTDA evaluates how accurately and efficiently these alerts are generated and resolved. False positives or negatives affect detection rates, so improving cloud-based threat intelligence and tuning systems to recognize legitimate traffic patterns can help improve CTDA scores.

10.5.3 Attack surface index

The more organizations' services are accessible from the internet, the larger the attack surface and the more vulnerable the organization is to cyberattacks. Attack surface index (ASI) quantifies the breadth of an organization's exposure to potential threats by measuring the number of internet-exposed assets, endpoints, and cloud services.

ASI helps track network exposure, indicating how well an organization manages to reduce its external-facing attack vectors. In practice, organizations with high ASI might expose many endpoints or services to the public internet, increasing the risk of exposure to cyberattacks. A lower ASI reflects a tighter control on exposure with fewer external vulnerabilities and a smaller attack surface.

External-facing attack vectors are vulnerabilities in systems accessible from outside an organization's network, making them prime targets for cyberattacks. One common example is web applications, which may be exploited through techniques such as SQL injection or cross-site scripting (XSS) if not properly secured. Remote access tools, such as VPNs or Remote Desktop Protocol (RDP), also present significant risks, especially when passwords are weak or repeatedly used. Similarly, cloud services, when misconfigured, can expose sensitive data to attackers via unsecured APIs or storage buckets. These attack vectors highlight the need for strong security practices to prevent unauthorized access and data breaches

10.5.4 Cloud and network threat management metric exercise

Consider the case of SecureCloud, a financial institution moving to the cloud. The left side of figure 10.4 shows the initial metrics dashboard reflecting SecureCloud's cloud and network security status. Their CTDA is low due to numerous false positives, and their ASI is high, as many services are exposed to the internet.

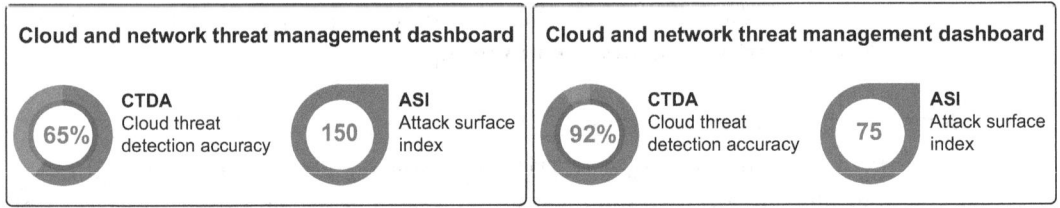

Figure 10.4 The left side shows the cloud and network threat management dashboard with the CTDA and ASI metrics prior to improvements. The right side shows the situation after the improvements.

SecureCloud's metrics indicated a CTDA of 65%, with a high rate of missed detections due to poorly tuned cloud monitoring tools. Their ASI was 150, meaning they had many exposed services, contributing to their high attack surface and vulnerability.

SecureCloud aimed to improve its CTDA to 90% and reduce its ASI to 80 by auditing exposed services and implementing cloud-specific security measures. To enhance SecureCloud's CTDA, they first audited their cloud services and monitoring tools. The initial step involved identifying and evaluating all cloud assets, services, and workloads, pinpointing which ones were not effectively monitored. Poorly tuned tools, such as those that missed activity due to insufficient rules or thresholds, were adjusted or replaced with cloud-native monitoring solutions that were better optimized for dynamic environments. SecureCloud used open source tools such as Wazuh or Elastic Stack, which integrate well with cloud services and provide enhanced visibility.

For reducing the ASI, SecureCloud conducted a thorough review of their internet-exposed services. The security team worked on eliminating unnecessary exposure by decommissioning unused services, strengthening access controls, and applying network segmentation. Cloud-specific security measures such as implementing Zero Trust Architecture, enforcing least privilege access, and deploying Web Application Firewalls (WAFs) were essential steps to achieve this reduction.

Through these processes, the company could achieve a measurable improvement, raising their CTDA to 90% by reducing missed detections and cutting down their ASI by almost half, reducing their overall attack surface and limiting vulnerabilities to external threats. The right side of figure 10.4 shows the improvements in their metrics.

After six months of remediation and fine-tuning cloud security measures, their CTDA improved to 92%, reflecting better detection capabilities. Their ASI dropped to 75 as they decommissioned unnecessary services, secured APIs, and limited access to sensitive data. These changes reduced their overall exposure, while improving threat detection accuracy in their cloud environment.

By consistently measuring and improving their cloud threat detection capabilities and reducing their attack surface, SecureCloud significantly enhanced its cybersecurity posture, reducing the likelihood of successful attacks on their cloud infrastructure.

10.6 Incident management

Measuring the effectiveness of an organization's incident-handling process helps determine the effectiveness of damage reduction and swift recovery. With the right metrics, we can proactively hunt for potential threats and estimate the effects of incidents after they occur. These metrics go beyond the traditional logging and response times to provide a more sophisticated view of threat detection and incident management.

10.6.1 Threat hunting

AI-based threat-hunting solutions can sift through large amounts of data, detecting subtle signs of malicious activities that traditional systems may overlook. For example, organizations using AI to hunt for advanced persistent threats or lateral movement in a network could see significant improvements as machine learning models learn from past incidents.

There are several open source AI-powered solutions for threat hunting that combine advanced machine learning models with cybersecurity monitoring. Tools such as Wazuh, Elastic Security (part of the Elastic Stack), and Apache Metron provide threat detection, monitoring, and response capabilities, using AI for enhanced threat hunting. Zeek (formerly Bro) and Cortex also integrate AI algorithms to analyze traffic, correlate events, and identify stealthy threats in real time. These platforms offer customizable rules and machine learning models, allowing improved detection and proactive threat hunting across various environments.

ADVANCED THREAT HUNTING SUCCESS RATE

The success of threat hunting operations can be measured by calculating the percentage of stealth threats identified and mitigated before they escalate into full incidents. This metric helps gauge the efficiency of AI-driven hunting techniques, the effectiveness of anomaly detection, behavioral analysis, and deep inspection of network traffic or endpoint activity.

Advanced threat hunting success rate (ATHSR) is calculated by determining the ratio of successful threat hunts to the total number of threat hunts conducted:

- *Determining the total number of threat hunts*—The total number of proactive threat-hunting activities conducted by the security team. Threat hunts can be initiated based on various triggers, such as suspicious activity, anomaly detection, or predefined threat-hunting campaigns.
- *Identifying the successful hunts*—A successful hunt is one in which a previously unknown or stealth threat (e.g., advanced persistent threats, malware, lateral movement) is identified and mitigated. This might involve detecting suspicious files, network traffic, or activities not picked up by traditional detection systems.
- *ATHSR formula*—As shown in equation 10.8, to obtain the ATHSR, we divide the number of successful threat hunts by the total number of threat hunts, multiplied by 100 to obtain a percentage.

$$\text{ATHSR} = \frac{\text{Number of Successful Threat Hunts}}{\text{Total Number of Threat Hunts}} \times 100 \tag{10.8}$$

10.6.2 Incident impact estimation

Incident impact estimation (IIE) is not just about financial losses but includes damage to brand reputation, customer trust, and compliance violations. These less tangible losses are difficult to measure in terms of cost to the organization. For example, if a ransomware attack takes down critical systems, it would be helpful to estimate the potential hours of downtime, the cost of restoring the systems from backup, and the broader financial implications. This predictive insight helps organizations prioritize their incident response and disaster recovery plans.

IIE focuses on predicting the potential consequences of an incident. It can be used to estimate the total impact, including downtime, financial losses, and data loss. IIE is valuable in helping organizations prepare for the aftermath of a breach to gauge the potential effects on business and design more effective recovery and mitigation strategies. It is calculated by considering several factors, including downtime, potential data loss, financial repercussions, and operational interruptions, as seen in equation 10.9:

$$\text{IIE} = \text{Downtime Cost} + \text{Data Loss Impact} + \text{Recovery Costs} \tag{10.9}$$

IIE data is gathered by analyzing several key factors. First, downtime costs are calculated by estimating the hourly financial losses due to business disruptions. This includes lost revenue and reduced productivity. Data loss effects are measured based on the sensitivity and volume of data compromised, factoring in regulatory penalties and reputational damage. Recovery costs encompass expenses for system restoration, legal fees, and communication with affected stakeholders. This information is typically obtained through financial reports, incident logs, and consultations with operational teams to estimate the broader consequences of an incident.

10.6.3 Incident management metric exercise

Consider CyberHealth, a healthcare provider experiencing frequent attempts at breaching its patient data systems. The left side of figure 10.5 shows CyberHealth's initial metrics dashboard before implementing advanced threat hunting and post-incident impact estimation measures.

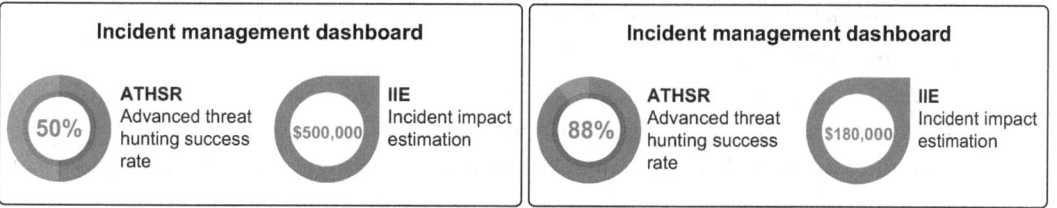

Figure 10.5 The left side shows the incident management dashboard with ATHSR and IIE metrics prior to improvements. On the right is the dashboard after implementing improvements.

The advanced threat hunting success rate was low at 50%, meaning half of the potential stealth threats went undetected, leaving the organization vulnerable. Meanwhile, their IIE score reflected an anticipated financial loss of $500,000 for every major breach due to patient data loss and system downtime.

CyberHealth aimed to increase its ATHSR to 85% by incorporating more advanced machine learning algorithms into its threat-hunting procedures. The IIE's goal was to reduce the predicted financial loss to $200,000 by implementing improved data backups, disaster recovery procedures, and business continuity plans, the results of which are presented on the right in figure 10.5.

CyberHealth's ATHSR increased to 88%, showing a more robust threat-hunting capability. The IIE dropped to $180,000, reflecting lower anticipated financial losses due to faster recovery times and better preparation for potential breaches. CyberHealth was able to improve its threat detection capabilities, mitigate potential damages, and better allocate resources to critical areas during incident recovery.

10.7 Continuous improvement

Each organization should strive to adapt and refine their information security posture over time. Threats are ever evolving, and this environment requires organizations to be agile and proactive in addressing new emerging threats. Continuous improvement ties directly to advanced cybersecurity metrics because as new threats emerge, organizations need metrics that track their ability to mitigate risks in real time. For example, if a vulnerability is detected on a critical server and it takes 48 hours to patch, that time is logged. By comparing this value across different risk categories (e.g., zero-day vulnerabilities, misconfigurations), organizations can assess whether they're becoming faster at mitigating risks, which is crucial in preventing small vulnerabilities from escalating into major incidents.

10.7.1 Risk mitigation

By reducing the average time it takes to patch a vulnerability or resolve an incident, organizations can minimize their exposure to cyberthreats. How quickly are identified risks mitigated after detection? The faster a risk is mitigated, the lower the likelihood of it evolving into a more significant threat.

RISK MITIGATION VELOCITY

Calculating risk mitigation velocity (RMV) involves tracking the time from risk identification to risk resolution, then comparing this across different types of risks and incidents. Consistently improving RMV indicates a stronger, more responsive security posture.

RMV is an important metric because it is closely tied to an organization's ability to respond to threats in real time. The faster risks are mitigated, the fewer opportunities attackers have to exploit vulnerabilities.

Now, let's walk through an example to calculate RMV. Imagine a company, DataSafe, that recently identified several vulnerabilities in its web applications. The vulnerabilities ranged in severity, with some classified as critical (e.g., SQL injection) and others as low risk (e.g., outdated software versions).

- *Incident 1 (critical vulnerability)*—Discovered on January 1st and resolved on January 3rd (two days)
- *Incident 2 (moderate vulnerability)*—Discovered on January 2nd and resolved on January 5th (three days)
- *Incident 3 (low vulnerability)*—Discovered on January 4th and resolved on January 10th (six days)

To calculate RMV, as shown in equation 10.10, the company tracks the time it took to resolve these vulnerabilities and computes the average time to resolve incidents across the month:

$$\text{RMV} = \frac{2 + 3 + 6}{3} = \frac{11}{3} = 3.67 \text{ days} \qquad (10.10)$$

This means that, on average, DataSafe mitigated risks in 3.67 days. Over time, by consistently reducing RMV, DataSafe can minimize its exposure to cyber threats.

10.7.2 Time to predict

Organizations can refine their predictive models to improve the speed and accuracy of threat forecasting to help them stay ahead of emerging risks. This can be achieved using various tools and frameworks designed for predictive analytics in cybersecurity, including open source platforms such as Wazuh or Elastic Stack, which integrate machine learning for anomaly detection and predictive analysis.

For example, by using Elastic Stack, an organization can collect real-time data on network traffic and feed it into machine learning models to identify patterns indicative of potential threats. These models can be retrained periodically with new data to refine predictions and improve the time it takes to forecast an attack. Similarly, Wazuh, which integrates with Elasticsearch, can predict potential security incidents based on logs, vulnerabilities, and system behavior over time.

The key is regularly assessing and optimizing the algorithms to minimize false positives and improve response times. Using this approach ensures continuous improvement, with data-driven decisions that enhance both speed and accuracy in threat prediction.

MEAN TIME TO PREDICT

Mean time to predict (MTP) measures the average time it takes for a predictive system, often driven by AI or machine learning, to forecast a threat before it occurs. This metric can assess the accuracy and efficiency of predictive analytics systems. The shorter the MTP, the more efficient the organization is at anticipating threats.

Organizations can implement a feedback loop for continuous improvement by regularly assessing these advanced metrics. As RMV and MTP are tracked over time, they should inform a constant cycle of learning, adapting, and refining strategies. When trends or inefficiencies are identified, teams can adjust their security protocols, invest in additional training, or deploy new tools to address these gaps. This process ensures that the organization is responding to current threats and proactively enhancing its overall security framework.

10.7.3 Continuous improvement metric exercise

Imagine you are the cybersecurity manager for a mid-sized financial services company, FinSecure Corp. Your company has recently implemented advanced AI-based predictive threat systems to detect potential risks. However, while the company effectively identifies threats, there's room for improvement in how quickly these risks are mitigated and how early the predictive system forecasts potential threats. These improvements can be measured using risk mitigation velocity (RMV) and mean time to predict (MTP).

The left side of figure 10.6, shows the status of FinSecure Corp.'s risk mitigation and threat prediction efforts.

The current RMV shows that it takes 15 hours to resolve identified risks, indicating a sluggish response time that leaves the organization exposed. The MTP of 5 hours means that the system is predicting threats with limited lead time, requiring a closer review of the predictive model.

Based on the initial metrics, FinSecure Corp. needs to reduce RMV and improve MTP to better manage risks and predict threats early. Over the next quarter, changes such as automating certain response protocols, refining the AI-based prediction

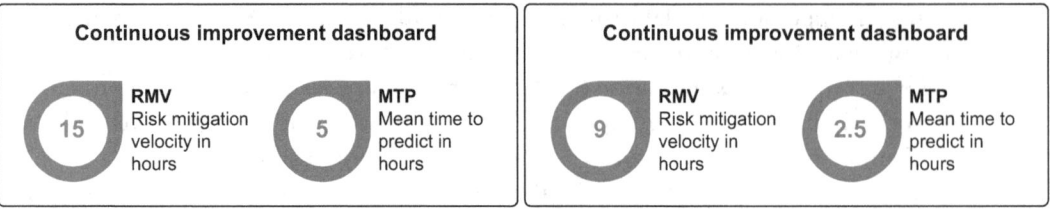

Figure 10.6 The left side shows the continuous improvement dashboard before the improvements. The right side shows the dashboard after implementation of the improvements.

models, and improving communication across teams are implemented. This includes enhanced training to shorten the response time and adjustments to the predictive models to make threat detection more precise and quicker. FinSecure Corp. has set target values for RMV to 10 hours or less and MTP to 3 hours or less. The right side of figure 10.6 shows FinSecure Corp's metrics after the improvement implementation.

FinSecure Corp. successfully reduced RMV from 15 to 9 hours by automating several response workflows and conducting targeted training for the incident response team. The quicker response time allowed the company to mitigate risks before they escalated. In terms of threat prediction, by refining AI models and using more comprehensive data, MTP dropped to 2.5 hours, giving the company more time to prepare for and defend against incoming threats.

By focusing on risk mitigation speeds and predictive capabilities, businesses can transition from a reactive security posture to a more proactive and resilient approach, continuously improving their defenses against cyber threats. Tracking these metrics empowers organizations to make informed decisions, fine-tune security processes, and reduce risk exposure.

While we have introduced advanced metrics in this chapter, it's important to understand that these are not the only metrics an organization should use. I am frequently asked what my top 10 metrics are, and my response remains the same: I don't have a definitive top 10. However, your organization does. The challenge lies in determining which metrics are relevant to your unique needs and aligning them with your business objectives. This approach will ensure your metrics provide actionable insights and drive continuous improvement in your cybersecurity posture. The next chapter examines how to select the most effective metrics for your organization and tie them directly to business goals.

Summary

- Advanced cybersecurity metrics provide a data-driven approach to anticipating and mitigating future threats.
- Predictive analytics, such as the risk exposure index (REI) and predictive threat index (PTI), help organizations estimate potential risks and prepare proactive defenses.

- Metrics such as anomalous behavior detection rate (ABDR) and dynamic risk scoring (DRS) enhance the accuracy of threat detection and response, especially when integrated with AI.
- False positive suppression rate (FPSR) and AI-based decision accuracy (AI-DA) assess the efficiency and accuracy of AI-driven cybersecurity systems.
- Continuous improvement through metrics such as risk mitigation velocity (RMV) ensures that organizations adapt quickly to emerging threats and vulnerabilities.

Advanced statistical analysis

This chapter covers
- Statistical techniques in practical terms
- Analyzing patterns in cybersecurity data
- Real-world examples to apply statistical tools
- Evaluating security strategies with actionable insights

This is not a mathematics book. Most cybersecurity practitioners will not be crunching numbers by hand or writing scripts to perform statistical data analysis. However, it is essential to understand the basic principles that underpin the metrics used to guide decision-making. These statistical calculations are often handled by a dedicated analyst or software solution, executing algorithms to generate actionable insights. Such in-depth understanding allows cybersecurity professionals at all levels to better interpret the data, identify trends, and make informed decisions about their security posture.

Statistics in cybersecurity help quantify risk, predict potential threats, and assess the effectiveness of security controls. For example, statistical trend analysis allows organizations to detect patterns in attack vectors, while correlation techniques can reveal relationships between seemingly distinct security incidents. These insights are invaluable for fine-tuning security strategies and making data-driven decisions.

Chapter 11 introduces the core statistical methods used in cybersecurity, explains their relevance, and shows how they directly affect key security decisions. Whether you monitor system vulnerabilities, analyze user behavior, or respond to incidents, understanding these concepts provides the context needed to make informed, strategic decisions. In today's data-driven world, having a grasp on statistics is not just for analysts—it's a skill every cybersecurity professional can benefit from.

I've included Python code examples and corresponding visualizations to make these principles practical and engaging. These examples are designed to let you see these concepts in action, making it easier to connect theory with real-world applications. If you're new to programming or statistics, don't worry—the examples are accessible and accompanied by detailed explanations to guide you through each step. All the code for this chapter, as well as for chapters 2, 3, 11, 12, and 13, is available in a Jupyter Notebook format in my GitHub repository at https://github.com/Mariano215/Security_Metrics. Whether you're an experienced coder or a beginner, this resource provides a hands-on way to follow along and practice these concepts.

> **Jupyter Notebooks**
>
> Jupyter Notebooks (https://jupyter.org/) is a free, open source web application, designed for creating and sharing documents that contain live code, equations, visualizations, and narrative text. It's ideal for demonstrating and running Python code because it integrates code, outputs, and explanations in a single, easy-to-use environment.
>
> In this book, we use Jupyter Notebooks to explore cybersecurity metrics concepts, while running real-time data analysis. You can install Jupyter by following the instructions on their official website at https://jupyter.org/install. Jupyter Notebooks enables step-by-step visualization of metric calculations, making it easier to understand the results and apply them to your cybersecurity analysis.

My goal is to ensure that by the end of this chapter, you feel confident in applying these methods to enhance your understanding of cybersecurity data and make well-informed decisions. Let's dive in together. Whether you find this topic interesting or intimidating, you'll discover how approachable and useful these tools can be.

11.1 Continuous improvement with statistical metrics

Continuous improvement is a core principle of cybersecurity, as the threat landscape evolves constantly. To stay ahead, organizations must implement effective security measures and use statistical metrics to gauge their success and make data-driven decisions. Statistical metrics enable organizations to monitor their security posture, identify areas for improvement, and adjust strategies to reduce vulnerabilities and increase resilience.

11.1.1 Key concepts for continuous improvement

The essence of continuous improvement is to track progress, analyze data, and refine processes. Statistical methods such as moving averages, trend analysis, regression models, and probability distributions help security teams stay vigilant by turning raw data into actionable insights:

- *Benchmarking*—Every improvement starts with knowing your baseline. Statistical analysis enables establishing performance benchmarks. For example, tracking how often patching is completed on time, or how many vulnerabilities are identified within a specific time frame, provides you with a baseline to compare against after implementing new security measures.
- *Monitoring trends*—Metrics should be continuously monitored over time using methods such as trend analysis or ARIMA forecasting. A steady increase in phishing attacks detected over time could indicate that existing email security measures must be strengthened.
- *Statistical testing*—Use statistical tests, such as t-tests or chi-square tests, to compare current metrics with historical data. For instance, if you've deployed a new intrusion detection system, statistical testing can help confirm whether the new system has statistically improved threat-detection rates.
- *Correlation analysis*—Identify relationships between different metrics. For example, correlation analysis can be used to see whether there's a link between server downtime and increased cyberattacks. This helps uncover patterns that might not be immediately obvious but are crucial for future planning.
- *Root cause analysis*—Whenever a breach or a near miss occurs, statistical tools such as Bayesian inference can help trace the root cause, showing which vulnerabilities were most likely exploited and predicting which future ones may be at risk.

11.1.2 Free resources for statistical analysis

In this chapter, we aim to empower readers by introducing statistical methods and guiding them on how to apply these techniques using free and accessible resources. The examples in this chapter are built with Python, and the code provided is designed to be executed and adapted by readers. To help you get started, here are some freely available resources that align with the content covered in this chapter:

- *Kaggle*—Kaggle is a well-known platform for data science and machine learning. It provides free datasets, tutorials, and examples of statistical analysis that can serve as a foundation for building and testing your cybersecurity metrics (see https://www.kaggle.com)
- *Statistical libraries in Python*—Libraries such as `pandas`, `statsmodels`, and `scikit-learn` are integral to performing the statistical analyses shown in this chapter.

These libraries are free, well-documented, and widely used, making them ideal tools for implementing and expanding on the Python code examples provided here (see https://pandas.pydata.org).

- *NIST Cybersecurity Framework*—While not a coding resource, the NIST Cybersecurity Framework offers guidelines and best practices that complement the statistical methods discussed here. By aligning your analysis with the NIST framework, it is possible to ensure your metrics support broader organizational security goals (see https://www.nist.gov/cyberframework).

11.2 Using statistical metrics for continuous improvement

Cybersecurity isn't static—it's a constant race against evolving threats. Statistical metrics help organizations measure progress, evaluate security strategies, and refine their processes. Here are some examples of key metrics:

- *Time to resolve incidents*—Tracks how quickly your team addresses security issues
- *Phishing detection rates*—Measures the effectiveness of email filters and user training
- *Vulnerability patch rates*—Evaluates the percentage of critical vulnerabilities patched within set timeframes

11.3 Implementing a feedback loop

The key to continuous improvement lies in closing the feedback loop, which involves regularly reviewing metrics, adjusting security protocols, and monitoring the effects of these changes. By incorporating statistical insights into your review process, you ensure that data, not intuition, drives decisions:

- *Set metrics-based goals.* For continuous improvement, use metrics to set specific, measurable, attainable, relevant, and time-bound goals (SMART). For example, aim to reduce the number of unpatched vulnerabilities by 20% in six months.
- *Track and analyze metrics regularly.* Use tools such as moving averages to smooth out fluctuations in data and identify long-term trends. Regularly tracking metrics such as time to resolve incidents or the number of detected threats helps identify what's working and what needs improvement.
- *Review and adapt.* Use historical data and statistical models, such as regression analysis, to predict future trends and adjust your security measures. If an analysis shows that a specific department has more incidents, you may need to review its security training or access controls.

11.4 Finding hidden relationships in data

In cybersecurity, identifying how different variables interact can be crucial for uncovering vulnerabilities or potential risks. For instance, you might notice a rise in failed login attempts coinciding with increased phishing emails targeting employees. These patterns may not be immediately apparent in raw data but can be uncovered through correlation analysis.

Correlation analysis is a statistical technique used to measure the strength and direction of the relationship between two variables. For example, if failed login attempts and phishing emails are positively correlated, it means that as one increases, the other tends to increase as well. This insight allows you to anticipate threats and implement preventive measures proactively.

Correlation analysis is often used to uncover hidden relationships in cybersecurity data. The following listing demonstrates how to compute and visualize correlations between two variables: the hour of login attempts and the number of failed logins. The dataset is synthetically generated for demonstration purposes and does not require any preprocessing.

The dataset includes

- *Login hour*—Represents the hour of the day when login attempts were recorded
- *Failed login attempts*—Counts of login failures for the corresponding hour

The following listing calculates a correlation matrix—a table showing the strength of the relationship between variables. A heatmap is then generated to visually represent these correlations. This technique is essential for identifying patterns or behaviors in data, such as higher failure rates during certain times of the day, which can guide your security measures.

Listing 11.1 Hidden relationships

```
#Import libraries
import seaborn as sns                                    ← Imports seaborn
import pandas as pd                                      ← Imports pandas
import matplotlib.pyplot as plt                          ← Imports matplotlib

#Example dataset: Login hours and failed attempts
data = {'Login_Hour': [8, 9, 10, 11, 12, 13, 14, 15,
                      16, 17, 18, 19, 20, 21, 22, 23,
                      0, 1, 2, 3],                       ← Defines login hour data
        'Failed_Login_Attempts': [2, 3, 4, 5, 3, 6, 7, 5,
                                 8, 9, 12, 13, 10, 8, 7,
                                 5, 2, 3, 4, 5]}         ← Defines failed login data

df = pd.DataFrame(data)                                  ← Creates DataFrame

#Calculate correlation matrix
correlation_matrix = df.corr()                           ← Calculates correlation

#Plot heatmap
plt.figure(figsize=(8, 6))                               ← Sets figure size
sns.heatmap(correlation_matrix, annot=True,
            cmap='Grays', cbar=True)                     ← Plots heatmap
plt.title('Correlation Between Login Hours and Failed \
          Login Attempts')                               ← Adds plot title
plt.show()                                               ← Shows plot
```

Figure 11.1 shows the output.

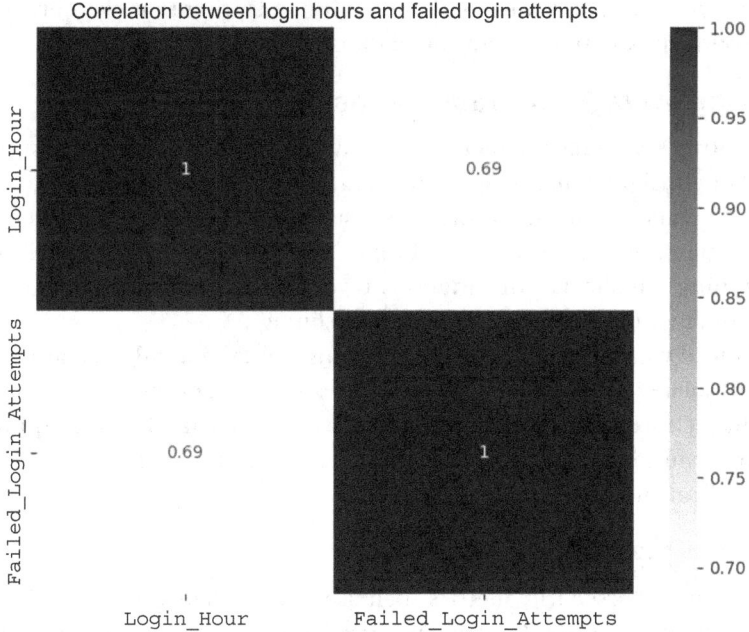

Figure 11.1 Heatmap showing correlation between login hours and failed login attempts.

The heatmap provided visually represents the correlation between two variables: `Login_Hour` and `Failed_Login_Attempts`. The values in the correlation matrix range from −1 to 1, where

- 1 indicates a perfect positive correlation, meaning both variables increase together.
- −1 signifies a perfect negative correlation, meaning one variable increases, while the other decreases.
- 0 indicates no correlation between the variables.

In this example, the correlation values inside each heatmap cell quantify the strength of the relationship. For instance, a higher correlation value between `Login_Hour` and `Failed_Login_Attempts` might suggest that failed login attempts tend to cluster during specific times of the day.

This analysis helps identify patterns that can inform incident response or improve authentication mechanisms. If you identify strong correlations, such as failed logins increasing during certain hours, you can adjust policies (e.g., stricter authentication controls during peak times) to mitigate risks.

Continuous improvement relies on systematically using statistical metrics to measure, analyze, and refine security processes. Organizations can adapt and enhance their security measures over time by benchmarking, tracking trends, and using statistical testing. Free resources can assist with implementation, ensuring that even organizations with limited budgets benefit from advanced statistical analysis.

11.5 Using moving averages to track trends

When monitoring cybersecurity incidents, daily fluctuations can obscure the bigger picture, making it challenging to spot meaningful trends. This is where moving averages become valuable. A moving average is a statistical technique that calculates the average of a dataset over a specific time frame, "moving" forward with each new data point. Smoothing out short-term variations reveals longer-term trends, helping analysts discern whether threats are escalating or declining.

For example, if you monitor malware detections daily, the numbers may vary significantly due to isolated events or anomalies—a moving average smooths these fluctuations, offering a clearer view of the overall trajectory. Understanding and applying this method allows you to anticipate patterns in cybersecurity incidents and better align your response strategies.

11.5.1 Moving averages example

When monitoring cybersecurity metrics such as malware detection, it can be difficult to interpret daily fluctuations. Moving averages help by smoothing the data to reveal long-term trends. In this example, we simulate daily malware detection counts over a month. Using Python, we calculate both a simple moving average (SMA) and an exponential moving average (EMA) to illustrate their differences.

The code generates a dataset representing daily malware detections over 30 days. It then calculates the SMA to show the average detection rate over a rolling five-day window. For comparison, the code also computes the EMA, which weights recent data more heavily, allowing quicker detection of sudden trends.

The data used here is simulated directly in the code, which ensures reproducibility and avoids dependency on external datasets. No preprocessing was necessary, as the data is clean and structured. Both SMA and EMA are computed from this simulated data.

The SMA is great for highlighting broader trends and smoothing out short-term variability. However, the EMA offers an added benefit by prioritizing recent events, which is crucial for detecting potential outbreaks or sudden spikes in malware activity. Both methods are valuable depending on the specific needs of the cybersecurity analyst.

Listing 11.2 Moving averages

```
import pandas as pd           ◄─── Imports pandas
import matplotlib.pyplot as plt   ◄─── Imports matplotlib

#Example malware detection data
```

```python
data = {'Day': range(1, 31),                          # Defines day range
        'Malware_Detections': [10, 8, 12, 15, 9, 11, 13, 8, 14,
                    16, 15, 13, 18, 20, 17, 14, 19,
                    21, 23, 17, 15, 14, 16, 13, 12,
                    18, 22, 25, 19, 9]}               # Defines malware data

df = pd.DataFrame(data)                               # Creates DataFrame

#Calculate SMA and EMA
df['SMA'] = df['Malware_Detections'].rolling(window=5)
        .mean()                                       # Calculates SMA
df['EMA'] = df['Malware_Detections'].ewm(span=5,
        adjust=False).mean()                          # Calculates EMA

#Plot the data
plt.figure(figsize=(10, 6))                           # Sets figure size
plt.plot(df['Day'], df['Malware_Detections'],
        label='Daily Malware Detections', color='blue',
        marker='o')                                   # Plots daily detections
plt.plot(df['Day'], df['SMA'], label='Simple Moving \
        Average', linestyle='--', color='green')      # Plots SMA
plt.plot(df['Day'], df['EMA'], label='Exponential \
        Moving Average', linestyle='-.',
            color='red')                              # Plots EMA
plt.title('Malware Detections: Daily vs. Moving \
        Averages')                                    # Sets plot title
plt.xlabel('Day')                                     # Labels x-axis
plt.ylabel('Malware Detections')                      # Labels y-axis
plt.legend()                                          # Adds legend
plt.grid()                                            # Adds grid
plt.show()                                            # Shows plot
```

By comparing SMA and EMA, you can decide whether long-term trends or immediate changes are more critical for your security planning, as shown in the output figure 11.2.

11.5.2 Detailed description of the plots

Figure 11.2 displays daily malware detections over 30 days, along with two types of moving averages:

- *Simple moving average (SMA)*—A dashed line represents the SMA, which smooths short-term fluctuations by averaging malware detection counts over a five-day window. It provides a clearer view of general trends in malware activity.
- *Exponential moving average (EMA)*—Represented by a dashed-dot line, the EMA gives more weight to recent data, making it more responsive to sudden changes in malware detection rates.

INTERPRETING THE PLOT

- The solid line with circular markers shows the raw daily malware detections.

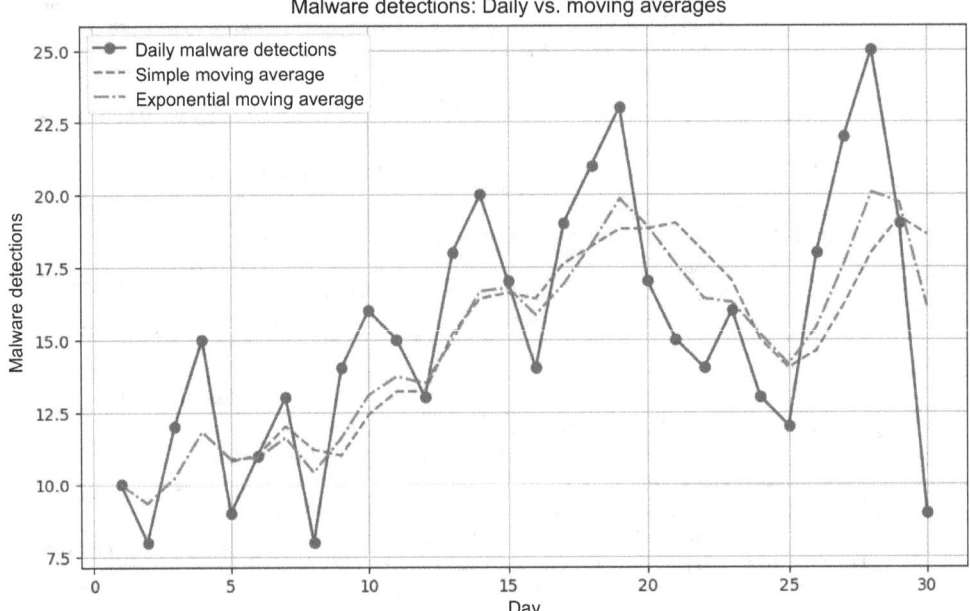

Figure 11.2   Malware detections output from sample code

- The dashed line (SMA) reflects a smoothed trend of malware activity, useful for identifying long-term patterns.
- The dot-dashed line (EMA) quickly highlights recent surges or drops in malware detections.
- As a key insight, spikes or dips in the dotted solid line that deviate significantly from the moving averages may indicate anomalies or unusual activity worth investigating.

11.6 Grouping similar events for better insights

Clustering techniques help organize large datasets by grouping similar elements. In cybersecurity, clustering can identify anomalies, segment network traffic, or classify threats based on behavior.

For example, imagine categorizing devices based on their login behavior. K-Means clustering groups devices into clusters, allowing you to spot unusual activity that doesn't fit any known group.

The following listing demonstrates using K-Means clustering, a popular unsupervised learning technique, to group devices based on their login behavior. The hypothetical dataset contains five devices with attributes for bandwidth usage and access times. These attributes represent measurable factors relevant to device activity, making the dataset practical for illustrating clustering techniques. Before diving into the code, let's clarify the meaning of the following terms:

- *Dataset origin*—The dataset is generated within the code, eliminating the need for external files. It includes two key features: Bandwidth_Usage (representing network activity) and Access_Times (frequency of logins).
- *Purpose*—The goal is to group devices with similar behavior into clusters. This helps cybersecurity professionals detect outliers or unusual activity, such as a device consuming an abnormally high bandwidth or logging in at irregular times.

Listing 11.3 Grouping similar events

```
#Import libraries
from sklearn.cluster import KMeans      ◁─── Imports K-Means
import pandas as pd                     ◁─── Imports pandas
import matplotlib.pyplot as plt         ◁─── Imports matplotlib

#Sample dataset: Device login activity
data = {'Device': ['Laptop_A', 'Phone_B', 'Printer_C',
        'Laptop_B', 'Server_D'],                          ◁─── Defines devices
        'Bandwidth_Usage': [100, 200, 50, 90, 300],       ◁─── Defines bandwidth data
        'Access_Times': [10, 12, 3, 9, 16]}               ◁─── Defines access times
df = pd.DataFrame(data)     ◁─── Creates DataFrame

#Extract features for clustering
X = df[['Bandwidth_Usage', 'Access_Times']]    ◁─── Selects features

#Apply K-means with 2 clusters
kmeans = KMeans(n_clusters=2, random_state=42)    ◁─── Creates K-Means model
df['Cluster'] = kmeans.fit_predict(X)             ◁─── Fits model, adds cluster

#Plot clusters
plt.scatter(df['Bandwidth_Usage'], df['Access_Times'],
        c=df['Cluster'], cmap='viridis',
        label='Clusters')                                  ◁─── Plots scatter with clusters
plt.title('K-Means Clustering of Login Activity')          ◁─── Sets plot title
plt.xlabel('Bandwidth Usage')                              ◁─── Labels x-axis
plt.ylabel('Access Times')                                 ◁─── Labels y-axis
plt.grid(True)                                             ◁─── Adds grid
plt.show()                                                 ◁─── Shows plot
```

Figure 11.3 shows the output.

The resulting scatter plot displays the devices grouped into clusters. Devices in the same cluster exhibit similar login behaviors, while outliers or anomalous devices are likelier to belong to separate clusters. For instance, a server with unusually high bandwidth usage might form its own distinct cluster, signaling potential misuse or abnormal activity.

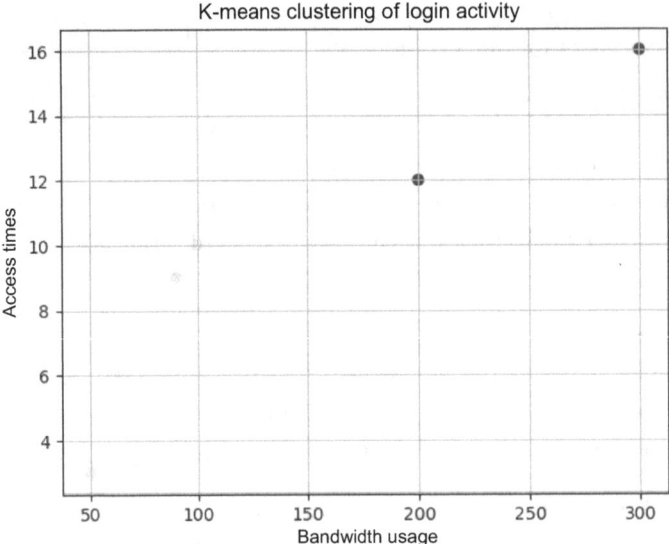

Figure 11.3 Clustering the output of login activity

Unusual behavior, such as a device with disproportionately high access times, could indicate a potential breach or misuse. The following visualizations are crucial for analyzing cybersecurity and network behavior:

- *Malware detection plot*—Helps visualize daily trends and anomalies in malware activity over time. It is useful for operational teams monitoring the effectiveness of malware detection systems.
- *Correlation heatmap*—Provides insights into patterns between login hours and failed attempts. It is useful for investigating whether certain times of the day pose higher security risks.
- *Clustering scatter plot*—Reveals behavioral patterns of devices on a network. It is useful for identifying anomalies, such as a device behaving differently from its expected cluster.

11.7 Forecasting cybersecurity trends

In cybersecurity, forecasting is like predicting the weather; it helps you prepare for future events by analyzing patterns in historical data. By using forecasting methods, organizations can predict trends such as the frequency of malware incidents, or the likelihood of specific threats, thus enabling proactive defense strategies.

One widely used forecasting technique is ARIMA (autoregressive integrated moving average). This statistical method combines historical data, trends, and patterns to predict future values. It's especially useful in cybersecurity for anticipating future attack volumes, resource requirements, or shifts in threat trends.

11.7.1 ARIMA in action

Let's consider an example where a security team wants to forecast monthly malware incidents using data from the past year. The code demonstrates how to use the ARIMA model to forecast the future frequency of malware incidents based on historical data. Forecasting cybersecurity trends such as this one can help organizations proactively allocate resources and prepare for potential threats.

The dataset is generated directly within the code and represents 12 months of malware incident counts for 2023. `pd.date_range()` creates the monthly timestamps, while the `Malware_Incidents` list provides the incident counts. No external data is required, making it easier for readers to run this code in their own environments. The dataset mimics a typical cybersecurity scenario where monthly incident counts are tracked.

Listing 11.4 Forecasting malware incidents

```python
import pandas as pd                                    # Imports pandas
import matplotlib.pyplot as plt                        # Imports matplotlib
from statsmodels.tsa.arima.model import ARIMA          # Imports ARIMA model

#Create a dataset for monthly malware incidents
data = {                                               # Defines dataset
    'Month': pd.date_range(start='1/1/2023', periods=12,
                           freq='M'),                  # Creates monthly dates
    'Malware_Incidents': [15, 18, 17, 20, 23, 21, 25, 28,
                          26, 30, 35, 33]              # Malwares counts
}
df = pd.DataFrame(data)                                # Creates DataFrame
df.set_index('Month', inplace=True)                    # Sets index

#Fit an ARIMA model
model = ARIMA(df['Malware_Incidents'],
              order=(2, 1, 2))                         # Inits ARIMA (2,1,2)
model_fit = model.fit()                                # Fits model

#Forecast the next 3 months
forecast = model_fit.forecast(steps=3)                 # Forecast 3 steps

#Plot the data and the forecast
plt.figure(figsize=(10, 6))                            # Setups plot
plt.plot(df.index, df['Malware_Incidents'], label=
                   'Historical Malware Incidents', color='blue',
                   marker='o')                         # Plots historical
plt.plot(pd.date_range(start='1/1/2024', periods=3,
                   freq='M'), forecast, label='Forecasted Malware \
                   Incidents', color='red',
                   linestyle='--', marker='x')         # Plots forecast
plt.title('Malware Incidents Forecast Using ARIMA')    # Adds title
plt.xlabel('Month')                                    # Labels x-axis
plt.ylabel('Malware Incidents')                        # Labels y-axis
```

```
plt.legend()
plt.grid(True)
plt.show()
```
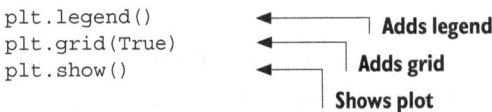

Figure 11.4 is the output.

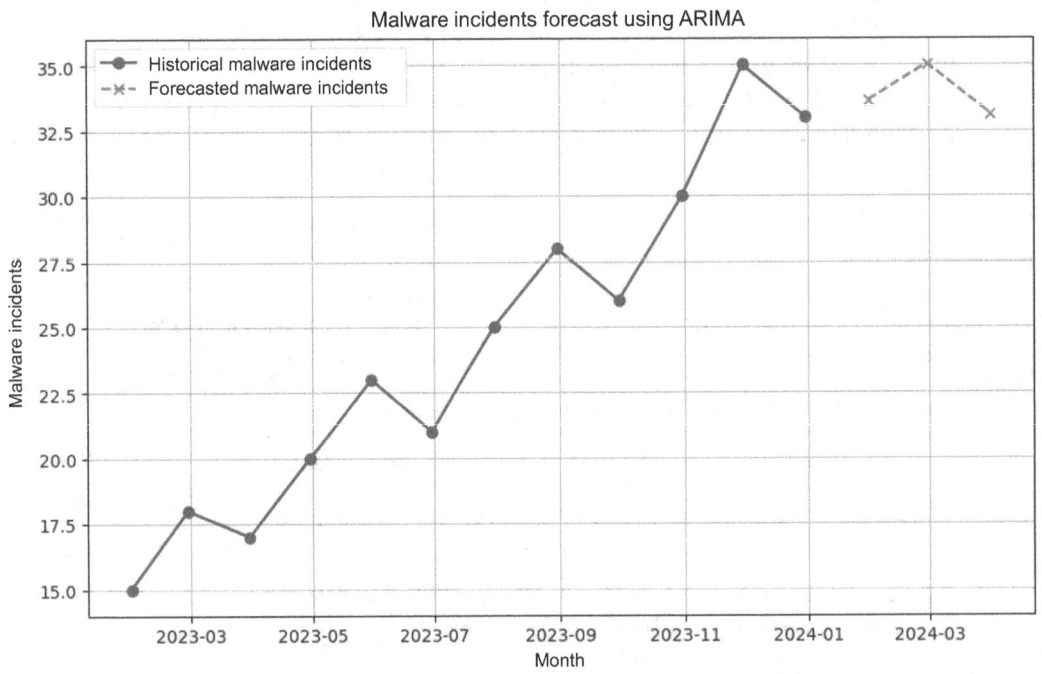

Figure 11.4 Malware incidents forecast, showing the forecasted malware incidents in dot-x and historical malware incidents in solid-dot lines

INTERPRETING THE RESULTS

The generated plot shows

- *Historical trends*—The solid line represents malware incidents recorded in 2023.
- *Forecasted data*—The dashed line predicts January through March 2024 incidents.
- *Actionable insights*—The upward trend in forecasted incidents indicates a need to allocate additional resources for threat monitoring and mitigation.

By using forecasting, security teams can

- Predict resource needs, such as staffing or tool enhancements
- Proactively address potential vulnerabilities before incidents occur
- Enhance incident response planning by preparing for likely scenarios

PRACTICAL APPLICATIONS

The forecast for malware incidents provides actionable insights for security leaders:

- *Resource allocation*—If malware incidents are predicted to rise, teams can prepare by scaling up defenses.
- *Risk mitigation*—Identifying trends early allows for adjustments in policies and practices to address specific risks.

This forecasting approach exemplifies how statistical methods can empower cybersecurity professionals to stay ahead in an ever-evolving threat landscape.

11.8 Bayesian inference

Bayesian inference is a statistical method that applies probability to infer the likelihood of a hypothesis based on prior knowledge and observed evidence. It allows you to update your belief as new data becomes available, which makes it a powerful tool for dynamic decision-making in cybersecurity.

Furthermore, in cybersecurity, Bayesian inference can help assess the probability of a security threat given new observations. For instance, suppose an unusual login pattern is detected—what's the likelihood that it indicates a malware infection? Based on prior data and current observations, Bayesian inference allows us to update the probability of the system being compromised.

False positives and false negatives are common challenges in cybersecurity. Bayesian inference offers a structured approach to weighing evidence and refining probabilities dynamically. This approach ensures that security teams focus on the most likely threats, reducing noise and enhancing decision-making efficiency.

The following code calculates the probability of a malware infection given observed unusual activity, using Bayes' theorem. The code demonstrates the application of Bayesian inference in a cybersecurity context. Specifically, it calculates the probability of a malware infection by detecting unusual activity, using Bayes' theorem. Based on new evidence, Bayesian inference is valuable for dynamically updating the probability of a hypothesis (e.g., a system being compromised).

While the data is supplied in the following listing for demonstration purposes, in a real-world scenario, these probabilities could be derived from

- Historical incident reports
- Data from intrusion detection systems (IDS) or security information and event management (SIEM) systems
- Domain-specific knowledge

Listing 11.5 Bayesian inference in cybersecurity

```
#Define the known probabilities     ◄──┐ Defines P(A)
P_A = 0.05
P_B_given_A = 0.9                   ◄──┘ Defines P(B|A)
P_B_given_not_A = 0.1               ◄──┐ Defines P(B|¬A)
```

```
#Calculate P(B), the marginal likelihood
P_B = P_B_given_A * P_A + P_B_given_not_A *
      (1 - P_A)                                  ◄── Calculates P(B)

#Apply Bayes' theorem to calculate P(A|B)
P_A_given_B = (P_B_given_A * P_A) / P_B          ◄── Calculates P(A|B)

#Print the result
print(f"Probability of malware infection given \
      unusual activity: {P_A_given_B:.2%}")      ◄── Prints result
```

We obtain the following output:

```
Probability of malware infection given unusual activity: 32.14%
```

11.8.1 Interpreting the results

The output provides the posterior probability that malware is present when unusual activity is observed. For instance, if the result is 31.25%, there's approximately a one-in-three chance that the unusual activity is due to malware.

PRACTICAL APPLICATIONS

- *High posterior probability*—Indicates immediate action, such as isolating the system or conducting further investigation, may be necessary
- *Low posterior probability*—Suggests the unusual activity is less likely to be a threat, allowing resources to be allocated elsewhere

11.9 Statistical models for vulnerability management

Statistical models are crucial in vulnerability management, helping organizations analyze risks, predict potential exploits, and prioritize remediation efforts. By using historical data and current threat landscapes, these models provide actionable insights supporting a more proactive cybersecurity approach. Statistical tools such as the Poisson distribution can quantify the likelihood and effects of vulnerabilities, enabling informed decision-making.

This section examines how statistical models can be applied to predict and manage vulnerabilities effectively. We illustrate this with Python code that uses the Poisson distribution to model the frequency of vulnerability exploits. The Poisson distribution is often employed to model the number of times an event occurs in a fixed interval, such as the number of monthly vulnerability exploits.

The following listing illustrates how the Poisson distribution can be used to model the frequency of vulnerability exploits over a fixed time interval, such as a month. The average rate (333) was chosen as a hypothetical example. Organizations can calculate this rate based on their historical records of exploit occurrences. The range from 0 to 10 captures a realistic spectrum of possible events without becoming too computationally intensive.

Statistical models for vulnerability management

Listing 11.6 Modeling exploits with the Poisson distribution

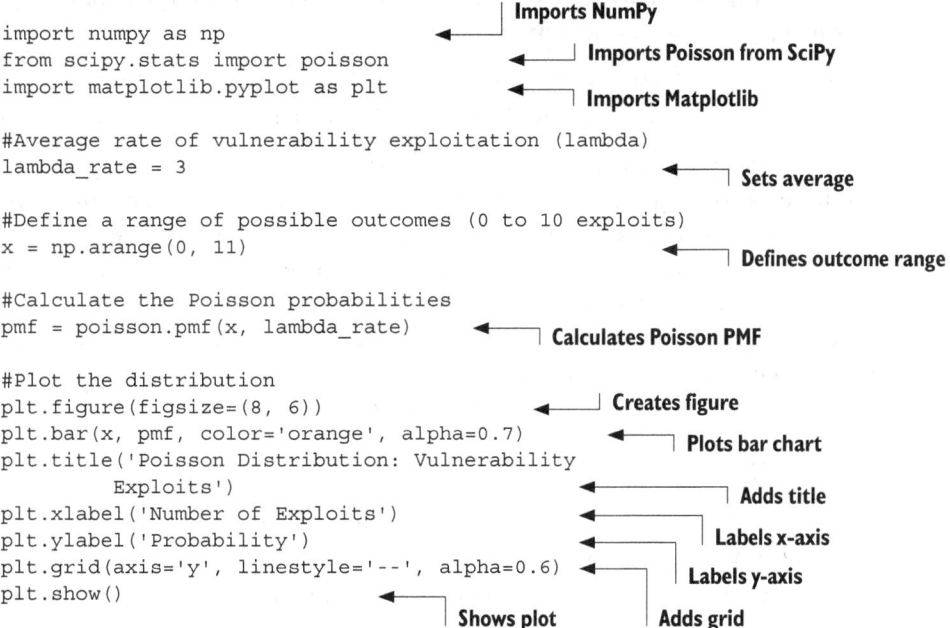

```
import numpy as np                              ◁── Imports NumPy
from scipy.stats import poisson                 ◁── Imports Poisson from SciPy
import matplotlib.pyplot as plt                 ◁── Imports Matplotlib

#Average rate of vulnerability exploitation (lambda)
lambda_rate = 3                                 ◁── Sets average

#Define a range of possible outcomes (0 to 10 exploits)
x = np.arange(0, 11)                            ◁── Defines outcome range

#Calculate the Poisson probabilities
pmf = poisson.pmf(x, lambda_rate)               ◁── Calculates Poisson PMF

#Plot the distribution
plt.figure(figsize=(8, 6))                      ◁── Creates figure
plt.bar(x, pmf, color='orange', alpha=0.7)      ◁── Plots bar chart
plt.title('Poisson Distribution: Vulnerability
          Exploits')                            ◁── Adds title
plt.xlabel('Number of Exploits')                ◁── Labels x-axis
plt.ylabel('Probability')                       ◁── Labels y-axis
plt.grid(axis='y', linestyle='--', alpha=0.6)   ◁── Adds grid
plt.show()                                      ◁── Shows plot
```

Figure 11.5 shows the output.

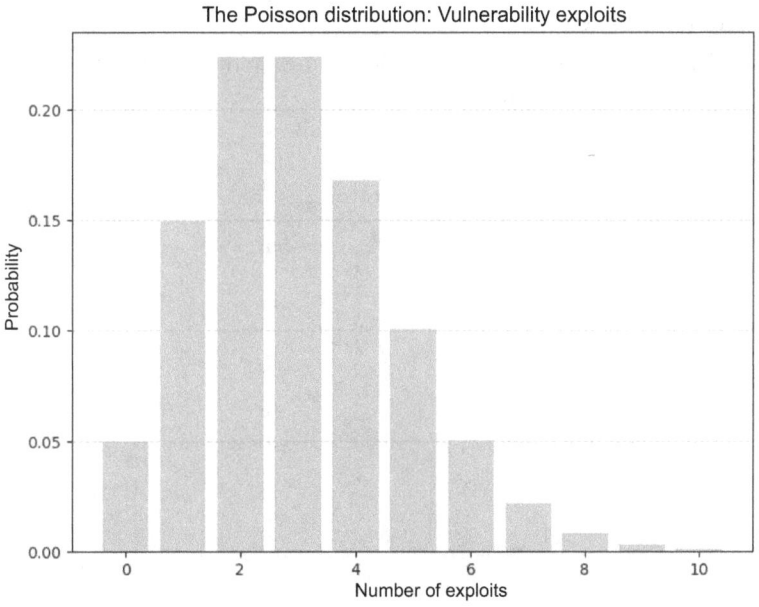

Figure 11.5 Poisson distribution of vulnerability exploits

11.9.1 Interpreting the results

The resulting bar chart shows the likelihood of different numbers of exploits occurring in a given time period. For example,

- The highest bar represents the most likely number of exploits (e.g., 3 exploits).
- Lower bars represent less likely scenarios, such as zero exploits or 10 exploits.

This visualization helps security teams predict exploit frequency and prioritize resources accordingly. For example, if 3 exploits are most likely in a month, the organization can proactively allocate resources to address those specific vulnerabilities.

This chapter focused on applying statistical techniques to enhance cybersecurity strategies. Through exercises, we explored how to uncover relationships between key variables to pinpoint risk factors and make data-driven decisions. In the next chapter, we shift our focus to machine learning techniques and their transformative role in identifying, predicting, and mitigating security incidents.

Summary

- Statistical techniques can be applied to analyze and strengthen cybersecurity measures effectively.
- Time series analysis can be used to forecast potential future threats and prepare proactive defense strategies.
- Correlation and clustering methods can be used to identify key risk factors by exploring relationships between variables.
- Bayesian inference can improve decision-making under uncertainty by updating probabilities with new data.
- The Poisson distribution can be applied to model and prioritize vulnerabilities based on their likelihood and effects.

Advanced machine learning analysis

This chapter covers
- The use of machine learning in cybersecurity
- Key machine learning algorithms for security applications
- Practical applications of AI in cybersecurity
- Implementing AI models in security systems
- Evaluating AI performance in cybersecurity

This chapter examines the transformative role that artificial intelligence (AI) and machine learning (ML) play in cybersecurity. AI and ML have changed the way organizations approach threat detection, response, and risk management. By learning from historical data and adapting to new patterns, AI can anticipate, identify, and respond to cyber threats far more rapidly and efficiently than traditional methods.

Here, we will explore some algorithms driving AI-powered cybersecurity solutions, their applications in real-world scenarios, and the practical steps required to implement and evaluate these models. Although AI and ML are complex technologies, this chapter aims to break them down into understandable components, providing security professionals with the knowledge they need to adopt AI-driven solutions effectively.

We will also discuss various algorithms, from supervised learning models such as decision trees to unsupervised clustering methods that help identify anomalous behavior. The chapter further explores methods for evaluating AI system performance to verify its reliability and effectiveness in cybersecurity, thus offering readers a solid foundation for integrating AI into their security strategies.

To fully engage with the exercises in this chapter, readers will need access to Python programming tools, such as Jupyter Notebook, and libraries including `scikit-learn`, `pandas`, and `matplotlib`. These resources will be essential for implementing, visualizing, and understanding the discussed machine learning models. The chapter also emphasizes evaluating AI performance to ensure the reliability and practical benefits of these systems in enhancing cybersecurity.

12.1 Code requirements

We'll continue utilizing Jupyter Notebooks for these exercises. Once installed, simply download this chapter's notebook and press play. Feel free to modify the code—make your changes and press play again to see the results.

The code examples and dependencies referenced in this book are available for download on the accompanying GitHub repository: https://github.com/Mariano215/Security_Metrics. This repository contains all code files, sample datasets, and setup instructions to ensure you have everything needed to follow along.

Make sure you have internet access during the setup process to download dependencies and any additional tools required for specific examples. For step-by-step instructions on setting up your environment, refer to the book's section on environment configuration.

12.1.1 What is AI

It is important to distinguish between the modern use of the term AI and what analysts have used for many years. With the popularity of generative AI, such as ChatGPT, many readers may confuse the terms. *AI* is a general term that includes various forms of algorithms mimicking human intelligence to perform tasks. Traditional AI analyzes and interprets existing data to help identify trends and patterns that might suggest new applications or solutions.

This distinction is critical for understanding AI's applications in this chapter's context. By clarifying the differences between traditional AI and modern generative AI, such as ChatGPT, we set the foundation for effectively using the correct type of AI in cybersecurity analytics and decision-making. This chapter focuses on how traditional AI techniques, such as ML and predictive analytics, can help identify patterns, assess risks, and optimize cybersecurity strategies. While generative AI holds promise for creative problem-solving, the examples and tools discussed here emphasize practical, data-driven AI approaches, tailored to analyzing trends, mitigating risks, and improving cybersecurity operations. The discussion in this chapter aims to ensure readers understand the capabilities and limitations of the AI tools they use. The next chapter will discuss generative AI.

Traditional AI does not possess the ability to conceive entirely new ideas from scratch. Different AI definitions are compared in figure 12.1.

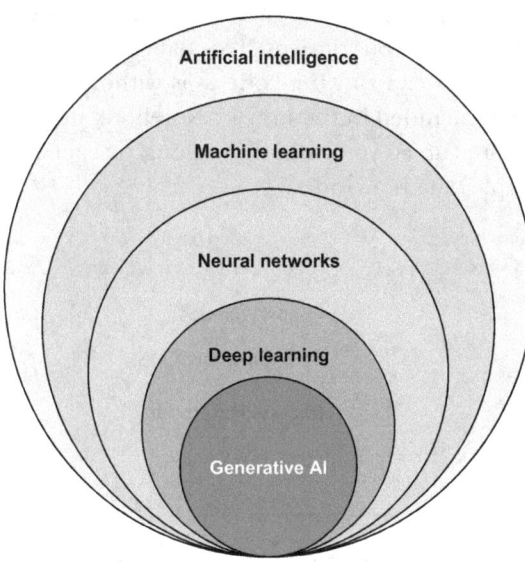

Artificial intelligence
A broad term that includes the development and use of computers to mimic human intelligence

Machine learning
A subset of AI that trains systems to learn from data and make decisions

Neural networks
A type of machine learning that uses algorithms similar to how the human brain functions

Deep learning
A subfield of machine learning that uses neural networks with multiple layers to learn and extract patterns from data

Generative AI
A subset of AI that focuses on generating new content, such as text or images, based on patterns learned from data

Figure 12.1 Artificial intelligence definitions compared

12.2 DBSCAN for threat detection

DBSCAN, which stands for Density-Based Spatial Clustering of Applications with Noise, is an unsupervised machine learning algorithm used to identify clusters in data and detect outliers. Unlike K-Means, DBSCAN does not require the number of clusters to be specified in advance. It excels at identifying clusters of varying shapes and detecting anomalies, making it particularly useful in cybersecurity applications. DBSCAN identifies clusters based on the following two parameters:

- *Epsilon*—The maximum distance between two points to be considered part of the same cluster is defined by epsilon (`eps`).
- *Minimum samples*—A minimum number of samples (`min_samples`) is the minimum number of points required to form a dense cluster.

DBSCAN groups points that are close to each other and have sufficient neighbors, forming clusters. Points that don't belong to any cluster due to their sparse surroundings are labeled as noise or anomalies. This makes DBSCAN highly effective in tasks such as anomaly detection in network traffic, where outliers could represent potential cyber threats.

12.2.1 DBSCAN example

The following listing demonstrates how DBSCAN can detect anomalies in a small dataset of network communication patterns. In this example, we analyze a sample dataset representing network communication patterns, such as the number of external and internal communications made by various devices. This data is synthetic and predefined in the script, meaning readers can run the code as-is without requiring any external data sources. Everything is included in the Jupyter Notebook provided in the GitHub repository. The cells are pre-run so you can follow along or execute the cells yourself. All the libraries and sample data is provided.

Listing 12.1 DBSCAN for threat detection

```python
import pandas as pd                                      # Imports pandas
from sklearn.cluster import DBSCAN                       # Imports DBSCAN
import matplotlib.pyplot as plt                          # Imports Matplotlib

# Create a sample dataset: Network communication patterns
data = {                                                 # Defines dataset
    'Device': ['Laptop_A', 'Phone_B', 'Printer_C', 'Laptop_B', 'Server_D'],
    'External_Comm': [10, 15, 3, 8, 120],
    #External communications (number of external IPs contacted)
    'Internal_Comm': [100, 95, 200, 90, 80]
    #Internal communications (number of internal IPs contacted)
}

df = pd.DataFrame(data)                                  # Creates DataFrame

# Extract features for clustering
X = df[['External_Comm', 'Internal_Comm']]               # Selects features

# Apply DBSCAN
dbscan = DBSCAN(eps=15, min_samples=2)                   # Sets DBSCAN params
df['Cluster'] = dbscan.fit_predict(X)                    # Fits model, assigns labels

#Plot the clusters
plt.figure(figsize=(8, 6))                               # Sets figure size
plt.scatter(df['External_Comm'], df['Internal_Comm'],
            c=df['Cluster'], cmap='Greys',
        label='Clusters')                                # Plots scatter by cluster
plt.title(('DBSCAN Clustering of Network '
        'Communications'))                               # Adds title
plt.xlabel('External Communications')                    # Labels x-axis
plt.ylabel('Internal Communications')                    # Labels y-axis
plt.grid(True)                                           # Adds grid
```

```
plt.show()                        ← Shows plot

#Display the resulting clusters
print(df)                         ← Prints DataFrame with clusters
```

Figure 12.2 shows the graphical output.

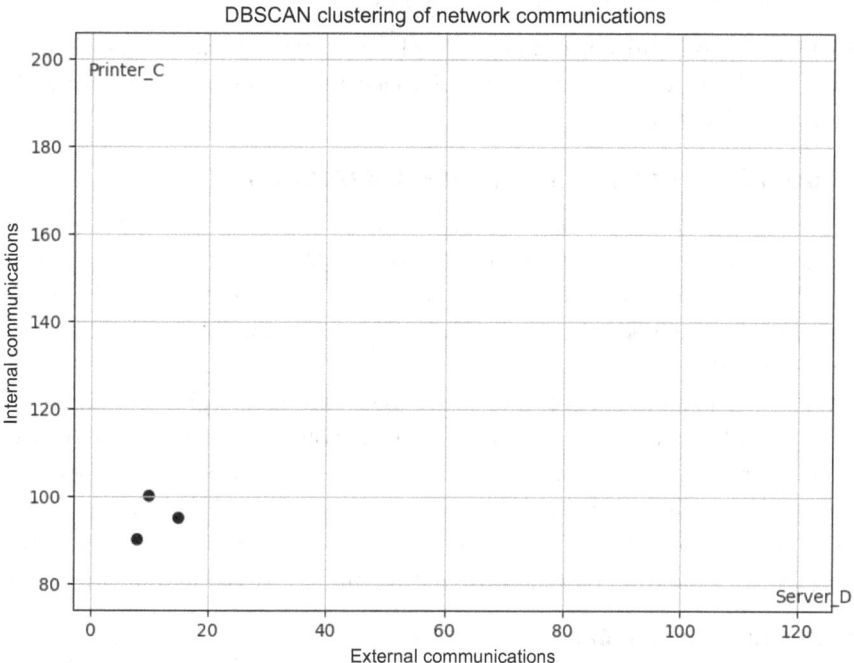

Figure 12.2 DBSCAN clustering of network devices showing outliers for `Printer_C` and `Server_D`

Here is a tabular output:

```
    Device  External_Comm  Internal_Comm  Cluster
0  Laptop_A             10            100        0
1   Phone_B             15             95        0
2 Printer_C              3            200       -1
3  Laptop_B              8             90        0
4  Server_D            120             80       -1
```

DBSCAN OUTPUT EXPLAINED

The graph plots `External_Comm` (x-axis) against `Internal_Comm` (y-axis) for each device in the dataset. Points are color-coded based on their cluster assignment. Devices belonging to a cluster are represented by the same color, while outliers are assigned the value –1 and are plotted separately.

In this example, the adjusted `eps` parameter allows `Server_D` to stand out as an outlier due to its significantly higher number of `External_Comm` compared to the other devices. The annotation explicitly labels `Server_D` on the graph for easy identification.

The tabular output lists each device along with its cluster label:

- Devices labeled 0 or other positive integers are part of a cluster.
- Devices with label –1 are classified as outliers, which might indicate unusual behavior warranting further investigation.

This visualization and clustering method help identify anomalous devices, such as `Server_D`, which could signify a potential security risk, such as unauthorized access or compromised systems.

12.3 Random forest and SVM for threat detection

Imagine trying to figure out whether a strange email you just received is a scam or not. Random forest and *support vector machines* (SVMs) are two smart tools that help us do that. They look at many different pieces of information about the email, such as who sent it, how it was written, and what kind of attachments it has. They then decide whether it's safe.

A *random forest* is like a group of smart trees that work together to make a decision. Each tree looks at different parts of the data and votes on whether something is a threat. The more trees that agree, the more likely they are correct. SVMs are like drawing a line that divides safe things from dangerous ones. The line is placed to clearly separate the two groups. These two algorithms can help detect malware, phishing, and other cyber threats by learning from past data and identifying patterns that indicate a threat.

12.3.1 Random forest and SVM exercise

Imagine you're monitoring incoming network traffic for potential threats. Some of the traffic might be normal, while other activity might be from a malicious source. By using random forest, you can create multiple decision trees, each analyzing different traffic attributes, such as IP address, traffic volume, and unusual login attempts. The combined results from these trees help you classify the traffic as safe or suspicious. In contrast, SVM can draw a line between safe traffic and malicious traffic, based on patterns learned from previous attacks. This helps predict which incoming data might be risky.

The elements of a decision tree are presented in figure 12.3.

This graphic represents a simplified decision tree structure. In a decision tree, each decision node represents a point where a question or decision is made based on certain criteria (e.g., "Is the email sender on a trusted list?"). The tree splits at each decision node, branching out into further decision nodes or leaf nodes.

Each leaf node represents an outcome or classification based on the decisions made along the path leading to it. For instance, in a cybersecurity application, a leaf node might classify an email as "safe" or "potential threat" after evaluating various criteria at the decision nodes.

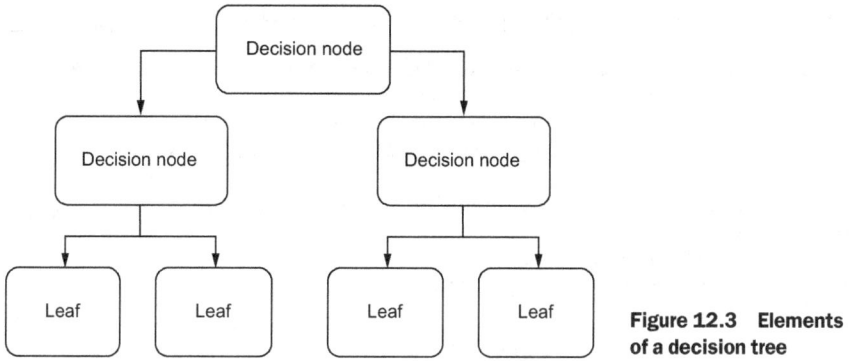

Figure 12.3 Elements of a decision tree

The path from the top of the tree (the root) to each leaf node represents a sequence of decisions that lead to a specific classification or result. Decision trees are commonly used in machine learning for classification tasks, such as detecting phishing attempts or categorizing network traffic, because they break down complex decisions into simpler, sequential choices.

The following listing uses two machine learning models—random forest and SVM—to classify network traffic data and detect potential threats. The dataset contains features that describe network traffic and labels that indicate if the data represents a benign (safe) or malicious (threat) activity. The code starts by preparing and cleaning the data, addressing missing values, and encoding labels for the classification task. After splitting the data into training and testing sets, the random forest and SVM models are trained on the data. Predictions are then made on the test set, and the accuracy of each model is calculated to evaluate how effectively they classify the network traffic as safe or suspicious. This code can help detect malicious activity in network traffic, a common use case in cybersecurity. What follows is a simplified example of how random forest and SVM can be applied to a network traffic dataset to detect threats.

Listing 12.2 Using random forest and SVM to detect threats

```
import numpy as np                                    ◀─── Imports numpy
import pandas as pd                                   ◀─── Imports pandas
from sklearn.model_selection import train_test_split  ◀─── Imports train/test split
from sklearn.ensemble import RandomForestClassifier   ◀─── Imports random forest
from sklearn.svm import SVC                           ◀─── Imports SVM
from sklearn.metrics import accuracy_score,
classification_report                                 ◀─── Imports accuracy, report

# Create a synthetic dataset for login activity (malicious vs. normal)
np.random.seed(42)                                    ◀─── Sets random seed
n_samples = 100                                       ◀─── Defines sample size

# Generate features: login hour and failed login attempts
login_hours = np.random.randint(0, 24, n_samples)     ◀─── Generates login hours
```

```
    failed_attempts = np.random.randint(0, 10, n_samples)    ◄─┐ Generates failed attempts

# Generate labels: 1 for malicious activity, 0 for normal activity
labels = np.array([1 if (hour > 20 or attempts > 5)
                   else 0 for hour, attempts in
                   zip(login_hours, failed_attempts)])    ◄─┐ Creates labels

# Create a DataFrame for visualization and model training
df = pd.DataFrame({
    'Login_Hour': login_hours,
    'Failed_Attempts': failed_attempts,
    'Label': labels
})    ◄─┐ Creates DataFrame

# Split the dataset into training and testing sets                    ◄─┐ Selects features
X = df[['Login_Hour', 'Failed_Attempts']]
y = df['Label']                                                       ◄─┐ Selects target
X_train, X_test, y_train, y_test = train_test_split(
    X, y, test_size=0.3, random_state=42)                             ◄─┐ Splits train/test

# Train a Random Forest model                                         ◄─┐ Inits random forest
rf_model = RandomForestClassifier(random_state=42)
rf_model.fit(X_train, y_train)                                        ◄─┐ Trains random forest

# Train an SVM model                                                  ◄─┐ Inits SVM
svm_model = SVC(kernel='linear', random_state=42)
svm_model.fit(X_train, y_train)                                       ◄─┐ Trains SVM

# Make predictions                                                    ◄─┐ Predicts with RF
rf_predictions = rf_model.predict(X_test)
svm_predictions = svm_model.predict(X_test)                           ◄─┐ Predicts with SVM

# Evaluate the models                                                 ◄─┐ Calculates RF accuracy
rf_accuracy = accuracy_score(y_test, rf_predictions)
svm_accuracy = accuracy_score(y_test, svm_predictions)                ◄─┐ Calculates SVM accuracy

# Display results                                                     ◄─┐ Prints RF accuracy
print("Random Forest Accuracy:", rf_accuracy)
print("SVM Accuracy:", svm_accuracy)                                  ◄─┐ Prints SVM accuracy
print("\nRandom Forest Classification Report:\n",
      classification_report(y_test, rf_predictions))                  ◄─┐ Prints classification
print("\nSVM Classification Report:\n",                                   reports
      classification_report(y_test, svm_predictions))
```

Here is a tabular output:

```
Random Forest Accuracy: 1.0
SVM Accuracy: 0.8666666666666667

Random Forest Classification Report:
              precision    recall  f1-score   support

           0       1.00      1.00      1.00        14
           1       1.00      1.00      1.00        16
```

```
            accuracy                           1.00        30
           macro avg       1.00      1.00      1.00        30
        weighted avg       1.00      1.00      1.00        30


SVM Classification Report:
               precision    recall  f1-score   support

           0       0.92      0.79      0.85        14
           1       0.83      0.94      0.88        16

    accuracy                           0.87        30
   macro avg       0.88      0.86      0.86        30
weighted avg       0.87      0.87      0.87        30
```

RANDOM FOREST AND SVM EXERCISE INTERPRETATION

The output from our random forest and SVM models gives us key insights into how well each algorithm is performing when classifying login activities as either *malicious* or *normal* based on the dataset we generated. The following list explains the meaning of accuracy scores:

- *Random forest accuracy = 1.0*—Indicates that the random forest model perfectly classified all test data with 100% accuracy. Every single instance in the test set was correctly labeled as either malicious or normal.
- *SVM accuracy = 0.8667 (≈ 87%)*—Indicates that the SVM misclassified some instances, achieving an overall accuracy of 86.7%. The performance is strong but lower than the random forest.
- *Lower recall for class 0 (normal)*—The SVM missed some normal login attempts and misclassified them as malicious.
- *High recall for class 1 (malicious)*—It correctly identified most malicious logins but made some mistakes with normal ones.
- *The meaning of results*—The SVM model is effective but less precise than the random forest model. However, it may generalize better to uncover unseen data in a real-world setting.

KEY TAKEAWAYS FOR APPLYING THIS IN YOUR ORGANIZATION

- *Random forest may be too perfect.* If your model achieves 100% accuracy, be cautious—it could be overfitting. Testing on a larger, more diverse dataset is necessary to validate its effectiveness.
- *SVM provides a more balanced result.* Although not perfect, SVM might generalize better, especially when data is limited.
- *Consider real-world scenarios.* If you deploy such a model for login anomaly detection, consider testing on live data to see how well it detects real threats.

12.3.2 Isolation forest and autoencoders exercise

Imagine you're a security guard at a museum, and your job is to watch the visitors. Most people behave normally—they walk around, look at art, and follow the rules. But occasionally, someone behaves strangely, for example, touches the art or tries entering restricted areas. Anomaly detection in cybersecurity is similar: it's all about identifying unusual behavior in a sea of normal activity.

Isolation forest and autoencoders are two algorithms that help tackle this problem:

- *Isolation forest* isolates or separates data points to identify outliers. Imagine building trees to group people by their behavior; if someone stands out and is quickly separated from the group, they're likely behaving unusually and could be an anomaly.
- *Autoencoders* learn what normal data looks like by trying to recreate it. When they encounter something that significantly deviates from what they've learned as normal, they flag this as a potential anomaly.

Let's say your organization is monitoring login activities on its network. Every day, thousands of users log in. Still, a handful of users exhibit strange behaviors, such as logging in from multiple locations within a short time or accessing data they usually don't. We can automatically flag these unusual login attempts as potential threats by applying isolation forest and autoencoders.

ISOLATION FOREST AND AUTOENCODERS PYTHON CODE

The following listing is an example of how you can use isolation forest and autoencoders to detect anomalies in login activities on a network. This code demonstrates two methods for detecting anomalies in a dataset—isolation forest and an autoencoder neural network. The dataset includes features such as login frequency, access levels, and failed logins for different users. The code first uses isolation forest to flag unusual data points and then trains an autoencoder model to identify anomalies based on how well it can reconstruct normal data patterns. Any data point with a high reconstruction error is flagged as an anomaly.

Listing 12.3 Using isolation forest and autoencoders to detect anomalies

```
# Import required libraries
import numpy as np
import pandas as pd
from sklearn.ensemble import IsolationForest          Imports libraries
from sklearn.preprocessing import StandardScaler
from tensorflow.keras.models import Sequential
from tensorflow.keras.layers import Dense
import matplotlib.pyplot as plt

# Step 1: Create a sample dataset
data = {                                              Defines dataset
    'Login_Frequency': [100, 98, 95, 150, 200, 105, 97, 99,
                       300, 50, 99, 98, 95, 105, 120, 110,
```

```
                    115, 600, 40],
    'Access_Levels': [1, 1, 1, 3, 2, 1, 1, 1,
                    4, 1, 1, 1, 1, 2, 3, 2,
                    2, 4, 1],
    'Failed_Logins': [2, 1, 0, 1, 3, 0, 1, 1,
                    5, 2, 1, 1, 0, 1, 1, 1,
                    1, 6, 0]
}
df = pd.DataFrame(data)                              ← Creates DataFrame

# Step 2: Apply Isolation Forest for anomaly detection
scaler = StandardScaler()                            Scales data
scaled_data = scaler.fit_transform(df)
isolation_forest = IsolationForest(
    contamination=0.1, random_state=42)              Runs isolation forest
df['Anomaly_IF'] = isolation_forest.fit_predict(
    scaled_data)

# Step 3: Plot the results from Isolation Forest
plt.figure(figsize=(8, 6))
plt.scatter(df.index, df['Login_Frequency'],
            c=df['Anomaly_IF'], cmap='coolwarm',
            label='Anomalies')
plt.title('Isolation Forest: Anomaly Detection')     Plots isolation forest
plt.xlabel('Index')
plt.ylabel('Login Frequency')
plt.legend()
plt.show()

# Step 4: Apply Autoencoder
input_dim = scaled_data.shape[1]
autoencoder = Sequential([
    Dense(10, activation='relu'),
    Dense(5, activation='relu'),
    Dense(2, activation='relu'),
    Dense(5, activation='relu'),
    Dense(10, activation='relu'),                    Builds/trains
    Dense(input_dim, activation='sigmoid')           autoencoder
])
autoencoder.compile(optimizer='adam',
                    loss='mean_squared_error')
autoencoder.fit(scaled_data, scaled_data, epochs=50,
                batch_size=16, verbose=0)

# Step 5: Evaluate reconstruction error
reconstructed = autoencoder.predict(scaled_data)
reconstruction_error = np.mean((scaled_data -
                        reconstructed) ** 2, axis=1) Calculates
threshold = reconstruction_error.mean() +            reconstruction error
            2 * reconstruction_error.std()
df['Anomaly_AE'] = reconstruction_error > threshold

# Step 6: Plot the results from Autoencoder
plt.figure(figsize=(8, 6))
plt.scatter(df.index, reconstruction_error,          Plots autoencoder results
```

```
            c=df['Anomaly_AE'], cmap='coolwarm',
            label='Reconstruction Error')
plt.axhline(y=threshold, color='r', linestyle='--',
            label='Anomaly Threshold')
plt.title('Autoencoder: Anomaly Detection')
plt.xlabel('Index')
plt.ylabel('Reconstruction Error')
plt.legend()
plt.show()
```
Plots autoencoder results

Figures 12.4 and 12.5 are the graphical output for isolation forest and autoencoder anomaly detection, respectively.

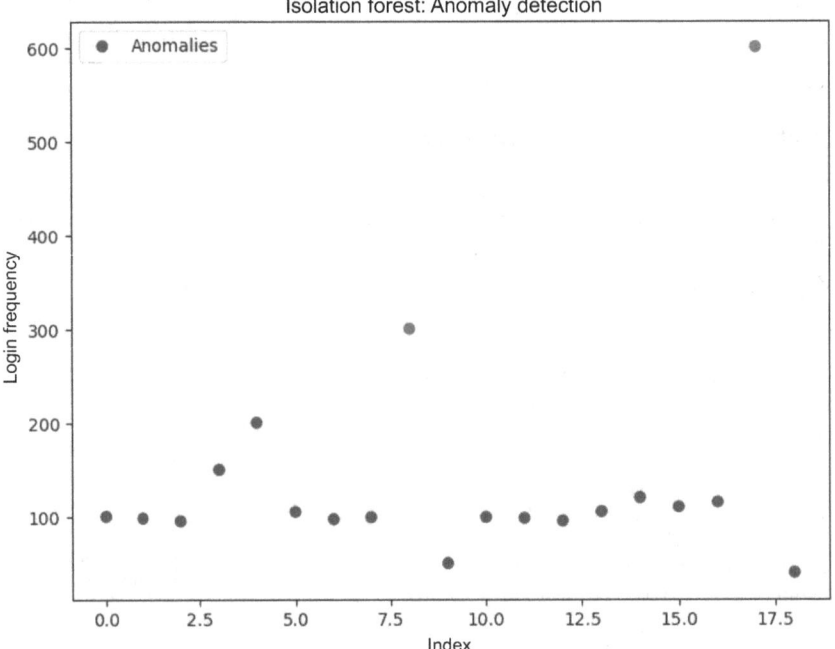

Figure 12.4 Isolation forest anomaly detection output

ISOLATION FOREST AND AUTOENCODERS EXERCISE INTERPRETATION

The outputs generated by this code illustrate two different approaches to anomaly detection—isolation forest and autoencoders. The isolation forest plot represents each data point (in this case, login frequencies) plotted against their index in the dataset. Points identified as normal are displayed in one color, while anomalies are highlighted in a contrasting color. Anomalies represent unusual login frequencies that differ significantly from the typical behavior observed in the dataset. For example, if most users attempt 100 logins, a user attempting 600 logins in a short period might be flagged as

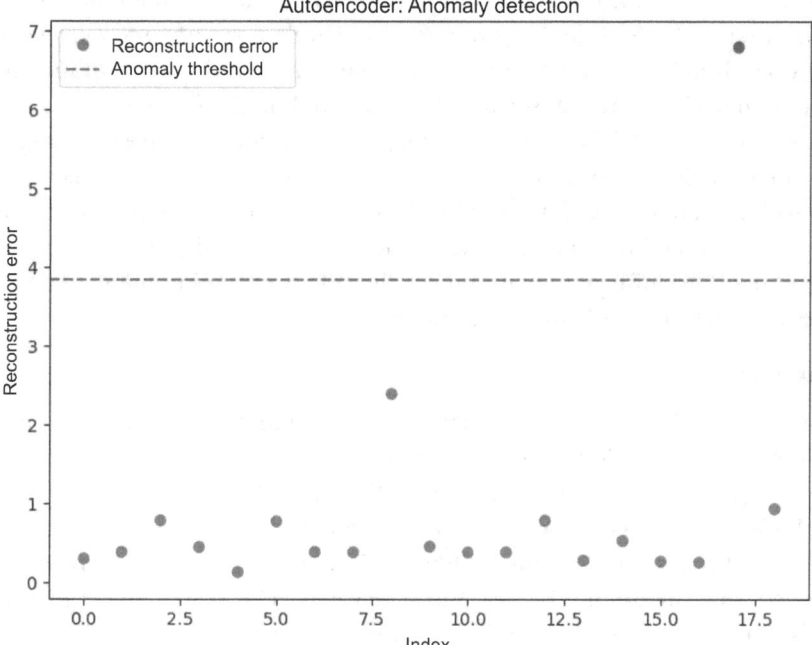

Figure 12.5 Autoencoder anomaly detction output

an anomaly. This visualization helps pinpoint which data entries are behaving abnormally, making it easier to investigate potential security problems.

The autoencoder reconstruction error plot provides another way to detect anomalies. Here, the reconstruction error is the difference between the original data and what the autoencoder model predicts as normal. Each point on the plot represents the reconstruction error for a specific data entry. The horizontal line indicates the anomaly threshold, calculated based on the average and standard deviation of the errors. Data points above this line are flagged as anomalies. This method is particularly useful because it identifies anomalies and shows the severity of the deviation from normal behavior. For example, a high reconstruction error for a specific data point may suggest that it significantly deviates from the patterns the model learned during training.

Both plots visually communicate how anomalies stand out against normal behavior, providing a clear and intuitive way to understand and interpret the results of these advanced analytical techniques. These outputs help analysts focus on the most suspicious data points, enabling faster and more targeted investigations into potential security problems.

12.4 Natural language processing

Imagine you're trying to read a lot of reports about bad things happening on the internet, such as hackers trying to steal information. But, instead of reading all those reports yourself, you have a smart computer program that can read them for you, telling you when it finds something dangerous. That's what *natural language processing* (NLP) does. It helps computers read, understand, and find important information in huge amounts of text, such as security reports or online discussions.

In cybersecurity, NLP helps us sift through vast amounts of threat intelligence data from sources such as news articles, blogs, research papers, and even social media posts. These sources often contain important details about new security threats, vulnerabilities, and attack methods being discussed in the cybersecurity community. With NLP, we can extract this information automatically and faster than humanly possible, which enables us to stay ahead of emerging threats.

12.4.1 NLP exercise

Let's imagine a cybersecurity team that uses NLP to monitor online threat intelligence feeds and news articles for information about new malware threats. Thousands of articles and reports are published daily, and it's impossible for the team to read all of them. With NLP, the system scans all the documents, identifies keywords such as "malware," "data breach," and "vulnerability," and pulls out relevant information that the team needs to be aware of. This way, the team can quickly react to emerging threats.

Let's assume we have a dataset containing different news articles on cybersecurity threats. We want to extract relevant keywords and classify the articles as "high risk" or "low risk," based on the language used. The code is presented in the following listing.

Listing 12.4 NLP exercise

```
# Import required libraries
import pandas as pd
from sklearn.feature_extraction.text import
    TfidfVectorizer
from sklearn.model_selection import train_test_split
from sklearn.linear_model import LogisticRegression
from sklearn.metrics import classification_report,
    confusion_matrix
import seaborn as sns
import matplotlib.pyplot as plt

# Step 1: Generate a balanced dataset
data = {
    'Article': [
        "Ransomware targets financial institutions",
        "Security patch released for major software vulnerability",
        "Hackers steal millions of customer data in breach",
        "Low-risk malware detected in corporate emails",
        "Phishing campaign aims to steal credentials",
        "Database vulnerability in hospital systems",
        "Encryption policies updated to prevent breaches",
        "Zero-day vulnerability in common software",
        "Mandatory security training after an attack",
        "Phishing attacks target large organizations"
```

Imports libraries

Defines dataset

```python
        ] * 2,  # Duplicate entries to balance classes
        'Label': ['high-risk', 'low-risk', 'high-risk',
                  'low-risk', 'high-risk',
                  'low-risk', 'low-risk', 'high-risk', 'low-risk',
                  'high-risk'] * 2  # Balanced labels
}

df = pd.DataFrame(data)          # ← Creates DataFrame

# Step 2: Convert labels to numeric
df['Label'] = df['Label'].apply(lambda x:
    1 if x == 'high-risk' else 0)   # ← Converts labels to numeric

# Step 3: Split data into training and testing sets
X_train, X_test, y_train, y_test = train_test_split(
    df['Article'], df['Label'], test_size=0.3,
    random_state=42)              # ← Splits into train/test

# Step 4: Apply TF-IDF and Logistic Regression      # ← Initializes TF-IDF
vectorizer = TfidfVectorizer(stop_words='english')
X_train_tfidf = vectorizer.fit_transform(X_train)
X_test_tfidf = vectorizer.transform(X_test)         # Transforms text
model = LogisticRegression()
model.fit(X_train_tfidf, y_train)                   # Trains logistic regression

# Step 5: Make predictions
y_pred = model.predict(X_test_tfidf)    # ← Predicts on test set

# Step 6: Evaluate the model
print("Classification Report:\n",                   # Shows classification report
      classification_report(y_test, y_pred))
conf_matrix = confusion_matrix(y_test, y_pred)      # Generates confusion matrix

# Step 7: Plot the confusion matrix (Grayscale)
plt.figure(figsize=(6, 4))
sns.heatmap(conf_matrix, annot=True, cmap='Greys',
            fmt='d',
            xticklabels=['Low-Risk', 'High-Risk'],
            yticklabels=['Low-Risk', 'High-Risk'])  # Plots confusion matrix
plt.title('Confusion Matrix (Grayscale)')
plt.xlabel('Predicted Labels')
plt.ylabel('True Labels')
plt.show()
```

What follows is a tabular output, and the graphical output is presented in figure 12.6:

```
Classification Report:
              precision    recall  f1-score   support

           0       1.00      0.50      0.67         4
           1       0.50      1.00      0.67         2

    accuracy                           0.67         6
   macro avg       0.75      0.75      0.67         6
weighted avg       0.83      0.67      0.67         6
```

280   CHAPTER 12   *Advanced machine learning analysis*

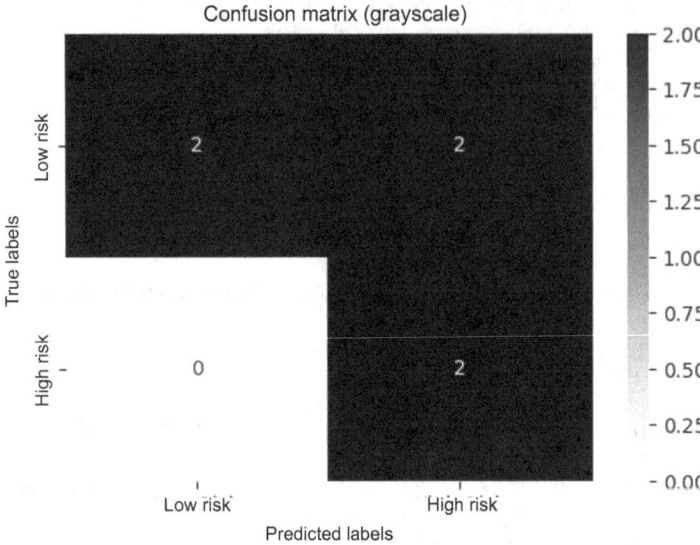

Figure 12.6 TF-IDF and logistic regression NLP model identifying high- and low-risk articles

NLP OUTPUT EXPLAINED

The output of this NLP threat classification code can be divided into two key components: the classification report and the confusion matrix. Together, they comprehensively evaluate the model's performance, making it easier to understand how well it identifies high- and low-risk cybersecurity articles.

CLASSIFICATION REPORT

The classification report includes precision, recall, F1-Score, and accuracy metrics. Each of these provides specific insights into the model's ability to distinguish between high- and low-risk articles:

- *Precision* tells us how many of the articles labeled as high-risk (or low-risk) by the model are correct. For example, if precision for high-risk is 80%, this means 80% of the articles predicted to be high-risk were accurate.
- *Recall* shows how many of the actual high-risk articles the model identified correctly. A high recall indicates that the model captures most of the real high-risk threats.
- *F1-Score* is a balanced measure that combines precision and recall, assessing the model's performance for each class. This is especially important when dealing with imbalanced datasets.
- *Accuracy* is the percentage of correctly classified articles overall. It gives a general idea of how well the model performed across both categories.

CONFUSION MATRIX

The confusion matrix is a table that visually represents the classification outcomes. The rows represent the articles' true labels (e.g., actual high- or low-risk articles). The columns represent the predicted labels (e.g., what the model predicted as high or low risk).

- *Diagonal cells* show the number of correct predictions, where the model's predictions match the true labels. For instance, the top-left cell represents articles correctly classified as low risk, while the bottom-right cell shows articles correctly classified as high risk.
- *Off-diagonal cells* indicate misclassifications. The top-right cell shows how many low-risk articles were incorrectly classified as high risk, and the bottom-left cell shows the reverse.

The grayscale heatmap enhances the confusion matrix's readability by visually distinguishing the intensity of each count. Darker cells indicate higher numbers, making it easy to spot where the model performs well (diagonal cells) or struggles (off-diagonal cells). For someone new to these concepts, the confusion matrix offers a tangible way to understand where the model succeeds and where it might need improvement, especially when identifying challenging edge cases between classes.

12.5 Deep learning

Deep learning, a subset of machine learning, is known for its ability to model complex patterns in data using neural networks with multiple layers. In cybersecurity, deep learning has become increasingly valuable owing to its power to automatically detect sophisticated and evolving threats that are difficult to identify using traditional methods.

Deep learning finds anomalies such as malware or unusual behavior on a computer network by looking at lots of data over time. The more data it sees, the better it detects these hidden threats. Deep learning models can analyze files and detect whether they are malware based on patterns too complex for traditional methods to recognize. Convolutional neural networks (CNNs) are often used to classify malware by treating code samples as images.

These models can detect unusual or suspicious activity in network traffic, which might indicate a cyberattack. Recurrent neural networks (RNNs) and long short-term memory (LSTM) models are used to detect sequences of events or network logs that signal malicious activity. These models can also analyze emails, websites, or social media posts to detect phishing attempts, even when attackers try to evade detection by using sophisticated techniques to hide their intent.

Deep learning models can monitor how users interact with systems. If someone suddenly starts doing something unusual (e.g., accessing sensitive files they've never touched), the system can flag this behavior for review.

12.5.1 Deep learning exercise

The following listing uses a neural network to classify network traffic data and detect potential security threats, such as a Distributed Denial of Service (DDoS) attack. Neural networks offer powerful capabilities for this type of classification because they can identify complex patterns within data, which enables them to effectively separate between benign and malicious traffic.

The listing first preprocesses the data, handling missing values and encoding labels for machine learning compatibility. It then splits the data into training and testing sets and standardizes the features crucial for neural networks to train effectively. The neural network model, built using TensorFlow/Keras, consists of three layers that help it learn relationships within the data. The model is trained over several epochs, which allows it to adjust and improve its accuracy. Finally, the model is evaluated on the test data, showing how accurately it can detect threats based on its learned patterns. This method is vital in cybersecurity, enabling accurate threat detection based on large volumes of network data.

Listing 12.5 Using neural networks to classify network traffic data

```
# Import required libraries
import pandas as pd                                          # Imports libraries
import numpy as np
import tensorflow as tf
from tensorflow.keras.layers import Input, Dense
from tensorflow.keras.models import Sequential
from sklearn.model_selection import train_test_split
from sklearn.preprocessing import StandardScaler
from sklearn.metrics import classification_report,
    confusion_matrix
import matplotlib.pyplot as plt
import seaborn as sns

# Step 1: Generate synthetic network traffic data
np.random.seed(42)                                           # Sets random seed
data = {
    'Packet_Size': np.random.randint(50, 1500, size=1000),
    'Connection_Duration': np.random.uniform(0.1,
                                          10.0, size=1000),  # Creates synthetic data
    'Protocol_Type': np.random.choice(
        [0, 1, 2], size=1000),
    'Threat': np.random.choice(
        [0, 1], size=1000, p=[0.7, 0.3])
}
df = pd.DataFrame(data)                                      # Makes DataFrame

# Step 2: Split data into features and labels
X = df.drop(columns=['Threat'])                              # Splits features/labels
y = df['Threat']

# Step 3: Preprocess the data
scaler = StandardScaler()                                    # Scales features
X_scaled = scaler.fit_transform(X)
```

```
X_train, X_test, y_train, y_test = train_test_split(
    X_scaled, y, test_size=0.2, random_state=42)                ◄─┐ Splits train/test

# Step 4: Define the neural network
model = Sequential([
    Input(shape=(X_train.shape[1],)),
    Dense(64, activation='relu'),                                  │ Defines neural network
    Dense(32, activation='relu'),
    Dense(1, activation='sigmoid')
])

# Step 5: Compile the model
model.compile(optimizer='adam',
              loss='binary_crossentropy',
              metrics=['accuracy'])                             ◄─┐ Compiles model

# Step 6: Train the model
history = model.fit(X_train, y_train, epochs=20,
                    batch_size=32,
                    validation_data=(X_test, y_test),
                    verbose=0)                                  ◄─┐ Trains model

# Step 7: Evaluate the model
y_pred = (model.predict(X_test) > 0.5).astype(int)
print(classification_report(                                       │ Predicts and evaluates
    y_test, y_pred, zero_division=1))

# Step 8: Plot the confusion matrix
conf_matrix = confusion_matrix(y_test, y_pred)
plt.figure(figsize=(8, 6))
sns.heatmap(conf_matrix, annot=True, fmt='d',
            cmap='Greys', xticklabels=['Normal', 'Threat'],        │ Plots confusion
            yticklabels=['Normal', 'Threat'])                      │ matrix
plt.title('Confusion Matrix')
plt.xlabel('Predicted Labels')
plt.ylabel('True Labels')
plt.show()
```

What follows is a tabular output, and the graphical output is presented in figure 12.7:

```
              precision    recall  f1-score   support

           0       0.63      1.00      0.77       126
           1       1.00      0.00      0.00        74

    accuracy                           0.63       200
   macro avg       0.81      0.50      0.39       200
weighted avg       0.77      0.63      0.49       200
```

DEEP LEARNING EXERCISE INTERPRETATION

The output from this neural network model provides two key insights: a classification report and a confusion matrix heatmap. Together, they help us understand how well the model predicts whether network traffic is normal or poses a threat.

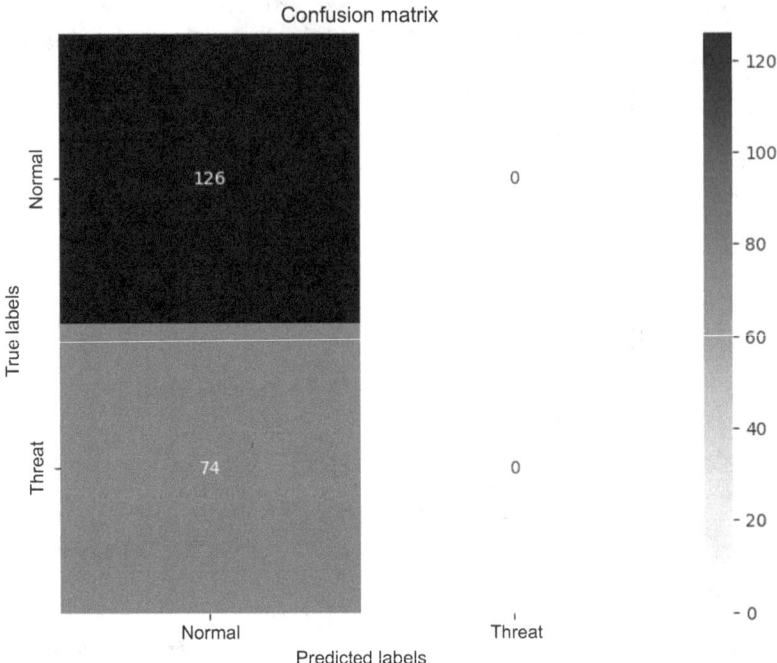

Figure 12.7 Classification report and confusion matrix heatmap obtained using deep learning

The classification report offers a numerical summary of the model's performance. It includes precision, recall, F1-Score, and accuracy. Precision tells us how many of the threats were flagged, helping assess the model's reliability when raising alerts. Recall shows how many actual threats were detected, reflecting the model's ability to identify problems. The F1-Score balances these two metrics, providing an overall measure of the model's accuracy in handling true positives and minimizing false positives or negatives. Accuracy indicates the percentage of all correct predictions, giving a general sense of the model's effectiveness.

The confusion matrix heatmap complements this by visually showing the breakdown of correct and incorrect predictions. The diagonal cells represent the accurate predictions, where the model correctly identified normal traffic or threats. The off-diagonal cells highlight the misclassifications: false positives (normal traffic misclassified as threats) and false negatives (threats missed by the model). For example, if the bottom-left cell shows a high value, it indicates many threats were incorrectly classified as normal, which could be a security concern.

Overall, this output helps assess not just how accurate the model is but also how it might behave in a real-world scenario, where false positives can create unnecessary alarms and false negatives could leave threats undetected. By analyzing these results, organizations can determine whether the model meets their requirements or needs further optimization.

12.6 Reinforcement learning

Imagine a security system that can learn from its own actions and make better decisions over time, just like a person who plays a video game repeatedly, learning what to do when bad things happen. In cybersecurity, we can use reinforcement learning to help a system figure out the best way to handle security incidents such as attacks or suspicious activity. The system gets rewards for making good decisions and penalties for making bad ones. Over time, it learns how to respond to incidents in the best possible way, without needing humans to tell it exactly what to do every time.

Reinforcement learning (RL) is a type of machine learning in which an agent learns to make decisions by interacting with its environment. The agent observes the environment, takes actions, and receives feedback in the form of rewards or penalties. The goal is for the agent to learn an optimal strategy or policy that maximizes the cumulative reward over time.

In the context of automated incident response, the agent is a cybersecurity system that can take various actions, such as quarantining a machine, blocking network traffic, or escalating an alert to a security analyst. The environment includes the network, endpoints, servers, and potential threats. The rewards are based on successful threat mitigation or prevention, while penalties might be triggered by false positives or escalating a threat too late.

Initially, the system might not know which action is best, but it learns over time as it tries different actions and sees the results. If blocking traffic stops an attack early, the system gets a reward and will likely choose that option next time. If quarantining a machine is too slow, it might get a penalty. The system will avoid that action unless necessary.

12.6.1 Reinforcement learning example in Python code

The following listing is a basic example of how reinforcement learning could be implemented for automated incident response using Q-learning. This code simulates a simple Q-learning algorithm, a type of reinforcement learning, to help a system make decisions in different states (e.g., "normal," "suspicious," and "attack"). Q-learning is often used in cybersecurity for adaptive threat response, where the system learns the best action (e.g., "quarantine," "block traffic," or "escalate"), based on a given state. The Q-table represents the learned "value" of each action in each state, guiding the system toward actions that yield the highest rewards over time. This approach allows the system to balance exploring new actions with exploiting known ones that have produced good outcomes, continuously improving its response to different security scenarios.

Listing 12.6 Using Q-learning for automated incident response

```
import numpy as np          ◄─── Imports numpy

# Define states and actions
```

```python
states = ['normal', 'suspicious', 'attack']          # Defines states
actions = ['quarantine', 'block_traffic', 'escalate']  # Defines actions

# Initialize the Q-table
Q_table = np.zeros((len(states), len(actions)))      # Inits Q-table

# Define the rewards for each action in each state
rewards = {                                          # Defines rewards
    ('normal', 'quarantine'): -10,
    ('normal', 'block_traffic'): -5,
    ('normal', 'escalate'): -1,
    ('suspicious', 'quarantine'): 5,
    ('suspicious', 'block_traffic'): 10,
    ('suspicious', 'escalate'): 1,
    ('attack', 'quarantine'): 20,
    ('attack', 'block_traffic'): 30,
    ('attack', 'escalate'): 15,
}

# Parameters for Q-learning
alpha = 0.1   #Learning rate        # Sets learning rate
gamma = 0.9   #Discount factor      # Sets discount factor
epsilon = 0.1 #Exploration rate     # Sets exploration rate

# Simulate the learning process
for episode in range(1000):                          # Runs episodes
    state = np.random.choice(states)                 # Picks random state

    # Choose an action (explore or exploit)
    if np.random.uniform(0, 1) < epsilon:            # Decides explore/exploit
        action = np.random.choice(actions)           # Chooses random action
    else:
        action = actions[np.argmax(Q_table[states.index(state)])]  # Chooses best action

    # Get the reward and update Q-values
    reward = rewards[(state, action)]                # Gets reward
    new_state = np.random.choice(states)
    # Randomly simulate a new state                  # Picks new random state
    Q_table[states.index(state), actions.index(action)] += \
    alpha * (reward + gamma * np.max(Q_table[
        states.index(new_state)]) - Q_table[
        states.index(state), actions.index(action)])  # Updates Q-table

# Print the learned Q-table                          # Prints label
print("Learned Q-table:")
print(Q_table)                                       # Prints Q-table
```

After running this code, we get the following output:

```
Learned Q-table: [[ 44.36507925 52.43335912 103.27555297] [ 44.85223654
119.38907614 61.2729418 ] [ 60.41160408 142.73065663 73.82460415]]
```

REINFORCEMENT LEARNING EXERCISE INTERPRETATION

The learned Q-table from the reinforcement learning model represents the optimal actions for each state. The values in the table indicate the expected cumulative reward for each action in a given state:

- Row 1 (normal):
  - Quarantine: 44.36
  - Block traffic: 52.43
  - Escalate: 103.28
- Row 2 (suspicious):
  - Quarantine: 44.85
  - Block traffic: 119.39
  - Escalate: 61.27
- Row 3 (attack):
  - Quarantine: 60.41
  - Block traffic: 142.73
  - Escalate: 73.82

The highest value for normal conditions is for the escalate action, indicating that when the system is in a normal state (i.e., no suspicious or malicious behavior detected), escalating an incident is considered the most beneficial action. This might reflect a cautious approach, where the system prefers to notify a human analyst when it cannot confidently handle a situation.

In suspicious states, the system has learned that blocking traffic is the best action, with a high value of 119.39. This means the system identifies that blocking network activity in suspicious cases effectively mitigates potential threats before they escalate.

When the system detects an outright attack, blocking traffic again is the optimal action with the highest reward value of 142.73. This is logical, as cutting off malicious traffic is a quick and effective way to mitigate an ongoing attack.

The Q-table shows that the system has effectively learned to escalate under normal conditions but aggressively blocks traffic during suspicious and attack states, which reflects appropriate responses to different security conditions.

Summary

- Artificial intelligence and machine learning automate data analysis in cybersecurity, enhancing threat detection and response capabilities.
- Clustering algorithms such as DBSCAN group similar behaviors to identify potential threats and anomalies in network data.
- Random forest and support vector machines (SVM) classify network activity, helping to distinguish safe behavior from suspicious patterns for automated threat identification.

- Isolation forest and autoencoders detect anomalies by isolating outliers and reconstructing normal behavior, flagging unusual activity that may indicate a threat.
- Natural language processing (NLP) processes unstructured data, extracting valuable insights from logs and threat reports for improved situational awareness.
- Deep learning models identify complex patterns, enabling the detection of network-based attacks by analyzing high-dimensional data.
- Reinforcement learning automates incident response by selecting the best actions based on past security outcomes.

Generative AI in cybersecurity metrics

> **This chapter covers**
> - Using generative AI to enhance cybersecurity metrics
> - Open source tools for AI analysis
> - Generating synthetic data for cybersecurity scenarios
> - Transforming datasets into actionable insights with AI

Generative AI has opened new possibilities in cybersecurity metrics, making it easier to analyze complex datasets, uncover hidden insights, and communicate findings effectively. This chapter explores how AI can become a practical tool in your cybersecurity toolkit. Instead of focusing on theoretical concepts, we'll demonstrate how you can use AI to solve real-world problems, such as assessing risk, monitoring compliance, and evaluating incident trends. Whether you're a cybersecurity professional or someone new to the field, this chapter will show you how to apply generative AI in meaningful ways, using simple tools and interactive exercises. By the end, you'll see how AI can help you simplify the challenging work of analyzing cybersecurity metrics and help you make informed decisions for your organization.

13.1 Understanding generative AI

Generative AI represents a transformative advancement in artificial intelligence. It is designed to create new content, such as text, images, or even predictions, based on patterns it has learned from existing data. Unlike traditional AI systems that focus on identifying patterns or making decisions from labeled datasets, generative AI has the unique ability to simulate creative processes. This capability introduces new opportunities to analyze data, simulate potential threats, and streamline reporting in cybersecurity.

Imagine a tool capable of generating detailed reports on cybersecurity metrics or simulating a potential breach scenario to better understand vulnerabilities, all based on your organization's historical data. Generative AI offers that potential by bridging data interpretation, reporting, and proactive planning gaps.

Key concepts behind generative AI include training models on large datasets, enabling them to mimic human-like text generation or synthesize realistic datasets. For example, a cybersecurity team can use generative AI to create realistic but synthetic login datasets to test anomaly detection algorithms without exposing sensitive real-world data.

This section explores how generative AI works, highlighting its practical applications in cybersecurity metrics. We'll examine its ability to streamline analysis, generate actionable insights, and transform the way we communicate findings to stakeholders. As we progress, you'll see how this cutting-edge technology can be accessible and effective, even for teams without a deep technical background.

13.2 Open source generative AI alternatives

Generative AI isn't limited to proprietary platforms. Open source tools such as LM Studio and Ollama offer robust solutions for organizations looking to integrate AI, while maintaining control over their data and infrastructure. These tools enable the use of local models, thus providing flexibility, privacy, and cost-effectiveness compared to cloud-based AI systems.

13.2.1 LM Studio

LM Studio is a powerful desktop application designed to run large language models (LLMs) locally on your machine. It supports popular models such as LLaMA, Falcon, and GPT-J, allowing you to fine-tune and query them without relying on external servers. This is particularly useful in industries where data privacy is paramount.

To get started with LM Studio

- *Download LM Studio*—Visit https://lmstudio.ai/ for installation instructions.
- *System requirements*—Ensure your system meets the requirements, including sufficient GPU memory for optimal performance.

- *Load a model*—LM Studio simplifies the process of loading and interacting with open source LLMs.

13.2.2 Ollama

Ollama focuses on simplicity and versatility. It allows users to interact with local language models directly from their desktop or a server environment. Ollama emphasizes privacy and performance, making it an excellent choice for professionals managing sensitive data.

- *Learn more about Ollama*—Visit https://ollama.com/ to explore installation guides and features.
- *Key features*—Ollama integrates seamlessly with existing workflows and customizes models for specific tasks, such as generating cybersecurity insights.

13.2.3 LM Studio vs. Ollama

Both tools have unique strengths. However, we decided to use LM Studio in this chapter because of its user-friendly features and accessibility, especially for readers who may be new to AI tools or programming.

LM Studio stands out for its graphical user interface (GUI), allowing users to interact with language models without extensive coding knowledge. This feature makes it an excellent choice for beginners or those who prefer a more visual approach. The GUI simplifies tasks such as

- *Model selection*—Users can choose from pre-trained models with just a few clicks.
- *Parameter adjustment*—Fine-tuning settings such as temperature or max tokens is straightforward and requires no scripting.
- *Real-time feedback*—LM Studio provides immediate results, which can help readers experiment and understand how inputs affect outputs.

The GUI also integrates well with various workflows, ensuring readers can follow along with examples even if they lack programming experience. This accessibility aligns with our goal of making the generative AI approachable to a wide audience, including cybersecurity professionals without a technical background.

While also open source, Ollama is more suited for users comfortable with APIs and command-line interfaces. It focuses on enabling LLMs to integrate into custom applications, making it ideal for developers building tailored solutions. Key features include

- *API integration*—Ollama's strengths lie in its flexibility to connect with custom systems and applications.
- *Lightweight setup*—It requires fewer resources compared to a GUI-based solution such as LM Studio.
- *Developer-friendly design*—Users with programming experience may find Ollama more efficient for automating workflows.

While Ollama offers powerful tools for developers, its lack of a GUI might pose a barrier for readers who are less familiar with coding.

13.2.4 Why we chose LM Studio for this chapter

The primary reason for selecting LM Studio over Ollama is its accessibility. The GUI lowers the entry barrier, allowing readers to focus on learning and applying generative AI rather than struggling with the technical setup. Additionally, LM Studio's real-time interaction provides immediate insights, making it easier to understand how different prompts and parameters affect outcomes.

For example, readers can experiment with cybersecurity scenarios in this chapter using LM Studio's intuitive interface. They can load pre-trained models, input prompts related to their metrics, and observe results—all without writing a single line of code. This simplicity encourages experimentation, fostering a deeper understanding of how generative AI can enhance cybersecurity metrics.

By contrast, while Ollama is excellent for advanced use cases, its API-driven approach might distract readers from the core concepts of this chapter. Introducing technical complexities too early could make the material feel inaccessible to those new to AI.

13.3 A note on LLMs

Choosing the appropriate LLM depends on the specific requirements of the task, as different models are designed with distinct strengths and tradeoffs. For example, smaller, locally deployed models such as LM Studio or Ollama are well-suited for organizations prioritizing data privacy and cost-effectiveness. These models are ideal for generating synthetic data or performing analyses where sensitive information cannot be shared externally. Conversely, cloud-based LLMs such as OpenAI's GPT-4 offer greater computational power, a broader knowledge base, and enhanced fine-tuning capabilities, making them a better fit for tasks requiring high accuracy or extensive contextual understanding.

Key considerations when selecting an LLM include:

- *Privacy and security*—Local models ensure data privacy by keeping sensitive data on-premises, while cloud-based models rely on third-party infrastructure.
- *Task complexity*—For computationally intensive or highly nuanced tasks, larger models typically outperform smaller, resource-constrained ones.
- *Cost*—Cloud-based services often charge per API call, whereas local models involve upfront hardware costs but no recurring fees.
- *Customization*—Open source models offer flexibility for fine-tuning and adapting to specific organizational needs, while proprietary models may limit customization.

By understanding each model's strengths and limitations, organizations can make informed decisions to align their LLM choice with their operational and business goals. This flexibility ensures that the model selection complements the task's unique challenges and priorities.

13.4 Prompt engineering

Prompt engineering is the art and science of crafting effective instructions to guide a language model's output. How you frame a prompt can significantly influence the quality and relevance of the AI's response. In cybersecurity, where precision and clarity are critical, mastering prompt engineering can make generative AI a powerful tool for analyzing metrics, generating reports, or identifying patterns.

13.4.1 Why prompt engineering matters

Effective prompts lead to actionable, precise outputs, thus saving time and resources. Whether you're summarizing data trends, generating synthetic datasets, or crafting stakeholder reports, understanding how to guide the model ensures success.

By exploring these open source tools and mastering prompt engineering, you unlock the potential of generative AI in a flexible, secure, and cost-efficient manner. Whether you choose LM Studio, Ollama, or OpenAI, the principles of effective AI utilization remain universal.

Key principles in prompt engineering are the following

1 *Be specific*—Provide clear and concise instructions. Ambiguity can lead to unhelpful or off-topic responses.
2 *Set context*—Include relevant details to help the AI understand the scenario or dataset.
3 *Guide the format*—If you need the response in a particular format (e.g., JSON, CSV, or a list), specify this explicitly, as AI-generated outputs don't always strictly adhere to the specified format. This requires post-generation validation.
4 *Iterate and refine*—Testing and tweaking prompts are often necessary to achieve optimal results.

13.5 Prompt engineering in cybersecurity

For those who prefer cloud-based generative AI solutions, OpenAI's API remains a leading choice for accessibility and reliability. Prompt engineering is the cornerstone of effectively using generative AI, and the principles remain consistent regardless of the platform or tool used.

13.5.1 Basics of prompt engineering

Prompt engineering involves crafting specific, clear, goal-oriented instructions to guide the AI model's responses. For example,

- An example of a weak prompt would be, "Analyze this login dataset."
- A strong prompt would be, "Using the provided login dataset, generate a summary that identifies unusual login patterns, includes the number of failed login attempts, and suggests potential causes."

13.5.2 Open source vs. cloud API integration

While OpenAI's cloud API is widely used, tools such as LM Studio and Ollama can be alternatives for local deployments.

The API key and base URL are the only changes required when switching between OpenAI and other platforms:

- *OpenAI base URL*—https://api.openai.com/v1
- *LM Studio base URL*—http://localhost:1234/v1
- *Ollama base URL*—http://localhost:11434/v1

The following listing is an example of switching between platforms.

Listing 13.1 Example Open AI API call

```
from openai import OpenAI                         # Imports OpenAI

# Point to the local server
client = OpenAI(base_url="http://localhost:1234/v1",
                api_key="lm-studio")              # Sets up client

completion = client.chat.completions.create(
    model=(
        "LM Studio Community/"
        "Meta-Llama-3-8B-Instruct-GGUF"
    ),                                            # Selects model
    messages=[
        {
            "role": "user",
            "content": (
                "Generate a sample cybersecurity risk "
                "report based on recent login data."
            )
        }
    ],                                            # Sets prompt
    temperature=0.7,                              # Sets temperature
)

print(completion.choices[0].message.content)      # Prints output
```

Keep in mind that your output may differ, as we are not basing this sample report on actual data. The LLM will create this each time with different data.

This code will communicate with the locally hosted LM Studio server using the specified model (`"Meta-Llama-3-8B-Instruct-GGUF"`). It generates a response based on the user-provided message, "Generate a sample cybersecurity risk report based on recent login data." The output, displayed on the console, will likely include a simulated risk report detailing potential threats, suspicious patterns, and suggested security measures based on the input topic.

By using the LM Studio local server, users can explore the capabilities of an open source generative AI model entirely within their own environment. This eliminates the need to send sensitive data to external APIs such as OpenAI's cloud service, ensuring full control over data privacy, security, and compliance, especially for organizations handling sensitive or regulated information.

One of the most significant risks of using public LLMs is data exposure. When data is sent to cloud-based AI services, it is processed on external servers, potentially subject to logging, retention policies, and third-party access. For industries such as finance, healthcare, and government, this can create compliance challenges and even security breaches if confidential data is inadvertently shared.

Offline AI models mitigate this risk entirely. With LM Studio, all inference and processing occur locally, meaning no data ever leaves the user's machine. This provides a significant security advantage, allowing organizations to use AI, while maintaining strict data governance policies and preventing unintentional data leaks.

For companies dealing with intellectual property, personally identifiable information (PII), or trade secrets, relying on locally hosted models is a necessity, not just a preference. Organizations should carefully assess whether their AI-powered workflows expose sensitive information and, when possible, default to private, self-hosted solutions like LM Studio to maintain the highest level of data security and control.

Cybersecurity Risk Report

Date: March 10, 2024

Introduction:
This report provides an analysis of recent login activity and identifies potential security risks to the organization's systems.

Login Activity Summary:

* Total logins: 15,432
* Unique users: 5,000
* Top 5 most active users:
    1. John Doe (123 logins)
    2. Jane Smith (98 logins)
    3. Bob Johnson (85 logins)
    4. Sarah Lee (70 logins)
    5. Michael Davis (65 logins)

Security Risks Identified:

1. **Weak Passwords:** 20% of users have weak or reused passwords, increasing the risk of successful brute-force attacks.
2. **Multi-Factor Authentication (MFA) Non-Compliance:** 15% of users do not use MFA, leaving their accounts vulnerable to phishing and other types of attacks.
3. **Unusual Login Locations:** 5% of logins originated from unusual locations, potentially indicating malicious activity or compromised user credentials.
4. **Suspicious Device Types:** 10% of logins were made from devices with suspicious operating systems or device types, which may indicate the use of compromised or malware-infected devices.

Recommendations:

1. **Password Reset Campaign:** Conduct a password reset campaign to enforce stronger passwords and encourage users to create unique passwords for each account.
2. **MFA Enforcement:** Implement MFA enforcement for all user accounts to prevent unauthorized access.
3. **Login Location Monitoring:** Monitor login locations more closely to detect and respond to potential security threats.
4. **Device Type Filtering:** Implement filtering rules to block logins from suspicious device types or operating systems.

Action Items:

1. IT Department:
    * Conduct a password reset campaign for all users
    * Implement MFA enforcement for all user accounts
2. Security Team:
    * Monitor login locations and investigate any unusual activity
    * Develop filtering rules to block logins from suspicious device types or operating systems
3. Management:
    * Review and approve the proposed action items
    * Provide additional resources as needed

Conclusion:
This report highlights several security risks related to recent login activity, including weak passwords, non-compliance with MFA, unusual login locations, and suspicious device types. Implementing the recommended action items will help mitigate these risks and improve overall cybersecurity posture.

Recommendations for Further Analysis:

1. Conduct a thorough review of login logs to identify any potential security incidents or suspicious activity.
2. Analyze user behavior and system logs to detect any anomalies that may indicate malicious activity.
3. Conduct regular security audits and penetration testing to identify vulnerabilities and weaknesses in the organization's systems.

Contact Information:
For any questions or concerns, please contact [Your Name] at [Email Address] or [Phone Number].

13.6 Generating and analyzing cybersecurity data

This section explores how generative AI can create and analyze synthetic cybersecurity data, simulating real-world scenarios to help organizations identify risks and improve their metrics. The purpose is to demonstrate how AI can assist in generating meaningful data and deriving actionable insights. We will be using AI to generate data for analysis following the pipeline in figure 13.1.

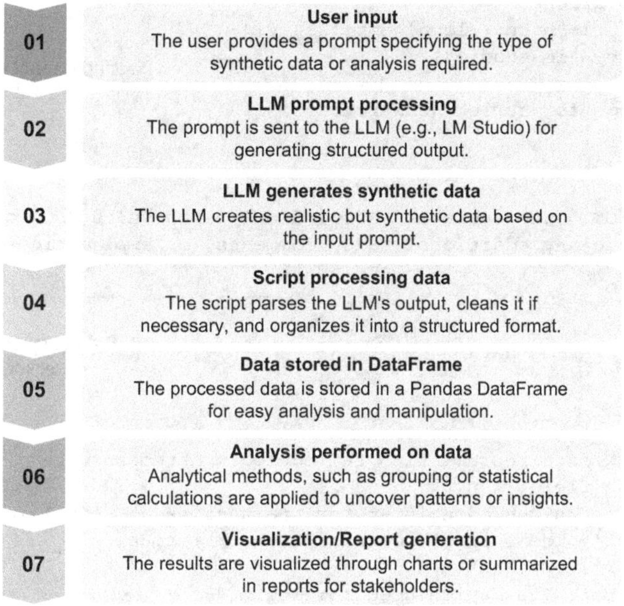

Figure 13.1 AI synthetically generated pipeline

01 User input — The user provides a prompt specifying the type of synthetic data or analysis required.

02 LLM prompt processing — The prompt is sent to the LLM (e.g., LM Studio) for generating structured output.

03 LLM generates synthetic data — The LLM creates realistic but synthetic data based on the input prompt.

04 Script processing data — The script parses the LLM's output, cleans it if necessary, and organizes it into a structured format.

05 Data stored in DataFrame — The processed data is stored in a Pandas DataFrame for easy analysis and manipulation.

06 Analysis performed on data — Analytical methods, such as grouping or statistical calculations are applied to uncover patterns or insights.

07 Visualization/Report generation — The results are visualized through charts or summarized in reports for stakeholders.

This pipeline demonstrates how to use a local LLM such as LM Studio to generate and analyze synthetic cybersecurity data. It begins with a user providing a structured prompt, which is processed by the LLM to create realistic but fictitious data. The generated output is then parsed and organized into a Pandas DataFrame for further analysis. Using Python scripts, the data undergoes statistical or categorical processing to identify patterns, trends, or insights. Finally, the results are visualized through charts or summarized in reports, enabling organizations to simulate real-world scenarios, test security strategies, and improve decision-making processes.

13.6.1 Generating synthetic cybersecurity data

Real-world data may not always be accessible due to privacy or regulatory concerns, especially in cybersecurity. Generative AI offers a practical solution by creating synthetic datasets. These datasets simulate realistic scenarios, such as failed logins, phishing attempts, or malware detections, and they can be used for training and testing security strategies.

The following listing is an example of generating and analyzing a dataset for failed login attempts using LM Studio.

Listing 13.2 Generating synthetic data for failed logins

```
# Import required libraries
from openai import OpenAI
import pandas as pd                    ◁── Imports libraries
import matplotlib.pyplot as plt
import json
```

```python
# Configure LM Studio client
client = OpenAI(base_url="http://localhost:1234/v1",
                api_key="lm-studio")                          # Sets up OpenAI client

# Define system message for strict JSON formatting
system_message = {
    "role": "system",
    "content": (
        "You are a JSON data generator. Respond only with valid JSON data. "
        "Do not include any additional text, comments, or explanations."
    )
}                                                              # Defines system and
                                                               # user messages
# User prompt for generating data
user_message = {
    "role": "user",
    "content": (
        "Generate JSON data representing failed login attempts with "
        "the following fields:\\n"
        "- 'User ID': A unique identifier for the user (e.g., 'U001').\n"
        "- 'Login Hour': The hour of login in 24-hour format "
        "(e.g., 13 for 1 PM).\\n"
        "- 'Device Type': The device used for login "
        "(e.g., 'Laptop', 'Mobile').\\n"
        "- 'Failed Login Reason': The reason for the failed login "
        "(e.g., 'Incorrect Password').\\n"
        "Generate 20 records in JSON format."
    )
}

# Request AI-generated JSON data
response = client.chat.completions.create(
    model="LM Studio Community/Meta-Llama-3-8B-Instruct-GGUF",  # Sends request
    messages=[system_message, user_message],                     # to model
    temperature=0.7,
)

# Process the AI response
try:
    raw_response = (
        response.choices[0].message.content.strip()
    )                                                           # Processes raw
    print("Raw AI Response:\n", raw_response)                   # AI response

    # Parse the JSON data
    json_data = json.loads(raw_response)                        # Parses JSON and
    data = pd.DataFrame(json_data)                              # load DataFrame
except json.JSONDecodeError as e:
    print("Error decoding JSON:", e)
    print("Raw response for debugging:", raw_response)          # Handles JSON or
    exit()                                                      # general errors
except Exception as e:
    print("Unexpected error:", e)
    exit()
```

```
# Debugging: Print the DataFrame to verify structure
print("Generated DataFrame:\n", data.head())    ◄──┐ Prints DataFrame preview

# Check for expected columns
if "Failed Login Reason" not in data.columns:
    print("The column 'Failed Login Reason' is missing. "   ┐ Checks required columns
          "Check the generated data.")
    exit()

# Analyze the data
failed_login_counts = data. \
    groupby("Failed Login Reason").size()    ◄──┐ Analyzes data (group by reason)

# Visualize the analysis
plt.figure(figsize=(8, 6))
failed_login_counts.plot(kind="bar", color="gray")
plt.title("Failed Login Reasons")
plt.xlabel("Reason")                              ┐ Plots bar chart
plt.ylabel("Count")
plt.grid(axis="y", linestyle="--")
plt.show()
```

After running the code, we get the following output, and figure 13.2 is its graphical presentation:

```
Raw AI Response:
[
    {"User ID": "U001", "Login Hour": 14, "Device Type": "Laptop", "Failed
     Login Reason": "Incorrect Password"},
    {"User ID": "U002", "Login Hour": 10, "Device Type": "Mobile", "Failed
     Login Reason": "Invalid Credentials"},
    {"User ID": "U003", "Login Hour": 15, "Device Type": "Desktop", "Failed
     Login Reason": "Account Locked"},
    {"User ID": "U004", "Login Hour": 16, "Device Type": "Tablet", "Failed
     Login Reason": "Incorrect Password"},
    {"User ID": "U005", "Login Hour": 11, "Device Type": "Laptop", "Failed
     Login Reason": "Invalid Credentials"},
    {"User ID": "U006", "Login Hour": 17, "Device Type": "Mobile", "Failed
     Login Reason": "Account Locked"},
    {"User ID": "U007", "Login Hour": 13, "Device Type": "Desktop", "Failed
     Login Reason": "Incorrect Password"},
    {"User ID": "U008", "Login Hour": 12, "Device Type": "Tablet", "Failed
     Login Reason": "Invalid Credentials"},
    {"User ID": "U009", "Login Hour": 18, "Device Type": "Laptop", "Failed
     Login Reason": "Account Locked"},
    {"User ID": "U010", "Login Hour": 14, "Device Type": "Mobile", "Failed
     Login Reason": "Incorrect Password"},
    {"User ID": "U011", "Login Hour": 16, "Device Type": "Desktop", "Failed
     Login Reason": "Invalid Credentials"},
    {"User ID": "U012", "Login Hour": 15, "Device Type": "Tablet", "Failed
     Login Reason": "Account Locked"},
    {"User ID": "U013", "Login Hour": 11, "Device Type": "Laptop", "Failed
     Login Reason": "Incorrect Password"},
    {"User ID": "U014", "Login Hour": 17, "Device Type": "Mobile", "Failed
     Login Reason": "Invalid Credentials"},
```

```
    {"User ID": "U015", "Login Hour": 13, "Device Type": "Desktop", "Failed
     Login Reason": "Account Locked"},
    {"User ID": "U016", "Login Hour": 12, "Device Type": "Tablet", "Failed
     Login Reason": "Incorrect Password"},
    {"User ID": "U017", "Login Hour": 18, "Device Type": "Laptop", "Failed
     Login Reason": "Invalid Credentials"},
    {"User ID": "U018", "Login Hour": 14, "Device Type": "Mobile", "Failed
     Login Reason": "Account Locked"},
    {"User ID": "U019", "Login Hour": 16, "Device Type": "Desktop", "Failed
     Login Reason": "Incorrect Password"},
    {"User ID": "U020", "Login Hour": 15, "Device Type": "Tablet", "Failed
     Login Reason": "Invalid Credentials"}
]
Generated DataFrame:
  User ID  Login Hour  Device Type   Failed Login Reason
0   U001          14       Laptop     Incorrect Password
1   U002          10       Mobile    Invalid Credentials
2   U003          15      Desktop         Account Locked
3   U004          16       Tablet     Incorrect Password
4   U005          11       Laptop    Invalid Credentials
```

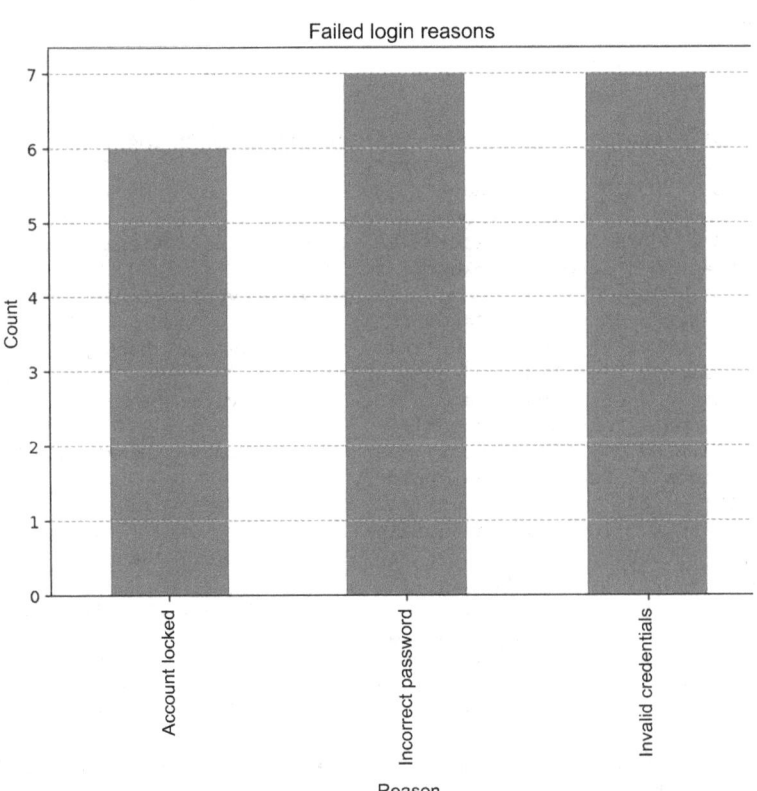

Figure 13.2 Gen AI-generated data and analysis for failed login attempts

The AI generates a dataset of failed login attempts with fields such as User ID, Login Hour, Device Type, and Failed Login Reason. This simulated dataset mimics real-world scenarios, while remaining entirely fictitious, ensuring safe experimentation.

The bar chart visualizes the frequency of reasons for failed logins. For instance, if "Incorrect password" appears most frequently, this indicates it is the primary reason for failed logins. This insight can help organizations prioritize user education or tighten password policies.

13.6.2 Analyzing the output

To effectively report on these findings, you can follow a structured approach that interprets the data, identifies patterns, and provides actionable insights.

SUMMARY OF FINDINGS

- The dataset includes failed login attempts categorized by user ID, login hour, device type, and the reason for failure.
- The most common reasons for failure are incorrect password, invalid credentials, and account locked.
- This dataset provides insights into patterns of login failures across different devices and times of the day.

HIGHLIGHT PATTERNS

- *Common reasons*—Report the most frequent failure reason. For example,
  - "Incorrect password" accounted for 40% of failures.
  - "Invalid credentials" and "Account locked" each contributed 30% to failed login attempts.
- *Device trends*—Analyze failures by device type to identify vulnerabilities. For example,
  - Laptops showed the highest number of failures due to incorrect passwords.
  - Mobile devices had a higher percentage of invalid credentials errors.

IDENTIFY TEMPORAL TRENDS

- Analyze the "Login hour" data to identify any time-based trends:
  - Are login failures clustered around specific hours?
  - For example: "The highest number of failed logins occurred between 10 AM and 2 PM, indicating potential problems during peak usage hours."

PROVIDE ACTIONABLE RECOMMENDATIONS

- *Training*—Employees should be trained on strong password practices to reduce "Incorrect password" errors.
- *Access controls*—Review and update account lockout policies to prevent unnecessary disruptions from repeated login attempts.

- *Device-specific security*—Investigate mobile device login procedures to address "Invalid credentials" problems.
- *Peak hour monitoring*—Implement additional monitoring during peak login hours to mitigate potential risks.

POTENTIAL FOLLOW-UP ANALYSIS

- Investigate whether specific users or departments show higher rates of failed logins.
- Examine the correlation between failed logins and attempted security breaches during the same period.
- Evaluate the effectiveness of password reset mechanisms to improve usability and reduce errors.

EXAMPLE REPORT

Title: Analysis of failed login attempts

Overview: This report analyzes failed login attempts across 20 sample records, focusing on reasons for failure, device types, and temporal trends. The objective is to uncover actionable insights to enhance security protocols and user experience.

Key findings

1. The most common reason for failure is "Incorrect password," accounting for 40% of all attempts.
2. Mobile devices frequently encounter "Invalid credentials" errors, highlighting potential gaps in authentication practices.
3. Peak login failures occur between 10 AM and 2 PM.

Recommendations

- Conduct password training to minimize errors.
- Strengthen account lockout policies to balance security and usability.
- Enhance authentication measures for mobile devices.
- Allocate additional monitoring resources during peak hours.

This approach ensures the findings are translated into meaningful actions, demonstrating the value of analyzing cybersecurity metrics.

13.7 Enhancing reporting and visualization

Reporting and visualization are critical for conveying complex cybersecurity data to diverse audiences, including executives, IT teams, and external auditors. Generative AI tools can automate parts of this process, transforming raw data into structured summaries, charts, and dashboards, as the next listing shows. This reduces the time and effort spent on manual reporting, while improving accuracy and engagement.

Listing 13.3 AI generated visualization with annotations

```
import pandas as pd                          ◀──┐ Imports pandas
import matplotlib.pyplot as plt              ◀──┤ Imports matplotlib
from openai import OpenAI                    ◀──┤ Imports OpenAI
from io import StringIO                      ◀──┤ Imports StringIO
import json                                  ◀──┘ Imports json

# Configure LM Studio or OpenAI API
client = OpenAI(
    base_url="http://localhost:1234/v1",
    api_key="lm-studio")                     ◀──── Sets up OpenAI client

# Prompt AI to generate JSON data
completion = client.chat.completions.create(  ◀──┐ Sends prompt
    model="TheBloke/Mistral-7B-Instruct-v0.2-GGUF",│ to generate JSON
    messages=[
        {
            "role": "system",
            "content": (
                "You are a JSON data generator. Respond ONLY with valid JSON \
                data. "
                "Ensure fields include UserID, LoginHour, DeviceType, and \
                FailedLoginReason."
            )
        },
        {
            "role": "user",
            "content": "Generate JSON data for 5 failed login attempts.",
        },
    ],
    temperature=0.7,
)

# Parse JSON data into a DataFrame
try:                                                          ┌─ Gets raw
    raw_response = completion.choices[0].message.content  ◀───┘  response
    print("Raw AI Response:\n", raw_response)  # Debugging step

    # Validate and clean JSON
    json_start = raw_response.find("[")       ◀──┐ Finds JSON array start/end
    json_end = raw_response.rfind("]") + 1
    if json_start == -1 or json_end == 0:
        raise ValueError("No valid JSON array found in the response.")

    clean_json = raw_response[json_start:json_end]  ◀──── Extracts JSON section
    json_data = json.loads(clean_json)              ◀──┐ Parses JSON
    df = pd.DataFrame(json_data)                    ◀──┤ Creates DataFrame
except Exception as e:
    print("Error processing JSON data:", e)
    exit()
```

```
# Summarize the data
try:
    failed_login_summary = df["FailedLoginReason"]. \
        value_counts()                                    # Counts failed login reasons
except KeyError:
    print("Error: Missing expected column 'FailedLoginReason'.")
    exit()

# Visualize the data
plt.figure(figsize=(10, 6))                               # Sets figure size
failed_login_summary.plot(kind="bar", color="gray")       # Plots bar chart
plt.title("Failed Login Reasons Summary")                 # Adds title
plt.xlabel("Failure Reason")                              # Labels x-axis
plt.ylabel("Count")                                       # Labels y-axis
plt.grid(axis="y", linestyle="--", alpha=0.7)             # Adds grid
plt.xticks(rotation=45, ha="right")                       # Rotates x labels
plt.tight_layout()                                        # Adjusts layout
plt.show()                                                # Shows chart
```

As shown in figure 13.3, "Incorrect password" is the most common failure reason, according to the failed login reasons summary.

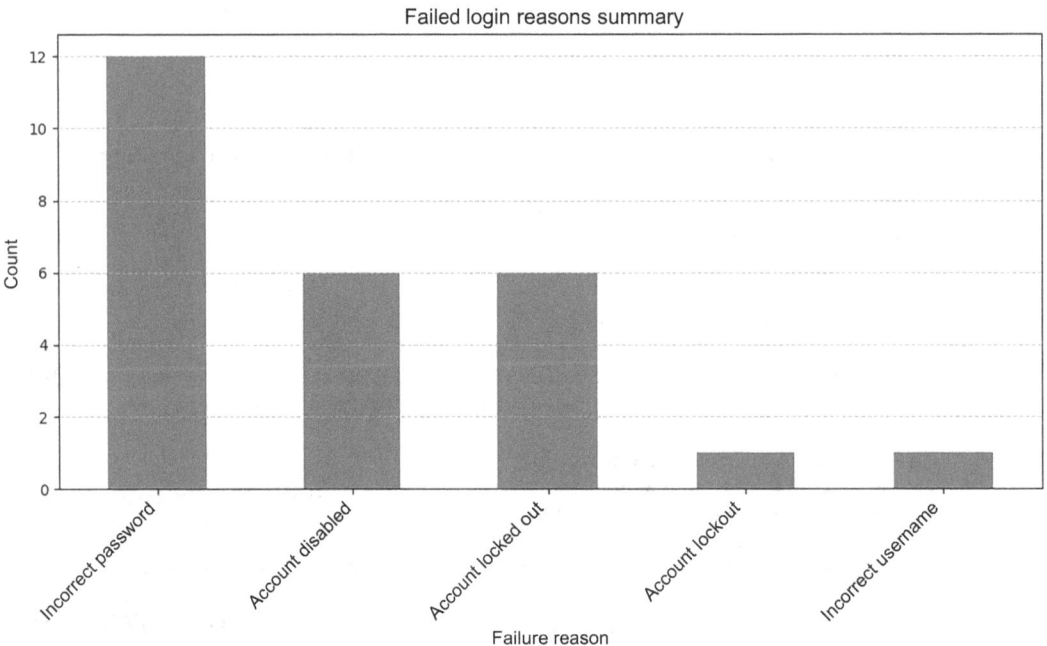

Figure 13.3 Failed login reasons summary showing incorrect password as the most common failure

13.7.1 Failed login reasons reporting

The bar chart output in our example summarizes the reasons for failed login attempts, with each bar representing a distinct reason and its corresponding count. The x-axis lists the failure reasons, such as "Incorrect password," "Account disabled," and "Account locked out," while the y-axis indicates the number of occurrences for each reason.

DOMINANT FAILURE REASONS

- The chart highlights that "Incorrect password" is the most common reason for failed logins, with a count of 12.
- "Account Disabled" and "Account locked out" also appear frequently, with nearly equal counts (6 each), indicating they are significant problems to monitor.

LESSER OBSERVED FAILURES

- Other reasons such as "Incorrect username" and "Account lockout" are far less frequent, suggesting they may not be as critical in this dataset but still require attention.

PATTERNS AND TRENDS

- Such visualizations allow security teams to quickly grasp trends and focus on mitigating the most common failure points, like incorrect passwords.

PRACTICAL APPLICATIONS OF THE VISUALIZATION

- *Policy adjustments*—If "Incorrect password" is prevalent, it may indicate that users need stronger guidance on creating and remembering passwords. Adjustments to password policies, such as reminders, strength indicators, or password managers, could mitigate this issue.
- *User education*—For reasons such as "Account disabled" or "Account locked out," there might be a lack of clarity on account recovery steps. Providing clear instructions or automated account unlock processes could reduce these incidents.
- *Infrastructure monitoring*—Frequent occurrences of reasons such as "Incorrect username" might indicate potential brute force or phishing attempts, requiring further investigation.

GENERATING A REPORT BASED ON THE FINDINGS

Executive summary

- State the total number of failed login attempts analyzed.
- Highlight the top failure reasons and their percentages.

Key findings

- Discuss the most frequent failure reason ("Incorrect password") and its implications.

- Outline other significant reasons such as "Account disabled" and "Account locked out."

Recommendations
- For users—Encourage better password management practices and provide educational resources.
- For security teams—Implement multi-factor authentication (MFA) and monitor for brute force attempts.
- For IT teams—Automate account recovery processes to minimize downtime.

Data summary table and graph
- Include a simple table summarizing the counts for each failure reason, as shown in table 13.1.

Table 13.1 An example table summarizing the counts for each failure reason

Failure reason	Count
Incorrect password	12
Account disabled	6
Account locked out	6
Account lockout	2
Incorrect username	2

The bar chart and the corresponding report provide actionable insights into reasons for failed logins. Organizations can use such analysis to strengthen their cybersecurity posture by identifying weak points and implementing tailored interventions. These insights also allow teams to prioritize resources and improve user experience and security.

13.8 Automating incident response and trend analysis

Automating incident response and analyzing trends is a game-changer for cybersecurity teams. Using generative AI, organizations can streamline their incident management workflows and uncover hidden patterns in their data. This section demonstrates how AI can respond to security incidents and identify trends over time, enabling proactive security measures.

13.8.1 Setting the context

Let's imagine a fictitious company, SecureSys, that faces a high volume of security incidents every month. These incidents include failed login attempts, malware detections, and data access violations. SecureSys wants to

- Automate the classification and prioritization of incidents
- Identify recurring patterns to mitigate similar problems in the future
- Generate actionable incident response recommendations

The following listing is a practical example illustrating how generative AI can help with these tasks.

Listing 13.4 Automating incident response

```
# Import required libraries
import pandas as pd                            # Imports Pandas for handling tabular data
import matplotlib.pyplot as plt                # Imports Matplotlib for plotting
from openai import OpenAI                      # Imports OpenAI for API interaction
from datetime import datetime                  # Imports datetime for timestamps

# Configure LM Studio or OpenAI API
client = OpenAI(base_url="http://localhost:1234/v1",\
                api_key="lm-studio")           # Configures OpenAI client with URL and API key

# Step 1: Generate synthetic incident data
incident_data = pd.DataFrame({                 # Creates synthetic incident dataset
    "Incident ID": range(1, 11),
    "Incident Type": [
        "Failed Login", "Malware Detected", "Data Exfiltration",
        "Phishing Attempt", "Malware Detected", "Data Exfiltration",
        "Failed Login", "Phishing Attempt", "Unauthorized Access",
        "Failed Login"
    ],
    "Severity": [
    "High", "Medium", "Critical", "High", "Medium",
    "Critical", "Low", "High", "Critical", "Low"
],
    "Timestamp": [
        datetime.now().strftime("%Y-%m-%d %H:%M:%S")
        for _ in range(10)]
})                                             # Formats data into DataFrame

# Step 2: Use AI to generate incident recommendations
recommendations = []
for index, row in incident_data.iterrows():    # Loops over each incident row
    prompt = (
        f"Based on the incident type '{row['Incident Type']}' "
        f"and severity '{row['Severity']}', provide an "
        "immediate response recommendation."
)
    completion = client.chat.completions.create(
        model="TheBloke/Mistral-7B-Instruct-v0.2-GGUF",    # Calls OpenAI API for recommendation
        messages=[
            {
                "role": "system",
                "content": "You are a cybersecurity incident handler."
            },
            {   "role": "user",
                "content": prompt},
        ],
        temperature=0.7,
)                                              # Appends AI recommendation to list
    response = completion.choices[0].message.content.strip()
    recommendations.append(response)
```

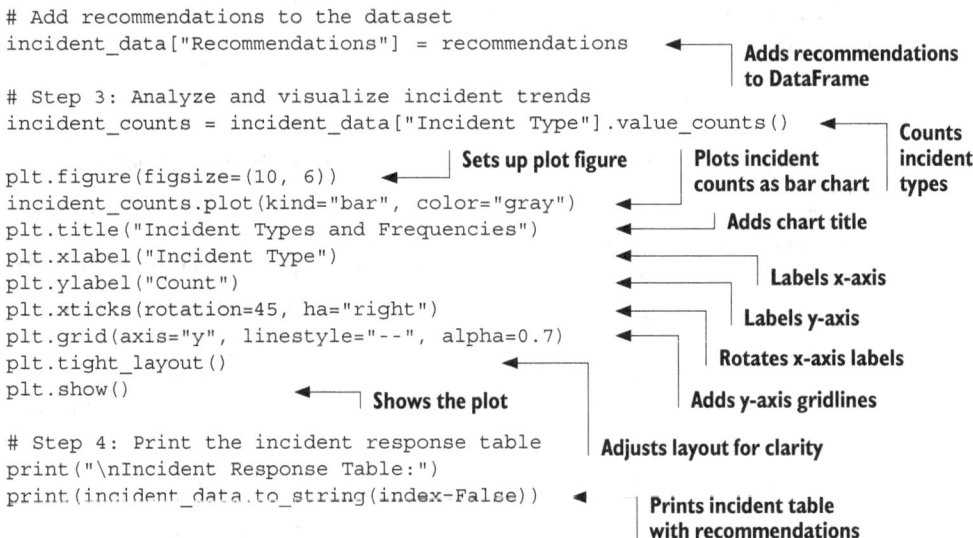

Figure 13.4 shows the output, an incident trends chart, where

- The bars show the frequency of each incident type, helping users identify patterns or recurring problems.
- "Failed login" incidents occur most frequently, indicating a possible brute force attack or poor password practices.

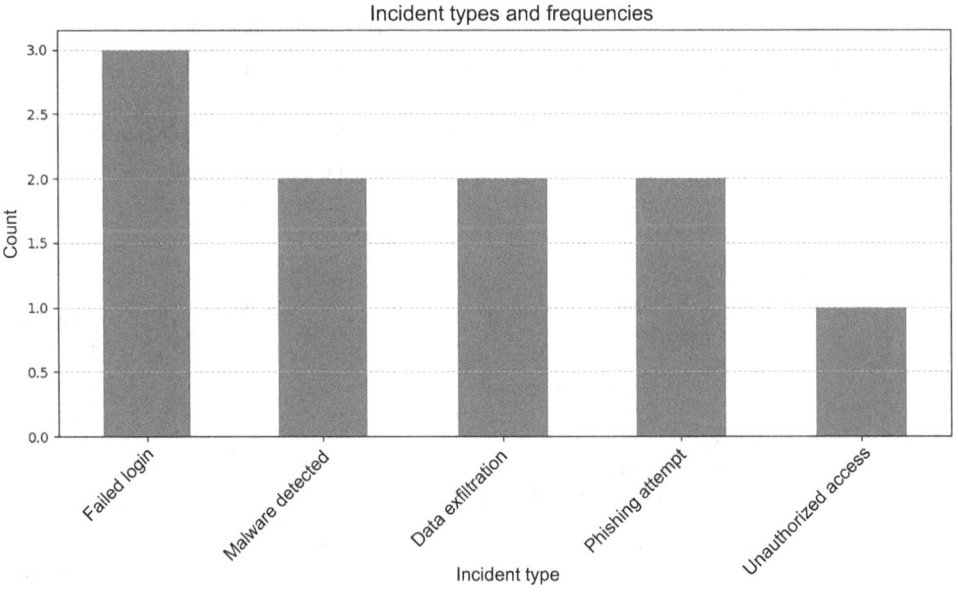

Figure 13.4 Incident types and frequencies from the sample code

Table 13.2 is the LLM output, an incident response table, where

- *Incident ID* is a unique identifier for each incident.
- *Incident type* is the category of the incident (e.g., failed login, malware detected).
- *Severity* indicates the urgency level of the incident (e.g., low, medium, high, critical)
- *Timestamp* shows the date and time of the incident.
- *Recommendations* are the AI-generated actions for resolving or mitigating the incident.

Table 13.2 Incident response example table (two entries)

Incident ID	Incident type	Severity	Timestamp	Recommendations
1	Failed login	High	2024-12-01 10:11:51	Immediate response recommendations 1. Verify the authenticity of the failed login report. 2. Investigate source IP addresses, usernames, and timestamps. 3. Block suspicious IPs and implement multi-factor authentication. 4. Inform affected users and recommend password changes. 5. Update and enforce access control policies and password requirements. 6. Review account lockout policies and monitor activity for unusual patterns. 7. Document the incident for future analysis and reporting.
2	Malware detected	Medium	2024-12-01 10:11:51	Immediate response recommendations 1. Isolate the infected system to prevent malware spread. 2. Perform a full system scan and update antivirus definitions. 3. Quarantine and analyze the malware to understand its behavior. 4. Restore affected files using clean backups. 5. Patch systems to close vulnerabilities. 6. Educate users on avoiding suspicious files and links. 7. Monitor network traffic for reinfection attempts.

13.9 Exploring generative AI

Generative AI is an evolving field that revolutionizes industries, including cybersecurity. For readers who want to deepen their understanding and experiment with generative AI, this section provides practical guidance and inspiration to encourage exploration and innovation. You should validate trends for statistical significance to avoid misleading conclusions from AI-identified patterns.

Generative AI is a powerful tool that can augment decision-making, automate repetitive tasks, and uncover new insights in cybersecurity metrics. By learning more about this technology, you can

- *Personalize your learning journey*—Tailor AI tools to meet your specific needs in cybersecurity and beyond.
- *Automate tedious processes*—Use AI to generate reports, visualize trends, or predict future incidents, saving valuable time.
- *Stay ahead of threats*—Enhance your ability to identify vulnerabilities and respond proactively.
- *Foster creativity*—Use generative AI to brainstorm innovative solutions and experiment with new ways of analyzing data.

13.9.1 Learning resources

To begin your journey, consider the following resources:

- Online tutorials and documentation
  - Hugging Face (https://huggingface.co/) offers a wealth of tutorials on natural language processing and generative AI with open-source models.
  - OpenAI API Documentation (https://platform.openai.com/docs/overview) provides step-by-step guides and examples for using GPT models.
  - DeepLearning.AI (https://www.deeplearning.ai/) offers free and paid courses covering AI fundamentals and generative AI techniques.
- Interactive learning platforms
  - Kaggle (https://www.kaggle.com/) features datasets and community-driven notebooks to practice AI in cybersecurity scenarios.
  - Coursera (https://www.coursera.org/) and edX (https://www.edx.org/) host structured courses taught by industry professionals and academic experts.
- Open source AI tools
  - LM Studio and Ollama provide downloadable models for local use, allowing you to experiment without relying on cloud-based APIs.
  - Open source libraries such as PyTorch and TensorFlow offer flexibility for advanced users.

13.9.2 Inspiration to experiment

Generative AI thrives on creativity and experimentation. Here are some practical ideas to get started:

- *Simulate scenarios*—Use generative AI to create simulated cybersecurity incidents, such as phishing attempts or malware infections. Analyze the outcomes and experiment with how AI could aid in incident response.
- *Create personalized reports*—Input sample cybersecurity metrics into a generative AI model and explore how it can format the data into executive summaries, charts, or trend analyses.
- *Enhance training programs*—Use AI to generate realistic phishing emails or attack scenarios for employee training, helping them recognize and avoid threats.
- *Experiment with AI prompts*—Challenge yourself to craft creative prompts for generative AI. For example,
  - "Generate a daily cybersecurity dashboard with recommendations for improving network defenses."
  - "Summarize a year's worth of login attempts and suggest three actionable improvements."
- *Collaborate with the community*—Engage with online forums and GitHub projects focused on cybersecurity and AI. Sharing your results and learning from others can accelerate your progress and inspire new ideas.

13.9.3 Your next steps

Start simple and set realistic goals. Generative AI is a tool to enhance, not replace, human ingenuity. Begin by choosing one use case that aligns with your professional interests. Spend time learning the nuances of model behavior, experiment with open source tools, and most importantly, have fun exploring the potential of generative AI in cybersecurity metrics.

Generative AI offers a wealth of possibilities limited only by your imagination. Dive in, explore, and see how this powerful technology can transform how you think about cybersecurity data and decision-making.

13.10 Limitations and ethical considerations

Generative AI offers remarkable potential for transforming how we analyze and report cybersecurity metrics, but it is essential to recognize its limitations and ethical challenges to use it responsibly and effectively. One of the primary challenges lies in its accuracy and reliability. The outputs it generates are based on patterns from its training data, which may not always reflect real-world situations. This can result in reports or recommendations that are incomplete or even misleading. Additionally, these models lack true contextual understanding. For instance, while they can detail failed login attempts, without additional inputs or clarifications, they cannot independently discern whether these failures are harmless user errors or part of a coordinated attack.

Another significant limitation involves the data itself. Generative AI depends on data to produce meaningful results, yet cybersecurity data often includes highly sensitive information. Using third-party systems or cloud-based APIs for processing, this data can introduce privacy risks, emphasizing the importance of anonymizing data and using local solutions when possible. Adapting AI models for specific cybersecurity scenarios, such as analyzing sophisticated threats, often requires advanced technical skills. Without proper customization, the results may feel too generalized or fail to address the nuances of a given situation.

Ethical considerations also play a critical role in using generative AI for cybersecurity. Bias in AI outputs is a notable concern, as the data used to train these models may inadvertently reinforce existing biases. For example, certain security incidents might be emphasized over others, not because of their actual risk but due to patterns in the training data. It is crucial to carefully validate AI outputs and involve human oversight in interpreting the results. There is also the inherent risk of misuse. AI tools could be exploited to simulate phishing attacks or create fake data, which underscores the need for secure implementation and clear boundaries around technology use.

Data privacy is a key concern when integrating AI into cybersecurity workflows. Processing sensitive security data requires strict adherence to regulations such as GDPR, CCPA, and industry-specific compliance standards. Even when using local AI tools such as LM Studio, organizations must prioritize data anonymization, secure storage, and access controls to protect sensitive information.

Beyond compliance, maintaining a human-in-the-loop approach is essential, particularly in high-stakes cybersecurity scenarios. While AI can streamline threat detection, automate security workflows, and provide valuable insights, it cannot fully understand business context, legal implications, or ethical considerations.

For example, AI-powered intrusion detection systems (IDS) can flag anomalies based on patterns, but they cannot always differentiate between a legitimate spike in activity (such as a system update) and an actual security breach. Similarly, an AI model might suggest revoking a user's access based on behavioral data, but without human oversight, it could trigger disruptions for legitimate users.

Decisions involving breach response, regulatory compliance, or insider threat detection require human expertise to interpret AI-generated outputs correctly. AI should serve as a decision-support tool rather than an autonomous decision-maker:

- To balance AI automation with human oversight, organizations should
- Implement review mechanisms where cybersecurity professionals must validate AI-generated alerts, policy changes, or risk assessments
- Ensure explainability in AI decisions, so security teams understand why AI flagged a problem before acting on it
- Incorporate human expertise in final decision-making, particularly in areas involving incident response, risk management, and compliance audits

AI is a powerful force multiplier in cybersecurity, but human judgment remains irreplaceable in making critical security decisions, mitigating false positives, and ensuring ethical AI deployment.

Ultimately, the responsible use of generative AI hinges on transparency, accountability, and human collaboration. Clear documentation of how AI tools are used in analyzing and reporting cybersecurity metrics builds trust among stakeholders and ensures the technology supports, rather than undermines organizational goals. By being aware of these challenges and considering them carefully, generative AI can become a powerful ally in navigating today's complex cybersecurity landscape.

Summary

- Generative AI introduces new opportunities to analyze data, simulate potential threats, and streamline reporting for cybersecurity metrics.
- Generative AI can generate, analyze, and visualize cybersecurity data through real-world scenarios.
- Open source tools such as LM Studio and Ollama enable the use of local models, providing flexibility, privacy, and cost-effectiveness compared to cloud-based AI systems.
- For those who prefer cloud-based generative AI solutions, OpenAI's API remains a leading choice for accessibility and reliability.
- AI can automate incident response and identify trends in security metrics.
- Prompt engineering involves crafting effective instructions to guide a language model's output. When creating prompts, be specific, set the context, guide the format, then iterate and refine as needed.
- Check generative AI outputs for accuracy and reliability; be aware of the data quality used. Also be aware of bias and data privacy concerns when using generative AI.

index

Numbers

2FA (two-factor authentication)   147

A

ABAC (attribute-based access control)   148
ABDR (anomalous behavior detection rate)   230
access control   146–156
    violations   58
accuracy, defined   280
ACLs (access control lists)   170
action items   204
administrative controls   153
adverse event analysis   188–189
AI (artificial intelligence)   266
    cybersecurity metrics and   19
    effectiveness of in cybersecurity   235–238
    predictive cybersecurity metrics   18–19
AI-DA (AI-based decision accuracy rate)   236
ALE (annualized loss expectancy)   138
AlienVault OSSIM   191
AlienVault OTX (Open Threat Exchange)   232
anomaly detection   230
    alerts   183
APIs (application programming interfaces)   38
APTs (advanced persistent threats)   137, 233

ARIMA (autoregressive integrated moving average)   259
ARO (annual rate of occurrence)   138
ASI (attack surface index)   239
assessments, cyber risk   132–140
    derived   136–138
    direct   135
    direct (vulnerabilities)   135
    metrics   134–138
    NIST 800-30   132–133
asset identification   127
asset management   128–131
    metrics   129
    metrics exercise   130
asset protection, configuration management   164–169
    hardware maintenance   164
    log maintenance   164
    platform metrics   167
    platform security metrics exercise   168
    software development   165–167
    software maintenance   164
    unauthorized software prevention   165
assets
    technology infrastructure resilience   170–171
    training and awareness   156–158
asymmetric encryption   159

ATHSR (advanced threat hunting success rate)   241
ATLAS (Alert Threshold Lifecycle Assessment System)   49, 182–184
authentication   146–156
autoencoders, for threat detection   274–277
   exercise interpretation   277
   Python code   274–276
Autopsy   206

B

BAA (Business Associate Agreement)   122
Bash, for metrics collection   63
Bayesian inference   261–262
BEC (business email compromise) attacks   9
benchmarking, defined   250
biometric authentication   147
board of directors   114
breach, defined   193–194
brute-force attack detection metrics   179
business alignment   69–72
business goals, misalignment with metrics programs   66
business impact factor   225
business strategy, aligning metrics with   72–75

C

C2 (command and control) beaconing   179
CEO (chief executive officer), executive summary report for   59, 75
chain of custody   204
CIO (chief information officer)   93
CIS (Center for Internet Security) Top 18 framework   14–16
CIS Critical Security Controls (CIS controls)   190
CISO (chief information security officer)   51, 93, 105, 115
   executive summary report for   58, 74
cloud and network threat management   238–241
   attack surface index   239
   cloud threat detection   238
   cloud threat detection accuracy   239
   metric exercise   240
clustering scatter plot   258
CNNs (convolutional neural networks)   233, 281
communication strategies   80–83
   communication exercise   83–86

navigating naysayers and resistance   80
proactively improving communication channels   82
starting the conversation   80
tailoring communication to different stakeholders   82
troubleshooting the conversation   81
compliance dashboard   26
compliance metrics   142
compliance risk   59
compliance status   28–29
configuration management   164–169
   hardware maintenance   164
   log maintenance   164
   platform metrics   167–168
   software development   165–167
   software maintenance   164
   unauthorized software prevention   165
continuous improvement   244–246, 250
   exercise   245
   key concepts for   250
   mean time to predict   245
   metrics   142
   risk mitigation   244
   statistical analysis free resources   250
   time to predict   245
continuous monitoring strategies   121
continuous threat detection   174
   adverse event analysis   188–189
   alternatives to ATLAS and Wazuh   190
   continuous monitoring metrics   179–181
   implementing continuous threat monitoring systems   175–178
   open source alternative to   178
   valid threat detections   185–188
contracts   121
corrective actions   207
correlation analysis   34–36, 250
   CISO report   36
   exercise   34
correlation heatmap   258
Cortex   228
Cortex XDR   231
Cortex XSOAR   233
Coursera   310
credential management   149–156
critical hardware and software assets   129

cross-site scripting (XSS)   240
CRR (compliance reporting rate)   217
crypto-mining detection metrics   179
CTDA (cloud threat detection accuracy)   239
CVEs (Common Vulnerabilities and Exposures)   132, 224
CVSS (Common Vulnerability Scoring System)   133, 135, 224
cyber risk   126
   assessments   132–140
   asset management   128–131
   continuous improvement   140–142
   identify phase   127
   identity metrics exercise   142
cybersecurity
   changing landscape of   9–11
   continuous threat detection   175–178
   foundational concepts   91
   machine learning   285–287
   NLP   278–281
   oversight   113–119
   policies   108–113
   procedures   108–113
   processes   108–113
   protecting assets   145
   supply chain risk management   120–124
cybersecurity analyst   115
cybersecurity analytics toolkit   21
   continuous improvement and iteration   39–42
   integrated security analytics environment   38–39
   statistical analysis   31–38
   tool selection   22–24
cybersecurity incidents, containing validated incidents   212
cybersecurity metrics   3
   advanced   221–229
   AI and   19
   cloud and network threat managemen   238–241
   continuous improvement   244–246
   effectiveness of AI in   235–238
   frameworks   11–17
   generating and analyzing cybersecurity data   296–302
   importance of   3
   incident management   241–243
   predictive cybersecurity metrics   18–19
   significance of   6
cybersecurity steering committee   115

cybersecurity supply chain risk management   120–124
   best practices   120–121
   metrics   122–123
Cybrary   133

D

DAC (discretionary access control)   148
dashboard development   25–31
   choosing right metrics   25–26
   example   27–31
   knowledge points   27
DAST (dynamic application security testing)   166
data, finding hidden relationships in   252–254
data collection   207
data encryption coverage   141
data exfiltration detection metrics   179
data security   158–164
   data at rest   159–160
   data backup and recovery   161
   data in transit   160
   data in use   161
   metrics   161–162
   metrics exercise   162–164
dataset origin   257
data summary table and graph   306
DBSCAN (Density-Based Spatial Clustering of Applications with Noise)   267–270
DDoS (Distributed Denial of Service), attack   282
   detection metrics   179
deep learning   281–284
DeepLearning.AI   310
derived asset management metrics   130
derived metrics   6, 130, 188
detection tool   203
diagonal cells   281
digital signatures   166
direct asset management metrics   129
direct metrics   6, 188
DoS (denial of service)   137
DPO (data protection officer)   116
DRS (dynamic risk scoring)   232

E

EDR (endpoint detection and response)   193
edX   310
EER (equal error rate)   185–188

EF (exposure factor)   136
EHRs (electronic health records)   70
Elastic Stack   60, 191, 206, 228, 231
EMA (exponential moving average)   254, 255
encryption algorithms   159
environmental threats   170
EPSS (Exploit Prediction Scoring System)   133, 134, 136
Equifax breach   4
event volume   188
evidence gathering   204
   and forensic analysis   213
executive dashboard   26
executive reports   76
executive summary   305
external notification   204
external/unknown IP communication over north/south   179

F

F1-Score   280
false positives/negatives   154
false positive rate   188
FAR (false acceptance rate)   185, 201
feedback loops   41, 251
FIM (file integrity monitoring)   207
financial consequences of security incidents   28
financial risk   59
firewall effectiveness   141
five-tier severity model   202
forecasting cybersecurity trends   258–261
   ARIMA   259
   practical application   261
forensic analysis   207
FPSR (false positive suppression rate)   236
frameworks   11–17
   CIS Top 18   14–16
   HITRUST   12–14
   NIST Cybersecurity Framework v2.0   16
FRR (false rejection rate)   185–188, 201

G

generative AI (artificial intelligence)   289, 290, 310
   automating incident response and trend analysis   306–309
   generating and analyzing cybersecurity data   296–302
   in cybersecurity metrics, LLM models   292
   inspiration to experiment   311
   learning resources   310
   limitations and ethical considerations   312
   metrics, reporting and visualization   302–306
   next steps   311
   open source generative AI alternatives   290–292
   prompt engineering   293–295
   prompt engineering, importance of   293
governance   92
   metrics   124
   structure of   114
Graylog   191
grouping similar events for better insights   256–258
GUI (graphical user interface)   291

H

hardware maintenance   164
hash functions   160
hashing algorithms   159
HIPAA (Healthcare and Health Information Portability and Accountability Act)   12, 58, 96
HITRUST (Health Information Trust Alliance)   12–14
HR manager (with a focus on cybersecurity)   116
Hugging Face   310

I

ICT (incident communication time)   217
IdM (identity management)   127, 146
   detection and documentation   201–206
   eradication of incidents   214–216
   incident triage and analysis   206–210
IDS (intrusion detection systems)   19, 22, 201, 261, 312
IDT (incident detection time)   204
ILM (identity life cycle management)   146
impact estimation   242
incident classification accuracy   189
incident ID   309
incident management   192
   containing validated incidents   212
   detection and documentation   202–205
   eradication of incidents   215

impact estimation   242
incident triage and analysis   208–210
metric exercise   243
notification and communication   210
post-incident and lessons learned   216–217
threat hunting, success rate   241
incident management and recovery
evidence gathering and forensic analysis   213
planning and preparation phase   195
recovering to operational status   216
incident response
and trend analysis, automating   306–309
metrics   215
table   309
testing incident response plan   196–200
incident response time   28
incident type   309
indirect metrics   6
individual identities   127
infrastructure monitoring   305
initial analysis   203
internal notification   204
IoCs (Indicators of Compromise)   188, 201, 203
IRP (incident response plan)   195
IRR (incident re-occurrence rate)   210
IRSR-I (incident response success rate incident)   215
IRT (incident response team)   195
ISACA (Information Systems Audit and Control Association)   52
ISCM (Information Security Continuous Monitoring)   175
isolation forest, for threat detection   274–277
exercise interpretation   277
Python code   274–276
ISSA (Information Systems Security Association)   52
IT security manager   116

J

Jupyter Notebooks   249

K

Kaggle   250, 310
key findings   305
K-Means clustering   256
KPIs (key performance indicators)   49, 70, 83

L

lagging indicators   6
leading indicators   6
legal and compliance officer   116
lesser observed failures   305
lessons learned   204
LLMs (large language models)   18, 290, 292
LM Studio   290–292, 310
log analysis   207
log maintenance   164
LSTM (long short-term memory)   281

M

MAC address   150
machine learning   265
advanced analysis   278–281
artificial intelligence   266
code requirements   266
DBSCAN for threat detection   267–270
deep learning   281–284
isolation forest and autoencoders for threat detection   274–277
random forest and SVM for threat detection   270–277
reinforcement learning   285–287
MAC (mandatory access control)   148
malware
analysis   207
communication detection   179
detection plot   258
Malware_Incidents list   259
matplotlib library   266
mean time to update software   167
metrics
advanced   223–235
aligning with business strategy   72–75
business alignment   69–72
cyber risk assessment   134–138
cybersecurity   110–113
defined   5–6
generative AI in, prompt engineering   293
governance metrics   124
integrating into business strategy   68
oversight   117–118
protection metrics   171
reporting   75–86

reporting and visualization 302–306
traditional vs. innovative 7
metrics collection, tools and technologies for 60–65
   automation and integration 61
   commercial tools for metrics collection 60
   open source tools for metrics collection 60
   scripting for metrics collection 61–65
metrics dashboard 57–59
   customizing for different stakeholders 57
   example 58–59
   executive summary report for CEO 59
   executive summary report for CISO 58
METRICS methodology 46–52
   communicate 51
   evaluate 48
   improve 49
   measure 47
   report 49
   sustain 51
   threshold 48
   using example 52–56
MFA (multifactor authentication) 14, 147, 306
MITRE ATT&CK 190, 232
ML (machine learning) 17–18
monitoring trends 250
moving averages 254–256
   detailed description of plots 255
   example 254
MSP (managed service provider) 208
MTP (mean time to predict) 245
MTTC-I (mean time to contain incident) 215
MTTC (mean time to contain) 136, 139
MTTD-I (mean time to detect incident) 205
MTTD (mean time to detect) 66, 136, 139
MTTI-I (mean time to identify incident) 205
MTTR-I (mean time to remediate incident) 215
MTTR (mean time to report) 136
MTTR (mean time to resolve) 27, 28, 29
MTTR (mean time to respond) 48, 58, 136, 139

N

Nessus 133
networks
   technology infrastructure resilience 170
   traffic analysis 207

NIST 800-30, guide for conducting risk assessments 132–133
NIST Cybersecurity Framework 16, 251
NIST (National Institute of Standards and Technology) 94, 175
NIST RMF (National Institute of Standards and Technology Risk Management Framework) 101
NLP (natural language processing) 18, 233, 278–281
   classification report 280
   confusion matrix 281
   exercise 278–280

O

off-diagonal cells 281
Ollama 291, 310
OpenAI API Documentation 310
open source alternative to continuous threat detection 178
open source generative AI alternatives 290–292
   LM Studio 290, 292
   LM Studio vs. Ollama 291
   Ollama 291
open source tools, for metrics collection 60
OpenVAS 60, 228
operational effects 59
organizational assets 127
organizational context 93–100
   mission, vision, and values 96
   organizational metrics 98–100
   strategic objectives 97
OSS (open source software) 72
oversight 113–119
   exercise 116
   governance structure 114
   metrics 117–118
   simulated governance structure 114

P

pandas library 251, 266
patch compliance 58
patterns and trends 305
PCI DSS (Payment Card Industry Data Security Standard) 96, 170
penetration testing 166
phishing detection rate 27–29

phishing simulation results 141
physical controls 153
PII (personally identifiable information) 197, 295
platform metrics 167–168
POAM (Plan of Action and Milestones) document 102
Poisson distribution 263
policies, cybersecurity 108–113
   exercise 111–113
   metrics 110
policy violation alerts 183
possible metrics 6
potential breach assessment, defined 194
PowerShell, for Windows metrics collection 64
precision, defined 280
predictive analysis 222
predictive cybersecurity metrics 18–19
probability distribution 36–38
procedures, cybersecurity 108–113
processes, cybersecurity 108–113
prompt engineering 293–295
   basics and importance of 293
   open source vs. cloud API integration 294
protection metrics 171
psutil library 61
PTI (predictive threat index) 223, 225
   cybersecurity teams working together with open source solutions 228
   using open source tools to calculate 228–229
PyRIT (Python Risk Identification Toolkit) 20
Python 222
   for metrics collection 61
   reinforcement learning example in 285–287
PyTorch 310

Q

qualitative metrics 5
Qualys 60, 133
quantitative metrics 5
   overreliance on 66

R

random forest, for threat detection 270–277
   exercise 270–273
ransomware detection metrics 179
Rapid7 InsightVM 133

RBAC (role-based access control) 148
RCAT (root cause analysis time) 210
RCE (remote code execution) 224
RDP (Remote Desktop Protocol) 240
real-time security alerts 27, 28
recall, defined 280
recommendations 309
   for IT teams, security teams, and users 306
recovery actions 204
REI (risk exposure index) 223, 224
   cybersecurity teams working together with open source solutions 228
   using open source tools to calculate 228–229
relationship mapping 127
reporting metrics 75–86
   communication exercise 83–86
   communication strategies 80–83
   demonstrating ROI 78
   presenting in executive reports 76
reporting and visualization 302–306
   failed login reasons reporting 305
residual risk 101, 137
resilience mechanisms 171
resource capacity 171
RES (risk exposure score) 27, 28, 137
   risk exposure 222
   risk exposure section 28
risk-based alerting 190
risk management strategy 100–105
   metrics 102–104
   mitigation 101, 244
RL (reinforcement learning), example in Python code 285–287
RMV (risk mitigation velocity) 244
RNNs (recurrent neural networks) 233, 281
ROI (return on investment), demonstrating 78
roles and responsibilities
   establishing foundation 105–108
   metrics 106–107
root cause
   analysis 207, 250
   identification 207
   resolution rate 189
RPOs (recovery point objectives) 161
RR (risk register) 102
RTOs (recovery time objectives) 161

S

SAML (security assertion markup language)   151
SANS Institute   133
SAST (static application security testing)   166
scatter plot   257
scikit-learn library   223, 251, 266
scripting, for metrics collection   61–65
    Bash   63
    PowerShell for Windows   64
    Python   61
SCRM (supply chain risk management)   120
SDLC (software development life cycle)   165
    testing exercise   169
secure coding practices   166
secure configurations   166
security analyst dashboard   26
security as code   166
security awareness and training metrics   141
security control effectiveness   141
security incident overview section   29
security metrics
    building metrics dashboard   57–59
    common pitfalls in metrics programs   65–66
    METRICS methodology   46–52
    program, designing   44–45
    tools and technologies for metrics collection   60–65
    using METRICS methodology example   52–56
service agreements   121
severity   309
SIEM (security information and event management)   10, 22, 48, 164, 190, 201, 261
signature-based threats   179
SLE (single loss expectancy)   136, 138
SMART (specific, measurable, attainable, relevant, and time-bound)   251
SMA (simple moving average)   254, 255
SOAR (security orchestration, automation, and response)   10, 38, 167
SOC (security operations center)   51, 184
software development   165–167
software maintenance   164
software patch management numbers per frequency   167
SOPs (standard operating procedures)   110
Splunk   60, 222, 231
SSR (stakeholder satisfaction rate)   217
stagnation and complacency   66
statistical analysis   31–38, 248
    Bayesian inference   261–262
    continuous improvement with statistical metrics   250
    correlation analysis   34–36
    feedback loops   251
    finding hidden relationships in data   252–254
    forecasting cybersecurity trends   258–261
    grouping similar events for better insights   256–258
    probability distribution   36–38
    statistical models for vulnerability management   262
    trend analysis   32–34
    using moving averages to track trends   254–256
    using statistical metrics for continuous improvement   251
statistical testing   250
statsmodels library   251
STRA (security threat and risk assessment)   193
SVM (support vector machines)   233
    for threat detection   270–277
symmetric encryption   159
synthetic cybersecurity data, generating   297–301
system resource usage   167
system restoration   204

T

TechMed Solutions   138
technical security controls   153
technology infrastructure resilience   170–171
Tenable   61
TensorFlow   223, 310
TheHive   228
third-party assessments   121
threat detection   229–235
    anomaly detection   230
    continuous, alternatives to ATLAS and Wazuh   190
    dynamic risk scoring   232
    isolation forest and autoencoders for   274–277
    random forest and SVM for   270–277
    time to predict   231
    valid threat detections   185–188
threat hunting, success rate   241

threat likelihood   226
threat modeling   166
three-tier severity model   202
Timesketch   206
timestamp   309
time to achieve compliance   142
time to implement improvements   142
title section   28, 29
TLS (Transport Layer Security)   159, 166
top attack vectors   27–29
top command   63
total hardware/software assets   129
total vulnerability score   225
TPM (trusted platform module)   150
training and awareness   156–158
trend analysis   32–34
TTD (time to detect)   188
TTP (time to predict)   231
TTR (target time to resolve)   105
TTR (time to respond)   188

U

unauthorized software prevention   165
UPS (uninterruptible supplies)   170
user education   305

V

VLANs (virtual local area networks)   170
VM (virtual machine)   175
vulnerability management, statistical models for   262
vulnerability status   28–29

W

WAFs (Web Application Firewalls)   240
Wazuh   60, 206, 222, 228, 231

X

XSS (cross-site scripting)   240

Z

zero tolerance alerts   183

RELATED MANNING TITLES

Grokking Web Application Security
by Malcolm McDonald
Foreword by Stuart McClure

ISBN 9781633438262
336 pages, $59.99
May 2024

Making Sense of Cybersecurity
by Thomas Kranz
Foreword by Naz Markuta

ISBN 9781617298004
288 pages, $49.99
October 2022

Cybersecurity Career Guide
by Alyssa Miller

ISBN 9781617298202
200 pages, $39.99
May 2022

For ordering information, go to www.manning.com